South Carolinians
in the Battle of Gettysburg

D1592246

South Carolinians in the Battle of Gettysburg

DEREK SMITH

McFarland & Company, Inc., Publishers
Jefferson, North Carolina

ISBN (print) 978-1-4766-8477-2
ISBN (ebook) 978-1-4766-4275-8

LIBRARY OF CONGRESS AND BRITISH LIBRARY
CATALOGUING DATA ARE AVAILABLE

Library of Congress Control Number 2021007023

© 2021 Derek Smith. All rights reserved

*No part of this book may be reproduced or transmitted in any form
or by any means, electronic or mechanical, including photocopying
or recording, or by any information storage and retrieval system,
without permission in writing from the publisher.*

Front cover image: "Pride of Erin"
by Dale Gallon www.gallon.com

Printed in the United States of America

*McFarland & Company, Inc., Publishers
Box 611, Jefferson, North Carolina 28640
www.mcfarlandpub.com*

To my mother,
Ella Willene Smith (1935–2019)

Table of Contents

Prologue

Brave son of Carolina! Thou art still in death;
On Gettysburg's red plains thou gavest up thy breath.
Where angels are now raising their sweet song,
There thou art gone to mingle with that throng.
Where bubbling waters glide beneath the tree of life,
Thou art gone where there is no bloody strife.
—Portion of poem by anonymous writer in obituary
of Pvt. W.D. Shirer, First South Carolina Cavalry,
mortally wounded at Gettysburg, July 3, 1863
(*Charleston Courier*, January 9, 1864).

Four days after the history-quaking battle of Gettysburg, Capt. Benjamin Roper, commander of Company I, Seventh South Carolina Volunteers, in Brig. Gen. Joseph B. Kershaw's brigade, sat down to write a letter to the father of one of his men killed in the epic fight. It was Tuesday, July 7, 1863, and the bloodied Confederate Army of Northern Virginia, led by Gen. Robert E. Lee, was encamped near Hagerstown, Maryland, retreating after the three-day battle. Cpl. Thomas Harling of Roper's company, whose family lived in Edgefield District, South Carolina, was one of about 28,000 Confederate casualties at Gettysburg. The ghastly losses were nearly as great in Maj. Gen. George G. Meade's Union Army of the Potomac, with casualties of some 23,000, but the Federals had held their high ground, blunting Lee's offensive into Pennsylvania. Coupled with the July 4 fall of Vicksburg, the rebel citadel on the Mississippi River, the past seven days had effectively torn the heart and soul out of the Confederacy's war fortunes and hopes for independence.

Yet foremost in the thoughts of Roper, at least for a brief period that Tuesday, was informing John Harling Sr. that his son Thomas would not be coming home. Roper wrote:

Dear Sir:

It is with grief and pain of heart that I seat myself to communicate to you the sad intelligence of the death of your son Thos. Harling, who fell in battle near Gettysburg…. He was a noble and gallant soldier, ever ready and willing to go forward in the discharge of his whole duty…. His loss to the Company is irreparable, and has cast a gloom over the hearts of us all…. May God comfort you in this, your sad bereavement, is the prayer of

Your sympathising friend
Benj. Roper, Capt., Co. I, 7th S.C. Reg't[1]

The tears of heartbreak and grief were threefold for relatives of 25-year-old Pvt. John Alexander Nisbet of Lancaster District, South Carolina, who were suffering through their third loss of a loved one within a few months. "Thrice in less than a year the shaft of death has pierced the affections of a now lonely and desolate widow … deprived of husband and children," the *Lancaster Ledger* noted on September 2. A militiaman in the Lancaster Hornets before the war, Nisbet had gone to Gettysburg in the ranks of the Twelfth South Carolina Volunteers in Col. Abner M. Perrin's brigade. He was severely wounded in the side during the 1862 battles around Richmond, but the tragedy was only in its first act. During his recovery, Nisbet's younger brother was killed at Second Bull Run; their father "died at home of disease" shortly afterward. John Nisbet was well enough to return to the army and fight at Fredericksburg and Chancellorsville. He also survived the butchery Perrin's South Carolinians suffered on July 1, 1863, Gettysburg's first day. His time, however, came in violent fashion when he was killed instantly the next day. Nisbet had "lived without reproach and died without fear," his obituary noted. He "was a constant sharer in all the toils and perils of his comrades till the day of death."[2]

About 5,000 South Carolina soldiers were in the ranks of the Army of Northern Virginia when Lee initiated his second offensive into the Union states in summer 1863. The majority were young men and boys such as Cpl. Harling and John Nisbet, who had never been more than a few miles from home but were now caught up in a nation born atop a volcano waiting to erupt with untold fury. The same could be said of thousands of Northerners, all ready for adventure, war, glory and the grand, romantic laurels of gallant heroes. Each would soon realize a vastly different reality of an armed conflict which no Americans on either side could ever have imagined.

The Carolinians mustered from all corners of the little state that had become the heartbeat of the secessionist cause when Fort Sumter was bombarded to spark the war. They were farmers, doctors, planters, lawyers, sheriffs, teachers, state legislators, storekeepers, college students and railroad workers, among other professions.

The troops were from local volunteer companies, including the Laurens Briars, Edgefield Rifles, Enoree Mosquitos, Carolina Bees, Meeting Street Saludas, Butler Guards, Jeffries Volunteers, Jasper Light Infantry, Darlington Guards, Edisto Rifles, Palmetto Riflemen, Calhoun Artillery, Secession Guards, Marion's Men of Winyah, Spartan Rifles, Columbia Greys, Boykin Rangers, Charleston Zouaves, DeKalb Rifle Guards, Cadet Rangers, Camden Volunteers, Campbell Rifles, and the Rutledge Mounted Riflemen. All of these units were assimilated into the Confederate army, most marshaling in and around Columbia, the state capital, or Charleston, where Fort Sumter was located.

"The very air seemed to be charged with electricity by the approaching storm of contest," Claudine Rhett, a Charleston belle, recalled of the autumn and winter of 1860–1861. "You could not walk more than a few steps down any thoroughfare without meeting young men wearing conspicuously on their breasts blue cockades or strips of plaited palmetto fastened to their button-holes, which attested that they were 'minute men' all ready for duty. Flags fluttered in every direction, and the adjacent islands were converted into camping grounds. Companies drilled and paraded daily on every open square of the city, and bands nightly serenaded all, the stately old homes echoing the strains of 'Dixie' and the 'Marseillaise.'"[3]

Among the young men who filled the city's streets was Simon Baruch of Camden, South Carolina. Baruch was a student at the Medical College of South Carolina in Charleston when the ordinance of secession was signed there on December 20, 1860. As the news spread like a lightning storm across the entire country, Baruch had joined in a jubilant procession the next night, celebrating Carolina's historic and daring move. In the parade he carried a lantern with the inscription "There is a point beyond which endurance ceases to be a virtue." Less than three years later, Baruch would be awash in a sanguine panorama of suffering at a country tavern outside Gettysburg.[4]

Such a scene was almost beyond comprehension on a splendid April morning in 1861, as C.P. Varner and other volunteers from his militia company who lived in or near Spartanburg, South Carolina, were ordered to muster with a blanket and three days of rations. The Carolinians had been drilling for weeks with their "old squirrel rifles" and now their time had come. The hounds of war were snarling ever louder, fiery words on both sides stoking the bubbling cauldron of a seemingly inevitable conflict between North and South. Varner and his 105 comrades were to gather at Spartanburg and then board a train for Columbia, where they would be organized as part of the Third Regiment, South Carolina Volunteers, ready to join the Confederate army. "We had lawyers, doctors, preachers, and West Pointers in our company—a rare combination of Southern chivalry," he recalled years later. The regiment also included men from Laurens, Colleton, Pickens and Newberry districts. Reaching Columbia, they prepared to take the train to Charleston, a day or so after Fort Sumter's bombardment. "As we marched up the main street that April morning, with bands playing, flags to the breeze, beautiful women waving handkerchiefs and throwing bouquets, I thought 'Is this war?'" he remembered.[5]

More than two years after that sweet-scented and sun-brushed day, the young men who survived the ensuing bloodbaths from First Bull Run to Antietam to Chancellorsville shouldered their muskets and followed their banners north in June 1863. Among them was Reuben Patterson of Liberty Hill, South Carolina, an infantryman in the Second South Carolina Volunteers. Unlike many of his comrades, Patterson had enjoyed a privileged life on his family's spread, savoring impromptu music recitals with his sisters. The house almost seemed to dance to the fruits of their talents, including Patterson's delicate and deft touch with his flute, an acquaintance describing how "in the old days at home the strains from his silver flute mingled with the music of the piano by his sisters." His world had changed dramatically in wartime. Still bothered by a leg wound sustained at Savage's Station the previous June, Patterson had endured the pain and become a good soldier among many in the ranks of Joe Kershaw's veteran brigade.[6]

Also in the Second were privates Charles and Edwin Kerrison, the brothers in Company I. "The army [is] in splendid condition; every soldier confident," Charles related. Another Confederate, W.B. Franklin of the First South Carolina Volunteers, was from Newberry, South Carolina, a stonecutter in peacetime. He left behind his wife and three young children to join the Southern cause and already had paid dearly with his blood. Shot down in the fighting around Richmond in 1862, he was thought to be mortally wounded, but survived and was now on the road that would end at Gettysburg.[7]

In the ranks of the Third S.C. Battalion was Virginia-born G.A. White who, at age 27, already had an interesting war résumé. Moving to Columbia in 1857, he worked as a stonemason on the columns of the new statehouse. When South Carolina seceded, however, he returned to Virginia, believing it would not leave the Union. After Virginia seceded, White joined a Virginia infantry regiment, most of the men in his company having been workers in the Norfolk navy yard. Because of this experience, White and his comrades were put to work on the damaged USS *Merrimac*, which would soon be repaired and converted into the formidable and historic ironclad CSS *Virginia* in the Confederate navy. White helped install iron armor plating on the *Virginia*'s sides and later greased the armor so that enemy rounds would deflect off it. Returning to South

Carolina, apparently after his Virginia enlistment expired, White joined the Third S.C. Battalion in Kershaw's command. His war experiences were soon to become even more interesting—if he lived.[8]

The German Volunteers of Charleston "were finely equipped with everything necessary to the comfort and efficiency of the soldier, whether in the camp or on the battle field" when they left the city for Virginia in September 1861. Each soldier was equipped with "one complete uniform, one great coat, one lined blanket, one piece ground oiled cloth and bed sack, one canteen and haversack, a best quality knapsack packed with one tin cup and plate, one knife, fork, spoon, a sewing pocket with pins, needles, buttons and thread, one pair scissors, and a two-blade pocket knife, one cased looking glass, one comb and tooth brush, two towels and soap, one box blacking and brush, two pair stout shoes, two pair woolen socks, one pair stout woolen gloves, two flannel shirts, two pair flannel drawers, one flannel stomach band. Each man carries, besides these articles, an extra pair [of] pants, three shirts, two handkerchiefs, and fatigue cap. The Company also carried a full assortment of camp equipage, cooking utensils and implements," supplied by the Confederate government. Later reconfigured as the German Artillery Volunteers and then the German Artillery, the Charlestonians were surely traveling with substantially fewer personal items on the road to Gettysburg.[9]

Lt. Col. Arthur Fremantle, a British army observer who was on a months-long tour of the Confederacy, headed north amid Lee's troops. On the morning of June 22, he found himself "entangled" on the road with soldiers of Maj. Gen. William Dorsey Pender's division, which included Col. Perrin's infantry brigade of South Carolinians and the Pee Dee Artillery, a South Carolina battery led by Lt. William E. Zimmerman. With an officer's keen eye, Fremantle gave a brief but detailed description of these Carolinians and their comrades on the march that day north of Front Royal, Virginia. "The soldiers of this division are a remarkably fine body of men, and look quite seasoned and ready for any work," he observed. "Their clothing is serviceable, so also are their boots; but there is the usual utter absence of uniformity as to color and shape of their garments and hats: gray of all shades, and brown clothing, with felt hats predominate. The Confederate troops are now entirely armed with excellent rifles, mostly Enfields. When they first turned out they were in the habit of wearing numerous revolvers and [B]owie-knives. General Lee is said to have mildly remarked: 'Gentlemen, I think you will find an Enfield rifle, a bayonet, and sixty rounds of ammunition, as much as you can conveniently carry in the way of arms.' They laughed and thought they knew better; but the six-shooters and [B]owie-knives gradually disappeared; and now none are to be seen among the infantry."[10]

Fremantle then turned his attention to the division artillery and other matters. "The artillery horses are in poor condition, and only get 3 lb. of corn a day," he related. "The artillery is of all kinds—Parrots [sic], Napoleons, rifled and smooth bores, all shapes and sizes; most of them bear the letters U.S., showing that they have changed masters," he noted of captured ordnance. "I saw no stragglers during the time I was with Pender's division; but although the Virginian army certainly does get over a deal of ground, yet they move at a slow, dragging pace, and are evidently not good marchers naturally."[11]

Hundreds of miles behind waited the wives, widows, daughters, mothers, grandmothers and sisters of South Carolina womanhood, ever supportive of their loved ones in uniform, just like women in the other seceded states. In more than two years of war, it was never a matter of victory or defeat on battlefields at First Bull Run, Shiloh, Antietam, Stones River or Fredericksburg, as many thousands of families—North and South—were touched by the death angel or by youngsters returning home without arms or legs, or with other myriad disfigurements.

"Did all these events, wringing our hearts with anguish and distress, daunt us and make us give up our 'Cause'?" Margaret Crawford Adams of Congaree, South Carolina, asked after the conflict. "No. We but clung the more closely to it; our sorrows purified us; our necessities kept us from sloth and selfishness; our thousands of hands were as one pair. 'Twere idle to try to tell of the tents … sandbags, socks, havelocks, shirts, drawers, etc. we made for our soldiers," along with boxes of food, other clothing, medicine, blankets sent to them.[12]

The bloody harvest at Gettysburg would test the faith and mettle of homes from Beaufort to Charleston to Edgefield to Greenville.

Lee's army began crossing the Potomac River into Maryland in mid–June, 75,000 tough, confident soldiers still heartened by their victory at Chancellorsville in early May. "At last we reach the mighty Potomac, the river we had always considered the great dividing line between the contending armies, and have to wade it, which we do to music from the band of the 14th S.C.V," noted a soldier in the Twelfth South Carolina; both the 12th and 14th were regiments in Perrin's brigade. Augustus Dickert, one of Kershaw's Carolinians, recalled the scene when he was among Confederates who crossed the river at Williamsport, Maryland, on June 25. "Here was shouting and yelling," he related. "Hats went into the air, flags dipped and swayed, the bands played 'Maryland, My Maryland,' while the men sang 'All Quiet on the Potomac To-night.' We were now in the enemy's country, and scarcely a shot had been fired."[13]

Lee's "right arm," Lt. Gen. Thomas "Stonewall" Jackson, was gone now, mortally wounded by friendly fire at Chancellorsville, but the Confederates were taking the fight into the enemy's homeland with his "army of veterans," as another of Kershaw's men, J. Russell Wright, said in describing the appearance and attitude of this Confederate army in the summer of 1863. "It was no longer a company of gay gallants, marching by amid music, waving scarfs, and showers of nosegays from fairy hands," Wright recalled years later. "It was a stormy wave of gaunt warriors in ragged clothes and begrimed faces, who clutched their shining muskets, rushed headlong over the breastworks [at Chancellorsville], and rolling through the blazing and crackling woods, swept the enemy at the point of the bayonet, with [the] hoarse and menacing cry, 'Remember Jackson.'"[14]

Lt. James F. Caldwell of Perrin's First South Carolina Volunteers added, "We were in excellent health, and more properly equipped than at any period prior or subsequent." The rebels' trust in their officers, especially Lee, and the valor of everyone in their ranks were unbridled. "The victories of 1862 and the great battle of Chancellorsville … had led us to believe scarcely anything [was] impossible to Lee's army," Caldwell noted, "and the management of our generals, which had wrung even from the North the highest encomiums, gave us assurance that every particle of our strength and courage would be most judiciously and powerfully applied. Lee, in himself was a tower of strength." "The army was never before or afterwards under better discipline nor in better fighting trim," recalled another of Kershaw's men.[15]

"We now had a fine army in all branches," added Lt. J.R. Boyles of the Twelfth South Carolina; "Our bands enlivened the march with strains of martial music." From the Potomac, the Confederates had only to traverse a few miles across a narrow portion of Maryland before reaching the Pennsylvania state line. Approaching the border, Boyles recalled a crowd of ladies were gathered to "see the Southern army in full force put their feet on the soil of Pennsylvania; we crossed the line without molestation and continued our march." Lee was optimistic that his offensive would draw substantial recruits to his army from Maryland, but he was disappointed. "We felt full of hope that now, being in such strong force in Maryland, her sons would rally by thousands to our standard—but they didn't rally worth much," Boyles related.[16]

In spearing north over the next few days, Lee scattered his forces from Chambersburg to York to Carlisle in southeastern Pennsylvania. With Jackson's death, Lee's faith and intuitive trust rested on the broad shoulders of a battle-wizened South Carolinian, Lt. Gen. James Longstreet, commander of the First Corps. Still, in the wake of Chancellorsville, Lee had had to select a general to replace the almost irreplaceable Jackson. The announcement came on May 23, well before the summer offensive: Maj. Gen. Richard S. Ewell, a career soldier who had lost a leg at the battle of Groveton in August 1862, was chosen to lead the Second Corps, Jackson's old command. More changes also were underway. The next day Lee unveiled plans to reorganize the army into three corps. A slightly built but hard-hitting Virginian, Maj. Gen. A.P. Hill, was to lead the newly minted Third Corps. Ewell and Hill were both promoted to lieutenant general, the assignment to go into effect immediately.[17]

Pennsylvania was a foreign land to most of the Confederates, but at least one Carolinian was impressed by the landscape. "Pennsylvania is one of the prettiest countries through which I ever passed," Tally Simpson of the Third South Carolina Volunteers wrote to his sister, Anna, back home in Pendleton, South Carolina. "The scenery is beautiful, and the soil is exceedingly fertile…. It is the finest wheat country in the world, & I believe I never saw as much before in all my life as I did passing through that rich and beautiful valley of Pennsylvania." Simpson continued that he had seen "very few negroes, the most of the labor being performed by the whites." The pastoral scenery aside, Simpson was much less enamored by the women and horses he encountered in Pennsylvania: "They have the fattest horses and the ugliest women I ever saw," he wrote Anna. "The horses are tremendous, some almost as large as elephants, but they are so bony and clumsy that they can't stand near as much as our smallest mules. The women are what you would call the flat-headed dutch, while the gals are ugly, broad-mouthed specimens of humanity. But they are always neat and clean and very industrious. In my trip … I don't believe I saw a single pretty woman, and it was remarked by several." Still, "it is certainly a delightful country to live in, to those who are firmly impressed with the abolition principle," Simpson conceded. "But give me the land of Dixie with a pretty and good little southern wife."[18]

"We are in Yankeedom this time, for certain, and a beautiful and magnificent country it is too," Spencer G. Welch, a surgeon in the Thirteenth South Carolina, wrote to his wife, Cordelia, on June 28, a few miles from Chambersburg. "Since we started we have traveled about fifteen miles a day, resting at night and drawing rations plentifully and regularly." Augustus Dickert added, "Many curious characters were found among the quaint old Quaker settlers, who viewed the army of Lee not with 'fear' or 'trembling' but more in wonder and Christian abhorrence."[19]

Lee had issued orders against stealing from civilians and the destruction of private property, but there were widespread incidents of thievery by the Confederates. In fact, the troops' overall restraint was amazing, since Union forces had ravaged many of their home states since the war opened. Yet one of Lee's main objectives was to collect food, livestock and forage to be taken back South. General Pender wrote his wife that the soldiers "have done nothing like the Yankees do in our country. They take poultry and hogs but in most cases pay our money for it. We take everything we want for government use." "The troops lived in clover," Dickert noted of this period. "The best of everything generally was given freely and willingly to them. Great herds of the finest and fattest beeves were continually being gathered together. Our broken down artillery horses and wagon mules were replaced by Pennsylvania's best. But in all, duly paid for in Confederate notes."[20]

"We fared first rate in Pennsylvania," Trooper William H. Perry of the Second South Carolina Cavalry wrote to his father on July 11, a week or so after the battle. "The Citizens gave us plenty of bread and milk, and we took all the horses we could lay hands on. Our cavalry so far as I saw behaved very well, but the Infantry they say plundered a good deal."[21]

"We had pretty fine times," John M. Steele of the Twelfth South Carolina later wrote to his brother, Hood, about the trek through Pennsylvania. "Some of the boys indulged pretty freely in bee gums, chickens, hogs; and cherry trees were torn to pieces. Cherries were just ripe and we stopped the growth all along the road we traveled."[22]

"The most of the soldiers seem to harbor a terrific spirit of revenge and steal and pillage in the most sinful manner," wrote Tally Simpson of the Third South Carolina. "They take poultry, hogs, vegetables, fruit, honey, and any and every thing they can lay their hands upon." Indeed, some Georgia troops in Longstreet's corps the previous night had "stole so much that they could not carry what rations they drew from the commissary," Simpson continued. "As for myself, I have not nor will I take one thing in such a manner."[23]

In a letter to his sister, Anna, written some three weeks after the campaign, Simpson again mentioned the Confederates' conduct on the march through Pennsylvania. As to orders against destruction of private property, "the soldiers paid no more attention to them than they would to the cries of a screech owl" he wrote. "Every thing in the shape of vegetables, from a cow pea up to a cabbage head, was 'pressed' without the least ceremony, and all animal flesh from a featherless fowl to full grown sheep and hogs were killed and devoured without the least compunction of conscience. The brigadiers and colonels made no attempt to enforce Lee's general orders."[24]

Maj. Gen. Richard H. Anderson, a Sumter County, South Carolina, native who led an infantry division in Hill's corps, had a much different assessment, especially of his own soldiers. "The conduct of the troops under my command was in the highest degree praiseworthy and commendable throughout the campaign," he related. "Obedient to the orders of the commanding general, they refrained from taking into their own hands retaliation upon the enemy for the inhuman wrongs and outrages inflicted upon them in the wanton destruction of their property and homes. Peaceable inhabitants suffered no molestation. In a land of plenty, they [his soldiers] often suffered hunger and want." Anderson also noted the poor condition of many troops who didn't take advantage of the possible spoils of war: "One-fourth of their number marched, ragged and barefooted, through towns in which it was well ascertained that the merchants had concealed supplies of clothing." Anderson had been one of the candidates to replace Stonewall Jackson in command of the Second Corps before Lee chose Ewell.[25]

The pilfering could have devolved into something far worse. James Longstreet explained it this way to the Britisher Fremantle on June 27: "Whilst speaking of entering upon the enemy's soil, he [Longstreet] said to me that although it might be fair [and] just retaliation, to apply the torch, yet that doing so would demoralize the army and ruin its now excellent discipline," Fremantle wrote. "Private property is to be therefore rigidly protected." Related to Longstreet's comments, the Twelfth South Carolina's Lt. J.R. Boyles claimed the rebels would have behaved much differently if they could have envisioned the scorched-earth destruction wrought by Union Maj. Gen. William T. Sherman in his flaming path through Georgia and South Carolina late in the war. "Private property was protected [in Pennsylvania], but if we had known what was in store for our homes and families by Sherman and his vandals, we would have made a clean sweep and left them homeless," Boyles wrote after the war.[26]

At Chambersburg on June 28, Lee was surprised to learn that his old nemesis, the Union Army of the Potomac, was across the Potomac and in Maryland with its 95,000 troops, possibly in position to threaten his separated corps. Lee immediately ordered a concentration of his army near Cashtown, Pennsylvania, a hamlet on the Chambersburg Pike about eight miles west of Gettysburg. "The long march from the Rappahannock had relieved both armies of all their weak and faint-hearted," noted an officer in the Fourteenth South Carolina, "and none but brave and strong men had marched there to battle."[27]

For days Lee had heard nothing from his flamboyant cavalry chief, Maj. Gen. J.E.B. Stuart, who was leading his 10,000 horsemen north but had not been in contact. Since the cavalry was the eyes and ears of the army, Stuart's absence essentially left Lee moving blindly through enemy country, unaware of the deployment of Union forces. The fact that Lee still believed the Army of the Potomac was still well to the south in Virginia shows how badly he missed Stuart's communications and reconnaissance, although the army did have two cavalry brigades to guard its flanks and rear. Another startling report reached Lee on or about June 30: Meade had replaced Maj. Gen. Joseph Hooker as commander of the Army of the Potomac. Thus Lee not only had to deal with the threat of a larger enemy army confronting him in hostile and unfamiliar territory, he also had to figure out Meade, the chess king in the other camp. And Stuart was still nowhere to be found. Yet, to the rebels in the ranks, it didn't seem to matter who led the enemy against Lee, be it Meade or his predecessors. The Virginian "had ruined every Northern general sent against him" even "in the eyes of their own people. McClellan, Pope, Burnside [and] Hooker had successively vanished before him, and he now appeared to be invincible, immoveable," wrote Lt. Caldwell of the First South Carolina.[28]

Like the Confederates from other states, the rank-and-file South Carolinians knew nothing of these command-level issues. Tally Simpson of the Third South Carolina was in a column that halted outside Chambersburg on the night of the 28th. There he wrote to his aunt, Caroline Miller, with more impressions about "Yankeedom" and its people. "We are still on the march northward, and there is no telling where we will stop—nor am I able to say to what point we are destined," he penned. "Our destiny and Lee's plan of operations are all a mystery and will only be developed by time.... All the fields are covered with beautiful green grass and clover, two and three feet high, and burdened with a rich growth of wheat ... and fine fields of young corn are seen every where." Simpson marveled at the large barns, bigger and "some handsomer than the hotels in Pendleton," South Carolina, but he remained unimpressed by the local citizenry, other than their general desire for peace. "The whole country is frightened almost to death," he wrote. "They won't take our money, but for fear that our boys will kill them, they give away what they can spare." "We hear nothing of Hooker's army at all, but General Lee knows what he is about," surgeon Spencer Welch wrote on June 28. "This is certainly a grand move of his [Lee's], and if any man can carry it out successfully he can, for he is cautious as well as bold.... I have never seen our army so healthy and in such gay spirits. How can they be whipped?"[29]

On June 29, elements of Hill's corps, including Maj. Gen. Henry Heth's division, were in Cashtown, with another of Hill's divisions—that of Maj. Gen. Pender—arriving just west of the village the next day. Heth on the 30th sent a brigade under Brig. Gen. J.J. Pettigrew toward the then-little-known town of Gettysburg to determine if there were any enemy troops in the vicinity. Founded in 1780 by Gen. James Getty, the borough was the county seat of Adams County and had about 2,100 residents at the time of the battle. Despite its size it was an important crossroads and farming community, ten roads converging there like the spokes on an artillery caisson wheel. Pettigrew's soldiers were not the first of Lee's army to reach Gettysburg. Late on the afternoon of June 26, Maj. Gen. Jubal Early's division of Ewell's Second Corps approached the town from a different direction. The only force opposing Early that day was a green regiment of Pennsylvania militia, which fled when confronted by Early's tough veterans. In town, Early demanded some $10,000 worth of goods and supplies, but most of these had been hidden earlier by Gettysburg merchants and local farmers. Impatient to continue his march toward York, Pennsylvania, Early abandoned his demand and ordered his infantry to move out. He did take note of a shoe factory and sent word to Hill that it could be a good source for badly needed shoes for the rebels.[30]

On the 30th, Pettigrew "encountered the enemy at Gettysburg (principally cavalry), but in what force he could not determine," Hill reported. Lee was informed of this development, and Hill prepared "to advance the next morning [July 1] and discover what was in my front." What Pettigrew's troops actually saw before withdrawing or engaging the enemy were elements of the Union cavalry division of Brig. Gen. John Buford, riding into Gettysburg amid the cheers and excitement of the townspeople. Buford, his troopers and many other Yankees would be there to give Hill and his troops—including hundreds of South Carolinians—a bloody greeting on July 1, 1863. The combat cataclysm would last for three days, forever haunting and forging American history.[31]

1

"Cover Themselves in Glory"

Wednesday, July 1

Drizzle and a gentle, cooling breeze from the south—perhaps an omen of good fortune—greeted the Confederates of Hill's Third Corps as they girded to march toward Gettysburg before sunrise.

Hill was sending two of his three divisions to try to ascertain the strength of the Union forces seen there the day before. Heth's division, almost 8,000 infantry, led the way on the Chambersburg Pike and marched out at about 5 a.m. Heth was to be supported by Pender's 6,500-man Light Division, Pender's First Brigade consisting of five South Carolina regiments commanded by Perrin. These Carolinians had reached Cashtown Gap through South Mountain the previous afternoon and encamped on the north side of the road about two miles west of Cashtown.[1]

Heth had a head start of some three hours before Pender's troops embarked. Moving on the pike with Heth was Maj. William J. Pegram's Battalion of Hill's artillery reserve. Among Pegram's five batteries—a total of twenty guns—was the Pee Dee Artillery, four 3-inch rifles and 65 South Carolinians who were also known as Zimmerman's Battery, their commander being Lt. William E. Zimmerman. The battalion was assigned to Pender, but at Cashtown the previous night had received orders to report to Heth and follow his division that morning. These artillerists would be the first South Carolinians to fire a shot at Gettysburg. Pegram, a Virginian, assumed command of the battalion that day, still recovering from an illness. He took over from Capt. Ervin B. Brunson, a South Carolinian.[2]

Zimmerman's gunners, all recruited from the Florence-Darlington area, had seen extensive combat, having been bloodied during the Seven Days Battles, Second Bull Run, Antietam, Fredericksburg and Chancellorsville. The rest of the battalion, combat tested as well, was composed of four Virginia batteries: the Crenshaw Battery, the Fredericksburg Artillery, the Letcher Artillery and the Purcell Artillery. Like many of the army's horses, the animals of the Pee Dee Artillery and the others of the battalion were in poor shape due to a chronic shortage of horseshoes. Brunson noted the "miserable condition of the horses' feet, for lack of shoes, on the limestone pikes, over which a large portion of our march was made." The battalion already had abandoned some twenty horses since embarking on the campaign from Fredericksburg on June 15. Efforts to procure fresh horses and shoes along the way were largely unsuccessful. Waving above the Pee Dee cannoneers was their flag, sent to Virginia by "Miss Louisa McIntosh and other ladies of Society Hill, S.C.," for presentation to the battery at Suffolk in 1861.[3]

11

About 7 a.m., Heth's infantry encountered Union cavalry vedettes along Marsh Creek, a slim stream some three miles west of Gettysburg. These Federals belonged to Col. William Gamble's First Brigade of John Buford's First Division. In the early light these Indiana, Illinois and New York troopers—some 1,600 men total—stung the gray columns with carbine and revolver fire before slowly falling back toward Gettysburg. Alerted to the enemy movement, Buford sent messages to Meade and to Maj. Gen. John F. Reynolds of the I Corps, who commanded the left wing of the army. The I Corps, led by Maj. Gen. Abner Doubleday, had bivouacked overnight a few miles from Gettysburg. It would be up to Buford to try to hold off the Confederates until reinforcements, primarily from the I Corps, could come up.[4]

For more than two hours after the Marsh Creek clash, Gamble's troopers did just that, slowing Heth's advance to a crawl. The first of Heth's troops reached Herr Ridge about 9 a.m. after covering only a mile and a half or so since Marsh Creek. Gettysburg was only two miles away, but Gamble's men, bolstered by a few fieldpieces, were assembled on McPherson's Ridge, bisected by the pike. Willoughby Run, a knee-deep branch in the valley between these two ridges, was occupied by Union skirmishers hidden in the thick underbrush.[5]

Pegram's artillery soon swung into line on Herr Ridge after firing a few shots in the moving battle since Marsh Creek. Zimmerman's Carolinians unlimbered three of their guns in a position on the ridge north of the pike. His fourth gun was disabled by accident as its crew hastily tried to join the fighting.[6]

Zimmerman's gunners and the rest of Pegram's battalion then engaged in an artillery duel with the greatly outnumbered Union cannon on McPherson's Ridge. As they did so, Heth readied his infantry to renew the attack about 9:30 a.m.—and hundreds of Abner Perrin's South Carolinians were on the road to Gettysburg.

Perrin's troops, along with the rest of Pender's division, received orders to march about 8 a.m. and were soon on the turnpike headed east, not knowing what to expect. They had been roused from their bivouac just after daybreak. "I soon came to the conclusion from the hurried & confused manner of our getting out of camp that the enemy was not far off," Perrin later wrote to his friend, South Carolina governor Milledge L. Bonham. "I do not suppose any army ever marched into an enemies [*sic*] country with greater confidence in its ability … and with more reasonable grounds for that confidence than the army of Gen. Lee." The previous night the men had been told to cook a day's rations. "We rolled up our blankets and [tent] flies in haste (knapsacks had been pretty generally dispensed with before this) and formed," related 25-year-old Lt. James F. Caldwell of the First South Carolina. The brigade of about 1,600 men consisted of the First South Carolina (Provisional Army) under Maj. Charles Wick McCreary; the First South Carolina Rifles, led by Capt. William M. Hadden; the Twelfth South Carolina Volunteers of Col. John L. Miller; Lt. Col. Benjamin T. Brockman's Thirteenth S.C. Volunteers; and the Fourteenth S.C. Volunteers, commanded by Lt. Col. Joseph N. Brown.[7]

Hadden's men, about 500 troops also known as Orr's Rifles, were left behind, assigned to help guard the army's wagon train. As they started out that morning, Perrin's brigade led Pender's division (with the Twelfth South Carolina in front), following in the footsteps of Heth's troops somewhere ahead.[8]

Perrin, 36, was a native of Edgefield District, South Carolina, and had fought in the Mexican War as an infantry lieutenant in the regular army. He later studied law and was an attorney in Columbia before the present conflict. He was captain in the Fourteenth

S.C. and went to Virginia in the spring of 1862. Perrin saw combat in the Seven Days battles, Cedar Mountain, Second Bull Run, Antietam and Fredericksburg. He was promoted to colonel in February 1863 and led the regiment at Chancellorsville. When the brigade's commander, Brig. Gen. Samuel McGowan, was wounded there, Perrin took over for the rest of the battle and led the brigade in the Gettysburg campaign.[9]

At least three of Perrin's five regimental commanders bore the scars from earlier battles in the war—and had paid for combat experience with their blood. Brockman, 31, was from the Greenville area and was a merchant in Spartanburg, South Carolina, before secession. He was wounded at Second Bull Run, as was Brown of the Fourteenth South Carolina. The latter was a 30-year-old native of Anderson, South Carolina, who was a grocer and later an attorney in Laurens, South Carolina, when war came. Before Second Bull Run, Brown also had suffered a wound to the arm at Gaines' Mill. Brown had assumed command of the Fourteenth when Perrin, the regiment's original commander, moved up to replace McGowan. John Miller, 34, of the Twelfth was born and raised in York District, South Carolina, and was an alum of Davidson College in North Carolina. Miller's prewar résumé included being a lawyer in Yorkville, South Carolina, editing the town's newspaper, the *Enquirer*, and serving as a state representative in 1860–1861. Miller survived wounds at Gaines' Mill and Antietam to be promoted colonel of the regiment in February 1863. He was a first cousin of wartime diarist Mary Boykin Chesnut. Maj. McCreary was from Barnwell District, South Carolina, and a graduate of the South Carolina Military Academy. He was an assistant teacher at a military school in Aiken when Fort Sumter was bombarded and, with his background, was urged to establish a company, which he did. The "Barnwell Volunteers" would become Company A of the First South Carolina Volunteers, with most of the men being from the area of Williston. McCreary was described as "every inch an officer and gentleman" in a news account shortly after his men left for Virginia in August 1861 to join Col. Maxcy Gregg's South Carolina regiment. Like many soldiers on both sides, McCreary carried a small copy of the New Testament into battle. Capt. Hadden of the First South Carolina Rifles was approximately thirty-six years old and a native of Pickens County.[10]

The Barnwell Volunteers were typical of the rank-and-file Carolinians and were the first company from Barnwell District to go to war. The command was "composed of the best young men in the district; and we are sure, if ever opportunity affords them a fight, they will cover themselves in glory," one officer wrote. In the weeks before the troops' departure by train, the Ladies' Association of Williston held regular meetings to ensure there were "fresh supplies of the various necessaries for the comfort and relief" of the soldiers, including "new made garments … a number of blankets, sheets, pillows, quilts" and "roller bandages." When McCreary's company readied for an August 14 departure, "the citizens of the village and vicinity prepared a handsome supper" and grand sendoff despite the rainy night. "Never before has so large a number of persons assembled in Williston," noted one observer. "Among them were a great number of the fair sex … and some older men who had organized as a home guard, calling themselves the 'Confederate Guards of Williston.'" After supper, everyone gathered at the local hotel, where the ladies threw bouquets to the soldiers and waved handkerchiefs from the balcony. There were speeches and resolutions and "parting sentiments with their loved ones" before the shrill of a whistle announced the train was approaching. Farewells were hastily concluded as the soldiers boarded the cars amid the strains of "Dixie Land." "Three cheers were given for Barnwell, and the cars moved off, amid the deafening sound of" many "voices, carrying with them the sympathies and prayers of many a loved one."[11]

Lt. Sidney Carter of Company A in the Fourteenth was one of five brothers in Confederate service, including Giles Carter, who was in his company moving on the Chambersburg Pike. Two of the Carters were already in their graves—Richard, the youngest, dying of disease in spring 1862, and James Morgan Carter, slain at Chancellorsville. A third, Capt. William Carter, suffered a serious head wound at Gaines' Mill—where Sidney also was slightly wounded—and had been forced to resign from active duty. The Carters were a prominent farming family, which also included six daughters, in Darlington District, South Carolina. Earlier in the war, Sidney wrote home—with a touch of braggadocio—to reassure his wife Bet and their children that he would eventually return home. "I was not born to be killed by the Yankees, all the Yankees born can't hurt me," he penned. "And if they kill me in battle remember I am fighting for God and country. When I think about being killed and leaving you and my dear little children it nerves me, for I feel like I am in the right and will come through safe and sound."[12]

An odd duck amid Perrin's ranks was Lt. James Armstrong of Company K (also known as the Irish Volunteers of Charleston) in McCreary's First South Carolina. Armstrong was a native Pennsylvanian, born in Philadelphia, but raised and educated in Charleston after his family moved south. Indeed, Armstrong had served as the Charleston harbor master before the war and took up the Southern cause. Armstrong was slightly wounded at Antietam and struck again at Fredericksburg, but he was well enough to join the army on the march into Pennsylvania.[13]

Another of Perrin's officers was 29-year-old Capt. Romulus L. Bowden, leading Company A of the Thirteenth South Carolina. Born on a farm near Spartanburg, South Carolina, he began clerking at a store in town when he was sixteen and had shown a knack for success in the mercantile field. By 1858, he was a partner in a general merchandise store in Laurens County, South Carolina, but the coming war changed his life forever. Bowden was in combat from Gaines' Mill to Malvern Hill to Second Bull Run, being wounded in the left leg at the latter battle. He had recovered enough by May 1863 to fight at Chancellorsville and join the gray hosts who once again thrust north across the Potomac. On this momentous summer day he was still bothered by his leg and no doubt had thoughts of his beloved, Mary, left behind so far away in the upstate Carolina hill country.[14]

The story of the First South Carolina's Lt. James Caldwell is also noteworthy. A native of Newberry and 1857 graduate of South Carolina College, he studied law in Charleston, traveled to Europe and returned to join the state troops just after secession. Caldwell served primarily as an aide for several South Carolina officers and was appointed ordnance officer by General McGowan after Fredericksburg. McGowan also chose him as brigade historian, possibly naming him as ordnance officer to keep him out of harm's way so that he could chronicle the brigade's war history. Early in 1863, however, he was promoted lieutenant and joined his old comrades in the First's Company B. Caldwell was very much in harm's way at Gettysburg.[15]

Sgt. Hugh G. Bullock, of the First South Carolina's Company F, was a 22-year-old schoolteacher living in Horry County, South Carolina, when war came. His great-grandfather fought in the American Revolution, and Bullock had been seriously wounded in the Seven Days battles. Bullock recovered to fight at Antietam, Harper's Ferry and Fredericksburg. At Chancellorsville, he claimed to have been near "Stonewall"

Jackson when the general suffered the wound that later cost him his life. Bullock would remember the coming hours of July 1 for the rest of his days.[16]

Also on the march was Pvt. James R. Harvey, who was "a mere stripling" when he ran away to join the Confederate cause. Harvey grew up in the country outside Winnsboro, South Carolina. Hearing that a trainload of men and boys was departing for the army, Harvey rushed "to town in his shirt sleeves … and managed to get aboard" just as the cars were moving away. Now he was in the ranks of the Twelfth South Carolina's Company F, tramping across this foreign land, the sounds of combat ever nearer.[17]

On this soon-to-be-eventful July day almost two years later, however, none of these quaint details mattered to anyone, as every step brought Perrin's Carolinians and other soldiers from the Palmetto State closer to the fighting. One of Brockman's rebs, Pvt. J.T.P. Crosson, described July 1–3, 1863, as "the grandest battle of the war, that of Gettysburg" in a postwar recollection. The spirits of those Carolinians who didn't survive that Wednesday may have disagreed with him.[18]

The Carolinians quickly sensed they were about to go into action. "The atmosphere had from the first a strong taint of battle to our experienced noses," Lt. Caldwell related, "and our suspicion was made conviction, after moving three or four miles, by the sound of artillery in front." Rufus Harling, a soldier in Co. K of the Fourteenth S.C., recalled, "It was not long before we heard the roar of the cannon and it became known that our advance lines had found the enemy and we would soon be engaged in battle." "We were all keen for a fight," added John Steele of Company H, in the Twelfth. By now the men were hearing artillery, small arms fire, "and then the well-known battle shout."[19]

Spencer Welch, the Thirteenth South Carolina surgeon, noted that Perrin's column had not moved more than a mile and a half before they heard the unmistakable booming of artillery. The faces of the Carolinians in the ranks told him what to expect ahead. "Upon looking around I at once noticed in the countenance of all an expression of intense seriousness and solemnity, which I have always perceived in the faces of men who are about to face death and the awful shock of battle," he later wrote to his wife, Cordelia.[20]

"The smell of battle was already in the air and the jocularity which always attends the early stages of a march was tempered by a secret feeling that serious business was ahead," South Carolina's Maj. David G. McIntosh noted. McIntosh led a sixteen-gun artillery battalion in Pender's division, the command composed of three Virginia batteries and one from Alabama, all clattering along with Pender's infantry. The 27 year old was a native of Darlington District, South Carolina, a graduate of South Carolina College, and was a lawyer before the war. He had been assigned to lead the artillery battalion after the battle of Fredericksburg in December 1862.[21]

Like Pegram's command, McIntosh's battalion belonged to Hill's artillery reserve, led by Col. R. Lindsay Walker, who was still on the road to reach Cashtown and accompanying South Carolina Maj. Gen. Richard H. Anderson's division. It was about this time—9 a.m.—that Pender's column was halted west of Marsh Creek, where Heth first encountered Gamble's Yankee cavalry. "The day was cloudy and close," Caldwell recalled. "The cannonade continued slowly." With Perrin's brigade still leading, the Confederates awaited orders and the results of the combat flaring ahead of them in this unfamiliar territory.[22]

From Herr Ridge, Heth launched his assault against McPherson's Ridge with two brigades—Brig. Gen. J.R. Davis's Mississippians and North Carolinians, and Brig. Gen. James Archer's Alabama and Tennessee troops—between 9:30 a.m. and 10:15 a.m., based on varying accounts. As these Confederates attacked across Willoughby Run on both sides of the pike, their task was about to become much more formidable and deadly. The Union's General Reynolds had reached Gettysburg an hour or so earlier and conferred with Buford. Realizing the grave peril of the situation, Reynolds sent a dispatch to Brig. Gen. James S. Wadsworth to hurry forward with his First Division of the I Corps. Wadsworth's division consisted of two infantry brigades, supported by a battery of Maine artillery. The Union XI Corps of Maj. Gen. Oliver O. Howard also was ordered to march for Gettysburg from Emmitsburg, Maryland, about ten miles to the south.[23]

Relieving Buford's exhausted cavalrymen, one of Wadsworth's brigades collided with Archer's men south of the pike, capturing Archer and shoving these Southerners off the ridge and back across Willoughby Run. It was a costly action for the Federals, Reynolds falling dead from his saddle with a bullet in his head. Gen. Doubleday, the senior officer on the field, assumed command. Davis's rebels, meanwhile, clashed with the other Federal brigade on the ridge north of the pike, forcing them to retreat. This threat prompted some of the Yanks to be hustled north to engage Davis. Their charge caught several hundred Confederates in a steep-banked and unfinished railroad cut where they had sought cover. Trapped there, many of these rebels surrendered, temporarily thwarting Heth's onslaught. Another Union brigade from the I Corps' Third Division, commanded by Brig. Gen. Thomas A. Rowley, had also come up by now and been heavily engaged. The Federals maintained their tenuous hold on McPherson's Ridge for the time being. Wadsworth's and Rowley's bluecoats were already tired from their march and drained by combat casualties as the unrelenting sun neared its noon apex. Their day in hell was just beginning.[24]

Continuing their advance, Perrin's troops and the rest of Pender's Confederates crossed Marsh Creek about 9:30 a.m. and halted on Knoxlyn Ridge, about a mile west of Heth's position on Herr Ridge. There Pender ordered the division to deploy in battle line. Perrin's brigade formed on Knoxlyn Road, a country lane to the right—or south—of the Chambersburg Pike, and along the ridge. From left to right were Brown's Fourteenth, McCreary's First, Miller's Twelfth and Brockman's Thirteenth South Carolina. Without Hadden's 500 troops on guard detail, the brigade numbered about 1,100 men. Brig. Gen. Alfred M. Scales's brigade fell into line to Perrin's left, on the same side of the pike. The brigades of Brig. Gen. James H. Lane and Brig. Gen. Edward L. Thomas spread out on the ridge north of the pike. By now the firing to the front was getting heavier, cannon blasts mixed in, as Heth battled the enemy. Pender ordered "a strong line of skirmishers" out in front. Still, however, there was no urgency to reach the fighting, and Pender, based on orders from Hill, halted the troops after proceeding "nearly a mile." "We moved down the Gettysburg road slowly," Perrin related. The stopping and starting in the July heat was exacting its toll on the rebels. "These advances in line of battle are the most fatiguing exercise I had in the army," Lt. Caldwell noted. "Now the perspiration poured from our bodies." Surgeon Welch was awed as he watched the battle line of Pender's entire division advancing at once. To his wife he wrote that he "could see from one end of the division to the other as it moved forward in line of battle. It was nearly a mile in length. The scene was certainly grand, taking all the surroundings into consideration."[25]

Lt. Col. Brown of the Fourteenth South Carolina recalled, "Perrin gave orders to the field and staff and then communicated to the rank and file, that they were to move forward without firing. That they were not to stop under any circumstances, but to close in, press the enemy close, and route (sic) it from its position…. Rumors of disaster and success alternately passed along the lines, derived from the wounded and prisoners," as the brigade marched ahead, he added. "But upon the whole the advantage was on our side." "Couriers began to pass to the rear, and orders given to hurry up—canteens to be filled with water," related Cpl. Thomas Littlejohn of the Twelfth South Carolina. He also recalled seeing local civilians fleeing the upcoming tempest: "I remember a woman leading a cow with some little children following crying." Not far from Littlejohn, the Twelfth's Lt. J.R. Boyles of Company C also heard the deadly symphony ahead as "the cannon were firing more rapidly, the musketry—pop, pop, pop—resembled fire in a canebrake."[26]

Pender's battle line reached Herr Ridge about 11 a.m., as Archer's command was being decimated, but was not ordered to bolster the attack, acting in its supporting role for Heth's infantry and Pegram's guns. Perrin's men and Pender's other brigades settled in on the ridge's western slope. The Carolina Maj. McIntosh, meanwhile, deployed his artillery along the ridge, sending a Virginia battery of Napoleons and a section of Whitworths in an Alabama battery just to the right of the turnpike and in proximity to some of Pegram's cannon. The fire by these gunners "was opened slowly upon the enemy wherever they brought into view considerable bodies of troops, and occasionally upon their" artillery, McIntosh noted. Some of McIntosh's fieldpieces were actually posted along the ridge on both sides of the Chambersburg Pike.[27]

In addition to Pender's troops, more reinforcements from both armies were arriving at Gettysburg while there was a lull of at least an hour or more in the fighting after Heth's failed assault. By early afternoon, some 40,000 soldiers total were taking positions north and west of town. Union General Howard rode into Gettysburg about 11:30 a.m. and assumed overall command of the Federal forces on hand. Howard's XI Corps infantry began arriving about an hour later and were posted in the hilly terrain north of town and on the right of the I Corps positions on McPherson's Ridge. There was good reason for this, Buford's cavalry scouts reporting before 1 p.m. the advance of Ewell's Confederates, pushing south toward Gettysburg from the Carlisle vicinity. The XI Corps Federals were desperately digging in to meet this threat.[28]

After the lull, Heth readied to resume his attack, based on orders from Lee himself, who had arrived on Herr Ridge just after 2 p.m. With Archer's and Davis's troops chewed up, his new bayonet point would be Brig. Gen. J.J. Pettigrew's North Carolina brigade and the Virginians of Col. J.M. Brockenbrough's command. Heth girded for the assault "with the notification that ... Pender's division would support me," he later reported. "Gen. Heath [Heth] formed line of battle & about one o'clock moved forward and soon became hotly engaged with the enemy, driving them slowly," Perrin stated. "Our division formed line in his rear within convenient supporting distance."[29]

Heth's thrust was made south of the pike about 2:30 p.m., Pettigrew and Brockenbrough, along with battered elements of Archer's brigade, attacking across Willoughby Run and up the west slope of McPherson's Ridge amid a sleet of musket and artillery fire. By this point, Doubleday's line on the ridge had been reinforced by more I Corps troops who had hustled to the battlefield. In the early stages of this assault, Heth was knocked senseless by a head wound, and Pettigrew assumed division command. Blue and gray killed and mangled each other, often at close quarters, both sides suffering horrific casualties. Slowly and violently, however, the Confederates gained the upper hand on the ridge.[30]

In its reserve role Pender's division, still in battle line, moved off Herr Ridge about 3 p.m. Scales's North Carolina brigade was on the left, his left close to the Chambersburg

Pike, Perrin's Palmettos in the center and Lane's North Carolinians expected to be coming up soon on the right of the line. Pender's fourth brigade, Thomas's Georgia troops, were left behind as a reserve and artillery support.[31]

Awaiting Lane, Perrin and Scales advanced about half a mile across an open wheat field, still west of Willoughby Run, before reaching the rear of Heth's position a mile or so ahead, again halting in "supporting distance of the troops in front," one of Pender's staff officers noted. Lane's troops came up to anchor Perrin's right about this time. From left to right, Perrin's line was composed of the Fourteenth, the First, the Twelfth and the Thirteenth South Carolina. Lt. Boyles of Company C, Twelfth South Carolina, said, "[We] advance at double quick over fences, gardens, hedges, &c, until we get in reach of their shells…. Here we rest and eat, the fight raging in our front." In the back of his mind, Boyles also must have recalled how he had been wounded in the fighting at White Oak Swamp in June 1862 and hoped to avoid being hit again in this battle. The sounds of combat ahead were heavier now, waves of musketry interspersed with the shrill yip of the rebel yell from Heth's men. "Many of the enemy's balls fell among us, but I recall no … result [other] than the startling of our nerves by their whistling past our ears and slapping the trees behind us," Lt. Caldwell said. "The artillery fire was slow on both sides."[32]

Outflanked and facing superior numbers, the Federals were overwhelmed and finally gave up McPherson's Ridge, falling back to Seminary Ridge about 3 p.m. There they regrouped behind makeshift breastworks on the grounds of the Lutheran Theological Seminary, some seven hundred yards west of Gettysburg. Bolstered by artillery, it would be the I Corps' last stand this day. Pettigrew occupied McPherson's Ridge, but his divisional onslaught lost steam about 3:30 p.m. due to his heavy casualties, exhaustion and the menace of the Union guns near the seminary buildings. He held the ridge, knowing that Pender's division was nearby and hopefully ready to seize the baton in the Confederates' combat relay. Pettigrew's halt and a brief lull before Pender's troops advanced gave Doubleday about fifteen precious minutes to further piece together his defenses along Seminary Ridge. But the Federals' overall situation in holding Gettysburg was becoming increasingly tenuous by the minute. On the Union right flank, elements of the XI Corps battling Ewell's Confederates north of town began breaking apart. This allowed some of Ewell's troops to link with Hill's troops and pressure the flank of the I Corps Yankees struggling to hold the portion of the ridges north of the Chambersburg Pike.[33]

2

"Go In, South Carolina!"

It was after 4 p.m. when Pender ordered Perrin, Scales and Lane forward again to bolster Heth's men to their front on McPherson's Ridge. The three brigades had "instructions to pass General Heth's division, if found at a halt, and charge the enemy's position," Maj. J.A. Engelhard, Pender's assistant adjutant-general reported. After crossing Willoughby Run—about one thousand yards west of Seminary Ridge—Perrin reorganized his line, telling his men to still hold their fire until ordered to do so. Sgt. B.F. Brown of Company L, First South Carolina, described what happened next: "Colonel Perrin, who was only a few paces from where my company … was lined up, said: 'Men, the order is to advance; you will go to the crest of the hill. If Heth does not need you, lie down and protect yourselves as well as you can; if he needs you, go to his assistance at once. Do not fire your guns; give them the bayonet; if they run, then see if they can outrun the bullet.'"

Perrin's troops continued up the combat-torn slope, the Fourteenth South Carolina on the left passing through the corpse-strewn portion of Herbst Woods where the Union general Reynolds had been killed that morning. Sgt. Brown continued his narrative: "When we reached the crest, it was plain that Heth did need us, for his men were at a standstill and exposed to a terrific fire" from Union guns on Seminary Ridge. Capt. Washington Shooter of the Twelfth South Carolina added that the "fire and smoke and dust and noise and confusion and disorder of battle had begun" for Pender's troops.[1]

Within minutes Perrin's ranks were passing through and around Heth's spent and bloodied troops, including Pettigrew's North Carolinians, who "seemed much exhausted by several hours' hard fighting," the colonel noted. The South Carolinians were now seeing even more effects of the gunfire they had been hearing earlier. "The field was thick with wounded hurrying to the rear and the ground was grey with dead and disabled," Lt. Caldwell wrote. "There was a general cheer for South Carolina as we moved past them," he said of Pettigrew's soldiers. Sgt. Brown also recalled this eventful moment: "As we swept through his [Heth's] lines, onward in our charge, the men cheered us with the stirring words, 'Go in, South Carolina! Go in, South Carolina!'" Other North Carolinians, retreating, offered a much different outlook, shouting to Perrin's men that "we would all be killed if we went forward," recalled a soldier in the Twelfth South Carolina. "The line did not halt for these men, but opened up to let them pass to the rear."[2]

"Our men moved as bravely forward as any troops ever did on earth," Perrin recalled. "We charged over Pettigrew's Brigade, the poor fellows could scarcely raise a cheer for us as we passed." Lt. Col. Brown of the Fourteenth South Carolina also noted this encounter: "Passing a burning house on our right [the Emmanuel Harman farmhouse] … the brigade mounted the hill [McPherson's Ridge] beyond and passed over the crippled lines of … Pettigrew's Brigade, which, after gallant fighting, had been with-drawn and were resting from their toils."[3]

The South Carolinians and Scales's troops descended the slope of east McPherson's Ridge, immediately coming under scattered artillery fire. "Our troops were in excellent spirits," Lt. James Armstrong of the First South Carolina wrote a few hours after the day's battle. "The enemy massed his artillery, and when we came within short range opened on our line with quite a variety of missiles, but did not stay our advance for a moment." On Perrin's right, Lane's brigade was being "annoyed" and held up by Gamble's dismounted Union troopers, who "kept up a severe enfilade fire." This delay put Lane to the rear of the attack by Perrin and Scales. Perrin's troops soon descended into a shallow depression between McPherson's Ridge and Seminary Ridge, which temporarily "sheltered us from the enemy's artillery" and allowed him "to reform my line." There, Perrin again "instructed regimental commanders when the advance was resumed not to allow a gun to be fired at the enemy until they received orders to do so." Advancing out of the ravine and "preserving an alignment" with Scales's brigade, the Carolinians started up the Seminary Ridge slope—and into the searing jaws of hell.[4]

As their battle line rose out of the ravine, the Carolinians could see up the slight western slope of Seminary Ridge, so named for the main brick building—Schmucker Hall—of the Lutheran Theological Seminary, crowning it among a cluster of shade trees and anchoring the enemy line. Atop this building, also known as the "Old Dorm," was a cupola where Buford and possibly Reynolds as well had observed the Confederate advance earlier that day. "In front and in view amid the grove of trees was the Seminary now changed from the halls of learning to a scene of bloodshed and carnage," Lt. Col. Brown related. "Beyond was a beautiful town partly concealed from view by the shade trees." The Yanks' defensive position along the ridge including a hastily built breastwork of "earth, rail and the like." This strongpoint on the western slope of the ridge and in front of the seminary was located a quarter mile west of Gettysburg and would be the Federals' last defense in this sector of the field. It was a menacing and deadly objective for the Confederates, who were soon looking into the maws of about twenty massed guns of Col. Charles Wainwright's I Corps artillery battalion, posted to the right of the Yank infantry and along the Chambersburg Pike. The Federals' line then ran south, bolstered by a stone fence beginning about 200 yards from the seminary and extending along the crest of the ridge. The fence actually was a short distance a little further back—or east—of the breastwork.[5]

Perrin's troops faced the makeshift defenses and would have to cross mainly open fields on the incline with some rail fences in their path. The breastwork was "full of Union soldiers pressed back, but not defeated, and replenished with fresh troops from the rear," Brown noted. Scales's brigade, on Perrin's left, had the Union artillery to its front and left flank. In front of Lane's left was a portion of the stone fence held by Gamble's cavalrymen, still fighting on foot with their carbines. At some point during Perrin's attack, these Union troopers contributed to the firestorm the South Carolinians endured. In all, the Federal line stretched some six hundred yards roughly from the Chambersburg Pike to the Fairfield Road. "Our line passed over Hill's [Heth's] and drove the enemy rapidly before us without firing a gun," Capt. Shooter of the Twelfth South Carolina recalled, adding, "We could see the Yankees running in wild disorder and everything went merry as a marriage bell until we ascended a hill [Seminary Ridge] where we saw their batteries and their last line of entrenchments—a stone wall."[6]

The Foe

The sweaty Union I Corps infantrymen settling into the Seminary Ridge defenses facing Perrin and Scales were Brig. Gen. Solomon Meredith's First Brigade of Wadsworth's division and Col. Chapman Biddle's First Brigade of Rowley's Third Division. Both brigades had been chewed up defending McPherson's Ridge, but remained full of fight, especially with Wainwright's artillery bolstering the seminary line. "What was left of the First Corps after all this slaughter rallied on Seminary Ridge," the interim corps commander, General Doubleday, related. Meredith's veterans, better known as the famed and combat-hardened "Iron Brigade"—a nickname earned on Antietam's sanguine fields—consisted of the 2nd, 6th, and 7th Wisconsin, the 19th Indiana and the 24th Michigan. The Midwestern warriors also were known as the "black hats" by friend and foe due to their distinctive and "own special non-regulation slouch hats," said one account.[7]

Biddle's regiments were the 80th York and the 121st, 142nd and 151st Pennsylvania. These Federals had not earned the battle prestige of Meredith's "black hats," but most were tough fighters whose own legend was already in the making this terrible day. Lt. Col. George F. McFarland's 151st Pennsylvania of Biddle's brigade was tasting battle for the first time at Gettysburg. The 151st was composed of "mostly solid, intelligent working men" from the villages and countryside of Berks, Juniata, Schuykill, Susquehanna and Pike counties. It was nicknamed the "Schoolteachers' Regiment" due to more than one hundred such educators in its ranks. About five months earlier these troops, most of whom were crack-shot hunters and woodsmen, had been issued new Springfield rifles, a stark contrast to the smoothbore long guns they used in the Pennsylvania wilds. McFarland realized the difference in weapons, and after hours and weeks of target practice and drills, the men became lethally proficient with the Springfields.[8]

Still, they were raw troops and were put in battery support near the seminary after reaching Gettysburg that morning. Around noon the 151st was posted as the I Corps' only remaining reserve. To that point the day had been relatively uneventful for McFarland's men, but this soon changed as they were sent to the front line. Many of the "Schoolteachers" never left McPherson's Ridge alive, the survivors now squaring off against Perrin's onrushing troops.[9]

A "furious storm of musketry and shells" from Yankee units to the left of the Chambersburg Pike assailed the Confederates charging up the slope, Perrin wrote. "The artillery of the enemy now opened upon us with fatal accuracy," Caldwell added. "They had a perfectly clear, unobstructed fire upon us." Capt. William S. Dunlop of the Twelfth South Carolina's Company B also remembered the "fearful accuracy" of the foe. "Shot and shell, succeeded by grape and canister, rained upon us," he recalled. As enemy rounds whipped into the ranks of the Twelfth's Company C, its commander, Capt. John A. Hinnant, "reeled and fell" when grapeshot tore into his left leg. Other rebels also crumpled, but the Confederates forged ahead.[10]

The Union gunners "began throwing grapeshot at us by the bushel it seems," noted Cpl. Thomas Littlejohn of the Twelfth. "They shot too high for us as the shot went over our heads. Had they been a little lower, I don't see how any of us could have escaped. As soon as we came in full sight we loaded and continued to advance." One of Littlejohn's comrades who didn't escape was Tom Willis, killed by a grapeshot to the head. The enemy "opened on us with grape and canister to our left, while the infantry poured leaden hail in front," recalled Lt. Boyles of the Twelfth, who saw Capt. Hinnant go down.

Shortly thereafter Boyles was hit by grapeshot in the right leg below the knee which "shattered the bone into splinters." Collapsing, the lieutenant saw "the shoe on that foot flying off some distance." Less than two yards from Boyles, two others from Company C, John A. Robertson and Jim Williamson, also fell victim to the Federals' fire. "Our brigade charged in splendid style, reserving our fire until we came to close quarters," recalled Lt. James Armstrong of the First South Carolina. "In advancing over the crest of a hill near the town, a most terrific fire of shell, grape, canister and small arms was poured into us. I never witnessed such firing before; it was providential how any of us escaped."[11]

Despite this punishment, "the instructions I had given were scrupulously observed," Perrin wrote in his battle report, and "not a gun was fired. The brigade received the enemy's fire without faltering; rushed up the hill at a charge, driving the enemy without difficulty to their last position." Ahead, some "lines of [Union] infantry had shown themselves across the field, but disappeared as we got within range of them." These Federals were apparently going into position along the Seminary Ridge defenses. The brigade "was met by a furious storm of musketry and shell," noted the division's battle report. The Carolinians "steadily advanced at a charge, reserving fire, as ordered."[12]

Roaring at the Confederates, Wainwright's guns included Battery B, First Pennsylvania Light Artillery, led by Capt. James H. Cooper, which had fallen back from McPherson's Ridge before the gray tide. Now Cooper's three rifled guns, unlimbered near the breastworks, were the Carolinians' primary tormentors. With Perrin's men edging closer, Cooper "caused our immediate front at the barricade to be cleared of our infantry," recalled Lt. James A. Gardner of Battery B. With these Yanks out of harm's way, Cooper then directed his guns "slightly to the left" and "poured into Perrin's troops a most disastrous fire of double charges of canister. Our immediate supports and the infantry to our left in the grove … at the same time fired deadly volleys of musketry. The severity of this fire staggered and checked Perrin and almost annihilated the left [the Fourteenth S.C.] of his brigade, his troops being wholly swept away from the front of our guns." Gardner also remembered the sight of "a single color bearer only, with a bravery to be admired," who "reached the rail barricade in front of us."[13]

Engulfed in this tornado of shell and canister that "continued to rain upon us," a Carolinian recalled, a "good many were killed and disabled," especially on the brigade's left, where Brown's Fourteenth South Carolina was closest to the blazing Yankee guns. Suddenly, the gray battle line "wavered under this murderous fire," the attack in peril of stalling even further. Seeing this, Perrin spurred his horse through the ranks of McCreary's troops and galloped to the head of the formation to lead the charge. "Filled with admiration for such courage as defied the whole fire of the enemy (naturally drawn to his horse, his uniform and his flashing sword) the brigade followed with a shout that was itself half a victory," Caldwell related. Rufus Harling in the Fourteenth also recalled this moment: "We were fired upon from right, left and center, and to retreat would have been complete destruction," he said. Perrin, "seeing our situation, came charging through our lines, at a time when it seemed no living being could escape the thick flying missiles of death, but the brave colonel dashed along our thin line, waving his sword and pointing at the enemy." John Steele added that Perrin "pulled his sword and waved it over us and said 'Follow me.' We raised the shout and charged." Lying helpless with his shattered leg, Lt. Boyles of the Twelfth also saw Perrin's dramatic moment, coming at a point as the "brigade wavered and [was] about to fall back."[14]

While Perrin's troops were dying or suffering greatly from the Federal rounds,

Scales's North Carolinians were being butchered by the bulk of the enemy artillery. Marching into the maws of Wainwright's guns, Scales's ranks were eviscerated in minutes by some of the most terrific artillery punishment of the war, and Scales himself was severely wounded in the leg. The survivors halted some distance to Perrin's left rear, many firing their muskets from a prone position. Perrin noted, "Scales Brigade came to a dead halt. The men lay down attempting to return the enemies fire." Seeing this, some soldiers in the Fourteenth South Carolina appeared to want to hug the ground as well. "The 14th for a moment seemed about to follow their example," Perrin wrote of Scales's troops, "but soon resumed the charge. The whole Brigade now moved forward with a yell."[15]

Lt. William H. Brunson of the Fourteenth was shot through both legs and fell on a Union captain who was on the ground and bleeding badly from a leg wound. Brunson, one of four brothers from Edgefield District, South Carolina, in the Confederate army, had the "ugly habit of constantly getting shot," wrote one of his comrades in Perrin's command. Brunson had been wounded twice at Gaines Mill, the more serious injury occurring when a bullet struck him in the mouth and exited the back of his neck. These gunshots were still healing when one of his hands was mangled by a projectile at Chancellorsville. At Gettysburg, he managed to crawl off the Federal officer and, seeing the other man's injury, offered his canteen. "Captain, you are bleeding profusely. I have some whiskey in my canteen which I thought I might need if badly wounded," Brunson told his enemy. "Drink it." The Yank took the canteen, but feeling its lightness, replied, "There is no more than a drink here. Have you had any?" When Brunson said he had not, the captain was reluctant to deprive the rebel, until Brunson convinced him that he might faint if he didn't drink. The tiny patch of civility where these men lay was surrounded by a horrific tempest of battle as blue and gray clawed at each other, the Yankees "all holding to the death," recalled an officer in the Fourteenth.[16]

Amid the screaming shells and zipping bullets, Perrin's men "rushed up the hill at a charge," driving off a few bluecoats "without difficulty," Perrin reported, not mentioning his role. The Confederates plunged forward as the Union cannoneers "maintained a constant and most galling fire upon us." Now his men were within some 300 yards of the Union line near the "theological college" and through the gun smoke could see blue infantry on the move in the distance across a field. The rebels surged ahead, crossing a "line of strong fencing" about 200 yards from the grove near the college. The Union guns poured forth "a perfect stream of grape and canister as our lines approached it," the Twelfth South Carolina's Capt. Dunlop remembered. The Carolinians "came over the ridge in front of the Seminary position on high-gear to within 200 yards of Biddle's line at the slight protection erected … earlier in the day," a Union officer recalled. Perrin's brigade "attacked us fiercely" with Scales's Confederates on Perrin's left, recalled the 151st Pennsylvania's Col. McFarland.[17]

Suddenly, the Federals in their front—the New Yorkers and Pennsylvanians of Biddle's brigade—struck like Thor's hammer. Perrin was no stranger to combat, having weathered all of the Army of Northern Virginia's major campaigns, but on this summer day in Pennsylvania, his Carolinians suffered "the most destructive fire of musketry I have ever been exposed to." "Men never fell faster in this brigade," Lt. Col. Brown of the Fourteenth wrote, "and perhaps never equally so." Brown also recalled how "the Union troops fired low, and their balls swept close to the ground on the dish-like field in their front." Brown continued: "To stop was destruction. To retreat was disaster. To go forward was orders," adding that the "minnie balls" were "sweeping the earth at every step."[18]

Dead, dying and wounded twisted and dropped, but the brigade "continued to press forward, however, without firing, until we reached the edge of the grove," Perrin noted. There, Biddle's troops triggered another lethal lightning strike. "At the charge bayonets, the enemy were behind a rock fence, and we could hear their officers distinctly encouraging their men to hold their fire, until the command to fire was given," another Carolinian related. "They obeyed their command implicitly, and rose to their feet and took as deliberate aim as if they were on dress parade." The hurricane of musketry was devastating. Perrin must have watched in stark horror as his old regiment, the Fourteenth South Carolina, was "staggered for a moment by the severity and destructiveness of the enemy's musketry. It looked to us as though this regiment was entirely destroyed." Dozens of men in the Fourteenth's Company K were hit by this scythe of bullets, noted Scott Allen, also a soldier in that company. Allen, whose brother, Lt. James H. Allen, led the company, had his uniform torn by several Miniés, but survived the day.[19]

"Here we met the most destructive fire of musketry, grape & canister I have ever been exposed to during the war," Perrin wrote to Gov. Bonham. "It was, however, but a volley." It is unclear which of the two deadly volleys Perrin referred to in his letter to Bonham—although it appears to be the second. Amid the violent mayhem the Carolinians were enduring, his description spanned only a matter of minutes and would have been appropriate for either volley. "The Federal infantry opened on us a repetition of the fire that had already slaughtered" so many other rebels, added Lt. Caldwell of the First South Carolina. "Still there was no giving back on our part," he said of the Confederates' not returning fire.[20]

With Scales's troops halted, Perrin realized that his beleaguered brigade was now without support on either flank. Lane's North Carolinians were still to the rear or off somewhere to the right, unable to dislodge Gamble's doughty cavalrymen, supported by a few pieces of artillery. "I here found myself without support either on the right or left," Perrin reported. "General Lane's brigade did not move upon my right at all, and was not at this time in sight of me." In his letter to Gov. Bonham, he added, "Lane's Brigade never came up at all." By this time, the Palmettos had advanced for some two miles, much of it "under a most terrific shelling & musketry," Perrin noted, "& without firing a gun until we came upon the enemies (*sic*) strong position at a breastwork & stone wall at the town of Gettysburg. We had lost many valuable men before we reached this point."[21]

"This gave the enemy an enfilading fire upon the Fourteenth," Perrin said of his naked left flank, but the men, led by Lt. Col. Brown and Maj. Edward Croft, held their ground despite heavy casualties. With the combat intensifying, there was "such a rattle of musketry I never heard surpassed," surgeon Welch related, adding, "How many brave fellows went down in death in this short period of time! Officers who have been in all the fights tell me they never saw our brigade act so gallantly before." With these developments and no support units coming up from the rear, the Palmettos would have to continue their attack alone.[22]

"The Yankees poured volley after volley of grapeshot and minnie ball into our ranks, but we still moved forward," said John Steele of the Twelfth South Carolina. Nearby, a comrade, W.M. Barton, dropped dead when a grapeshot ripped into his head. "We never shot or said one word until we got within about 100 yards of where they were behind a rock fence."[23]

With two of the Twelfth's flag bearers already casualties, Sgt. S.H. Huey of Company I "acted gallantly in seizing the colors of the Regiment, after it had fallen twice and bore them until he was shot down" with a severe neck wound, one account stated. An officer wrote, "One color bearer after another was shot ... until four were killed and two others wounded. And a scarcely less fatality [rate] attended the colors of the other regiments." At least four of the Twelfth's color bearers, Huey, Kimbrell, Davis and Rains, fell within ten minutes, stated another account.[24]

"With unabated ardor the Confederates pushed forward their battle-flags through the storm of deadly missiles that swept the open plain," added Capt. Dunlop of the Twelfth's Company B. "The line passed on, many of the men throwing away their knapsacks and blankets to keep up," related the First South Carolina's Lt. Caldwell. "Struggling and panting, but cheering and closing up, they went through the shell, through the Minie balls, heeding neither the dead who sank down by their sides, nor the fire from the front which killed them, until they threw themselves desperately on the line of Federals." In the "immediate front" of the 151st Pennsylvania was the battle line of the Fourteenth South Carolina. The close-quarters fighting in this sector was brief but no less deadly. "For ten or more minutes we successfully contested the position, breaking the lines in front from our better position behind the intrenchment and the trees of the grove," Col. McFarland related.[25]

Amid the confusion and uproar of combat and the dense smoke cloaking the field, Perrin apparently was initially unaware of the Union infantry in the defenses to his front as his line closed in, especially since his troops were enduring fire from several directions. Once he "discovered the enemy was posted" behind a "breastwork of rails," he took decisive action.[26]

Perrin ordered McCreary's First South Carolina to change position and launch a flank attack on this position. In the former's words, he "directed" McCreary's men "to oblique to the right ... and then to change front to the left, and attack in his [the enemy's] flank. This was done most effectually, under the lead of this gallant officer." "Finding that he could not cross our works, Perrin by a movement placed one of his regiments on the left of our barricade, and turned our position," wrote the Pennsylvanian James Gardner. McCreary's Carolinians sprang forward and overran the breastwork, routing the Yankee infantry defending it. Amid the gun smoke and mayhem, Sgt. Hugh Bullock of the First South Carolina found himself leading the survivors of his Company F and "was the first man over the breast works." The Carolinians of the First and Fourteenth regiments triggered a wave of bullets into the bluecoats, and the Union line in this area began to melt away. "The enemy, however, did not fly readily," Lt. Caldwell wrote. "They fought obstinately everywhere, and particularly against our right. In fact, it was not possible to dislodge them from that point, until having broken the portion of their line opposed to our left, we threw an enfilade fire along the wall."[27]

Col. McFarland ordered his Pennsylvanians "back in time to escape the flank fire" as "the enemy extended far to our left and soon made it impossible for us to remain longer in our enfiladed position." McFarland's horse was shot from under him, but he was uninjured. On foot he accompanied his Pennsylvanians withdrawing around the seminary. The Palmettos' breakthrough prompted Wainwright's gun crews on Perrin's left to hastily limber up, preparing to retreat. "The brigade set its heart upon the artillery that had so severely tried it," Lt. Caldwell noted. "The men closed upon the guns with all the rapidity their exhausted limbs would permit. The artillerists limbered up with commendable expedition, and applied whip and spur vigorously to their horses." McCreary's men were the closest to the Union cannon at this point. Musketry from the Carolinians toppled some of the gunners as they tried to withdraw, also killing several of the horses, which immobilized one of the fieldpieces. "There was now a race for who should first lay hand upon the piece," Caldwell wrote. "This was so entirely a matter of legs."[28]

While the First and Fourteenth South Carolina were thus engaged, Perrin sent Miller's Twelfth and Brockman's Thirteenth regiments to assail another portion of the stone wall to the right of the college where bluecoats—Gamble's dismounted troopers—had kept up a "constant and withering fire of musketry" on the brigade's front and right flank. To meet this menace, Capt. Dunlop of the Twelfth wheeled companies B and K to the right after a brief advance, the Palmetto soldiers aiming at the massed Federals behind the fence. They "delivered volley after volley into the naked flank of the enemy with such deadly effect that they began to break, at first a few, then a greater number and then the whole line," Dunlop related. "The yankees stood until we got close to them and then they ran like fine fellows," the Twelfth's John Steele remembered. In the assault along the fence he lost several friends, including P.B. Lindsay, James B. Fleming and John A. Nisbet, whose contorted corpses now lay on the sun-baked field with many others.[29]

As Miller's men gained the fence, and unleashed this enfilading fire, primarily against troopers of the Eighth New York Cavalry posted along the north end of the wall, the Thirteenth South Carolina rushed up as well. Brockman's soldiers also paid in death for possession of this position. J.T.P. Crosson, of the Thirteenth's Company G, related the tragic story of four of his comrades, including Pvt. Joe Matthews, a regimental color bearer, as the five of them neared the wall. Seeing enemy artillerists pointing a fieldpiece in their direction, one of the Carolinians said, "They are leveling a cannon on us; let us get behind the wall," Crosson recalled. One of the others replied that he wanted to take cover there but didn't want to be shot in the back in doing so. The five men were clambering atop the wall when the cannon blast ripped them, killing Matthews, Lt. Will C. McNinch and Pvt. R. Brown Moore, both of Company G, and Pvt. J.P. Rickard of Company D. Crosson, who had a hand resting on a small oak tree growing beside the wall, was shocked by the bloody carnage but otherwise uninjured. "They rushed up to the crest of the hill and the stone fence, driving everything before them," Perrin noted of Brockman's and Miller's regiments. "The Thirteenth now coming up, made it an easy task to drive the enemy down the opposite slope and across the open field west of Gettysburg." "Our entire line now swept down the hill in pursuit," added Capt. Dunlop of the Twelfth.[30]

Surgeon Welch of the Thirteenth wrote of the carnage: "When the order was given to charge upon the enemy, who were lying behind stone fences and other places of concealment, our men rushed forward with a perfect fury, yelling and driving them, though with great slaughter to themselves as well as to the Yankees…. As the enemy was concealed, they killed a great many of our men before we could get to them."[31]

Closer to the seminary, Lt. James Armstrong of the First South Carolina was shot in the left arm in the opening moments of the Yankee retreat. "We continued to advance," he wrote. "I was wounded just as the enemy began to fall back." Earlier, when one of the color bearers, Sgt. James Larkin, went down near the stone wall with a grapeshot puncturing a lung, the lieutenant grabbed the regimental flag and continued forward before he was wounded. Another color bearer, Cpl. Albert P. Owens of the First's Company E, fell with the Confederate and South Carolina banners in his flag belt.[32]

Meanwhile, Lt. Gardner and the other Pennsylvanians in Cooper's Battery were still fighting and initially unaware of the Carolinians' double breaches, possibly due to the combat smoke. "At a most opportune time," however, a Union officer arrived, informing

Capt. Cooper that the Union line was broken and that unless he withdrew immediately he and his battery would be captured. Gardner related that the gunners quickly limbered and trundled to the rear, passing "on the north side of the seminary," and "narrowly escaping capture, the enemy being around both flanks."[33]

McCreary's troops and the remnants of the Fourteenth South Carolina continued forward but were momentarily slowed by enemy infantry posted behind a stone wall to the left but nearer the college. There was a brief but savage fight there—likely saving some of Wainwright's fieldpieces from being captured—before the Carolinians overpowered the defenders. As the Union line dissolved, Col. McFarland of the 151st Pennsylvania stopped a "rod or two" from the north end of the building and stooped to check on the Confederates' progress. It was 4:20 p.m. At that point, McFarland related, "I received the volley from the left flank." The blast of musketry "knocked both legs from under me, badly shattering both, and I fell over on my left side towards the enemy," he recalled. The onrushing Carolinians barely missed scooping up the wounded McFarland. A private in the 151st Pennsylvania carried the colonel into a north entrance to the building, a bullet clipping off a button from McFarland's coat sleeve, barely missing the soldier, while some of Brown's troops began entering through a south-side door. "The shattered remnant of our regiment went to the rear, the enemy pursuing," McFarland remembered, adding in another account that the 151st was "as brave a regiment as ever entered the field." The 151st went into the battle with 466 officers and men, losing 337, including 99 killed. The vast majority of these casualties occurred on July 1.[34]

Sgt. B.F. Brown of McCreary's regiment recalled that as the rebels blanketed this portion of Seminary Ridge, his "schoolmate and classmate" P.H. Reilly barged into the Old Dorm and captured ten or more "panic stricken" Federals who had sought shelter in the rooms. By now, both the First and Fourteenth regiments had lost more than half their men, but had captured two artillery pieces, dozens of prisoners (Perrin reported "hundreds" of captives), and a number of caissons. The Federals "gave back at all points, and the rebel turn came to kill," stated the First's Lt. Caldwell. "As the disorganized mass fled towards Gettysburg, they suffered a far greater loss than they had previously been able to inflict upon us."[35]

The Fourteenth South Carolina swarmed over the ridge crest, passing on both sides of the seminary. Lt. Col. Brown led part of the regiment on the left side of the building while Major Edward Croft advanced past the right end with the rest of the troops. Croft apparently reached one of the enemy guns first and secured the only uninjured horse of the battery. He mounted it with the harness still on. Shortly afterward, the major handed a captured sword to Lt. Col. Brown and "loaned" the horse to Capt. T.P. Alston of the First South Carolina so that he could lead a squad of skirmishers into the town. Croft and other elements of the Fourteenth also continued toward Gettysburg. "But there was no crossing of swords or bayonets, for this is seldom done except on paper," Brown related. "It was no time for a thousand hair-breadth escapes with nobody hurt. It was not the clipping off of clothing, but the bodies of men that were struck." An unidentified soldier in the Fourteenth captured a large flag of the 149th Pennsylvania in the Union defenses, its slain color guard sprawled with it. Another Carolinian seized a smaller enemy banner and folded it against his chest inside his shirt. The retreat was well underway when the veterans of the shot-up Iron Brigade were caught up in the withdrawal. Capt. R.K. Beecham of the Second Wisconsin and others saw that "the Chambersburg Pike all the way from Seminary Ridge to the city was black with our troops in swift retreat. To our brigade no order for retreat was given that we can remember. In fact there was no time to waste; so we stood not on the order of our going, but went at once," he recalled.[36]

The Union commander, General Doubleday, apparently exaggerated in describing his role in the last stages of the retreat, writing: "I remained at the seminary superintending the final movement until thousands of hostile bayonets made their appearance around the sides of the building." Years later, Lt. Col. Brown of the Fourteenth took issue with this claim, stating in his memoir that only a few hundred South Carolinians swept past the "Old Dorm" after suffering some 600 casualties in the assault.[37]

Watching the action and the "close fighting throughout," General Pender rode onto smoke-shrouded Seminary Ridge within minutes of its capture and saw elements of Perrin's brigade "almost mingle with the Union soldiers" they were pursuing and suddenly disappear from his view in the combat haze. When the firing ceased soon afterward, he initially supposed the brigade had been overwhelmed, especially since he saw a large body of Federals in the distance. Riding forward, Pender met Lt. Richard L. Simmons of the Twelfth South Carolina, wounded and heading to the rear. Inquiring about the possible capture of Perrin's command, Simmons told Pender, "No, it is over the hill yonder."[38]

Brown and Maj. Croft led the Fourteenth South Carolina into Gettysburg between North Boundary Street and the old railroad bed. That regiment and McCreary's First each pushed toward the town square amid a flurry of confused combat in the streets. "By this time, the churches and the halls were filled with the disabled and wounded, and dying men lay on the streets and sidewalks," a Pennsylvania officer recalled. "Over these latter, and into the bewildered, retreating throng, there was sharp fighting … but there was no panic, —no rout. Remnants of regiments driven around this corner and that corner, kept by their colors the best they could, and then fell back to Cemetery Hill." The blue silk flag of the First South Carolina was the first Confederate banner to fly in the town after its skirmishers, under the mounted Capt. Alston, entered on Chambersburg Street. McCreary's men "dashed forward without a halt until their banner was floating in the town" square, related J.C. Lynes of the First's Company I. It was between 4:30 and 5 p.m. It is unclear who actually planted the First's flag at the square, but it appears to be W.A. Chatman of Company K. The soldier from Barnwell, South Carolina, apparently took up the banner when Lt. Armstrong was wounded in the seminary combat. Armstrong later described Chatman as "one of the most daring and dashing of men."[39]

The chaos continued a few minutes longer as Federals from the I and XI corps struggled to escape the pursuing Southerners, mainly Perrin's men and possibly a few lead elements of Ewell's corps. "We were surely greatly hurried and badly tangled in the streets of Gettysburg on that retreat … and many a brave Union soldier went to Richmond and to his death on that account," noted the Wisconsin Capt. Beecham. Hundreds of Yankees were captured. "We saw only Federal soldiers, some crossing the streets, but mostly in backyards, outhouses and places of concealment," one Carolinian recalled, "whence our soldiers were taking them in and sending them to the rear." "The enemy completely routed and driven from every point, Gettysburg was now completely in our possession," Perrin stated.[40]

3

"All the Yankees Born Can't Hurt Me"

In their relatively brief occupation of the town, Perrin's men rounded up prisoners and interacted with some of Gettysburg's civilians with mixed results. "No violence was offered to the citizens by our troops," Lt. Caldwell of the First South Carolina noted. "With the exception of the wheat trampled [in the fields during the attack] and one or two houses fired on the outskirts … by our shells, to dislodge sharpshooters, they were uninjured. They were so badly frightened, that they contributed many articles of food to pacify us, but there was nothing like a levy made upon them. Some light-fingered persons helped themselves secretly to fowls and other dainties, of course, but even these things were done gently." Caldwell's impressions were not so complimentary later in reproaching some Confederates who were behind the front line. "The bad behavior was in the rear, about the hospitals," he related, himself among the wounded. "There was a general uprooting of gardens and depopulation of hen-houses. But there, no insult was offered, nor was there any wanton destruction whatever." Of the day's battle, the lieutenant noted: "Federals and Confederates, both, seemed to be rather surprised at the sudden and violent collision—especially the former, who had been broken and driven from an admirable position, with a heavy loss in killed and wounded, and some four thousand prisoners."[1]

Surgeon Welch of the Thirteenth was touched by the sight of some civilian homes torched by Confederates after Union soldiers used them for cover amid the fighting. "I think this was wrong, because the families could not prevent the Yankees seeking shelter in their houses," he wrote to Cordelia. "I saw some of the poor women who had been thus treated. They were greatly distressed, and it excited my sympathy very much." Nevertheless, Welch and some colleagues entered a home from which the family, other than an elderly man, had fled, and were delighted by what they found inside. "A churn of excellent buttermilk had been left, and I with some other doctors helped ourselves," he penned. "Someone near by shot at us as we came out and barely missed us."[2]

With his brigade split in half, Perrin ordered the First and Fourteenth regiments—exhausted and decimated—to withdraw from the town and wait to reunite with the Twelfth and Thirteenth. He later would send a small detachment, led by Lt. E.B. Simmons of the Fourteenth, into Gettysburg to help round up any other prisoners. By now, Confederate units of Ewell's Second Corps were arriving in town, including Brig. Gen. Stephen Ramseur's brigade of Maj. Gen. Robert Rodes's division, entering from the left, or north. "What troops are those?" Perrin asked. A staff officer coming up just then replied that it was Rodes's division, to which Perrin "showed displeasure on account of their going in and taking the place captured by us," a Carolinian remembered. Still, the most immediate need for the Carolinians was to pull back and recuperate. Perrin "told us we had fought enough; that we might rest," the Twelfth's John Steele related. In addition to the untold number of dead in the Twelfth's Company H, sixteen others had been wounded in the day's action. "From the fatigue and somewhat disorganized condition of the troops engaged, it was thought inadvisable to continue the pursuit," said Capt. William Dunlop of the Twelfth's Company B. He added, "Although our loss was heavy our success was complete." In his company, Dunlop noted that James S. Ware, James Brigman, John Quinton and J.H. Smith were killed, while Lt. R.L. Simmons—mentioned earlier—was among the wounded.[3]

General Pender, after encountering the wounded Lt. Simmons, "rode forward with speed," found the Twelfth and Thirteenth South Carolina, and ordered these regiments back to a point between the town and the seminary to protect the division's right flank. He then rode into Gettysburg. At some point, Pender rode by the South Carolinians— it's unclear if this occurred while the First and Fourteenth regiments were still in Gettysburg or after the brigade regrouped west of town—"raised his hat to it, and complimented Col. Perrin on its performances that afternoon," Lt. Caldwell of the First related. "It is only the language of sober truth to say that it [the brigade] had covered itself in glory." Perrin recalled that Pender "soon came up and ordered me to put my men in some safer position. He rode amongst us, telling us we had acted most nobly." An unidentified correspondent with the Columbia (S.C.) *Guardian*, who mingled with these Palmettos a few weeks after the battle, gave another account of this incident: The troops were "highly complimented by Maj. Gen. Pender, a soldier of the 'Old Roman School,' who said it had saved the credit of his division. As he was riding by the 1st Regiment South Carolina Volunteers, which were resting after the battle, the warrior reined up his steed and waved his hat to their colors—a large blue Palmetto flag—in token of respect and admiration." Lt. Col. Brown of the Fourteenth recalled that his troops were still in Gettysburg when they were passed by Pender "at some shade trees on the right," the general complimenting the men.[4]

The First and Fourteenth South Carolina withdrew from the town and rejoined the Twelfth and Thirteenth regiments in the fields between Gettysburg and the seminary, where they rested. With Thomas's brigade coming up, the rest of Pender's division was brought in line with Perrin's troops along Seminary Ridge, facing the town and Cemetery Hill with its right on the Fairfield Road. "The sun was setting on that bloody field," an unidentified Carolinian wrote. "Each stone of some two miles was reeking with the warm blood of friends and foes. Each step of the way was counted with a corpse."[5]

General Lee rode by the position where Pender's men were resting, saluted him and said, "All honor to the noble North Carolinians." Pender, a born and bred Tarheel himself, replied, "Permit me, General, to correct an error—the brave *South* Carolinians saved my Division today." Lt. Col. Brown of the Fourteenth wrote of this incident: "General Lee then came up, and all honor was then given to 'the South Carolina brigade that captured Gettysburg.'" Pender at some point conversed with Col. Miller, Lt. Col. H.C. Davis and several other officers of the Twelfth S.C. who were discussing the day's battle. Of Perrin's command, Pender is said to have remarked, "Your Brigade has done *the fighting of my Division* today." As the Carolinians recuperated and bound their wounds, Perrin saw Union artillery on Cemetery Hill, southwest of town, one of the pieces firing at his brigade. He recognized it as "the same artillery which we had driven from our left near Gettysburg."[6]

Brown estimated the "terrible strife" he and the rest of Perrin's brigade endured that afternoon "was over in a few minutes—fifteen, say twenty at most." Years later he also saluted the stubbornness and combat prowess of the Union troops they battled on July 1. "It was no ordinary soldier that we had met," he wrote. "The prisoners captured were more intelligent than on other fields. They were mostly Pennsylvanians fighting for everything they held dear." Still, Perrin's rebels had singlehandedly pushed these Federals off Seminary Ridge, displaying their own moxie, courage and confidence as the veterans they were and with the toll they inflicted. When Brown returned to Gettysburg in 1882—nineteen years after the battle—he took special note of the trees. "On our side the firing was not slack nor wild," he recalled of his infantry's musketry reply that long-ago afternoon. "The trees in the Seminary grounds where the Union lines ran are still thickly covered with scars, from the ground to the height of a man, made with the bullets of our unerring rifles…. And the ground strewn with their dead and wounded well attested [to] the accuracy of the deadly aim" on the day of battle.[7]

"We captured the town of Gettysburg & hundreds of prisoners, thousands of small arms, two field pieces … a number of caisons and four standards," Perrin wrote to Gov. Bonham a few weeks after the battle. The most impressive flags taken were a banner of the U.S. First Corps "commanded by Reynolds, whom we killed" and the "beautiful flag" of the 104th New York, the "Wadsworth Guards." Perrin intended to send these standards to Bonham, "to be placed in the State House at Columbia," but higher authorities "ordered me to turn them in … to be sent to Richmond, I suppose."[8]

"Under the impression that the enemy were entirely routed, my own two divisions exhausted by some six hours' hard fighting, prudence led me to be content with what had been gained, and not push forward troops exhausted and necessarily disordered, probably to encounter fresh troops of the enemy," A.P. Hill noted. Pender's and Heth's soldiers "were bivouacked in the positions won," Hill continued, while Dick Anderson's division, which "had just come up," encamped about two miles west of the battlefield. Hill also praised Perrin and his Carolinians for their work and sacrifice on the day, writing of "Perrin's brigade taking position after position of the enemy and driving him through … Gettysburg." The corps commander added, "The want of cavalry had been and was again seriously felt," an obvious swipe at the absence of Jeb Stuart's cavalry. Yet Hill's troops had had a successful day, Hill described the results as a "brilliant victory" and the "almost total annihilation of the First Corps of the enemy." This was only a slight exaggeration, since Hill's corps had figured greatly in inflicting 5,750 casualties among the 8,200 Union First Corps troops in the battle that day.[9]

Maj. McCreary of the First had a terrifying moment at some point during the day's combat. A bullet struck him in the chest, stunning him and knocking him to the ground. "After recovering from the shock he crawled to his feet and was surprised to find neither blood nor wound." Continuing his examination he found the bullet, still hot, had torn into the leather-bound New Testament he carried in the breast pocket of his uniform coat. Replacing it in his pocket, he resumed the fight with his troops. Later it was determined that the round had torn through about half the pages. The story went that relatives went to the first page that was not torn and was immediately in the bullet's path. There they found Acts, chapter 27, verse 22: "Now I exhort you to be of good cheer, for there shall be no loss of any man's life."[10]

If Maj. Croft was among the first Confederates to enter Gettysburg, the sanguine events of the day did not allow him much time or respite to savor the honor. Croft, 28, was a Greenville native and an 1856 graduate of the S.C. Military Academy. He had settled near Aiken, where he was a planter, but the onslaught of war prompted him to raise a local company called the "Ryan Guards," which would eventually become Company H in the Fourteenth South Carolina. One of his brothers, Lt. Randell Croft, died while in service at Fort Sumter in 1862. Croft himself had been severely wounded in the arm and shoulder in the Seven Days battles but had recuperated enough to fight at Gettysburg.[11]

All of this was ancient history now as the Fourteenth and the rest of Perrin's brigade tallied their losses. The butcher's bill was indeed ghastly. Of the 1,100 or more Carolinians who fought that day, almost six hundred were casualties. "The Brigade now had been reduced to 500 men," Perrin wrote to Bonham on July 29. "Those we had left were so much exhausted that they could make no further effort." In his campaign report composed on August 13, Perrin reported that his casualties of killed and wounded on July 1 "did not fall short of 500," including a sanguine toll of color-bearers. "Better conduct was never exhibited on any field than was shown by both officers and men in this engagement," he noted of the day's action. "Each one of the color-sergeants taken into the fight was killed, in front of his regiment. Some regiments had a number of color-bearers shot down one after another. The officers generally were conspicuous in leading their men everywhere in the hottest of the fight."[12]

"The losses were immense," Lt. Col. Brown of the Fourteenth recalled. The Fourteenth, the largest regiment in the brigade, went into battle with 475 troops and lost over 200 dead and wounded. "There was no loss of prisoners" among the Carolinians, Brown stated. "They were all killed or wounded," he wrote, adding that more than 600 men fell in front of the makeshift breastworks. Each of the regiments in the brigade lost over one-third of its number. The Fourteenth's Company K was especially hard hit. Of 39 officers and men present, 34 were out of action, including four killed and 30 wounded, the latter including lieutenants B.B. Bryan and Simeon Cogburn, who suffered a severe foot wound. Five-foot-tall Pvt. George Ouzts, one of a number of men from his extended family serving in the Fourteenth, was slain in the attack. The Allen brothers were among the few unscathed. The decimation of this outfit would bring hard news to many loved ones in Edgefield District, where 72 men had joined up in organizing the company in August 1861. Overall, the regiment stacked 82 muskets—to remember the casualties amid the Carolinians who went into battle on July 1.[13]

Also among the Fourteenth's slain was Thomas R. Owens, of Company F. His father, Capt. Robert S. Owens, had raised the company from the young men of Laurens County, South Carolina, many from the town of Clinton, and led it to war. The captain had been mortally wounded at Frayser's Farm on June 30, 1862, almost exactly a year before his son's death. Thomas Owens was a mere fourteen years old when he enlisted at the beginning of the war. The teenager was killed still clutching the regimental colors, all but one member of the color guard dying as well. Another Laurens County soldier, William B. Parson of the Fourteenth's Company E, was wounded in the right thigh and captured. His brother, Pvt. Richmond E. Parson in the same company, died of a fever within months of the battle.[14]

Lt. Robert Briggs Watson of Company B in the Fourteenth was shot in the thigh about 3 p.m. and watched helplessly as his comrades continued the assault. "After a few hours I was carried off the field and laid under a tree," he recalled. Some six hours after being hit he was taken to the rear, but he received minimal care over the next two days due to the heavy fighting and the overwhelming numbers of wounded. "I was so saturated with blood that I had my drawers and trousers taken off and I was wrapped in a blanket," he remembered. The two Carter brothers from Darlington District—who were mentioned earlier—added to the casualties in the Fourteenth as well. Lt. Sidney Carter, who boasted that "all the Yankees born can't hurt me," fell with a Federal bullet piercing his chest, ripping down through his body. Giles Carter crumpled with a leg wound, and both brothers were captured in the process.[15]

The young entrepreneur Capt. Romulus Bowden was also down, shot in the left arm and left hand while leading the Thirteenth South Carolina's Company A. In agony from his second and third major wounds of the war, he undoubtedly must have questioned whether he would ever again see his parents and his beloved Mary. One of Bowden's comrades, 30-year-old Capt. John Dewberry of the Thirteenth's Company E, had fallen as well, one of his arms maimed. Dewberry had been one of the best farmers in the Cowpens section of Spartanburg County, South Carolina, before the war. Lying helpless, he was captured by the Federals before their retreat through the town.[16]

Lying on the field with his smashed leg, Lt. J.R. Boyles of the Twelfth's Company C was not out of peril after Perrin's battle line swept up Seminary Ridge. "Here I lay, bullets falling around like hail, still no infirmary or ambulance corps to carry me off for a length of time"; he recalled years later, "finally two of them ventured up; danger over, as they thought, but they had no stretcher to carry me; the July sun was broiling hot and I [was] famishing for water." Boyles told the men to get two poles, cut his sword belt into strips and use them to tie his blanket to the poles, to fashion a stretcher. This they did, starting for the rear, but the blanket "sagged so much that it came near smothering me," Boyles said. On reaching the "branch" (probably Willoughby Run), the Carolinians "had so recently crossed in all the pride of manhood, I begged the men to lay me down in the water to cool," the lieutenant recalled, "and for a time my life's blood caused the water to run red—I knew that if I lived I was ruined forever."[17]

Also fallen was Pvt. James R. Harvey of the Twelfth's Company F, the Winnsboro "stripling" who hopped a troop train to join the army. Harvey was wounded simultaneously in the thigh and in the opposite hip. Faint from blood loss, he lay on the battlefield until sometime the next day.[18]

Artillery

The Carolinians of the Pee Dee Artillery in Pegram's artillery reserve, Hill's corps, were engaged for much of the day, as was the rest of the battalion. Despite "the heavy fire to which the battalion was exposed" along Herr Ridge, losses were surprisingly low, consisting of two dead, eight wounded and six horses killed, the battalion's second-in-command, Capt. E.B. Brunson, reported. Lt. Zimmerman's major loss was a rifled gun disabled while rushing into action. During the combat, Pegram's men saw some enemy batteries posted "behind the crest of a hill"—apparently McPherson's Ridge—and "partially concealed." The battalion opened on these cannon with "ten Napoleons and seven rifled guns," The Carolinians, with their other three guns were actively engaged and did good service throughout the day. They and the rest of Pegram's cannoneers pounded the Union batteries, forcing them to limber up and retreat three times, Brunson reported.

But the bluecoats hung tough, twice bringing their guns back "under shelter of the hills" and into position to support Union infantry coming forward. Zimmerman's men joined the rest of the battalion in blasting away at the "advancing infantry, whose lines our guns played upon … with telling effect," Brunson noted. The battalion bivouacked for the night near Herr Ridge. General Heth took special notice of Pegram's command in his battle report written a few weeks later. "At the same time that it would afford me much gratification, I would be doing but justice to the several batteries of Pegram's battalion in mentioning the assistance they rendered during this battle, but I have been unable to find out the names of the commanders of those batteries stationed at the points where important service was rendered," Heth related.[19]

Meanwhile, South Carolina Maj. David McIntosh and his reserve artillery battalion, also in Hill's corps, had for the most part held their position on Herr Ridge through much of the day, assisting Ewell's troops as well as Hill's infantry. "The artillery fire on both sides was occasionally brisk, but deliberate on our part," he reported. At different times, his Virginia and Alabama gunners opened a flank fire against Union cannon engaging Ewell's artillery, "which caused them to leave the position in haste." Another "fine opportunity" came when the battalion, assisted by Pegram's artillery, blasted away at a "heavy column" of Yankee infantry formed in one of the railroad cuts and along a fence line. The enemy troops were "entirely discomfited" and "disappeared from the field," McIntosh said. He had earlier advanced two of his batteries "to the intervening hollow," where they "followed close upon the enemy as he left the hills." Six of McIntosh's guns from two batteries also assisted Lane's infantry of Pender's division in trying to uproot Gamble's dismounted Union cavalrymen along Seminary Ridge. "The Whitworth guns were used to shell the woods to the right of the town" as well as "distant points wherever the enemy could be seen." McIntosh's losses were one Virginian killed, another man wounded and "several horses disabled." Two of his guns were damaged, one by a solid shot "striking it full in the face," he noted. His battalion was "at times severely engaged and doing effective work against masses of infantry of the enemy," McIntosh added in a postwar account. The "guns of either battalion [were] being used in the advance whenever a favorable opportunity offered," McIntosh added. Col. Walker, Hill's reserve artillery chief, also noted the fine job done by Pegram's and McIntosh's gunners, stating that they "opened fire on the enemy with marked effect, finally driving them back out of range."[20]

As the hot afternoon waned, Longstreet joined Lee on Seminary Ridge about 5 p.m. The generals had ridden together earlier in the day before Lee rushed ahead to gauge what was happening amid the combat cacophony. The stately Virginian was watching the last of the retreating Federals streaming away from Gettysburg and up the slopes of Cemetery Hill, which Longstreet later described as "the rock-ribbed hill that served as a burying ground for the city." Lee pointed out the enemy concentration on the heights, and for five to ten minutes Longstreet used his field-glasses to study the Federals gathering there as well as the terrain in the Confederates' front. The Carolinian was excited, believing the Yankees were in a position greatly suited for the defensive, two-steps-ahead matchup he envisioned for Lee's army. In so many words, he advised Lee that the Confederates should move around the Union left, putting themselves between the Federals and Washington, D.C. Taking a strong position somewhere in the Pennsylvania countryside, they would await Meade's attack. If the enemy balked, the army would march closer to Washington and occupy another defensive line. With the capital thus threatened, Meade would have little choice but to attack then. Longstreet was confident of another monumental triumph, telling Lee, "The probabilities are that the fruits of our success will be great." Lee, however, disagreed, replying, "No … the enemy is there, and I am going to attack him there." Longstreet persisted, saying that his proposed move would allow the Confederates to control roads leading to Washington and Baltimore, but Lee was adamant: "No, they are there in position, and I am going to whip them or they are going to whip me." Longstreet knew his opinion was lost, at least temporarily. "I saw he was in no frame of mind to listen to further argument at that time, so I did not push the matter, but determined to renew the subject the next morning," he related.[21]

Perrin's Carolinians and other rebels on Seminary Ridge watched the continuous Union buildup unfolding on the high ground in front of them. "There may have been a lack of tactical military knowledge on the part of the men in the ranks, but there certainly was no lack of military common sense among them, and there was a general condemnation of the failure to seize Cemetery Ridge, which could have easily been done after the rout of the enemy," one of Perrin's men recalled years later. "For an hour or two before dark, the long columns of the enemy could be plainly seen with the naked eye moving in and occupying the Ridge. Not a single effort was made to impede them. Not one shot was fired. 'Oh for one hour of Stonewall Jackson,' said some of the boys, as they looked on from the Seminary grounds." Perrin himself was incensed about the lack of aggression shown in following up the Confederate successes of the day. "The enemy during this eventful time was taking their new position at the Cemetery Hill which afterwards baffled all our efforts to take," he wrote to Governor Bonham on July 29. "The very batteries which we had run off … were the first to fire a shot from their new position. The very infantry that we had run from the stone walls that surround Gettysburg were the first to form a line of battle in their new position. The first shell fired by them from that position was aimed at my Brigade."[22]

Perrin also was highly critical Dick Anderson's failure to reach the field and potentially help shove the Federals off Cemetery Hill. He claimed that when Pender told him to reform his brigade after its attack, the general also said "he had sent back for Anderson's Division, supposing as I suppose[d] of course that Anderson was not far off. But neither Anderson nor his Division was anywhere to be found," Perrin wrote to Bonham. "I suppose you will be curious to know where Anderson was & why he was out of the way at so important a juncture. His failure to be up was the cause of the failure of the campaign. I know he [Anderson] had camped some miles in our rear that night preceding the battle, but I know not why. It may have been Gen. Hill's fault & it may have been the fault of Anderson himself. I saw nothing of him until the next day."[23]

Anderson's command fell into column just after daylight on July 1 from their encampments at Fayetteville, Pennsylvania, a few miles east of Chambersburg. Anderson's five brigades—composed of soldiers from Alabama, Virginia, Georgia, Mississippi and Florida, along with a Georgia artillery battalion—passed through the South Mountain gap and reached Cashtown by early afternoon, where it "halted for further orders." Anderson, 41, was a native of the Stateburg section of Sumter County, South Carolina, an 1842 West Point graduate in an outstanding class that included 22 men who would eventually become either Union or Confederate generals (out of 37 graduates alive in 1861). Anderson fought well in the Mexican War and was a captain of U.S. dragoons when he resigned his commission to join the Confederacy in March 1861. Within four months he was promoted brigadier and assumed command at Charleston. Early in 1862, he was sent to Virginia to lead a brigade in Longstreet's command and was with the Army of

Northern Virginia for the rest of the war, his battle tenacity earning him the nickname "Fighting Dick" from his men. Appointed major general in July 1862, he led his division in the major battles leading up to Gettysburg. "Tall, strong, and of fine background, Anderson never was disposed to quibble over authority or to indulge in any sort of boastfulness," historian Douglas Southall Freeman wrote of him. Anderson was "beloved in the army for his kindness, amiability, and unselfishness." The war already had seen him wounded twice, a bullet breaking his left arm at Santa Rosa Island, Florida, in October 1861, and a shot to the thigh knocking him from his horse at Antietam.

Nearing Cashtown, Anderson's men heard "the sound of brisk cannonading near Gettysburg."[24] The troops rested for about an hour at the village before Anderson received orders from Hill to come to Gettysburg. Approaching the battlefield and the Confederate units west of town, Anderson was instructed to post his brigades in battle line in a position "just vacated by Pender's division." The Palmetto general's troops who settled in on the already bloody terrain were Brig. Gen. Cadmus Wilcox's Alabamians, Brig. Gen. A.R. Wright's Georgians, Brig. Gen. William Mahone's Virginians, Brig. Gen. Carnot Posey's Mississippians and Col. David Lang's understrength Florida brigade. The artillery, the Sumter Battalion under Maj. John Lane, was composed mainly of men from Sumter County, Georgia. Wilcox's soldiers and one of Lane's batteries were to be posted in a "detached position" about a mile to the right of Anderson's main line, apparently as a defensive precaution. Thus, Perrin's ire toward Anderson appears to be misplaced and possibly better aimed at A.P. Hill. With Heth's and Pender's divisions "exhausted" and believing the enemy "entirely routed," Hill decided not to push these troops any further over unknown ground and likely to clash with "fresh" Federal forces. He also decided to halt Anderson's division "some 2 miles in rear of the battle-ground." Anderson's report states basically the same facts.[25]

"Late in the evening" that day, Pvt. J.A. Walker of the Forty-fifth Georgia in Thomas's brigade was ordered to lead a platoon over the ground covered by Perrin's attack, burying the dead and caring for the wounded. "In the rapidity and confusion of the day's work the dead and wounded were left much as they fell," he later related. Many of the slain Carolinians "were still unburied and a few wounded [were] sitting about the fence corners." One of the first bodies to be buried was a "young man of perhaps thirty years, who did not die suddenly. There was evidence of a struggle, and the torn fragments of letters lying around" the soldier, along with "the broken pieces" of a daguerreotype. Curious about the Carolinian's identity, Walker said that he examined the shattered frame and found inside a piece of pink paper. On it, "written in a feminine hand," was the name and address of a woman living in Warrenton, South Carolina. He pocketed the paper, the Georgians burying the soldier where he lay.[26]

The platoon pressed on, interring gray and some blue, before coming upon the corpse of one of Perrin's officers. The Georgians first noticed a white handkerchief covering the man's face. "We approached to find that in the hour of his death some kind friend had fastened this handkerchief to a few straws, which kept the sun from burning his face, and his death had been so calmly [that] he had not broken down the frail canopy," Walker recalled. The detail somehow determined that the man was a captain from Charleston, but "his name was nowhere to be found."[27]

Near nightfall, surgeon Welch of the Thirteenth South Carolina made his way through the ranks of the Confederates just getting to the field and reached the regiment's field hospital. It would be a horrific night for the 29-year-old doctor from Newberry

County, South Carolina, but one that was not unfamiliar. "When I arrived at the hospital my ears were greeted as usual at such time with the moans and cries of the wounded," he later wrote to his wife. "I went to work and did not pretend to rest until next morning after daylight." Also somewhere behind the Confederate line, Dr. Louis V. Huot, surgeon for the Fourteenth South Carolina, faced a huge task over the coming days. Huot "performed many skillful operations, drawing praise from Union surgeons," Lt. Col. Brown of the Fourteenth recalled.[28]

Among the many beyond the care of these physicians was Capt. Thomas J. Warren, commander of the Fifteenth South Carolina's Company D, who was killed this day. Warren, 38, was from Camden, South Carolina, and had been "editor and proprietor" of the *Camden Journal* newspaper for some years before the war. Warren was later described as "a high spirited and Christian gentleman" who was "a warm advocate of secession." Another of Perrin's men, Pvt. John B. Bagwell of the Fourteenth's Company C, had hustled toward Gettysburg that morning but had fallen out due to an ankle badly injured shortly before the battle. "I could not follow," he recalled years later of watching his comrades march into harm's way. Later in the day Bagwell was taken to a brigade field hospital where he saw some of the gruesome results of the butchery the Fourteenth had endured. One of his buddies in the company, Pvt. H.A. "Hamp" Phillips, had a gaping chest wound. "I saw a silk handkerchief pulled through his body," Bagwell related. He spent the next two nights tending to another Carolinian, Pvt. John R. Smith, trying to keep him from bleeding to death. Bagwell also mentioned Sgt. John P. Pool of McCreary's First South Carolina and Lt. N. Austin of the Fourteenth's Company E, both of whom were wounded.[29]

D.J. Carter of Company I, Twelfth South Carolina, kept a diary of the campaign and, apparently that night, penned a brief description of the hard combat. Carter, however, was more affected by the loss of five comrades in his company, some of whom were mentioned by Pvt. John Coxe of the Twelfth's Company H. in his recollections. Carter lamented the deaths of Sgt. P.B. Lindsay, Cpl. W.M. Barton and privates James B. Fleming, J.P. Caskey and J.A. Nesbit. His July 1 diary entry about his lost buddies would have been a fitting requiem for the many on both sides who fell that day: "The five young men were as worthy and reliable as the Regiment afforded," he wrote. "We mourn their loss as brothers—they were brave to a fault."[30]

Lt. Col. Brown of the Fourteenth, meanwhile, never forgot the gory uniqueness of the day's struggle. "The nature of the ground was such and the contest so brief that the wounded could not be moved, and were wounded twice, thrice and as many as four times, after being first stricken down," he recalled years later. "A few who, with shattered arms or wounded bodies ran back in safety to the surgeons, have not ceased to appreciate their legs for good service rendered. It was the only battlefield in which all avenues of escape for our wounded were closed. There was nothing that the ambulance corps could do. The ground was swept at every point by the deadly minnie balls. The artillery fire is terrible, but the almost silent whirl of the minnie ball is the death-dealing missile in battle. Not a foot of ground presented a place of safety."[31]

Cavalry

The bone-tired horsemen of Jeb Stuart's cavalry curled into positions around Carlisle, Pennsylvania, on the afternoon of July 1, trying to locate Lee's army. A day earlier, on the morning of June 30, Stuart's troopers had unexpectedly collided with Union cavalry at Hanover, some sixteen miles east of Gettysburg. There was sharp fighting in the town's streets as the blue and gray horsemen clawed at each other, carbine and revolver fire reverberating among the homes and stores. The Federals hung on to the town, Stuart's column veered northwest toward Carlisle, some thirty miles to the northwest. This movement mutely illustrates that Stuart had absolutely no clue as to the whereabouts of Lee's forces, his cavalry riding further away from a linkup with Lee. Among Stuart's horsemen was a South Carolina brigade led by Brig. Gen. Wade Hampton, a larger-than-life citizen soldier who was one of the wealthiest men in the Palmetto State. A landowner and politician before the war, he had evolved into a savvy and battle-scarred cavalry chieftain, who would flirt with death at Gettysburg hours later.[32]

At Carlisle, the Stuart Horse Artillery, commanded by Maj. R.F. Beckham, shelled the town, the cannoneers including the South Carolinians of Capt. James F. Hart's battery. The bombardment was due to riflemen, apparently state militia, who peppered the Confederates from buildings in town, but who drew little, if any, blood. The gray troopers soon gained control of the town, the highlight of their carnage being the burning of the U.S. Cavalry barracks there. By now Stuart's men were past the point of exhaustion after seemingly endless hours in the saddle, little sleep and scant rations. "Whole regiments slept in the saddle, their faithful animals keeping the road unguided," Stuart reported. "In some instances they fell from their horses, overcome with physical fatigue and sleepiness."[33]

Some thirty or so miles southwest of Carlisle, the South Carolinians of Brig. Gen. Joseph Kershaw's brigade in Maj. Gen. Lafayette McLaws's division of Longstreet's corps were on the move to reach Gettysburg. The British army observer Lt. Col. Arthur Fremantle had the opportunity to see this division on the march on June 25 north of Winchester, Virginia. The gray-clad columns "were composed of Georgians, Mississippians and South Carolinians," he related.

> They marched very well, and there was no attempt at straggling; quite a different state of things from [General Joseph E.] Johnston's men in Mississippi. All were well shod and efficiently clothed. In rear of each regiment were from twenty to thirty [N]egro slaves, and a certain number of unarmed men carrying stretchers and wearing in their hats the red badges of the ambulance corps;—this is an excellent institution, for it prevents unwounded men falling out on pretence of taking wounded to the rear. The knapsacks of the men still bear the names of Massachusetts, Vermont, New Jersey or other regiments to which they originally belonged. There were about twenty wagons to each brigade, most of which were marked U.S., and each of these brigades was about 2,800 strong…. All the men seem in the highest spirits, and were cheering and yelling most vociferously.[34]

By the night of June 30, Kershaw's troops were encamped at the village of Fayetteville on the Chambersburg Pike. On July 1, they remained in camp most of the day while Dick Anderson's division—which had bivouacked nearby—and other components of Lee's army occupied the road. It had rained heavily the night before, and the Carolinians spent the forenoon resting, cooking, eating and drying out their wet blankets. The "sun ushered in a beautiful morning," recalled Pvt. Daniel T. Hargrove of the Eighth South Carolina's Company K. "The business of the day was assumed as usual, but with a feeling of apprehension as cavalrymen were dashing up and down the roads…. The plowman watched with anxious eye, the housekeeper gazed out in anxious wonder, while panting steeds with soldierly riders dashed to and fro."[35]

"The distance intervening and the mountainous … country prevented us from hearing the roar of the guns, and little did any of us think, while enjoying the rest in our tents, [that] one portion of our army was in the throes of a desperate battle," another Carolinian recalled. Kershaw's troops finally were on the march by 4 p.m. They made good progress, but after dark were held up again by Confederate troops and wagons ahead of them. At one point, they heard the distant grumble of artillery fire. As they listened, Capt. R.C. Pulliam of the Second Carolina's Company B remarked, "Boys, that sounds familiar," one of his men, Pvt. John Coxe, recalled. The lead elements of the brigade reached a point about two miles from Gettysburg and bivouacked near midnight on the left side of the Chambersburg Pike. The men of Maj. Robert C. Maffett's Third South Carolina Infantry found themselves settling down on the western fringe of the battleground, where they rested for a few hours. Some of the Carolinians, however, apparently did not reach the brigade's camp until hours later, the darkness lending confusion as to whether they had even reached the battlefield. Augustus Dickert of Kershaw's command noted that he was among soldiers who topped a hill and beheld "a great sea of white tents, silent and still," which was one of A.P. Hill's field hospitals. Here Kershaw's men heard about that day's horrific combat and began inquiring about the fate of friends and relatives in Hill's corps, especially Perrin's brigade. The Southerners "listened with no little pride to the report of their desperate struggle through the streets of Gettysburg, and to learn that the flag … of a Palmetto regiment first waved over the city," Dickert related. Despite the late hour and fatigue from the march, Dickert heard that an old friend and schoolmate, Lieutenant W.L. Leitsey, had been desperately wounded. Dickert searched among the tents and eventually located his friend. "I found him severely wounded, so much so that I never met him afterwards," he wrote. Kershaw's brigade had orders to march at 4 a.m. on the 2nd.[36]

Other reunions were taking place as well. Tending to the many wounded, surgeon Spencer Welch of the Thirteenth South Carolina in Perrin's brigade learned that Longstreet's corps had reached the field and that McLaws's division was encamped near the hospital, Kershaw's troops almost on the grounds. Welch apparently took a short break outside and almost immediately found himself amid some old friends from Laurens, South Carolina, who were now in Kershaw's command and whom he had not seen since the war began. "They all seemed surprised and glad to see me; but I had work to do and they had fighting, so we could not remain long together," the doctor later wrote his wife. "They were all lively and jocose." Welch was especially struck by the happy mood of one of these friends who "was in a gay humor and left me as one going on some pleasant excursion…." Hours later, on the afternoon of July 2, the light-hearted Carolinian would be a corpse, killed by the concussion of a shell burst.[37]

Col. John D. Kennedy's Second South Carolina Infantry in Kershaw's brigade halted near a large house just off the pike and saw a number of wounded men, most of them Confederates, lying in the front yard, Private Coxe remembered. Three women who lived in the home were tending to the wounded, as were several doctors who were in and out of the house. "The lights, being candles, were rather dim, and occasionally we heard groans of the wounded," Coxe related. Kennedy's soldiers spread out near the pike and stacked arms. "As we had nothing to cook, no fires were lighted, and so we lay down and slept," said Coxe. Pvt. William T. Shumate, also of the Second, bedded down with his comrades in a clover field, recalling that it was "the last natural sleep many of the brave boys ever enjoyed." Nearby, Daniel Hargrove and his comrades in the Eighth South Carolina were "cracking 'hard tack' and writing letters home. Here and there were little groups around candles, writing letters that to many a one was to be his last message to loved ones at home."[38]

Stuart was still at Carlisle after midnight on Thursday, July 2, when he received word from Lee that the army was at Gettysburg and was in battle on Wednesday. "I instantly dispatched to [Wade] Hampton" and his South Carolinians to march ten miles toward Gettysburg overnight, Stuart noted, and he "gave orders to the other brigades" to be prepared to reach the battlefield early that day. He immediately ordered his horsemen on the thirty-mile trek to finally link up with the Army of Northern Virginia. Stuart himself started out for Gettysburg in advance of the other brigades. Incredibly, the cavalry chieftain had not been in contact with the main army since June 25, leaving Lee uninformed as to what enemy movements and threats he faced in this unfamiliar territory. Still, Lee had the two other cavalry brigades—under brigadier generals William E. "Grumble" Jones and Beverly H. Robertson—with his main force. The question lingers even today of why Lee did not use these horsemen more effectively in Stuart's absence.[39]

His cavalry issues aside, Lee later summed up Wednesday's results: "The enemy was driven through Gettysburg with heavy loss, including about 5,000 prisoners and several pieces of artillery," he noted in his July 31 campaign report. "He retired to a high range of hills south and east of the town. The attack was not pressed that afternoon, the enemy's force being unknown, and it being considered advisable to await the arrival of the rest our troops." Lee sent orders to "hasten the march" of the rest of his army and tried to determine the enemy's strength, positions and "the most favorable point of attack. It had not been intended to fight a general battle at such a distance from our base, unless attacked by the enemy, but finding ourselves unexpectedly confronted by the Federal Army, it became a matter of difficulty to withdraw through the mountains with our large trains. At the same time, the country was unfavorable for collecting supplies while in the presence of the enemy's main body, as he was enabled to restrain our foraging parties."[40]

Still, the Confederates had squandered an opportunity to seize at least more of the high ground around Gettysburg before the Federals became more organized and reinforced there. Lee's orders to avoid a general engagement—even though that is exactly what occurred on July 1—caused hesitation among some officers, including Ewell, to take further offensive action until the rest of the army reached the field. Both sides had been greatly bloodied when they essentially blundered into each other this day, but Abner Perrin's troops had led the rebels to victory, taking Seminary Ridge and being first to enter the town of Gettysburg itself.

From different directions, hundreds of other South Carolinians—as well as other Confederates—were converging on this soon-to-be hallowed field of national destiny. For Lee, they were all crucial elements in how he could build on the momentum of Wednesday. "Encouraged by the successful issue of the engagement…, and in view of the valuable results that would ensue from the defeat of the army of General Meade, it was thought advisable to renew the attack" the next day, he related.[41]

4

"Tomorrow I Am Going to Lose My Life"

Thursday, July 2

The enemy titans, both injured and exhausted, sized up each other through the early morning as more lethal chess pieces—blue and gray—reached the battlefield. The line of Lee's army on Seminary Ridge was extended north and northeast by Ewell's corps. A.P. Hill's corps, including Pender's division and Perrin's brigade, was in the center, and the troops of Longstreet's corps, with McLaws's division, including Joe Kershaw's Carolinians, came up within the next few hours to form Lee's right flank. One of Longstreet's other two divisions, Maj. Gen. John B. Hood's command, also was nearing the field, while his third division, commanded by Maj. Gen. George Pickett, remained at Chambersburg destroying enemy property and supplies. Stuart's cavalry was also beginning to return to the Confederate fold, and most of the artillery was being massed as well.[1]

Longstreet rose about 3 a.m. and again joined Lee on Seminary Ridge, both anxious to see the extent of Union reinforcements during the night. The most immediate problem for Lee was that elements of six Union infantry corps—the I, II, III, V, VI and XI—plus cavalry and artillery were either on the field or filtering into position as well. Union Maj. Gen. George G. Meade, the newly minted commander of the Army of the Potomac, was also present, arriving overnight.

Meade, a 47-year-old Pennsylvanian, was West Point tough—class of 1835—a scarred, seasoned and savvy leader who had fought in the Mexican War. He had been handed the reins of this fearsome weapon—at the very least on paper—only a few days earlier, on June 28. Its previous commander, Joseph Hooker, had resigned three days earlier, but his days had been numbered since the Confederate triumph at Chancellorsville in early May. Meade recovered from severe wounds in the Seven Days battles in 1862, seeing action at Second Bull Run, Antietam and Fredericksburg. Ironically, he had led the Union V Corps at Chancellorsville under Hooker's leadership. After learning of Meade's promotion, Lee is reported to have said, "General Meade will commit no blunder in my front, and if I make one he will make haste to take advantage of it."[2]

From prisoners taken the previous day, Lee knew that he had fought two Union corps and that the rest of Meade's army was on the way to Gettysburg, but he remained without "information as to its proximity." The situation remained fluid that morning as these Federal troops were arriving but were not yet fully deployed from Cemetery Hill, along the southern reaches of Cemetery Ridge and beyond. Within hours, however, most

41

of these Yanks would be looking down at the rebels in a fishhook-shaped defensive line from Culp's Hill to the north, to Cemetery Hill and south along Cemetery Ridge, the latter generally paralleling Seminary Ridge across a broad valley of woods, fields and orchards bisected by the north-south Emmitsburg Road.[3]

As he had the previous afternoon, Longstreet again proposed a movement around the Union left to reach the Federals' rear, allowing the Confederates to control roads to Washington and Baltimore. Lee, however, remained firm and—"unwilling to consider the proposition"—rode to confer with Ewell on the Confederate left about the possibility of making an assault there. Presently, Lee returned from Ewell and found Longstreet on Seminary Ridge. The commander had reached a decision: Longstreet would assail the seemingly exposed left flank of the enemy with the divisions of Hood and McLaws. These Confederates would extend Lee's right flank upon their arrival on the field and attempt to roll up the Union line, basically attacking from south to north parallel to the Emmitsburg Road. Lee had earlier sent two engineer officers to find the best route for McLaws and Hood to march south and get into positions for the attack without being seen by Union signalmen on Cemetery Ridge. Lee ordered this movement to begin about 11 a.m., McLaws's division in front followed by Hood's troops, all led by the engineer officers. Very little went as planned. The attack would be delayed for hours and hundreds of men would pay with their blood.[4]

Hampton

The cavalrymen of Wade Hampton's brigade were nearing the village of Hunterstown, some six miles northeast of Gettysburg, about 2 p.m. after rejoining Stuart's main force that morning. By this time the rest of the mounted column was nearing Gettysburg at Brinkerhoff's Ridge, Stuart and the main body having passed through Hunterstown about noon. The Georgians of Cobb's Legion in Hampton's command had been in the area doing reconnaissance since June 29 and were now reunited with their brigade, which also included the First and Second South Carolina Cavalry, First North Carolina Cavalry, the Jeff Davis Legion (composed of Alabama, Georgia and Mississippi troopers), and Phillips's Legion (of Georgians). Stuart dispatched orders for Hampton, whose troopers were at the rear of the column, to come up and take position on the left of the rebel infantry with the main army.[5]

The First South Carolina was commanded by Lt. Col. John D. Twiggs, replacing Col. John Logan Black, who was wounded in the cavalry clash at Upperville in June. Black returned to the army during the Gettysburg battle, fighting with an independent and temporary command, but did not reach his regiment in time to lead it in action. The Second South Carolina was led by 30-year-old Maj. Thomas J. Lipscomb, who had taken over the reins after Col. Matthew C. Butler lost a foot to an artillery round and Lt. Col. Frank Hampton, General Hampton's younger brother, was mortally wounded, both at Brandy Station less than a month earlier. Lipscomb, one of five brothers in the Confederate army, was from Abbeville District, South Carolina, and attended South Carolina College and the University of Virginia before graduating from the Medical College of Charleston in 1857. He saw action at First Bull Run, and served on the staffs of generals M.L. Bonham, Kershaw and Jubal Early. He also had been sent back to South Carolina to recruit a cavalry company before being attached to Hampton's brigade. The attrition at Brandy Station had placed him in this historic moment and what would be the most unforgettable episode of his life, if he survived.[6]

Cobb's Legion was led by 26-year-old Col. Pierce M.B. Young, a Spartanburg, South Carolina, native whose family moved to Bartow County, Georgia, when he was a child. In the blockbuster 1930s novel and movie *Gone with the Wind*, one of the main characters, Ashley Wilkes, was a cavalry officer in Cobb's Legion. Hampton's other commanders were Col. Laurence S. Baker of the First North Carolina, Lt. Col. W.W. Rich of the Phillips Legion and Lt. Col. J.F. Waring of the Jeff Davis Legion.[7]

Born in Charleston, the 45-year-old Wade Hampton, the third member of his prestigious family to have the name, was a natural gladiator and was considered one of the physically strongest men in the army. He was a flesh-and-blood legend, bearing scars of death struggles with bears he had killed with a knife in his youth, roaming the Carolina backwoods and deep swamps. He was also still saddened and seething over the death of his brother Frank. On that same day at Brandy Station, however, Hampton had shown his humane side, galloping up to a Union colonel to sabre the life out him, but holding up when he saw the officer was helpless, his sword arm disabled. Hampton saluted him, veering away to reenter the fray. A citizen soldier with no formal military education, Hampton "was rather a soldier by inheritance and natural aptitude," recalled Lt. George W. Beale of the Ninth Virginia Cavalry, who also served with Stuart. "Like [General Nathan Bedford] Forrest, he seemed to know by instinct when and how to strike." Beale also noted of the Palmetto titan: "No cooler man in the heat and rush of mortal combat perhaps ever wielded a sword than Wade Hampton." On June 8, 1863, the eve of the Brandy Station battle, Stuart held a grand cavalry review for Robert Lee, other generals and some infantry divisions of the army. It was an impressive martial display, and the Carolinian cut a memorable figure on his warhorse. "Hampton appeared to splendid advantage, and to hundreds of young and admiring soldiers he seemed the beau ideal of Southern grace and chivalry," Beale recalled.[8]

One of the late Stonewall Jackson's staff officers, Henry Kyd Douglas of Virginia, added this description of the Southern Ivanhoe in his famous postwar memoir: "It was said of Wade Hampton that he looked as knightly when mounted as if he had stepped out from an old canvas, horse and all." Gilbert Moxley Sorrel, an officer on Longstreet's staff, related that Hampton "had served from the very beginning of the war with high distinction, had proved himself a careful, vigilant, as well as enterprising cavalry leader, and possessed the confidence of the cavalry troops." The Carolinian "was of fine presence, a bold horseman, a swordsman and of the most undaunted courage."[9]

Having graduated South Carolina College in 1836, Hampton served in both houses of the state legislature from 1852 to 1861 and, by the war's outbreak, was said to be the largest landowner in the South. At his own expense, he organized and equipped the Hampton Legion, of which he became colonel, taking the command to Virginia in time to join in the battle of First Bull Run in July 1861 Hampton suffered a slight wound to the scalp there, but was soon back in the fight after having his head bandaged. He was not so fortunate at Seven Pines in May 1862, a bullet tearing into his foot about a week after he was promoted brigadier general. Refusing to leave the field, Hampton remained on his horse under heavy fire while a doctor removed the slug. The surgeon himself was then wounded in the arm, later requiring amputation. The newly forged general, meanwhile, had his boot put back on and continued the battle. By the next day, however, his foot was so swollen and inflamed that the boot had to be cut away. He was sent to Columbia on crutches, returning to duty in less than a month. "He was the beau-ideal of a cavalry commander," one Southerner said of Hampton, "of tall, heroic form, a superb horseman, brave and enterprising without being rash, and with daring always tempered by sound judgment." One of Stuart's staff officers, John Esten Cooke, watched Hampton's troopers crossing the Potomac at night during the strike into Pennsylvania: "The spectacle was picturesque. The broad river glittered in the moon, and on the bright surface was seen the long, wavering line of dark figures, moving in 'single file,' the water washing to and fro across the backs of the horses, which kept their feet with difficulty."[10]

Leaving Hunterstown about 4 p.m., Hampton's troopers were riding toward Gettysburg when the brigadier received word that "a heavy force of [Union] cavalry was advancing on Hunterstown with a view to get in the rear of our army." Hampton sent word of this development to Stuart, who changed his plans, instructing Hampton's to return to the hamlet and "hold the enemy in check." The Confederates wheeled back toward the village and encountered Union horsemen between Hunterstown and Gettysburg. There was brief skirmishing before the Federals launched a charge, met head on by Cobb's Legion. At about the same time, Hampton hurled Rich's Phillips Legion and the Second South Carolina against both flanks of the Yankees in support of Young's horsemen. "The charge was most gallantly made," Hampton noted of his troopers, the Federals being "driven back in confusion" toward their supporting line of artillery and sharpshooters, "both of which opened on me heavily." Hampton had no guns with him, but two fieldpieces were soon sent to him (apparently by Stuart) and did "good service" in keeping the enemy at bay. With night coming on, Hampton's men held their ground until the morning of July 3 when they saw that the Federals were gone, leaving behind some wounded officers and men in the village. Cobb's Legion, meanwhile, had been chewed up in leading the counterattack. The Georgians "suffered quite severely," Hampton reported, adding that the regiment "lost in killed quite a number of brave officers and men," although he gave no specific numbers. Stuart described the Hunterstown combat as "a fierce engagement in which Hampton's brigade performed gallant service, a series of charges compelling the enemy to leave the field and abandon his purpose" of menacing the Confederate rear. Stuart and the rest of his cavalry, meanwhile, took position on the York and Heidlersburg roads on the left flank of Lee's army.[11]

Perrin

Perrin's Carolinians bivouacked overnight on Seminary Ridge slightly north of their position after they had regrouped the previous day, still staggered by their ghastly losses. By sunup on Thursday, they were posted in woods behind a stone fence on the ridge crest and to the rear of some Confederate artillery, which Perrin did not identify in his battle report. "We rested on the field of battle," wrote Joseph Brown, the Fourteenth South Carolina's lieutenant colonel, adding that the stone wall had been held by Union troops facing Lane's Confederates on the 1st. In this position on the 2nd, Perrin's men suffered a few more casualties from enemy shelling, which erupted at dawn. "During the night the enemy had received heavy reinforcements and had greatly strengthened their already strong position," noted Capt. William S. Dunlop of the Twelfth South Carolina.[12]

The night had not been particularly restful for the Carolinians. "All night it was tramp, tramp, tramp," recalled Cpl. Thomas Littlejohn, also of the Twelfth. "The rumble of artillery moving to positions, wagons with supplies of all kinds needed by soldiers, coming up." Within Perrin's position was the David McMillan farm, which contained a large apple orchard. McMillan and his family had left the property on the morning of July 1, along with a quantity of canned apples, and the Carolinians took full advantage of the situation. "Abandoned property is [a] lawful prize of war, and our weary soldiers enjoyed these fruits, on the volunteer system, in the intervals of quiet," Lt. Col. Brown recalled.[13]

From a field hospital behind the Confederate lines, Lt. James Armstrong of the First South Carolina wrote one of the earliest personal accounts of the July 1 combat, in which he was wounded:

> I am again indebted to an Almighty and kind Providence, for sparing my life in battle. I am severely wounded in the left arm. The Doctor thinks no bones are broken. We engaged the enemy [Reynolds' First Army Corps] yesterday … and drove him from a strong position, compelling him to fall back to the rear of Gettysburg…. The casualties in the Regiment are considerable…. Our wounded are well attended to under the immediate care of Dr. F.L. Frost, Regimental Surgeon. I do not know what disposition will be made of our wounded when the army moves forward. The people here entertain anything but friendship for us.

As he wrote, Armstrong didn't yet know that the fighting would last three days: "The battle of Gettysburg, Pa., was certainly the hardest engagement I ever participated in. The enemy, as usual, had every advantage of position, and acted entirely on the defensive. Some of their wounded say that it was the first time they ever turned their backs on the enemy. Quite a number of prisoners passed … last evening."[14]

Somewhere on the blood-stained fields and slopes west of the Lutheran Seminary, Confederate soldiers found Pvt. James Harvey of the Twelfth South Carolina, wounded in both legs. "After [the] considerable delay" of remaining unattended for twenty-four hours or so, Harvey "was removed to the hospital in Gettysburg, the delay and exposure throwing him into a fever," said one account.[15]

Artillery

The Pee Dee Artillery and the rest of Pegram's battalion in Hill's artillery reserve, meanwhile, were on the hoof early on the morning of the 2nd, rumbling into a position southwest of Gettysburg on Seminary Ridge and well in advance of the Herr's Ridge line they occupied the day before. Now the battalion's gunners were opposite the center of the Union line on the opposite ridge, about 1,400 yards from the crest, where much of the Federal artillery was massing. Lt. Zimmerman's Carolinians were still excited but also were exhausted from their action on the 1st. Nearby, Maj. David McIntosh's four-battery battalion, also in Hill's reserve artillery, reined in on Seminary Ridge south of the college, the guns—minus two damaged Whitworths—unlimbered behind a "rough, irregular" stone wall.[16]

Kershaw

About two miles from Gettysburg, the Carolinians of Joe Kershaw's infantry brigade had spent the night along the Chambersburg Pike, with orders to move at 4 a.m. on Thursday. However, they did not break camp until almost sunup, apparently due to other troop movements in front of them and the Carolinians' late overnight arrival. It was "a beautiful clear morning," Augustus Dickert recalled of the July 2 advance years later; "the sun had long since shot its rays over that quaint old, now historic, town of Gettysburg." After the march on July 1 and "a hard day's work before them, the troops were allowed all the rest and repose possible," he added. "Resting on the eve, every heart beating with hope and determination, the regiment and the brigade were ready," related Pvt. Charles Kerrison of the Second South Carolina. Soon these troops were marching to the front along the right side of the pike; it would be the last summer morning many of the Carolinians would ever know. "We reached the hill overlooking Gettysburg, with only a slight detention from trains in the way" Kershaw reported, not noting the time, but apparently about 9 a.m. Longstreet had been waiting for Law's brigade of Hood's division to reach the field late that morning before advancing about noon. "We were then directed to move under cover of the hills toward the right, with a view to flanking the enemy in that direction, if cover could be found to conceal the movement," Kershaw noted.[17]

The Palmettos were excited, marching with "quick step and beating hearts" as they "moved in the direction of the enemy, thinking that we would soon be engaged in mortal combat," recalled Pvt. William Shumate of the Second. With Kershaw's brigade in the lead, the gray column—McLaws followed by Hood—marched west on the Chambersburg Pike to the hamlet of Seven Stars, and then turned south on a narrow road running along Marsh Creek to the Black Horse Tavern on the Fairfield Road (also known as the Hagerstown Road). Kershaw's troops headed east toward the Emmitsburg Road but halted near Herr Ridge as Kershaw realized they could be seen by the enemy if they advanced further. Longstreet rode forward and was told that a portion of the road in their front was in view of the Union signal station on Round Top. Longstreet showed "considerable irritation" after surveying the terrain ahead, according to Kershaw, and ordered the troops to retrace their steps to the Chambersburg Pike.[18]

"We marched and countermarched, first to the right, then to the left" with "a slow and halting gait," a Carolinian recalled. "As we thus marched we had little opportunity as yet to view the strongholds of the enemy on the opposite ridge … and everything was quiet and still save the tread of the thousands in motion, as if preparing for a great review." Longstreet rode past several times, "but he had his eyes cast to the ground, as if in a deep study, his mind disturbed…. Well might the great chieftain look cast down with the weight of this great responsibility resting upon him. There seemed to be an air of heaviness hanging around all."[19]

The troops then took a road south along Willoughby Run to again try to reach well past the right flank of Lee's army. By then the column had been marching and countermarching for three hours or more in the heat and still were not in position to fight. Frustrated, Longstreet decided to forge ahead, secrecy be damned. "It seemed to me useless, therefore, to delay the troops any longer with the idea of concealing the movement, and the two divisions advanced." The barrel-chested Carolinian must have cut a striking figure as he rode along his line, "putting my troops in the best position we could find."[20]

Followed by the other brigades of McLaws's division—led by generals William Barksdale, Paul Semmes and William Wofford, in that marching order—Kershaw's troops passed Pitzer's Schoolhouse and pressed east on the Millerstown Road in the last stages of their trek. "Arriving at the school-house, on the road leading across the Emmitsburg road by the peach orchard, then in possession of the enemy," Longstreet "directed me to advance my brigade and attack the enemy at that point, turn his flank, and extend along the cross-road, with my left resting toward the Emmitsburg road," Kershaw noted. Reaching the slight western slope and crest of Seminary Ridge about 3:15 p.m., the lead ranks of the Carolinians halted with an open field in their front and "in view of the enemy" some six hundred yards distant in and around a peach orchard. With the rest of his troops coming up, Kershaw studied the enemy's position in his front and sent out skirmishers. The Federals appeared to have a "superior force in the orchard" and had artillery support. Their main line of battle was entrenched to the rear, "extending to and upon the rocky mountain to the left far beyond the point at which his flank was supposed to rest."[21]

None of the Confederates, especially the high command, had expected to encounter a strong Union force stretched this far south on and in front of Cemetery Ridge. But shoddy reconnaissance and the lengthy delays due to miscommunication and the countermarching had seriously disrupted Lee's attack plans in this sector. Of course, the alertness of the Federals in eventually putting troops on Little Round Top, and the epic concentration of Meade's army throughout the day and the previous night, greatly contributed to this disruption. "Everything was quiet in our front, as if the enemy had put his house in order and awaited our coming," Dickert remembered. Hundreds of miles from their homes, these Carolinians, many of them already combat-weathered, were soon to enter a hellish furnace of battle none had ever survived or experienced before.[22]

Still, the Palmetto soldiers were loose and ready to fight. "The boys were in the best spirits. Many jokes were cracked," recalled an unidentified Confederate from the Newberry area who was in the Third South Carolina. The brunt of one highly popular joke that day was a long-haired and splendidly attired officer, apparently a general, riding into position. Spying the unidentified general, a Carolinian shouted to him in words to the effect of: "Come out from under that hair; we know you're there because we can see your legs sticking out." The general was furious and tried to find the catcaller, but to no avail. "He never found his man, but we got the last laugh," the Newberry soldier related. Dickert gave his own version of the encounter: "The head of the column was lead by a doughty General clad in a brilliant new uniform, a crimson sash encircling his waist … while great gold curls hung in maiden ringlets to his very shoulders. His movement was superb and he sat his horse in true Knightly manner." Incensed by the unknown heckler, the general wheeled his horse and "demanded in an angry tone, 'Who was that [who] spoke? Who commands this company?'" Getting no reply the general turned to leave, "saying 'D——d if I only knew who it was that insulted me, I would put a ball in him.' But as he rode off the soldier gave him a Parthian shot by calling after him, 'Say, Mister, don't get so mad about it, I thought you were some d——n wagon master.'"[23]

Almost certainly there was little levity on the mind of Joseph Kershaw as he contemplated all that lay ahead for his troops that afternoon. The 41-year-old brigadier was a native of Camden, South Carolina, and had fought in the Mexican War as a lieutenant in the famed Palmetto Regiment. He had been a lawyer and politician before the present conflict and had participated in the South Carolina secession convention in 1860. After Fort Sumter, Kershaw was named colonel of the Second South Carolina Volunteers and led it at First Bull Run. He was promoted brigadier general as of February 1862, and was in action in the Seven Days' battles, Antietam and Fredericksburg. Kershaw "had been distinguished in almost every battle he had shared," Douglas Southall Freeman wrote of the Carolinian. "Pious, intelligent, a clear blond of high-bred, clean-cut features, Kershaw had the bearing of command and a clear voice that seemed to inspire courage when it was raised in battle." "In person not more than five feet ten inches in height, straight as an arrow, with a sunshiny face whose effect was quickened by a beautiful deep blue eye," recalled a fellow soldier. "His voice was clear and always well in hand."[24]

After Kershaw and his regiment departed for Virginia in summer 1861, his wife, Lucretia, had "her Joe's" hair made into a bracelet and a necklace for herself, related Mary Chesnut, a Camden resident best known for her famous Civil War diary. Kershaw "was one of the most distinguished and efficient officers of the Virginia army," noted Gilbert Moxley Sorrel, one of Longstreet's top staff officers. The brigadier "was of most attractive appearance, soldierly and handsome … well set up, light hair and moustache, with clean-cut, high-bred features."[25]

Emma Holmes of Camden remembered a visit from the Kershaws at her home in February 1863. The general had news about Emma's cousin, Rutledge Holmes and the Palmetto Guard, which were in his brigade. "He is, I think, about the middle height & [has] a small but compact frame, very clear healthy complexion, good features, & a large clear blue eye, which I am sure would flash and burn in excitement," she recorded in her diary. "I like his appearance & modest, unassuming manners very much, & I'm sure, though not a distinguished looking man, he must look 'born to command' when at the head of his brigade." The Second South Carolina's predecessor was the Palmetto Regiment itself, which earned its record of combat fierceness in the Mexican War. This regiment of about 1,000 Carolinians lost almost half its number in battle.[26]

At Gettysburg, the Second South Carolina was commanded by Col. John D. Kennedy, like Kershaw a Camden native. The Third South Carolina Volunteers were led by Maj. R.C. Maffett, the Seventh South Carolina Volunteers by Col. D. Wyatt Aiken and the Eighth South Carolina Volunteers by Col. John W. Henagan. Col. William D. De Saussure commanded the Fifteenth South Carolina Volunteers, and the brigade was rounded out by Lt. Col. William G. Rice's Third South Carolina Battalion.[27]

Exemplifying all of these seasoned regiments, the Eighth was a proud and combat-tough organization, its résumé written in blood and courage from First Bull Run to Savage Station to Antietam, Fredericksburg and Chancellorsville. One Carolinian recalled the "bright day" in May 1861 when the regiment, numbering 980 men—"the best young blood of the Pee Dee"—departed for Virginia, where "high hopes and noble deeds accompanied and were expected of us."[28]

Kennedy, 23, and Kershaw both shared a January 5 birthday, although Kershaw was eighteen years older. Also like Kershaw, he was a lawyer, having been admitted to the bar a few weeks before the war erupted. He fought at First Bull Run as captain of a company in Kershaw's Second South Carolina Infantry and was slightly wounded. After Kershaw's promotion to brigadier, Kennedy rose to colonel of the regiment. Kennedy saw action in the June, fighting near Richmond, including Savage's Station, but was soon disabled by fever. He recovered enough to lead his regiment at Antietam but was wounded early in the battle. Kennedy fought at Fredericksburg three months later. His health, his wounds or a combination of both caused him to be away from the army for a month in early 1863, but he was in action at Chancellorsville and soon moved north into Pennsylvania in Lee's army. Kennedy's second-in-command was Lt. Col. Franklin Gaillard. The native of Pineville in Berkeley County, South Carolina, graduated South Carolina College in 1849 and journeyed to California that same year to join in the great gold rush there. Three years later he returned to his home state, working as a newspaper editor in Winnsboro and Columbia.[29]

Aiken, 35, was from Winnsboro and was a college instructor and newspaperman before the war. He was shot through the lungs at Antietam, his severe injuries for a long time believed to be fatal. Years later his family still kept printed accounts of his death. After months of recovery, however, Aiken was able to rejoin his regiment in June, in time for the march to Gettysburg. One of Aiken's top subordinates was Lt. Col. Elbert Bland, who called the Seventh South Carolina his "hell cats." In battle, Bland was known to shout, "Aim low men and shoot 'em in the stomach and make them die hard." To the end of his days Bland would be pained by a severe wound to his right arm, suffered at Savage's Station in June 1862. He narrowly averted death at Fredericksburg in December when a bullet slammed against his chest, destroying a "spy glass" in his left breast pocket but leaving him unharmed. The 40-year-old Henagan was a former sheriff of his native Marlboro County, South Carolina. Described as "a very quiet man" but one who "expressed his views firmly and candidly when called upon, Henagan was a farmer and also had been twice elected to the state legislature before the war. Maffett, in his late 20s, was from Newberry County, his father, James, a long-time member of the state general assembly. Henagan and Maffett had both been longtime officers in the state militia. Maffett had fought in most of the army's major battles and been wounded several times, but not seriously."[30]

Rice, 31, was one of four sons whose family roots were in Union County, South Carolina, living along the Broad River in his early years. He graduated South Carolina College, studied law and was engaged in planting after moving to Laurens County. In the Antietam campaign, Rice was severely wounded and his battalion, composed mostly of men from Laurens County, was almost wiped out in fighting at Crampton's Gap. Still, he was credited for saving his command from destruction by ordering a retreat to a less exposed position before he fell. Rice recovered to lead his men at Fredericksburg and Chancellorsville. Within the army, the Third Battalion was generally known as "James' Battalion" for its first commander, Col. George S. James, who was killed at South Mountain. James commanded a mortar battery at Fort Johnson in Charleston harbor and either fired—or gave the order to fire—the first shot of the Civil War in the bombardment of Fort Sumter. Rice had just returned from an "enjoyable leave of absence" a few days earlier, reaching his command at Chambersburg.[31]

The cream of Kershaw's regimental commanders had to be the 45-year-old De Saussure, a Mexican War hero in the Palmetto Regiment who also had years of service with the U.S. cavalry on the western plains. De Saussure "was certainly the Bayard of South Carolina," Dickert wrote, while another Carolinian described the colonel as "like a game cock in battle…. He understood men, was clear sighted, quick and sound of judgment, and seemed never to be at a loss what to do in emergencies." Born and raised in Columbia, De Saussure was a South Carolina College graduate and had studied law in his father's office before raising a company of Columbians that was part of the Palmetto Regiment in the Mexican conflict. His wife was a member of the prominent Ravenel family of Charleston. In Mexico, De Saussure's uniform was pierced several times by enemy projectiles, but he was unharmed. Still, he may have sensed that Gettysburg would be his last fight. Sgt. Richard O'Neale of the Fifteenth South Carolina's Company A claimed years later that the colonel voiced this feeling to him in a conversation between the two Columbians on the eve of battle. Based on O'Neale's recollection, De Saussure "appeared rather sad and morose that day" (apparently July 1) and told O'Neale, "'Tomorrow I am going to lose my life." "A hard charge and a desperate fight confronts us, and we all feel that way,"

I answered. "It is probable that many of us will be lying dead on the field before another day has passed."[32]

Another of the more notable soldiers in Kershaw's ranks was Sgt. Richard R. Kirkland of Co. B, Second South Carolina. Kirkland's family was from the Flat Rock community near Camden, his three brothers in the Seventh S.C. Cavalry. Richard had fought in basically all of the army's major engagements, emerging unscathed thus far. His unassuming fame had been won at Fredericksburg the previous December when waves of Union troops were mown down while storming Confederate defenses on Marye's Heights, primarily the infamous stone wall there. The slope was carpeted with dead and wounded Federals, many of the latter crying out for water. Kirkland was affected by these pleas and requested permission from Kershaw to bring the fallen enemy some relief. When permission was granted, Kirkland gathered canteens of water and climbed over the wall despite Union fire. He aided as many of the wounded as he could, while other Federals, realizing what he was doing, ceased their fire. He is immortalized as the "Angel of Marye's Heights." Somewhat surprisingly, one of the Seventh South Carolina's color bearers was a New Jersey native. Sgt. Alfred D. Clark of the Seventh's Company D was known for his "great coolness" under fire in leading the troops in battle. Born in Elizabeth City, New Jersey, he moved to Lowndesville in Abbeville District, South Carolina, in 1859 to become a clerk in a store owned by his uncle, later joining the Confederate cause.[33]

Kershaw's left flank lay near the James Flaherty farm south of the Millerstown Road. The brigade's right flank was posted in the vicinity of the Philip Snyder house, west of the Emmitsburg Road. Left to right were the Eighth South Carolina, the Third S.C. Battalion, the Third South Carolina, the Seventh South Carolina and the Fifteenth. In the stifling heat and amid a tangle of orders, Kershaw "received in various messages from the lieutenant-general [Longstreet] and the major-general [McLaws] commanding, and in part by personal communications with them," Kershaw was to proceed with the instructions he had previously received. The troops of Hood's division were hustling to the right of the Confederate positions passing behind the South Carolinians and still intent on gaining the Union left flank. Kershaw had orders to begin his assault as soon as Hood was engaged, swinging his brigade toward the peach orchard. Hood, meanwhile, was to "sweep down the enemy's line in a direction perpendicular to our then line of battle," the Carolinians joining Hood's division in rolling up the Union positions, Kershaw related. Barksdale, posted to Kershaw's left along the ridge, "would move with me and conform to my movement."[34]

If Kershaw's men had time to closely examine Hood's sweaty and dust-caked column as it passed to their rear, they would have seen a sword-slender, young brigadier from South Carolina accompanying his infantry brigade of five Alabama regiments. Within a few hours, this general, Evander M. Law, would carve his name with the other notables of Gettysburg. Two South Carolina batteries also clattered along in Hood's ranks, their stories also yet to unfold that day.

Hood's Attack

Law's brigade had already endured an early and exhausting but historic day. These troops were at New Guilford, some twenty-four miles from Gettysburg, when Law received orders about 3 a.m. to rejoin Hood and the rest of the main army. The

Alabamians covered the distance in about nine hours, Longstreet stating the feat was "the best marching done in either army to reach the field of Gettysburg." With McLaws's men in position, Hood's troops completed their march past them to a point further south, reaching the Emmitsburg Road in front of Round Top. Hood then posted his command "in an acute angle with the road," Law noted, and on the partially wooded Warfield Ridge. His battle formation was in two lines, Law's Alabamians on the right and the Texas Brigade of Brig. Gen. J.B. Robertson on the left in front. Some two hundred yards behind was the second line, composed of two Georgia brigades, Brig. Gen. H.L. Benning's men supporting Law while Brig. Gen. G.T. Anderson's command was to bolster Robertson.[35]

Law "in his prime was one of the handsomest of men, as straight as an arrow, with jet black beard, and of dashing appearance," one of his soldiers recalled. "The grace of his manner was flawless." The brigadier was about a month short of his 27th birthday (August 7) when he fought at Gettysburg. Born in Darlington, South Carolina, he graduated from the South Carolina Military Academy in 1856, spending the next few years organizing and teaching at a military school in Tuskegee, Alabama. He raised a company of state troops and served as lieutenant colonel of the Fourth Alabama at First Bull Run, where he was seriously wounded in the left arm. Promoted colonel of the regiment, he led his troops in the Seven Days battles, Second Bull Run and Antietam. Law was promoted brigadier as of early October 1862.[36]

Hood's division artillery battalion was commanded by Maj. M.W. Henry and consisted of two batteries each from South and North Carolina. Of the South Carolina units, Capt. William K. Bachman led the German Artillery and Capt. Hugh R. Garden commanded the Palmetto Light Artillery. Bachman's command was with Law's brigade at New Guilford that morning before heading to Gettysburg.

Bachman was a 33-year-old Charlestonian, an attorney in Columbia before the war and the son of a Charleston clergyman. He graduated Charleston College in 1850 and studied for three years in Germany before returning to South Carolina. He had artillery training as well, joining in the 1861 bombardment of Fort Sumter. In September 1861, he accepted command of a group of some one hundred and ten young German Americans from the Charleston area—the German Volunteers—assigned to the Hampton Legion. The "brave young men" were "mostly citizens by adoption, and some the very flower of the family hearths of our oldest German citizens," the *Charleston Courier* said of the Volunteers when they left the city on September 10, 1861, for the war front. It was a grand and jubilant sendoff, with a parade and a flag presentation ceremony at Institute Hall. In accepting the banner, Bachman thanked the "German ladies of Charleston" for its creation, adding, "When this flag, in our hands, shall no longer wave in honor, the last of those manly and brave hearts shall have ceased to beat," his words punctuated by great applause. The troops then marched to the Northeastern Railroad depot for their departure and there, among an immense crowd, families said their goodbyes. "Tears were shed; fathers, mothers, wives, sisters and brothers bade adieu to each other; friends shook hands … and amid the shrill of the steam whistle, the waving of handkerchiefs and the music … the cars bore off their precious burden," the *Courier* stated. "May they return safe and triumphant in the good cause is the prayer of our people."[37]

"This fine Charleston Company arrived in Richmond … in excellent health and spirits," the *Charleston Mercury* noted about a week later when these Carolinians arrived in Virginia. Later, Bachman's men would be organized as light artillerists and assigned to a battalion under Capt. Stephen D. Lee for about two years before being transferred to

Hood's command. Also known as the German Light Artillery and the Charleston Artillery Battery, their combat résumé included the Seven Days Battles, Second Bull Run, Antietam and Fredericksburg. Garden's and Bachman's cannoneers excelled at Second Bull Run, and had "handled their batteries with great skill," noted Maj. B.W. Frobel, Longstreet's artillery chief. Bachman's men readied their four 12-pounder Napoleons for action on the 2nd.[38]

Typical of these Carolinians was 20-year-old Louis Jacobs, who was born into a Jewish family in Germany and emigrated to the United States in spring 1860, landing in Charleston. He obtained employment as a clerk there and enlisted in the German Volunteers when war came. Another immigrant, Anton William Jager, was also German born, and beginning in 1849 was raised and educated in Charleston. As a youth he worked in a drygoods store. Joining the German Volunteers, he was made color bearer, carrying the battery's flag from the banner presentation in Charleston to Gettysburg. He was 22 or 23—his exact birthdate is unknown—when he and his comrades unlimbered their pieces on July 2.[39]

The Palmetto Light, also known as Garden's Battery, boasted two Napoleons and two 10-pounder Parrotts. Most of the cannoneers were volunteers from Sumter, Chesterfield and Darlington counties who had great respect for the youthful gallantry of their commander, as well as their own pluck. "Capt. Garden was unquestionably a brave boy, (for he was but a boy of bare majority then, with but a downy 'bang' upon [his] upper lip and the roseate hues of babyhood yet in his cheeks)," wrote Pvt. J. Merrick Reid, one of Garden's men, "and he had followers every whit as brave as he." The battery was well represented by the Haynesworth family of Sumter, three soldiers, Sgt. Matthew E., Cpl. James H. and Pvt. Charles Haynesworth, all serving a gun commanded by Lt. William Alexander McQueen, another Sumter native. The Palmettos reached the battlefield that day "under a fierce Pennsylvania sun" and with combat already raging to their front. "As we approached the mighty drama was in full progress and the field already stained and scarred from the intermittent combats of the morning and preceding day," related Pvt. Reid. The Palmettos unlimbered for action "with the Round Top in our front and the peach orchard and wheat field bristling with bayonets while the heights above glowered with guns."[40]

Longstreet's artillery reserve, under Col. J.B. Walton, also was coming into battle line. Walton's command consisted of a 26-gun battalion of South Carolina, Virginia, and Louisiana cannoneers under Col. Edward P. Alexander and four companies of the Washington Artillery of New Orleans. Alexander's Carolinians belonged to the Brooks Artillery from the Charleston area, led by Lt. Stephen Capers Gilbert. Born in Colleton County, South Carolina, but raised in Charleston, the 25-year-old Gilbert already had experienced an eventful—even charmed—life. He had been a conductor on the South Carolina Railroad before the war and served with the Brooks Guards artillery in the forces which battered Fort Sumter. Reorganized, the Guards were sent to Virginia soon afterward, fighting as infantry in Kershaw's brigade at First Bull Run. When their 12-month enlistment expired, most of them reenlisted, their command reorganized as the Brooks Light Artillery battery, also known by June 1862 as the Brooks Artillery, under Capt. A.B. Rhett, and Rhett's Battery. Gilbert rose from private to lieutenant as the Carolinians battled through the major campaigns in the east. On one of these sanguine fields, Gilbert evaded death by inches on two occasions. He escaped a mortal wound once when a projectile crushed his canteen. Later, he was holding his horse's bridle when a shot carried it away, his mount then being gored by a cannonball. Another officer remarked, "'Gilbert, they are certainly after you today." He replied with his "usual quiet smile," as one source noted, "Well it certainly does look so." His luck would run out at Gettysburg.[41]

The Brooks artillerists may have fought without colors until late 1862 when the "patriotic ladies of Charleston" enlisted the services of an "accomplished embroiderer," a Mrs. Schuckmann, whose family ran a store downtown on King Street. The flag "was begun some time ago, and could not be finished before, as the materials could not be got in the Confederacy, and had to be sent for to Paris," the *Charleston Mercury* noted. "It is a peculiar and handsome banner." On one side "in beautifully shaded green silk against a crimson background, was a leafy wreath tied with a blue ribbon. Inside the wreath, in gold letters, were the names of the battles in which the Carolinians were engaged prior to Antietam. The other side displayed a Palmetto tree with a rattlesnake coiled around the trunk and a crescent in the upper corner, the tree and crescent in gold, contrasting with the crimson background. The banner was displayed at Schuckmann's store in early November 1862 before being presented to the battery."[42]

To further explain the Confederate attack plan, Lee wanted to capitalize on the wrecking ball momentum of the first day's action by assailing the Union left flank on Cemetery Ridge and rolling up the enemy line north toward Gettysburg. The battle was to open on the right by two of Longstreet's First Corps divisions—McLaws's and Hood's—supported on their left by four brigades of Richard Anderson's division. This movement was to be "promptly followed" on Lee's left by Ewell's Second Corps feinting and attacking "if the opportunity occurred," although in another account Longstreet states that Ewell was to make a "simultaneous attack." In Lee's center Hill's Third Corps was to threaten the Union line and take advantage of the opportunity to attack or, as Longstreet also wrote in another account, Hill "should watch closely and engage so as to prevent heavy massing [by the enemy] in front of me." The movements of the Second and Third Corps were to be prompt and in close cooperation, so as "to prevent concentration against the battle of the right."[43]

As mentioned earlier, Anderson's division bivouacked overnight on the fringe of the battleground, some two miles west of Gettysburg. About 6 a.m. on July 2, Anderson received orders to move forward and form a new battle line to the right of Pender's division, relieving Heth's men along Seminary Ridge. Wilcox's brigade had returned from its "detached" service by now, as had Ross's battery, but Lane's entire Sumter Battalion of artillery, including Ross's gunners, had again been detailed for detached duty that morning. In taking the new position, the Tenth Alabama of Wilcox's command engaged in a sharp skirmish with some Yanks who occupied a wooded hill on the extreme right of Anderson's line. The Alabamians soon ousted these bluecoats from the woods and Anderson established his position. "The enemy's line was plainly in view, about 1,200 yards in our front, extending along an opposite ridge [Cemetery] somewhat more elevated than that which we occupied, the intervening ground being slightly undulating, inclosed by rail and plank fences, and under cultivation," Anderson reported.[44]

Skirmishers on both sides soon began their lethal feud, keeping up "an irregular fire upon one another." Shortly after getting his troops posted, Anderson was notified that Longstreet's men would occupy ground to the right of Anderson to attack the Union extreme left flank. As the Carolinian understood his orders, Longstreet intended to push the enemy toward Gettysburg "and I was at the same time ordered to put the troops of my division into action by brigades as soon as … Longstreet's corps had progressed so far in their assault as to be connected with my right flank." Hill went over the orders three times with the Carolinian, realizing this was Anderson's first battle as part of the Third Corps. One of Anderson's men later wrote of him: "He was cool in the face of every danger, and heroic when it came. He was not a fiery, impetuous fighter, but struck hard, and being cool and clear headed, knew where to strike so as to attain the very best results. Seldom his blows were fruitless." "Fighting Dick," however, would not live up to his nickname this day at Gettysburg.[45]

The situation was much more ominous on the Confederate right. Evander Law, looking toward Round Top in the distance, could see that his men and the rest of Hood's troops faced an almost impossible task in assailing the enemy uphill, over rugged, rocky terrain, segments of the Union line partially hidden in summer greenery. "The position occupied by the Federal left wing in front of us ... was certainly one of the most formidable it had ever been the fortune of any troops to confront," he related. Law sent six scouts on foot across the valley and into the woods and boulder-strewn ground to his front to see what the Confederates were facing. Shortly thereafter, information from these men and from several Yankees taken prisoner in the vicinity presented the Confederates with an opportunity that—if accurate—might change the course of the battle. The scouts and captives reported that no Union troops were on the summit of Round Top. Thus, if Hood altered plans for a frontal attack and instead moved around the enemy's unprotected left flank at Round Top, the rebels would have a foothold to the south and rear of Meade's army, possibly forcing him to abandon his strong positions all along Cemetery Ridge.[46]

The Gettysburg campaign has myriad controversies still debated today, and exactly what transpired among the Confederate high command from about 3:30 p.m. to 4:30 p.m. this day is among these puzzles. Law's version is that he went to Hood, told him of the Federals' naked left flank, and urged a shift around Round Top, averting a costly frontal assault. Hood listened and seemed to support the change, but he had orders to attack as planned. When Law protested, Hood sent a messenger to Longstreet, informing him of the new information. Within ten minutes the messenger returned with one of Longstreet's staff officers who confirmed that Hood was to attack at once, as ordered. By then the rebel artillery supporting Hood was dueling with its blue foe in the distance. Pvt. Reid of the Palmetto Light Artillery recalled that the "shrill bugle blast of our own command sounded in quick succession" and soon "with a whirl and rush, and scarce breathing time, our own guns were joining in the grim war music."[47]

About 4:15 p.m., Hood moved to the attack, Law's brigade and Robertson's Texans plunging down the slope into tilled fields. "The artillery on both sides had been warmly engaged for about fifteen minutes, and continued to fire heavily until we became engaged with the Federal infantry, when the Confederate batteries ceased firing to avoid injury to our own troops," Law reported. The South Carolina artillerists watched the fate of some of these infantrymen "while shot and shell from Cemetery Heights [Ridge] ploughed through the ranks and we remember the flying hats and scattered limbs of the dead and wounded as hideous gaps were made through the files, also the steady 'Close up' and continued firm and confident tread of these oaken-hearted troops, nearer to danger and surer death," recalled the Carolinian Pvt. Reid.[48]

Most of Hood's soldiers were soon obscured in the woods along the base of Big Round Top "and the spurs to the north of it." The Confederates had already advanced rapidly across the valley in their front—despite taking losses from Union artillery and infantry on Houck's Ridge—brushing away Yankee skirmishers and crashing into a battle line of Federals on the rocky lower slopes of the hills. Strewn with wagon-size boulders, with trees and undergrowth carpeting gullies and beds of sharp stones, this was the Devil's Den. "The ground was rough and difficult, broken by rocks and boulders which rendered an orderly advance impossible," Law recalled. Most pressing, however, was an immediate command crisis as the fighting intensified. Some twenty minutes into the assault, Hood was severely wounded by an enemy artillery round ripping his left arm and hand in four places. Law assumed division command, his brigade now led by Col. James L. Sheffield of the 48th Alabama. Ironically, Law himself was still suffering from the long-term effects of the severe left arm wound he suffered at First Bull Run, almost two years earlier, his injuries then having incapacitated him for about three months.[49]

A rugged area south of Houck's Ridge, between Devil's Den and Big Round Top, would forever be known as the "Slaughter Pen," after the Fourth Maine clashed with Alabamians and Texans in a nightmare of butchery. The outnumbered Federals were hurled back, allowing the Confederates to advance toward the west slope of Little Round Top, but the Southerners were being thinned considerably due to heavy casualties, the regiments being unable to maintain cohesion due to the tough terrain. Their long march through the earlier part of the day, coupled with the scarcity of any water, compounded the troops' issues. There was brutal combat among the boulders and trees on the slopes, Law hurling the two Georgia brigades—Benning's and Anderson's—ahead to strengthen his troops in the first wave. Within half an hour Law's division had seized a hill adjacent to Devil's Den—capturing three guns—while Law's brigade under Sheffield had cleared the northern slope of Big Round Top and was advancing toward Little Round Top. The Alabamians, however, quickly came under a terrific flank fire on their right from Union Col. Strong Vincent's Third Brigade of the U.S. Fifth Corps. Alerted to the threat to Little Round Top, Vincent's troops hurried into positions near the crest. The firepower from these fresh troops repelled Sheffield's rebels, while George Anderson's Georgians on the left were being cut up as well.[50]

At this point, Law had not heard anything from McLaws's division, which was supposed to have extended the left of Hood's line and "moved to the attack at the same time," Law wrote. His account continues that he halted the division to rest and regroup and went to check on McLaws, whose troops had not yet advanced. Law met with Joe Kershaw, whose brigade formed the right flank of McLaws's position. The Carolina brigadiers conferred, Kershaw stating that he had not yet received orders to attack, Law claimed. "I pointed out the position of Hood's division, and urged the necessity of immediate support on its left," Law wrote. Kershaw then requested that he be shown the point where "his right flank should be directed, and promptly moved to the attack, the movement being taken up by the whole division," Law's postwar account states. As will be seen, this is not how the battle evolved, nor how Kershaw responded. Still, Hood later had high praise for Law, noting in his memoir that the Carolinian "assumed command of the division, and proved himself, by his courage and ability, fully equal to the responsibilities of the position."[51]

5

"Shrieking, Crushing, Tearing, Comes the Artillery Fire"

Marching through the unfamiliar Pennsylvania countryside earlier in the day, Kershaw's Carolinians sensed this could be the war's decisive battle, many of them never again to see the Palmetto State. "Soldiers looked into the faces of their fellow-soldiers with a silent sympathy that spoke more eloquently than words an exhibition of brotherly love," Augustus Dickert related. "They felt a sympathy for those whom they knew, before the setting of the sun, would feel the touch of the elbow for the last time, and who must fall upon this distant field and in an enemy country."[1]

The time of destiny had come. Kershaw's troops formed the right of McLaws's front with Brig. Gen. William Barksdale's brigade of Mississippians on the left. Brig. Gen. Paul J. Semmes's four regiments of Georgians were in support of Kershaw, posted about two hundred yards to the rear of the Carolinians, while Brig. Gen. W.T. Wofford's Georgia brigade was behind Barksdale. Meanwhile, McLaws's artillery battalion, led by Col. Henry C. Cabell, had rumbled into position to Kershaw's right along the road and in front of an oak grove. Kershaw sent De Saussure's Fifteenth South Carolina as infantry support for Cabell's guns. Soon afterward Union artillery trundled from the distant woods and into the wheat field, where the cannoneers deployed and unlimbered their pieces as if in response to this threat.[2]

"All troops in line, the batteries in position, nothing was wanting but the signal gun to put these mighty forces in motion," a Carolinian wrote. Suddenly, the Carolinians and the rest of McLaws's troops heard the blasts of Hood's artillery off to their right along with the "furious reply" of the enemy cannon. Shortly thereafter, "a few sharp bugle notes were heard and then boom! boom! boom! blazed away Cabell's guns" at the Union batteries near the peach orchard, Pvt. John Coxe of the Second South Carolina recalled. It was about 4 p.m., and the Union artillerists wasted little time before answering. "The Yankees were ready and replied with spirit, and in less time than it takes to tell it our ears were deafened by the noise of the guns and exploding shells," Coxe recalled. He added that Longstreet and his staff, dismounted, were behind the stone wall to the right, watching the effects of the rebel shelling through their field glasses. Amid the bombardment, McLaws's men listened to the sounds of combat off to the right—or south—where Hood's division was engaged. Said Dickert: "We could easily determine their progress by the 'rebel yell' as it rang out in triumph along the mountain sides."[3]

Listening to the battle symphony, Kershaw, Barksdale and the rest of McLaws's division steeled for their attack. "The Confederate artillery opening along the entire line the boys all ready, hopeful, yea, joyous over the prospect of success," recalled Pvt. Charles Kerrison of the Second South Carolina. Still, there had to be some trepidation as the Carolinians, including Pvt. Wesley P. Nichols in Henagan's regiment, watched Union cannon devastate some of the Confederate artillery, killing all the horses before the rebels could get them out of range.[4]

Among Kershaw's soldiers was Pvt. Thomas W. Sligh, a teenaged orderly in the Third South Carolina's Company E. Sligh left Newberry College to join the army and had quickly become a favorite around Kershaw's campfires. Sligh was "witty, very ready, and always kind," Dickert said of him. "His was a brave heart, too. Still he was rather girlish in appearance, for physically he was not strong." For the latter reason, Sligh was assigned as an orderly. As Kershaw's brigade girded for battle, the private was ordered to keep the horses of some of the regiment's officers, now dismounted, well to the rear. "Now, Tom, get behind some hill and the moment we call you, bring up the horses," the regiment's adjutant told him. To the officer's surprise, Sligh burst into tears, pleading for him not to be left behind but to join his company in battle. At first the adjutant denied the request, but Sligh persisted so strongly that the officer finally relented, telling him, "Well, Tom, for this one time you may go, but don't ask again."[5]

Also in the ranks was 25-year-old Capt. Thomas E. Powe, leading Company C of the Eighth South Carolina. Powe "was the son of pious parents" and raised "in religious nurture around the venerable altar" at St. David's Church in Cheraw, South Carolina, a comrade wrote of him. Powe had graduated South Carolina College in 1857 and was admitted to the bar shortly before the war. "No one, perhaps, in his regiment possessed so completely the respect and love … as did Captain Powe, actuated, as he always was, by just and pure principles." Powe also had "a courage preeminently conspicuous" and "an intellect clear and quick." Color Sgt. Elisha Adams of the Eighth South Carolina stepped forward with his combat-tattered flag ahead of Company G. Known for cheerfulness "under every trying circumstance," Adams, from Marlboro District, South Carolina, "always longed for the battlefield," a comrade noted, "and never was more happy than when amid the smoke and thunder and carnage of battle."[6]

Among Kershaw's objectives was farmer Joseph Sherfy's peach orchard (now known as the Peach Orchard), occupied by "an advanced line" of Union infantry and artillery. The Carolinian counted six enemy batteries: three in the orchard near the crest of a hill and three about 200 yards further to the rear in a line extending toward Little Round Top. Federal infantry of undetermined strength were posted along the front of the orchard and also on the face of the orchard hill, looking south toward the George Rose farm.[7]

These Yankees, more than 10,000 in number, belonged to Maj. Gen. Daniel Sickles's III Corps. With drums beating and flags flying, they had marched into this advanced position, forming a salient in the Union line about 3 p.m., even as Longstreet's column was still in route to this portion of the field. Sickles had made the move without orders but believed the high ground in the orchard would be quite important to the Union defenses, even though it was exposed and well beyond immediate support from the rest of Meade's forces on the ridge, a half to three-quarters of a mile to his rear. Indeed, the orchard was some 70 feet higher than the position Sickles's corps held before moving forward. Sickles's two divisions were led by Brig. Gen. Andrew A. Humphreys and Maj. Gen. David B. Birney. Humphreys's troops were posted on the right along the Emmitsburg Road and facing northwest, linking with Birney's line near the John Wentz farm and the orchard. On the left, Birney's position looked southwest, the Federals spread dangerously thin from the orchard to Devil's Den in front of Little Round Top. Sickles's line—almost 3,500 yards in total length—also ran along the front of a wheat field, but there were undefended gaps vulnerable to attack. Sickles's new position also left a sizeable vacancy in the Federals' ridge line, exposing the left of Hancock's II Corps, posted to the north. Still, the turtle-slow and confused Confederate movements allowed Sickles to occupy this salient, post his troops and artillery and develop their fields of fire. If the rebels assailed the Peach Orchard, Sickles would be on his own, at least in the initial stages, since Maj. Gen. George Sykes's V Corps of about 11,000 troops was in reserve well to his rear. If needed, it would take some time for Sykes to come forward with reinforcements.[8]

From a distance of 500 to 600 yards, Kershaw's Carolinians saw the Rose family's stone house, large stone barn and a stone fence. Beyond the house was another rise, defended by another enemy battery, and behind this was a rocky hill, "wooded and rough," said one Confederate account. The men in the center of Kershaw's line saw that beyond this hill was a large wheat field spreading east to the slopes of the main Federal line on Cemetery Ridge, north of Little Round Top.[9]

"Under my instructions I determined to move upon the stony hill, so as to strike it with my center, and thus attack the orchard on its left rear," Kershaw explained. He would cross the Emmitsburg Road, wheel left (north) generally parallel with the Wheatfield Road, running east-west, and, linking with Hood's troops, attack the Federal left. A new concern for the Carolinians was a Union battery posted apart from Sickles's main line but which "commanded every foot of our advance," recalled Pvt. William T. Shumate of the Second South Carolina. Surrounded by aides, Longstreet stood out in front of Kershaw's line, studying the enemy with a "glass," Shumate continued. Their presence attracted the attention of some Federal gunners, who "threw shot and shell uncomfortably near … Longstreet": however, he "never flinched or changed his position until he got through with his observation … walking to the rear of our lines."[10]

With Hood's assault well underway, Cabell's artillery ceased fire about 5 p.m., then boomed the three-gun signal to attack, the assault commencing about 5:30 p.m. Kershaw immediately ordered his regiments—some 1,800 men in all—to step over the stone wall, file to the right, along and in front of it and form a battle line. From left to right the regiments were Henagan's Eighth, near the Warfield house, Rice's Third S.C. Battalion, Kennedy's Second South Carolina, Maffett's Third S.C. and Aiken's Seventh. De Saussure's Fifteenth remained in support of Cabell's artillery near the Snyder farmhouse. Kershaw noted, "The men leaped over the wall and were promptly aligned; the word was given, and the brigade moved off … with great steadiness and precision," passing between Cabell's and Alexander's guns. Semmes's Georgians followed the Carolinians "with equal promptness." To their front the brigade skirmishers, commanded by Maj. William M. Wallace of the Second South Carolina, sniped with their Union rivals along the Emmitsburg Road, some 350 to 400 yards in front of Kershaw's oncoming line. Wallace's force was composed of sharpshooters from each of Kershaw's regiments, including Capt. R.E. Richardson's Company A of the Third South Carolina, which distinguished itself later in the day. The general "next gave the command, 'forward,' and the men sprang to their work with a will and determination," Dickert recalled. Kershaw was on foot as were all the brigade's officers due to the rocky, uneven nature of the terrain. The Carolinian was "prepared to follow the line of battle immediately in rear, looking cool, composed and grand, his steel-gray eyes flashing the fire he felt in his soul." With Kershaw was Longstreet, also on foot, whipping his hat in the air and encouraging the troops. "As the order to move forward is issued to the line, the artillery ceases, a calm comes, only to be banished by the carnage to follow," Pvt. Kerrison remembered. "With rifles at the 'right shoulder shift,' the march common time, the infantry advances in steady column."[11]

Another of the many Confederate missteps at Gettysburg occurred here, some historians point out, Hood's troops fighting for more than an hour before McLaws's division attacked. Historian Jeffry Wert notes that the reasons for the time lapse were "never satisfactorily explained" but that Longstreet was ultimately responsible. None of this mattered to the Carolinians marching into the open knowing Union gunners were already sighting their fieldpieces on them. Early in the advance, Pvt. W.A. Johnson of the Second South Carolina was mildly shaken by the sight of a comrade's corpse in his path. "As we marched forward, I discovered just in front of me, one of my company stiff in death, killed on the skirmish line," the Carolinian recollected. Maj. Maffett of the Third South Carolina noted that the enemy positions were "at the foot and upon the sides of a mountain range," an understandably general description, since he and his men were seeing the terrain for the first time as they girded for battle. The Third and the rest of the brigade were "ordered forward to the attack" across an "open plain" some 1,500 yards wide.[12]

Almost immediately after Kershaw's attack began, several Union guns in the orchard opened on the Confederates. "As soon as we started we came under fire of the enemy's batteries," noted Lt. Col. Franklin Gaillard of the Second South Carolina. The artillery fire against the Carolinians could have been worse, but the enemy cannoneers were also occupied in engaging Cabell's and Alexander's fieldpieces. Aiken's Seventh South Carolina was "ordered to advance … which we did in fine stile [sic]," the colonel wrote to his wife, Virginia, a few days after the battle. His men were "directly in front of the cannon, not 1,000 yds distant, which immediately began playing on" Kershaw's troops, who were "the most exposed, having to advance from behind the stone wall just in the edge of the woods through a large level clover field."[13]

Longstreet returned to the rear as Kershaw's men neared the Emmitsburg Road, bordered by rail fences on each side. It was about this time that the Carolinians heard Barksdale's drummers beating assembly for the Mississippians, who were supposed to advance in tandem with Kershaw's brigade. The drumming to his left and rear was an ominous and shocking sound to Kershaw: "I knew then that I should have no immediate support on my left, about to be squarely presented to the heavy force of infantry and artillery at and in rear of the Peach Orchard," he recalled. Barksdale may have been unaware that the signal guns would be used to initiate the assault, McLaws sending him an order to attack. If this was so, it was yet another example of miscommunication and piecemeal, uncoordinated movements plaguing the Confederates. McLaws later claimed that Barksdale's and Wofford's brigades were "mixed up with the batteries" posted in the area and were "temporarily delayed in extricating themselves therefrom." Whatever caused the tardiness, it was already beginning to soak that portion of the battleground with the blood of Kershaw's Carolinians.[14]

A Minié smacked into the right knee of Color Sgt. Elisha Adams soon after the assault began, but he refused to give up his flag to soldiers of his guard. Clutching the banner with one hand and supported on the other, Adams continued in the assault with the Eighth's Company G. Another bullet "goes crushing through the same leg," a comrade noted, "but still he pressed on with his banner, assisted by others." At some point in the attack, Henry C. Miller, "a stalwart lad from Darlington, S.C.," in Henagan's Eighth, "was advancing into heavy fire when a shot ripped off one of his fingers. An officer ordered

Miller to the rear, but he replied, 'No sir, they will call me a coward if I go back for that.' Seconds later, a shell fragment tore off one of his arms above the elbow. Miller was caught by another soldier as he fell, gasping, 'I will go back now, but I would rather lose my arm than to be called a coward.'"[15]

"Directly we were ordered to move on and under a most fearful shelling in the very face of two batteries plainly in our sight," recalled Col. Aiken of the Seventh South Carolina. A Company I color sergeant was advancing with the Seventh's regimental flag but was wounded, and Cpl. Thomas Harling grabbed the banner. "It fell to his lot … to bear the colors, and it was nobly done by him until he was pierced through the head by a minie ball and fell dead upon the field," Capt. Benjamin Roper later wrote to the boy's father. The New Jersey–born Sgt. Alfred D. Clark of Company D also apparently bore the Seventh's colors at some point during the battle. He was in front of the ranks as usual when a shell struck his haversack, containing uncooked rations. Clark was unscathed, but the rations, including a quantity of flour, "was scattered in every direction," his messmate J.S. Gilbert recalled years later.[16]

Pvt. John Coxe of the Second South Carolina kept in step with the men on either side of him as they crossed the now shell-splintered fences and the Emmitsburg Road, eyeing the Union guns in the distance. "We went along in perfect order," Coxe recalled, the battle line nearing a slight depression in the terrain. No Federal infantry were to be seen in their immediate front, but the enemy fieldpieces ahead and to their left were obviously the most imminent threat. The rebels "saw plainly that their artillerists were loading their guns to meet our assault, while their mounted officers were dashing wildly from gun to gun, apparently to be sure that all were ready." Some Confederate cannon off to the left opened fire and Coxe heard another Carolinian remark, "That will help us out," but the shelling was aimed at another target in the enemy's Peach Orchard position.[17]

The Carolinians looking north toward the orchard and further to the east saw elements of six Union batteries—some thirty guns in all—belonging to the Union army's First Volunteer Brigade, Artillery Reserve, commanded by Lt. Col. Freeman McGilvery. Also bracing to engage the Confederates were the Yankee infantry of Birney's First Division in Sickles's corps. Reinforcements from the Union II and V corps were also soon on the move toward this increasingly dangerous bulge in Meade's line. Most of the Union guns were still not in action; those that were targeted Kershaw's troops and Cabell's and Alexander's batteries; Semmes's brigade, in support, was also in the bullseye.[18]

Now on the east side of the Emmitsburg Road, the Carolinians advanced along a narrow dirt lane leading to the Rose farm and beyond. They were well south of the Peach Orchard, passing over fields of rye and young corn with the Rose farm and the wooded stony hill in their front. Amid this rocky terrain of greenery and gullies ahead were a great many Federals, many disorganized by Hood's assault and now in Kershaw's path. "For four hundred yards our line moved beautifully forward not wavering or hesitating in the slightest degree," wrote Lt. Col. Gaillard of the Second South Carolina.[19]

Despite the artillery fire, Kershaw's left wing—Henagan's Eighth, Rice's Third S.C. Battalion and Kennedy's Second—advanced along the left side of Rose's lane, "moving majestically across the fields … with the steadiness of troops on parade," the brigadier recalled years later. Still with no Barksdale on his unprotected left, Kershaw made a desperately bold decision—he ordered the left wing to "change direction to the left"—or north. Reaching the vicinity just north of the Rose barn, this wing was halted briefly, apparently to reorganize and close ranks. These Carolinians then wheeled left toward the enemy infantry and batteries facing them to the rear—or east—of the Peach Orchard and near the edge of the Wheatfield. Minus the Fifteenth South Carolina, the rest of the brigade, along with Kershaw himself, continued through the Rose yard toward the stony hill, which will be covered later.[20]

The Carolinians of the left wing marched down the grassy slope toward a depression. After that they would have to advance uphill for a few hundred yards to reach the Union line at the Orchard and along the Wheatfield Road. "We were to take a battery immediately in our front. I never saw men more resolved upon an accomplishment. We had crossed two fences and our line was unbroken although many gaps had been in the ranks," recalled Gaillard of the Second.[21]

"The storm breaks," Pvt. Kerrison, also in the Second, said of the next few moments. As the gray line neared the depression, the Yank artillerists in their front jerked their lanyards, a lethal tornado of grapeshot inundating the attackers. "Shrieking, crushing, tearing, comes the artillery fire," Kerrison continued. "Grape, cannister, shell and minnies from the Federals heap their destruction upon the devoted Confederates." Kershaw's rebs were charging some sixteen enemy guns in their immediate front which were shredding the oncoming gray mass, the whizzing grape and canister slashing more gory gaps in the ranks. The "very grass under our feet was being cut to pieces by these missiles of death," one of the Carolinians recalled, "and it looked as if mortal men could not possibly live there." Col. Kennedy was shot down while "gallantly leading his command to the charge," Kershaw later said. Among other wounded was Capt. William Z. Leitner of the Second South Carolina, who slumped to the ground while leading his Company E. Some of his soldiers stopped to carry him to the rear, but Leitner would have none of it, refusing to be moved. "Men I am ruined but never give up the battle. I was shot down at the head of my company, and I would to God that I was there yet," he gasped to those surrounding him.[22]

The Palmettos marched "in perfect order and with the precision of a brigade drill, while upon my right and left comrades were stricken down by grape and canister which went crashing through our ranks," recalled Pvt. William Shumate of the Second South Carolina. The bluecoats "let fly at us with grape," Pvt. Coxe related. "O the awful deathly surging sounds of those little, black balls as they flew by us, through us, between our legs, and over us! Many of course were struck down," including Capt. R.C. Pulliam of Coxe's Company B, who was hit in the head and mortally wounded.[23]

Coxe and his comrades were now moving on the "double quick," out of the depression and again on somewhat level ground. The field behind them was draped with the dead and wounded Carolinians who fell in the first blast of grapeshot from the Union gunners. Coxe noted, "We were mad and fully determined to take and silence those batteries at once." Moments later the "next fusillade of grape met us," the private recalled, never forgetting the sight of a grapeshot whooshing between his legs. Kennedy's troops were now drawing ever closer to the Union cannon and their artillerists, who "seemed bewildered and were apparently trying to get their guns to the rear," Coxe wrote.[24]

The Carolinians moved "steady, onward, without firing a gun till the charge," added Charles Kerrison of the Second's Company I. "Many a brave fellow bit the dust long before the regiment opened. The bravery and courage exhibited were almost superhuman. Color-bearers were shot down one after another." In the company's ranks nearby, Kerrison's brother, Edwin, later recalled that the men "advanced on a battery in an open field under a most terrific fire of grape, shell and canister." The "grape and canister made great swaths," remembered another soldier in the Second South Carolina, and "you could see as many as a score fall at once. 'Dixie' 'Land of the orange and cotton bloom' thy sons were dying for thy cause, which they loved so well." Lt. Alex McNeill of the Second added that this was "the most terrible fire to which they ever were exposed."[25]

The Eighth South Carolina, on Kershaw's extreme left, found itself assailed on the front and flank. Maj. Donald M. McLeod led the Eighth in the desperate drive against the massed enemy guns, his men toppling in heaps with every step. At 6'4" McLeod, a school teacher from Marlboro District, South Carolina, was an inviting target. He had survived Malvern Hill, Antietam and Fredericksburg, but his time ran out near the Peach Orchard, where he fell, mortally wounded by an artillery round. "On the field of battle his gallantry was conspicuous, and he exhibited undaunted courage," Augustus Dickert noted of McLeod. Capt. Thomas Powe rushed ahead of his oncoming troops in the Eighth South Carolina's Company C, a fellow soldier noting Powe's "gallantry, his coolness and distinguished courage in a great carnival of death." Suddenly a shell seared through the gray ranks with devastatingly efficient results, at least one account stating that sixteen or so of Powe's men and the adjoining company of Carolinians toppling in a bloody swath. Powe was among them, desperately wounded, his right leg gone. This section of Henagan's line was stunned, the advance stymied. "A momentary halt, a slight confusion, when his cheering voice is heard ringing along his ranks, 'forward boys—forward,'" an unidentified comrade penned of Powe. "The ranks close up firmly; 'forward,' they bravely press on."[26]

The Second and Eighth South Carolina, with Rice's battalion, charged close enough to the Yankee artillery to drive away many—if not all—of the gunners. Kershaw, who was with his right wing and did not see this action, noted, "The movement was reported to have been magnificently conducted," the cannoneers fleeing "and the caissons were moving off." It was likely about this time that Color Sgt. Adams suffered his third wound in the right leg, a bullet striking him in the thigh. "It did seem to me that none could escape," Pvt. Shumate of the Second noted of himself and his comrades. "My face was fanned time and again by the deadly missiles. We had arrived within one hundred yards of the battery and had not fired a shot. The artillerists were limbering up their pieces to retire, for in a few moments they would have been in our possession."[27]

Then occurred one of the many—if lesser known—enigmas of Gettysburg, one that cost many of the Palmettos their lives. Someone shouted out an order for the left-wing troops to shift front and move by the right flank, away from the abandoned enemy cannon. No one has ever been identified as the man who gave the order or for what reason, but Kennedy's, Rice's and Henagan's men did as they were told, now marching generally east and parallel to the Union line. Seeing this, the surprised Federal artillerists scrambled back to their pieces, quickly unleashing a torrent of grape and canister into the exposed flank of the two rebel regiments and Rice's battalion. Capt. S.G. Malloy of the Eighth's Company C wrote: "We occupied the extreme left of the brigade, just fronting the celebrated 'Peach Orchard'…. We began the fatal charge, and soon had driven the enemy from their guns in the orchard, when a command was given to 'move to the right,' which fatal order was obeyed under a terrible fire, this leaving the 'Peach Orchard' partly uncovered. The enemy soon rallied to their guns and turned them on the flank of our brigade." "The Federals … opened on these doomed regiments a raking fire … at short distance, which proved disastrous, and for a time destroyed their usefulness," Kershaw wrote of this situation. "Hundreds of the bravest and best men of Carolina fell, victims of this fatal blunder." Years later, the brigadier only knew that the "move by the right flank" order had been issued "by some unauthorized person" but that it "was immediately obeyed by the men."[28]

William Shumate of the Second also never forgot this sudden and incredible turn of events: "At this particular minute we heard in a clear, ringing tone, above the din … the command, 'By the right-flank!' True to our sense of duty we immediately obeyed … but why it was given, or by whom, the private soldiers and company officers could never ascertain. The artillerists, seeing our change of position, returned to their guns and poured death and destruction into our fast-thinning ranks." Charles Kerrison of the Second recalled one color-bearer, "a gallant, youthful looking boy, when the order was given to rally on the colors, in anticipation of his death, pushed his staff into the ground, and when struck by the death dealing minnie, his colors were there on which his battalion rallied and dressed." Kerrison continued: "'Charge after charge, but impossible….' The very dust around the feet, from the grape and cannister rises as if from a Sirocco."[29]

Kershaw claimed that the shift by his right wing at the Rose farm likely caused this sanguine error: "It was, no doubt, this movement, observed by some one from the left, that led to the terrible mistake which cost us so dearly." "The consequences were fatal," Lt. Col. Gaillard of the Second South Carolina wrote home after the battle. "We were, in ten minutes or less time, terribly butchered. A body of infantry to our left opened on us; and as a volley of grape would strike our line, I saw half a dozen at a time knocked up and flung to the ground like trifles…. There were familiar forms and faces with parts of their heads shot away, legs shattered, arms torn off, etc."[30]

This deafening hell of whizzing, lethal projectiles and gore was too much for mere mortals, at least for the surviving Palmettos, who withdrew in an effort to reach some semblance of safety and possibly regroup. This was not an easy task on the acres of open, undulating fields, already dotted by the dead and maimed of their comrades. Some of the Carolinians recoiled to the cover of the Rose farm buildings, but most dodged into woods along the northern edge of Stony Hill, close to Kershaw's right wing. A number of the Second South Carolina's soldiers sheltered in the depression between the Peach Orchard and the Rose farm, but this lowland also quickly became a killing ground, a Union gun positioned to fire down its length. It was a desperate situation for the Second, the Palmettos steeling for a last stand as their numbers rapidly dwindled amid the blaze from Union artillery and infantry. Pvt. Coxe of the Second's Company B saw a comrade, Pvt. Charles "Charley" Markley, collapse when a bullet pierced his forehead. "Many others fell; but our 'spunk' was up to white heat, and we didn't care, but made up our minds to die right there[,] to the last man if necessary," Coxe recalled. More Confederates were mown down, but this damage was soon limited as the Carolinians hugged the ground, some also trying to pick off the Federal cannoneers. One of the premiere experts on Gettysburg, historian Harry W. Pfanz, described the area where the Second rallied as "the woods on the left of the Third [South Carolina], in the swale that drains the area east of the Peach Orchard into the thumb of trees west of the stony hill."[31]

After regrouping, the Eighth South Carolina and the Third S.C. Battalion resumed their attack on the Peach Orchard from the south. The Eighth attacked Clark's and Bigelow's batteries, supported by Col. Henry J. Madill's 141st Pennsylvania, which was lying in concealment in a depression or sunken portion of a lane. "Kershaw charges the skirmish line and the batteries," stated one Union account. "The skirmishers fall back behind the guns and come in line" with the Pennsylvanians, who belonged to Brig. Gen. Charles Graham's First Brigade in Birney's division. "The batteries vomit double canister into the

Johnnies. On they come." The Pennsylvanians then "raise to their feet and give Kershaw a sheet of leaden flame and drive him back." At about the same time, Barksdale's brigade finally assailed the Union positions in the orchard from the west. Barksdale's assault was overwhelming and, combined with Kershaw's renewed strike, caused Graham's position in and around the orchard to fall apart. Adding to the Federals' woes, survivors of the Second South Carolina, hidden among the rocks and greenery of this terrain were among Confederates dropping Union artillerists and horses amid the guns lining Wheatfield Road. With his cannon in jeopardy, Lt. Col. McGilvery, the artillery brigade commander, ordered his batteries to withdraw about 6 p.m., the position becoming too hazardous to hold.[32]

Kershaw's Right Wing

The Palmettos of Kershaw's right wing—Aiken's Seventh and Maffett's Third South Carolina—meanwhile swarmed over the rocky grounds of the Rose farm, their ranks disrupted by the stone house, barn and outbuildings. With the brigade's left wing already in the initial stages of its wheel movement, Kershaw ordered the Third South Carolina to shift gradually to the left, so that it could navigate between the house and the barn and reconnect with the Seventh, which was moving to the right—or south—of the residence. These regiments would then align and continue their eastward advance toward the Stony Hill. "The wheel was accomplished in gallant style by the regiment, when we moved forward under a galling fire of grape, shell and cannister," Maffett related.[33]

The hill, sometimes referred to as Rose Hill, was some distance to the left and rear of the Rose place and was between the Peach Orchard and the Wheatfield. It was defended by two brigades of Union troops in Brig. Gen. James Barnes's First Division of the V Corps. These brigades—the First led by Col. William S. Tilton and the Second commanded by Col. Jacob B. Sweitzer—consisted of Michigan, Massachusetts and Pennsylvania soldiers who had arrived at Gettysburg about 5 a.m. after an exhausting sixty-mile march beginning on the morning of June 29. In short order, they were cast into the cauldron to bolster Sickles. "Shot, shell and musketry raged terrifically," recalled one of the Pennsylvanians. "The familiar piercing rebel yell, incapable of description, conceivable only by those who knew it, dominated the uproar."[34]

During its advance Kershaw's right wing managed to connect with Hood's left brigade, that of "Tige" Anderson. These Georgians already had clashed with Federals west of Devil's Den while attacking with Robertson's and Benning's troops, now under Evander Law. With the Third and Seventh South Carolina aiming for Stony Hill, Anderson's Georgians, on Kershaw's right, advanced toward the Wheatfield. By this time a pall of gun smoke and dust shrouded the thickets and depressions hindering the vision of Barnes's Yankees on the hill. Union skirmishers trotted back uphill into the position before Kershaw's ranks appeared like a line of ghosts in the battle haze. J.L. Smith of the 118th Pennsylvania in Tilton's ranks recalled: "The skirmishers came in hurriedly, and then … a column of the enemy appeared through the smoke, moving with shout, shriek, curse and yell…. They were moving obliquely, loading and firing with deliberation as they advanced, begrimed and dirty-looking fellows, in all sorts of garb, some without hats, others without coats, none apparently in the real dress or uniform of a soldier."[35]

Kershaw's men were nearing woods in their front when the Third South Carolina came under a "deadly fire" from Union artillery near the orchard and Barnes's riflemen on the hill ahead. Some of the Confederates thought their flag was attracting this lethal attention, since four soldiers of the color guard were shot down, and a Carolinian in the ranks called out, "Lower the colors, down with the flag." The color bearer, Sgt. William B. Lamb, however, would have none of this. Lamb, nicknamed "Squire" by his comrades, "waved the flag aloft and moving to the front where all could see, called out in loud tones, 'This flag never goes down until I am down.'" The Carolinians could see a Union officer directing the fire of the battery's guns; each time, "the grape shot would come plunging into our very faces," Augustus Dickert wrote. Soon word went up and down the line—"Shoot that officer, down him, shoot him." Some sharpshooters who joined Kershaw's ranks as they advanced began blazing away, and the artillerists quickly sought cover to the rear, leaving the officer to his fate. "This officer finding himself deserted by his men, waved his sword defiantly over his head and walked away as deliberately as on dress parade, while the sharpshooters were plowing up the dirt all around him, but all failed to bring him down," Dickert related.[36]

At some point in the attack, Dickert sensed that his Company H—nicknamed the "Dutch"—in the Third regiment was about to "flicker," or break, according to Pvt. Allen Barksdale in the Third's Company G. Dickert ran from his place in the ranks and grabbed Lamb's banner before the bearer knew what was happening. Facing his company and "waving the colors over his head," Dickert shouted to the men so he could be heard over the battle cacophony, "'Look here, Dutch, are you going to run?'" The orderly sergeant, Perry Fulmer, whom Barksdale described as "big hearted and big bodied," replied, "What do you mean, Gus? Don't you know we'll follow you to h——?" "All right," Dickert answered, "dress to the right and come ahead." Barksdale recalled that Company H "took step with the color guard and marched across that field toward the cannon we could see and count with all the precision of cadets in a prize drill. This too, while 'grape and canister' appeared to me to be coming at us by the bushel."[37]

In minutes the enemy musketry slackened. Kershaw's Third and Seventh South Carolina were surprised when the hill's bluecoat defenders—Tilton's and Sweitzer's brigades—suddenly and unexpectedly withdrew. General Barnes apparently felt this enemy assault, coupled with the pressure of Tige Anderson's onslaught against Federal units in the Wheatfield, to his left, and the Second South Carolina's musketry from the low ground near Tilton's right was too much of a threat for his brigades to hold their ground.[38]

Occupying the height, Kershaw directed some of Maffett's Palmettos to turn their muskets on two Massachusetts batteries posted on the Wheatfield Road and still punishing Kershaw's left wing. On the hill itself, Maffett's troops were deployed on the left with Aiken's Seventh to the right. Maffett wrote: "Sheltering ourselves behind some rocks and trees, the left of the regiment was directed" to try to pick off the enemy artillerists while the right triggered their muskets at Yankees in their front. Shortly after, however, the Carolinians saw a new and much more immediate menace. A strong force of Union infantry in two battle lines began advancing across the Wheatfield toward Kershaw's regiments on the hill.[39]

General Birney had earlier called for assistance, Meade, through Hancock, sending elements of the II Corps First Division of Brig. Gen. John C. Caldwell. These reinforcements were what the Carolinians saw as they reached the vicinity of the Wheatfield about 6 p.m. The brigade of Col. Edward E. Cross was the first to get into action, followed by Col. John R. Brooke's brigade coming up on his left and the famed Irish Brigade, led by

Col. Patrick Kelly, going into line on the division's right. The troops of Brig. Gen. Samuel K. Zook's brigade, also in Caldwell's command, were heading into action as well. Moving southwest, Cross's troops advanced diagonally through the Wheatfield, under rebel fire, a Pennsylvania soldier recalling "how the ears of wheat flew in the air all over the field as they were cut off by the enemy's bullets."[40]

The rugged nature of the terrain, however, prevented Caldwell's brigades from cohesive and coordinated efforts. Zook and Kelly moved toward the Stony Hill—where Kershaw's Seventh and Third South Carolina awaited. Composed of New York and Pennsylvania soldiers, Zook's brigade was first to assail this position—described by one Pennsylvanian as a "knoll of boulders"—and immediately encountered a storm of enemy musketry. "In our front, and but a few rods away, there was an almost continuous blaze of light, behind which we could dimly discern the forms of the men who confronted us," recalled Pvt. Robert L. Stewart of the 140th Pennsylvania. Zook's troops benefited from much of the Carolinians' fire initially being over their heads, the "first volleys" being "aimed too high [as] the balls rattled and crashed among the limbs of the trees behind and above us," Stewart related. "This was not long, however." Kershaw's muskets soon found the range and "awful was the carnage which followed. Men reeled and fell on either side" of Stewart, toppling amid the rocks and undergrowth. Zook himself fell mortally wounded by a bullet to the stomach, and was taken to the rear, Stewart noting that "the casualties among the officers were unusually large." Zook's loss, coupled with the heavy fire from the hill, blunted the brigade's advance.[41]

With Zook's troops temporarily stymied, Kelly's Irishmen were still in the Wheatfield, coming toward the hill on the left of where Zook attacked. The Carolinians, among them Col. Aiken and Lt. Col. Elbert Bland of the Seventh South Carolina, watched the enemy's martial spectacle in front of them. "Is that not a magnificent sight?" Bland exclaimed to Aiken. The colonel recalled that Bland was "pointing to the line of gayly dressed Union forces in the wheatfield whose almost perfect line was preserved though enfiladed by our fire from the woods, decimating the front line, whose gaps were promptly filled by each file-closer." Shielded by the greenery and gun smoke, the Federals did not initially see Kershaw's men immediately to their front. "Suddenly someone in the ranks cried out 'there they are!'" recalled Maj. St. Clair Mulholland in the Irish Brigade's 116th Pennsylvania. "Sure enough, not forty feet up from us towards the crest, behind the trees and big rocks … was the enemy; no orders were given, but in an instant every musket on the line was at its deadly work." As was the case during Zook's assault, some of the Carolinians fired too high, many of their rounds zipping over the kepis of the Irish, who also had another advantage. Said Mulholland, "The enemy having to rise to fire over the rocks, their shots for the most part passed over our heads, but as they exposed themselves to our men at such close quarters, armed with smoothbore muskets firing 'buck and ball' [one large and three buck shot] the effect of our fire was deadly in the extreme … under such circumstances a blind man could not have missed his mark."[42]

Zook's brigade, meanwhile, had reassembled and resumed its advance. These Yankees assailed the front of the Carolinians' position, primarily the Third South Carolina, while Kelly punished the right flank of the Seventh South Carolina. The Irish were taking advantage of a gap between the Seventh and Tige Anderson's Georgians. Amid this added pressure, Kershaw, who was in the thick of the combat, divided the Seventh South Carolina into two wings, the left led by Col. Aiken and the right by Lt. Col. Bland. After conferring with Bland about defending his portion of the hill, Kershaw hurried to find Brig.

Gen. Paul Semmes, whose Georgians were to his right and about 150 yards to the rear. Kershaw implored Semmes to bring his brigade in line on the Carolinians' right—Bland's troops—who were under the heaviest pressure. This would allow the Fifteenth South Carolina—separated by Semmes's command and the latter's earlier artillery support assignment—to also come up, filling the gap between Kershaw's right and the left of Anderson's Georgians.[43]

Semmes "promptly responded to my call, and put his brigade in motion toward the right, preparatory to moving to the front," Kershaw related. Semmes was mortally wounded shortly afterward, but his troops continued to advance.[44]

His brief discussion with Semmes ended, Kershaw, still on foot, then rushed to the Fifteenth South Carolina in an effort to bring it forward, finding that Col. De Saussure had been killed moments earlier. De Saussure "was rather a small man, physically, but his appearance and bearing were extremely martial, and [he] had a stentorian voice that could be heard above the din of battle," one of his officers noted. "In the act of leading his regiment, this gallant and accomplished commander … had just fallen when I reached it," Kershaw recalled. "He fell some paces in front of the line, with sword drawn." Sgt. Richard O'Neale of the Fifteenth related: "Lying near him was another of our best officers and over to one side a young boy—he was of such a tender age that he looked like a girl—lay dead." O'Neale claimed the colonel had foretold his own death in their conversation the previous day. With De Saussure's fall, the regiment's leadership went to 23-year-old Maj. William M. Gist, son of former state governor W.H. Gist. A Union County native and South Carolina College graduate in 1859, the younger Gist was active in the state's military mobilization up to and after Fort Sumter, organizing a company of Union County men that was eventually assigned to the Fifteenth. Gist "was a young man of rare qualities," noted one of Kershaw's veterans, "open, frank, generous, and brave." He would need all of these attributes and great good fortune to survive this day.[45]

Kershaw then "hastened back" to his beleaguered troops, as the oncoming Union infantry were then within some 200 yards of the Stony Hill. He quickly rearranged the Seventh South Carolina's right flank to make it stronger and more compact. Minutes later, the Federals halted, "poured into us a volley from their whole line, and advanced to the charge," Kershaw stated. The Carolinians received the attack "handsomely, and long kept him [the enemy] in check in their front." He later added that the attacking bluecoats were "received and entertained by this veteran regiment [the Seventh] which long kept them at bay in its front."[46]

On Kershaw's right wing, about 40 men from one of Semmes's regiments—Col. W.R. Manning's Fiftieth Georgia, by most accounts—meanwhile had hustled into position to the right rear of the Seventh South Carolina. These Georgians outpaced the rest of Semmes's troops in reaching Kershaw, temporarily fending off elements of the Irish Brigade in their front. Kershaw's problem was that a gap of about 100 yards still remained between these Georgians and the right of Aiken's command, "and into this the enemy was forcing their way." This lethal pressure forced the Seventh "to swing back more and more, still fighting at a distance not exceeding 30 paces, until the two wings were doubled on each other, or nearly so." In line to the left of the Seventh, Maffett's Third South Carolina was battling equally as hard as the foes poured deadly lead into each other in basically a point-blank firefight. Maffett related that "the enemy advanced to within 30 yards of us, and, for more than an hour, we held him in check, notwithstanding the repeated re-enforcements brought up by him." Still, Maffett's troops were "gradually being pressed back" by enfilading fire, the major related. To get these soldiers out of the crossfire, "and prevent its flank from being too much cut up," these men were ordered to fall back, as the regiment's left was held "firmly in its place. This made the line to be at nearly an acute angle to the first line," Maffett stated. As he had done with Aiken's troops, Kershaw "gradually swung around its [the Third's] right as the enemy made progress around our flank."[47]

It was about this time that Kershaw sent for Kennedy's Second South Carolina to reinforce Aiken's and Maffett's men on Stony Hill, telling Kennedy to "come to the right" from the Second's position with the brigade's left wing. Before Kennedy responded— or if he did, since he was wounded at some point in the fighting—Kershaw realized that "the enemy had swung around and lapped my whole line at close quarters, and the fighting was general and desperate all along the line, and so continued for some time." Still, Kershaw had deep confidence in these stressed but combat-hardened regiments. "These men were brave veterans who had fought from Bull Run to Gettysburg, and knew the strength of their position, and so held it as long as it was tenable," he recalled. Under increasingly heavy pressure, however, the Seventh South Carolina finally "gave way," Kershaw telling Aiken to reform his men at the stone wall on the Rose farm, some two hundred yards to the right rear. The Seventh's breaking point on Stony Hill may have been attributed as much to the rebels' reinforcements as to the foe. Aiken noted that as Semmes's Georgians and the Fifteenth South Carolina hustled into position they triggered friendly fire into the rear of his troops. They "fired over or at us, we never could tell, & wounded many of my men," Aiken wrote of Semmes's and Maj. Gist's soldiers. "We drove the enemy easily until then, when my men, feeling the effects of the balls from the rear began to waver."[48]

With their revolvers, the Irish Brigade officers joined their infantry in blasting away at the Palmettos on the slight slope above. To Mulholland, it seemed his Pennsylvanians—and possibly the rest of Kelly's bluecoats—were loading and firing "twice as fast" as their foe. After some ten minutes of trading lead and blood, Kelly ordered an uphill charge through the hovering gun smoke. The Yankee line surged forward "with a cheer," Mulholland recalled, "a few quick strides, and we are on the crest among the enemy." An Irish sergeant shot a Carolinian "within six feet of his bayonet," while Sgt. Francis Malin, a tall Federal "conspicuous for his dash and bravery," towered over the struggling men around him before crumpling with a bullet in his brain. "For a few moments it was hand-to-hand," Mulholland recalled.[49]

Kershaw personally led the embattled Third South Carolina, "then hotly engaged on the crest of the stony hill," as Federals clawed through the underbrush and rocks to engulf the hilltop. By this point, Semmes's advanced regiment had broken, but some of the individual Georgians stood with Maffett's men in the close-range combat. Amid his troops in this maelstrom, Kershaw later recalled, "Among the rocks and trees, within a few feet of each other, a desperate conflict ensued." The Yankees "could make no progress" in front of the Confederates' position but were gradually curling around Kershaw's right. The Palmettos' crisis was at flood tide. His vision obscured by trees, smoke and the undulating terrain, Kershaw couldn't determine how his left wing was faring; all of his staff officers were with that portion of his brigade and the position of the Fifteenth South Carolina was unknown to him, despite his earlier order to advance. Likewise Kennedy's Second South Carolina had yet to respond to his call for assistance. Aiken's Seventh had already fallen back to the Rose farm, and the Federals assailing Maffett were swarming like angry bees from a mule-kicked hive. In this dire situation, Kershaw made the decision to abandon Stony Hill to the enemy. He later explained: "I feared the brave men about me would be surrounded by the large force pressing around them," and ordered the Third South Carolina and the rest of the Fiftieth Georgia "to fall back to the [Rose] stone house, whither I followed them."[50]

Then occurred an "extraordinary scene" that, if Mulholland's account is true, would be one of the most remarkable episodes of the entire battle. "Our men and their opponents were mingled together," he related. "Firing instantly ceased, and we found there were as many of the enemy as there were of ourselves. Officers and men of both sides looked, for a time, at each other utterly bewildered; the fighting had stopped, yet the Confederates stood there facing us, still retaining their arms and showing no disposition to surrender." Breaking this odd stalemate, Mulholland shouted, "'Confederate troops lay down your arms and go to the [Union] rear.' This ended a scene that was becoming embarrassing. The order was promptly obeyed and a large number of … Kershaw's Brigade became our prisoners." He claimed that some of the Confederates "seemed to have no stomach for the fight; they were tired, weary and glad to call 'enough,'" which is not hard to believe, considering everything the Carolinians had previously endured that day.[51]

The other three regiments of Semmes's brigade, meanwhile, had already met a similar fate. They had gone into line to the right of their comrades in the Fiftieth Georgia and soon crashed head-on into the Federals of John Brooke's brigade. Amid the big rocks, slopes and summer foliage, Brooke's bluecoats ousted the Georgians from the Rose Woods. At least temporarily, intermixed Yanks of the Irish Brigade and Zook's command found themselves in possession of the smoky hill, among the bodies of Kershaw's men. Many of the slain Carolinians had fallen in the first scything volley of the Irish, claimed Maj. Mulholland. "Behind one large rock five men lay dead in a heap," he recalled. "They had evidently fallen at the first volley and all at the same time. One of them in his dying agony had torn his blouse and shirt open, exposing his breast and showing a great hole from which his heart's blood was flowing."[52]

The "buck and ball"—three buckshot and a 69-caliber bullet—had done its lethal work at close quarters. It was "wretched ammunition for distant firing," Mulholland noted, adding, "The fire of the Regiment was terrible in its effect, while the small rifle balls of the South Carolina men went whistling over the heads" of the Irish. At some point, Kelly's Federals realized the enemy they faced were their brothers in blood, since they had battled the Carolinians at Fredericksburg. These Confederates were "the same who, at Fredericksburg, had poured their deadly fire into the Regiment from the stone wall at the base of Marye's Heights," Mulholland related of the 116th Pennsylvania.[53]

A hundred yards or so away, Kershaw trotted toward the Rose farm on the heels of his bloodied and decimated Third South Carolina. Since his assault began from Seminary Ridge, the brigadier had been all over this sector of the battlefield on foot, acting as a messenger, to bring up reinforcements—since his staff accompanied the brigade's left wing—and commanding his right-wing regiments in face-to-face combat with the Yankees. He was unscathed but had to be mentally and physically exhausted from the summer day's many trials. Thousands of soldiers on either side could claim the same sufferings, but such a situation was unheard of for most generals in this war or perhaps any other since. Emerging from a patch of woods, however, Kershaw was heartened by the sight of "Wofford riding at the head of his fine brigade, then coming in." What was more surprising was that Wofford's Georgians were advancing east near the Peach Orchard, "which was then clear of the enemy."[54]

The orchard was "clear" due to the fierce onslaught of Barksdale's brigade, the Mississippians overwhelming the Pennsylvania infantry in that portion of Sickles's salient near the Wentz farm. Supporting Barksdale, and advancing shortly after the Mississippians attacked, Wofford veered to the right, his ranks moving along and on both sides of the Wheatfield Road. A lethal combination of Barksdale's and Wofford's thrusts and continuing punishment from Confederate shelling was the deciding blow against the other Federal units—infantry and artillery—in the orchard, forcing them to fall back. Among these Yanks were the Third Maine, the Third Michigan, the Second New Hampshire and the 141st Pennsylvania, which had been battling the Carolinians of Kershaw's left wing.[55]

At some point, Wofford reined in next to men of Kershaw's Second South Carolina, asking that the regiment form up on his right and join his assault, which they did. "Wofford took off his hat and, waving it at us, turned back and charged along his line," recalled Carolinian John Coxe of the Second. "And here was seen how the right sort of officer can inspire his men to accomplish next to superhuman results." Wofford "calmly brave as ever, throughout, riding up, assured them [Kershaw's men] that the Georgians, instead of the enemy were on their left; they rallied and, joining his brigade, all moved rapidly on after the fleeing foe," one of Wofford's soldiers recalled. The Second's Lt. Col. Gaillard added, "We charged upon the party opposed to us and drove them pell-mell through the woods, shooting them down and taking prisoners at every step." "The enemy gave way at Wofford's advance, and with him, the whole of my left wing advanced to the charge, sweeping the enemy before them, without a moment's stand … beyond the wheat-field, up to the foot of the mountain," Kershaw noted. "At the same time, my Fifteenth Regiment, and part of Semmes' brigade, pressed forward on the right to the same point."[56]

Only about fifteen minutes had passed since Kershaw abandoned Stony Hill, but Wofford's advance had reinvigorated the Carolinians and the other Confederates in this sector to recapture their earlier momentum and aggressiveness. The arrival of Maj. Gist's Fifteenth South Carolina further stoked them, as the Palmettos and Semmes's Georgians rallied and regrouped at and around the Rose farm. The counterattack came quickly, Wofford's Georgians thrusting east along the Wheatfield Road, accompanied by what was left of Kennedy's Second South Carolina, Henagan's Eighth South Carolina and Rice's Third S.C. Battalion. From the Rose farm vicinity came the Fifteenth South Carolina and three regiments of Semmes's brigade—the Tenth, Fifty-first and Fifty-third Georgia. Additionally, Tige Anderson's Georgians of Hood's division moved forward further to the east. "The victorious Rebel hordes for the first time sweep over the bloody Wheat Field, filling the air with demonical yells," a Union soldier recalled.[57]

This was not an assault like a Currier and Ives print—few, if any, were in this war. The regiments were tangled together in helter-skelter ranks, Wofford being the only general actively leading the Confederate riposte. Semmes was gravely wounded and Tige Anderson also was down, shot in the thigh. As the Fifteenth South Carolina advanced, its Company G, led by Capt. James McCutchen, found itself in the bullseye of Union cannoneers. Pvt. Gabriel G. Gist, in close proximity to the captain, was hit and crumpled to the ground. "He was standing [with]in two feet of me when he was stricken down by a grape shot," McCutchen recalled. "As he fell, he called out: 'Captain, I am wounded.' I looked down and saw that his leg was shot nearly off just at the knee."[58]

J.W. Lokay in the Fifteenth South Carolina's Company B encountered a wounded

Carolinian lying on the ground, the man telling him, "'You had better not go up there, you will get shot."' He continued uphill and "was taking deliberate aim at a Yankee with my old Enfield rifle when a minie ball passed through my thigh," Lokay recalled. "I felt as if lightning had struck me." Tossing his rifle aside, Lokay tried to make his way down the hill. Suddenly he saw a Union sergeant running, and apparently disoriented, since the Yank was within the Confederate lines. Lokay called for help and the sergeant came over, telling him, "'Put your arm around my neck and throw all your weight on me. Don't be afraid of me. Hurry up, this is a dangerous place."' As the Federal helped him, the "balls were striking the trees like hail all around us, and as we went back, he said, 'If you and I had this to settle we could soon do it, couldn't we?'" Lokay replied "that he was a prisoner and I a wounded man, so I felt we could come to terms pretty quick."[59]

The rebels swept forward in a disjointed but effective assault against Barnes's and Caldwell's overmatched Federals, including the Yankees on Stony Hill, who quickly relinquished their prize. Also caught up in this maelstrom were two brigades of U.S. regulars in Brig. Gen. Romeyn B. Ayres's Second Division of the V Corps. One of Kershaw's Carolinians described the regulars as "the stubbornest and most determined troops in the Federal army," but Ayres's men didn't have much of a chance facing elements of four Confederate brigades. Kershaw, meanwhile, headed to the stone wall at Rose's place, where he found Aiken and the Seventh South Carolina in position. We "poured it into the enemy," Aiken wrote of watching the assault. "In a few minutes the blue whelps were" retreating. Kershaw then reached the "stone building"—either the Rose farmhouse or barn—where Maffett's Third South Carolina and the Fiftieth Georgia were resting and binding their wounds. He ordered these soldiers to join Aiken's men at the stone wall in a defensive posture if the counterattack failed.[60]

Most of the Yankees fell back in various degrees of disorder, with Ayres's troops, along with the brigades of Sweitzer, Zook and Kelly, in danger of being cut off before fighting their way out. In some instances, blue and gray fought hand-to-hand amid the boulders and thickets, as the Federals swarmed over Plum Run and its swampy gorge toward the relative safety of the Union lines on Little Round Top. On reaching the crest, a number of the bluecoats filtered through the position of Brig. Gen. Samuel W. Crawford's Third Division of the V Corps. At Gettysburg, this division consisted of two brigades of Pennsylvania Reserves, its other brigade posted in the Washington defenses. "We pursued them [the Union fugitives] to the foot of the stone mountain," recalled Lt. Col. Gaillard of the Second South Carolina. By now, however, the rebels were already being hit by Federal artillery on the heights. Once the disorganized Yanks cleared his ranks, Crawford led his troops down the slope, attacking the intermingled Confederate pursuers, Gaillard writing, "Here the bullets literally came down upon us as thick as hailstones." The Pennsylvanians blasted the gray line with two volleys before charging.[61]

The Carolinians and Georgians fought savagely for a few minutes, but Crawford's counterstroke was overpowering, and most of the Confederates withdrew beyond the Wheatfield. "It is scarcely necessary to say we fell back," Gaillard related. "But the Yankees did not venture to pursue." It was about 6:30 or 7 p.m., based on varying accounts. Apparently during this see-saw action, Pvt. Wesley Nichols of the Eighth South Carolina recalled moving through "an old field" toward some woods, but then "a ball struck me in the head and blood soon blinded me." Lying on the ground, Nichols apparently wiped away the blood enough to see the Federals drive back the Confederates, now finding himself between the foes: "Both sides were throwing balls toward me."[62]

The brief, but hellish, firefight had been devastating to the antagonists. "The whole fight from the moment the infantry met was not more than [a] half hour, & I have never seen the same destruction on both sides in any battle before," related Col. Aiken of the Seventh South Carolina. As he limped to the Confederate lines, assisted by the Union sergeant, J.W. Lokay of the Fifteenth South Carolina soon saw a soldier from Kershaw's rear guard approaching them across a field. The soldier took custody of the kindly Federal, who he learned was in the Fourth Maine, but did not get his name before the Yank was escorted away. Lokay, meanwhile, lay down to rest under some trees.[63]

Pvt. Young P. Reagan of the Seventh South Carolina's Company C also was headed to the rear with a severe hand wound but was still "full of humor," at least one comrade recalled years later. Reagan had three fingers on his right hand shot off, his thumb and little finger injured. Later he told fellow Carolinians that he had outrun three cannonballs as he retreated. It had been "a fair race" because the projectiles "started about the same time he did, but never gained on him an inch." The fighting in this sector had raged for more than three hours by this point, the Confederates holding the Peach Orchard, Wheatfield, Abraham Trostle's farm and Devil's Den. "Amid a storm of shot and shell from flank and front, our gallant old brigade pushed towards the Round Top, driving all before them, till night put an end to the awful slaughter," recalled Capt. S.G. Mallory of the Eighth South Carolina. Near dusk, Kershaw regrouped his battered brigade and Semmes's Georgians behind the stone wall at the Rose farm. "It was now near nightfall, and the operations of the day were over," he recalled, adding, "We occupied the ground over which we had fought." That ground also was occupied by about 6,000 dead and wounded from both sides.[64]

6

"The Ghastly Dead
Upon the Fields of Blood"

The Brooks Artillery had been in the thick of the action even before McLaws's infantry—including Kershaw's brigade—engaged the enemy forces in and around the Peach Orchard. "Our battery is on the extreme left of the battalion," Pvt. Albert H. Prince later scrawled in his diary. Minutes earlier he had watched Lt. S.C. Gilbert ride ahead of the battery and consult with their battalion's colonel, E.P. Alexander, about where the guns should be placed. "In we go, and unlimber on the outskirts of the woods" with Barksdale's troops in their rear. Alexander put four of his batteries into action there under overall command of Virginian Maj. Frank Huger, Alexander "having been ordered to control also the other battalions of artillery on the field." The task in front of these artillerists was to engage "a heavy artillery and infantry force of the enemy, about 500 yards distant" in the Peach Orchard, Alexander reported.[1]

With the rest of the supporting artillery, Gilbert's four 12-pound howitzers blasted away after getting into position about 4 p.m. "The fight is opened, our battery I think, was the first to fire. Then commenced one of the most terrible fire of artillery I ever heard. Men and horses are falling on every hand," Prince wrote. "Three of our caissons were blown up." Two howitzers were soon put out of action, but "Lieut. Gilbert orders the men to man the two remaining guns which are working with diminished numbers." These Carolinians ceased firing as Barksdale's Mississippians attacked toward the Peach Orchard, Prince describing it as a "grand magnificent charge." He also noted that he saw Alexander approach Lt. Gilbert, telling him, "Your battery has held the hottest position of the day, few men would have stood, make up a section and follow up the charge," Prince wrote in his diary. It had been a "spirited engagement." Gilbert's Carolinians and Huger's other batteries now watched as the orchard was "immediately carried by the infantry," causing the Federals to fall back toward Cemetery Ridge, Alexander reported. By then Alexander "annoyed by his [the enemy's] obstinacy," had ordered up his two remaining batteries, Virginians led by Captains Pichegru Woolfork, Jr., and T.C. Jordan. "Limber to the front is heard from Lieut. Gilbert. In to the Peach Orchard we go," Prince related. Other guns from Alexander's battalion also rumbled into the thunderstruck orchard, all blasting the withdrawing Federals. "Action front again we pour shot and shell," into the enemy, Prince wrote. He added that Barksdale pushed the Yankees back "beyond our range and sends his aide back to tell us our shot is now falling short, and to move up."[2]

The Pee Dee Artillery, meanwhile, dueled with Union batteries trying to focus their fire against Confederate guns supporting Longstreet's attack. "From this position a fire

73

was opened at intervals, enfilading the enemy's guns when they were attempting to be concentrated, and also diverting their attention from the infantry of the First Corps," related Col. R.L. Walker, commander of A.P. Hill's artillery reserve.[3]

The artillery battalion of South Carolina Maj. David McIntosh occupied a section of stone wall along Seminary Ridge. The wall, two to three feet high, also fronted Pender's infantry, and had gaps in it a few feet across. Unfortunately for McIntosh, and his Virginia and Alabama batteries, their position became a prime target for Union guns after Longstreet opened his assault. "Our line remained quiet until a movement forward being made by the First Corps, [part of the Peach Orchard–Wheatfield action] a few rounds were fired by us to draw the enemy's attention, which never failed to do so." With Longstreet's attack well underway, the "firing in the afternoon became extremely warm, and resulted in considerable loss," he related in a postwar account. "There was more or less fighting all day on our front." The most notable casualties were two Alabama lieutenants in "Hurt's battery," officially known as the Hardaway Artillery, led by Capt. W.B. Hurt. One of these officers had the misfortune to be hit by a shell crashing through a gap in the wall and tearing off a leg, "from the effects of which he died," McIntosh recalled. Two guns were also put out of action, one "struck upon its face" by a Federal round, and a Whitworth with a broken axle, the latter sent to the rear to be repaired. "The enemy opened upon this spot at various times throughout the two succeeding days a terrible artillery fire, accompanied by a galling fire of musketry from their sharpshooters," the major noted.[4]

Gilbert's two guns of the Brooks Artillery joined elements of Huger's other batteries in moving forward to support the infantry assault, but not before "the teams could be disencumbered of killed and wounded animals (for his loss had been serious)," Alexander noted. The two newly arrived Virginia batteries also plunged forward. The South Carolinians unlimbered again to add their firepower to Alexander's other advanced artillery in punishing the retreating Federals, causing them to temporarily abandon several guns. This cannonade lasted until near dark, the rebel gunners preventing the pursuing Federals from becoming too aggressive in their chase. Gilbert was wounded in the left arm during the combat but remained on the field until he was hit in the left leg.[5]

With night descending, Gilbert's cannoneers trundled off the field, their ammunition exhausted. Earlier the lieutenant, nursing his arm wound, had seen an abandoned gun from another battery in danger of being captured. He called for volunteers and, under heavy fire, led a detachment back to retrieve the fieldpiece and haul it to safety. During the night some of the Carolinians went back to their first position of the day and gathered a supply of shells from their wrecked caissons, Pvt. Prince recorded. Gilbert's gunners had done a commendable job in supporting the Confederate infantry assaults in this sector, harassing Union troops as they retreated. With their last shots, they also helped stall any semblance of a pursuit of the Confederates' advanced lines, which pulled back after dark. His 70 or so Carolinians had put up a brave fight but had paid the butcher's bill—ten were killed, twenty mortally or severely wounded, twelve others less seriously injured. Additionally, the battery had lost twenty-five horses, two caissons and two guns dismounted.[6]

Anderson's Attack—5:45 p.m.

With Longstreet's divisions of McLaws and Hood in a desperate cockfight, "Fighting Dick" Anderson's infantry finally moved forward from the leafy woods behind Seminary

Ridge about 5:45 p.m. The troops had waited and listened as the rival artillery commenced fire almost two hours earlier, followed by "furious and sustained musketry." Yet it was not until 5:30 p.m. that "McLaws' division (by which the movement of my division was to be regulated) had advanced so far as to call for the movement of my troops," the Palmetto general recalled. "The advance of McLaws' division was immediately followed by the brigades of mine, in the manner directed. Never did troops go into action with greater spirit or more determined courage."[7]

Anderson's objective was the center of Cemetery Ridge in the same sector where the Pettigrew-Pickett-Trimble Charge—more popularly but less accurately known as Pickett's Charge—would be made less than 24 hours later. Wilcox's brigade was on the right, followed en echelon by Lang's Floridians, Wright's brigade and Posey's troops, Mahone's brigade being held in reserve. The open ground provided no cover, but Anderson's soldiers plunged forward for almost three-quarters of a mile as "they were compelled to face a storm of shot and shell and bullets; but there was no hesitation nor faltering." Wilcox's Alabamians crossed the Emmitsburg Road, crashing into the Federal positions and captured eight guns, driving some Yankees from their entrenchments, A.P. Hill reported. Wright's Georgians, however, overran a first line of Federals, grabbing some prisoners and about twenty artillery pieces on the ridge—but the success was short lived. Wright found himself without support, Lang's brigade falling back on his right and Posey's Mississippians not coming up on his left. Confronted by enemy artillery and infantry in front and on both flanks, Wright sent a desperate call to Anderson for reinforcements. Anderson sent a message to Wright to hold on, as Mahone's brigade was being sent to support him. Wilcox also had requested backup, Anderson telling him to "hold his own, things would change."[8]

Based on Wilcox's account, Anderson then sent one of Wilcox's staff officers to Mahone with orders to attack, but the Virginian refused to move, stating that he had instructions from Anderson to remain in reserve. Thus stranded, Wilcox and Wright were pulverized with a "destructive fire of grape" and bloodily punished by Union infantry rushing to fill the gap. With the ridge toehold now "untenable," Wright as well as Wilcox fell back, returning to their positions in the battle line along Seminary Ridge. There was no pursuit by the Federals, so both sides again posted pickets, while Anderson's "troops lay upon their arms." Losses in the brigades of Wilcox, Wright and Lang were "very heavy," Anderson reported. It had been an uncoordinated, hodge-podge attack, the brigades seemingly advancing on their own and unsupported, Mahone inexplicably staying out of the action.[9]

Mahone himself offered no answers as to why his troops were not engaged. His battle report had to be the shortest of any brigade commander on either side who fought at Gettysburg and could "be summed up in a few brief remarks," he noted. "The brigade took no special or active parts in the actions of that battle beyond" its contribution as skirmishers, he wrote. His men were in battle line, primarily as support for Pegram's batteries. Most of his 102 casualties, including killed, wounded and missing, were due to the "terrific shelling" on July 2–3.[10]

One of the few positives of Anderson's strike was that he acted in a timely manner in following Lee's orders to proceed in tandem after Hood and McLaws attacked. Yet "Fighting Dick" had not acted with his usual effective and reliable leadership, and his conduct on this evening at Gettysburg followed him to the grave and into the twenty-first century. "Left to his own devices in his first battle under Hill, Anderson was indecisive and sloppy in his actions," wrote historian James I. Robertson, Jr., in his biography of Hill. Yet as Robertson points out, others were to be blamed as well: Hill understanding that Anderson would be under Longstreet's control in the attack, Longstreet assuming that Hill would direct his own troops, and Lee not making his orders emphatically clear. Cadmus Wilcox, who had seen so many of his Alabamians lost this day, remained bitter toward Anderson in a postwar letter to Lee. "I am quite certain that Gen'l A., never saw a foot of the ground on which his three brigades fought on the 2nd of July," he wrote. "I may be wrong [about] Gen'l A., but I always believed that he was too indifferent to his duties at Gettysburg." Wilcox's accusation was based on his adjutant general's report of encountering Anderson as the combat raged on July 2. The officer, according to Wilcox, "found Gen'l A. back in the woods which were in the rear of Emmitsburg Road several hundred yards in a ravene [sic], his horse tied, and all his stuff lying on the ground (indifferent) as tho' nothing was going on, horses all tied." Hill summed up the attack thusly, placing no blame: "The enemy threw forward heavy re-enforcements, and no supports coming to these brigades, the ground so hardly won had to be given up." Of this combat, General Lee reported on July 31: "General Hill was instructed to threaten the center of the Federal line, in order to prevent re-enforcements being sent to either wing, and to avail himself of any opportunity that might present itself to attack."[11]

C. Irvine Walker, who wrote an Anderson biography published in 1917 and who knew the general personally, contended that Anderson's attack could have exploited the gap torn in the Union center, and greatly altered the battle's outcome if the assault had been reinforced. "The position thus captured by these three Brigades of Anderson's Division was the same which Pickett's and Pettigrew's two Divisions failed to carry the next day," Walker wrote. "If Anderson's Brigade had been properly supported they would have held a crucial point in Meade's line, after having pierced and broken it and there never would have been a necessity for the galling assault of the third day's battle…. Three Brigades of Anderson's … had captured a position which two solid Divisions, the next day, failed to reach!"[12]

More than a century and a half after the battle, it is risky to second guess Walker's contention, but this much is known: the Federal center was not nearly as strong late on July 2 as it would be by the next afternoon as Meade continued to concentrate his forces; and even if Anderson's troops held their ground, there were numbers of Federals on three sides of them; the nature of Lee's front-wide attack demanded a synchronization of efforts the Confederates grandly botched, one of their many damning mistakes at Gettysburg.

Perrin

After earning accolades—and sustaining heavy casualties—on July 1, Abner Perrin's Carolinians rested and bound their wounds on the 2nd, alert for the enemy artillery rounds that came their way. The troops listened to the battle crescendo well to the south as Longstreet's divisions were engaged and came even closer with Dick Anderson's attack.

Still, there was a chance that Perrin's brigade, along with other elements of Pender's division, could join in the assault "should the opportunity offer" in Lee's ongoing attempt to roll up the enemy line. The "opportunity" was all but lost, however, when Pender, considered one of the best and most promising young generals in the army, fell wounded. Riding near his troops and paying no mind to Union artillery rounds exploding in the vicinity, he suddenly went down, a shell fragment tearing into his left thigh. Brig. Gen. James Lane assumed division command.[13]

Anderson's men were some fifteen minutes into their onslaught about 6 p.m. when Perrin was ordered to send out a skirmish line to deal with Union pickets along the Emmitsburg Road in front of Cemetery Hill. Perrin assigned the task to Capt. William T. Haskell of the First South Carolina Volunteers, who commanded a "select battalion of sharpshooters" and sent the rest of McCreary's regiment—the First South Carolina— now carved down to about 100 troops, to deploy behind Haskell's men as their support. Haskell, 26, was from a prominent family in Abbeville District and was well liked and respected by the men of the brigade. He had served in all of the army's campaigns and had never been wounded, ill, or away from his command other than a month or so spent in South Carolina the previous winter to round up absentees from the brigade. One officer noted of Haskell, "In battle he was the very spirit of gallantry and self-possession." Led by "the gallant Haskell," as Perrin described him, the sharpshooters charged, pushing the Yankee skirmishers away from the road and up the slope, back toward their batteries. It was quick and good work, but not without cost. Haskell was "boldly walking along the front line of his command" along the road, "encouraging his men and selecting favorable positions for them to defend," when a Union sniper shot him in the chest. The captain fell, dying within moments or "in a few minutes," based on varying accounts. Perrin was clearly affected by Haskell's loss, stating that he "was educated and accomplished, possessing in a high degree every virtuous quality of the true gentleman and Christian. He was an officer of most excellent judgment, and a soldier of the coolest and most chivalrous daring." Others Carolinians were equally stunned by his demise. It was "the greatest individual loss to the brigade," Lt. Col. Brown of the Fourteenth observed, adding, "The gravity of his loss can scarcely be estimated. It was only known to those who knew him best." "It was everywhere conceded that we could have sustained no heavier loss in the line than in him," James Caldwell wrote. The captain's body was buried on the battlefield "near the scene of his exploits." Years after the war, former Brig. Gen. Ellison Capers of South Carolina, who wrote a history of the state's participation in the conflict, summed up the high esteem felt by so many for Haskell: "South Carolina gave no better, purer, nobler man as a sacrifice to the cause of Southern independence at Gettysburg."[14]

Among the sharpshooters most affected by Haskell's loss was Pvt. James Ouzts of Company K, Fourteenth South Carolina, whose brother George was killed on July 1. Nicknamed "Limber Jim," Ouzts was devoted to Haskell, often saying that he would die for the captain if necessary. If he was aware of his brother's death, his grief and anger also may have contributed to Limber Jim's daredevil state of mind. As the fighting continued in the ever-dimming light, Ouzts "seemed to be regardless of fear" and "fought with desperation as if to avenge the death of his fallen chief," said one account. Late in the day, he was struck down and killed almost instantly. Some comrades noted the smile on his face, "as if he had courted death to be again with his Captain." Despite the shock of Haskell's death, his other sharpshooters held their position until about 10 p.m., when Perrin was ordered to put his troops into line of battle to the right of Ramseur's brigade and on the left of Brig. Gen. Edward Thomas's four Georgia regiments. "I remained quietly in this position during the remainder of the night, having thrown forward skirmishers again," Perrin reported. At some point, however, Capt. T. Frank Clyburn led two companies of the Twelfth South Carolina to push back a small force of Federals and restore some pickets to posts they had relinquished, Lt. Col. Brown of the Fourteenth related.[15]

Earlier in the day a handful of men in the Thirteenth South Carolina risked their lives for a wounded Union soldier left between the enemies' positions. Lying on the field in the sun, the Federal pleaded for help. Lt. Alexander S. Douglass of the Thirteenth's Company C was in charge of the brigade's ambulance corps. This unit was composed of two soldiers from each company in each regiment whose duty was to bring off wounded men during battle and get them to ambulances to be taken to field hospitals. Douglass, 29, and four volunteers from the Thirteenth left the relative safety of Seminary Ridge and headed toward the fallen bluecoat, immediately attracting fire from some Union sharpshooters. The shooting ceased when the Federals realized the intent of the Carolinians' mission of mercy. They retrieved the Yankee, carrying him back into the Confederate lines and to the seminary building, where many other wounded from both sides were being treated.[16]

The action in which Haskell fell did not merit a mention in Perrin's battle report, but the night still held some self-inflicted bloodshed for the brigade's Twelfth South Carolina. Capt. Dunlop's Company B pulled back to replenish their ammunition, rest and clean their muskets. One soldier, R.A. Mullineaux, saw that a bullet was lodged in the barrel of his gun and tried to extract it using his ramrod while another man held the butt of the weapon. The musket accidentally fired, sending the ball and part of the ramrod through Mullineaux's body. "He screamed and fell," Dunlop recalled, "and when we rushed to his relief we found the rammer lodged in his body, but projecting through his back, and it had to be drawn through." The other piece of the ramrod whipped through the air and struck another Company B Carolinian, Pvt. George Sherrer, in the head, inflicting serious injury. Mullineaux died shortly afterward, Dunlop relating his last words: "'Captain, tell my mother I was a good soldier.' And a good soldier he was."[17]

Another of Perrin's Carolinians who was more fortunate to weather the battle's first two days unscathed was Scott Allen of Company K, Fourteenth South Carolina, whose brother, James, led the company, as noted earlier. Scott had been preparing to enter South Carolina College when the war came. By luck and God's grace, he evaded the lethal storm that eviscerated his company and the rest of Col. Brown's Fourteenth on July 1. Still, Scott had already used up more than his share of four-leaf clovers in combat. He had been severely wounded at Gaines Mill, but recovered enough to fight at Chancellorsville, where he was hit in the chest but not seriously injured. In Gettysburg's second day, still wearing the uniform riddled by bullets on the battle's first day, his gunstock was shattered in his hand, although the shock did not knock the musket from his grip. Less fortunate and lying in a Union field hospital was Capt. John Dewberry of the Thirteenth South Carolina. His arm wound was so severe that the limb had to be amputated, the operation performed by captured Confederate surgeon Tazewell Tyler, son of former U.S. president John Tyler. Dewberry would need time to recover, if he ever did, and he was a long way from the farm fields and hills of Spartanburg County.[18]

Lt. J.R. Boyles, of the Twelfth South Carolina's Company C, finally made it to a field hospital after reddening Willoughby Run with his blood on July 1. The two soldiers who carried him there on his makeshift stretcher laid him on a pile of straw that day. Boyles lay there in a torturous haze before his mangled right leg was amputated either on the 2nd or 3rd of July, his memory fogged by his severe injury and time's passage. He awoke lying on his back in some straw in a tent, his leg missing. Nearby "some parties were whispering that I was gone, no chance for me; I felt that my time had come and was resigned to my fate, but thought it hard," he related.[19]

Kershaw

Twenty-two-year-old Capt. Simon Baruch, the assistant surgeon for Rice's battalion, was watching from his aid station as Kershaw's attack unfolded earlier in the day. When several enemy shells burst in close proximity, Baruch was ordered to withdraw to Kershaw's brigade hospital set up at the Black Horse Tavern, well to the Confederate rear. Baruch's family had immigrated to America from Germany when he was a youth and had settled in Camden, South Carolina. He had already spent several months in Union confinement after being captured while attending wounded after Second Bull Run. Another healer was also at work. With the battle raging, word reached Dr. T.W. Salmond, Kershaw's brigade surgeon, that his friend Capt. Leitner had been seriously wounded and was still on the field. The 37-year-old physician was a family man with a medical practice in his native Camden before the war, but he did not hesitate to go in harm's way to aid his comrade. Salmond immediately mounted his horse and rode to the front, dodging enemy projectiles and finding Leitner. Salmond helped the captain onto his horse and brought him off the field. Another wounded Carolinian making his way to the rear recalled seeing Salmond on his "mission of mercy," the doctor "ordering those to the front who were not wounded, as he went along." Soon Kershaw's wounded began to arrive at the tavern where Baruch and other medical personnel awaited. What was immediately noticeable was that a number of soldiers had been hit in the left side of the body. Some of the men explained this oddity—of how their left flank had been exposed to Union artillery. Baruch's labors would last through the night, as he worked by candlelight, and well beyond.[20]

Infantryman Charles O. Wheeler of Kennedy's command was among the many injured who lay helplessly on the battlefield on July 2. Wheeler was hit in the upper left thigh but, unlike some others, was not under fire as he awaited aid. A chaplain from the Eighth South Carolina came by and gave him a swallow of brandy before an ambulance arrived to take him to a field hospital. Wheeler, who had also been wounded at Savage's Station a year earlier, would spend the night there, but his long road home was just beginning. Another casualty in Kennedy's Second South Carolina was Reuben Patterson, the affluent, young flute player from Liberty Hill. Ironically, the fingers on one of his hands were shot away, prompting Patterson to casually remark to his comrades, "No more playing the flute now."[21]

In the Eighth's Company G, Lt. H.R. Adams and privates Alex McIntosh and Josiah K. Easterling, along with Color Sgt. Elisha Adams, all were among the casualties not returning home. "Rarely does death, even in such great carnivals of slaughter, demand of one company so many of its choicest and bravest members," a fellow Carolinian later wrote of his comrades. Of Lt. Adams, the unidentified soldier wrote: "Of singularly pure morals, gentle, quiet and brave, he has gone to his rest," earlier adding that no "purer or nobler young man has drawn his sword in this great contest for liberty" than Adams. Pvt. McIntosh, "young, of a noble and commanding appearance, full of life and spirit," who fell in the attack on the Union artillery. His last words, according to at least one account, were, "Boys, we must take that battery or die in the attempt." "Young, frail and fragile as a flower," was the description of Easterling, "whose spirit and unyielding will always enabled him to undergo laborious fatigues and marches before which the stoutest and ablest among us quailed," the unidentified soldier wrote of him. Despite the "hand of disease" which "seemed always upon him," Easterling fought at Gettysburg, his last battle.

He, Lt. Adams and McIntosh all died on the field. Thrice wounded in the same leg, Color Sgt. Adams would hold on awhile longer.[22]

Among Kershaw's other dozens of dead was Capt. D.H.M. Langston of Company I in Maffett's Third South Carolina. Langston was from Laurens County, South Carolina, and had been wounded three times at Savage's Station in June 1862. With "little hope for his recovery," said one account, he was sent home either to die or survive. He lived and in January 1863 was well enough to rejoin his command. A short distance from where the captain fell, his brother, Sgt. G.M. Langston of the same company in the Third, crumpled to the ground, his thigh shattered by a Minié. Unable to move, Langston was "exposed to a terrible fire and his clothing and blanket riddled," but he survived. Another officer in the Third, Lt. Pickens B. Langford of Company E, was also slain. The 21 year old was a student at Newberry College before the war and had been severely wounded at Malvern Hill, recovering to amass an impressive combat record. The hourglass of his life ran out at Gettysburg, where he was riddled by grapeshot. One ball struck a tin plate in his haversack, but another pierced his heart. Langford's schoolmate at Newberry, Pvt. Thomas W. Sligh, the popular orderly from Company E, was dead as well, falling near the Peach Orchard, his first and last combat. Also amid the fallen was Lt. William Bearden of Maffett's Company K. Bearden was one of nine brothers from Spartanburg, South Carolina, in the Confederate army. Seven of them eventually made it back home, but his brother David had been killed earlier at Second Bull Run.[23]

Lt. M.R. Hinson and his brother, Pvt. Elijah Hinson of Company H in the Second South Carolina, were from Lancaster District, South Carolina, but neither would go home again. They left behind their parents, two other brothers, and at least two sisters, and the lieutenant also was survived by "two darling little babes to mourn over his absence." He "fell a victim to death, under the murderous shower of shot and shell," that day, a comrade noted. "Thus has our country lost a noble young man and gallant officer." Pvt. Hinson had his "chin shot off," the *Lancaster Ledger* related on July 29, adding that the company's Capt. B.R. Clyburn was severely wounded in the face and leg. There was no mention of whether Elijah was still with the army, had been taken prisoner or was recovering from his ghastly wound, and the already grieving family apparently suffered for weeks wondering about his well-being. With some finality, the September 2 edition of the *Ledger* contained a small notice about captured soldiers from Lancaster District "who are officially reported to have died in the hands of the enemy." Among them were Elijah Hinson, Lt. G.C. Brazington, Cpl. J.H. Small Pvt. W.C. Horton, all of Company H, and Pvt. J.Q Croxton of the Second's Company G.[24]

Pvt. Gabriel G. Gist, of the Fifteenth South Carolina's Company G, lived only a short time after a grapeshot nearly severed one of his legs. "The nervous shock was so great that he died in about four hours," related Capt. James McCutchen, his company commander. "I had him and another gallant comrade buried, side by side, under a large elm tree on the battlefield."[25]

Also listed in Kershaw's slain was Lt. James M. Daniel, 27, of Co. E., Seventh South Carolina. Daniel's 30-year-old brother, Lt. William Lowndes Daniel of Co. I, Second South Carolina, had been a doctor in Orangeburg County before the war. Joining the Palmetto Guards of Charleston, he had risen through the ranks from private to lieutenant in Aiken's regiment. A year or so earlier, Dr. Daniel had expressed his war weariness in a letter to his mother, written after the battles of the Peninsular Campaign near Richmond. "I have given you an imperfect sketch of what we have done and suffered in the last three weeks," he wrote. "But no description can give you an idea of the suffering and anxiety … to which we have been exposed. Nothing but actual experience will suffice. I have seen the ghastly dead upon the fields of blood and the suffering wounded till I am sick and tired of it and trust I may never see the like again. The sight hardens some, but I must say it deeply wounds my sympathies. God grant that this terrible war may soon be brought to a close and that its survivors may soon be permitted to join their families, never more to be parted on such a dark errand…. I have seen enough to make a heart of stone bleed and such sights trouble me much, but I bear them with seeming fortitude." He joined his brother in death at Gettysburg. Eighteen-year-old Pvt. John M. Reynolds already had earned a reputation for bravery and leadership among his buddies in Company F of the Second South Carolina. The youngest of eight children in a Greenwood, South Carolina, family, his promising military career ended abruptly when he was killed instantly on July 2.[26]

Lt. Milton P. Buzhardt, of the Third South Carolina's Company B, was killed by the "jar of a ball striking a tree near him." Buzhardt had three brothers in the Confederate military, all from the Newberry area.[27]

Capt. Benjamin Roper of the Seventh South Carolina oversaw the burial of Cpl. Thomas Harling, killed while carrying the regimental flag on July 2. "After the battle was over I had his remains put away as well as circumstances would admit," he wrote to Harling's father, "and the spot marked so it can be pointed out in after days." Cpl. Humphrey D. Ruston of the Seventh's Company H must have considered himself lucky to come through the day unscathed, although he "suffered a very narrow escape, part of his clothing having been cut off by a bomb shell," a newspaper account stated. Ruston was not so lucky some two and a half months later—on September 20, when he was killed at Chickamauga. His right leg blown away, Capt. Thomas Powe of the Eighth South Carolina was among the many taken to the brigade hospital at the Black Horse Tavern. Fighting for his life, Powe fell "with his harness on, struggling for the State of his birth and his love, and above all, ready to meet his God," a comrade remembered.[28]

In the gathering darkness, other Carolinians were in enemy hands, among them Pvt. Thomas Jefferson Young, Company B, Fifteenth South Carolina. Young, a native of Union County, South Carolina, who was in his early 20s, was married and the father of three children when he volunteered for the army in 1861. He had been in many battles, had been seriously wounded at Antietam, and was hit again at Chancellorsville. The latter injury had not prevented him from being at Gettysburg. In the fighting this day he was wounded again, this time in the wrist, and was taken prisoner. Injured, in enemy hands and so far from home, Young had to wonder if he would ever see his family again. Lt. William S. Bissell of Company I, Second South Carolina, was severely wounded and also captured. He was one of five brothers in the Confederate service. As he lay in a hospital, Bissell must have wondered if he or any of his brothers would live through this terrible conflict.[29]

"Our Brigade suffered very severely," Lt. Col. Franklin Gaillard of the Second South Carolina wrote home about three weeks after the battle. "The 2nd Regiment I have no hesitation in saying was the hero Regiment of the Brigade…. I cannot recur, even in thought, to their gallantry without the proudest emotions." The skirmishers of Capt. R.E. Richardson's Company A, Third South Carolina, meanwhile, had been in action since early in the day on the 2nd, stepping into Kershaw's ranks as the brigade attacked. These men "did good service as sharpshooters" and, with "other companies from the brigade," had confronted and stalled "a column of the enemy's infantry … endeavoring to gain our rear," Maffett reported. Other companies from the Third were later sent out as sharp-shooters and "performed the duty assigned them satisfactorily."[30]

The Seventh South Carolina's Col. Aiken later recalled his informal inspection of the ravaged terrain after nightfall. "We held the battlefield, and about dark I walked over the field," stopping to talk to some of the many fallen Federals still alive but awaiting medical attention, he wrote. Aiken spoke with wounded "representatives" from twelve Union volunteer regiments and a regiment of U.S. Regulars, somewhat impressed by the latter: "Those Regs fight splendidly, but won't stand a charge," he penned days after the battle.[31]

"The wheat field and woods were blue with dead and wounded Federals," related John Coxe of the Second South Carolina. "The ground was covered with dead, dying and wounded, Confederates and Federals alike," noted another Carolinian. "The red earth of Pa., was made crimson, pouring from the veins of several thousand soldiers. The earth truly drank blood." As the fighting died down, the Carolinians were met at the edge of some woods by General McLaws, the exhausted men giving him a hearty cheer. The division commander "seemed well pleased with the evidences of our victory lying around him," Coxe wrote of the Union casualties. The private, however, was shaken by the sufferings of the stricken Yankees he saw: "I felt sorry for the wounded enemy, but we could do little to help them." Just before dark, Coxe passed a "large and fine-looking" Union officer with a gruesome leg injury, sitting with his back against a large oak tree. The man called out to Coxe and "politely asked me to give him some water. There was precious little in my canteen, but I let him empty it." The officer's left leg had been crushed just above the ankle, his foot lying sideways on the ground, and he asked Coxe to straighten it out and use some rocks to prop up what was left of the limb. The Carolinian complied, asking if the movement was painful, to which the Federal quietly replied, "There isn't much feeling in it just now,'" Before leaving the officer, Coxe said, "Isn't this war awful?' 'Yes, yes, said he, and all of us should be in better business.'"[32]

In the fading light the Carolinians and other soldiers on both sides listened to the clatter of musketry to the north as Ewell's corps began its assault against the Federals on Cemetery Hill and Culp's Hill. The battle symphony flamed out there before midnight, Ewell's troops seizing and tenuously holding some ground at Culp's Hill.

Kershaw's men settled down to build campfires and "from the haversacks of the dead enemy all about us got something to eat," Coxe noted. About 9 p.m. cooks came up from the rear carrying camp kettles of boiled beef. The cooks did not issue any salt or bread, but the men still ate heartily. "We had not eaten anything since seven o' clock in the morning," recalled one of Coxe's comrades in the Second. Before the battle opened, this unidentified soldier was getting rid of unnecessary items to lighten his load going into combat. He thought about discarding a plug of "fine Virginia tobacco," but reconsidered. Now, some five or six hours later he retrieved it for a well-deserved chaw. "I took it from the bosom of my shirt and I could almost squeeze the perspiration out of it…. I took a chew and put it by to dry. We were soon asleep, waiting for the coming day."[33]

Shortly afterward began the process of retrieving the wounded, a task that would last late into the night for some of Kershaw's men. Dr. Salmond, the brigade surgeon, directed the effort from the outset. "Our loss in regimental and line officers was very great," recalled Augustus Dickert of the Third South Carolina. "The dead were left to take care of the dead" until the next day. A detail from the Second South Carolina brought in

Sgt. R.W. Pool of Company B, who had been terribly mutilated by the Union artillery. "Poor First Sergeant Pool of my company!" Coxe remembered. "He was brought into our ranks suffering horribly from the grapeshot in his stomach. The surgeons could do nothing for him." Many of the men in the Second's Company B were comrades from Greenville, South Carolina, who belonged to the "Butler Guards" before entering Confederate service. The day's devastation was beyond anything they had ever experienced before. "It has been the most heart rending engagement we have yet had," Lt. William Holland wrote days later. "We all mourn the loss of our dead and I apprehend the people of Greenville will feel as much the effect of this battle as any of the war."[34]

"Our troops were severely punished, particularly my company and regiment," related William Shumate of the Second. "Night put an end to the conflict, and when my regiment was reformed, but a handful of men answered to their names at roll-call." Indeed, Company B had basically ceased to exist as a fighting unit. Out of the forty-nine Carolinians who went into the battle, only three—Lt. Holland, Shumate and Coxe—were left who were not killed, wounded or captured. Lt. W.E. James of the Eighth's Company F wanted to find wounded men of his company, also nearly destroyed, and bring them in. With some difficulty he procured an ambulance. James located the fallen Capt. John K. McIver and Sgt. I.D. Wilson, loaded them in the wagon and headed to the brigade field hospital at Black Horse Tavern, some two miles distant. En route, he also discovered Henry Bozeman, another Company F soldier, lying on the porch of a house with a broken arm. James did all he could for Bozeman, telling him that he would send someone back for him, since he had no more room in the ambulance. He then continued toward the tavern.[35]

Privates Charles and Edwin Kerrison of the Second South Carolina's Company I survived the day, Charles sustaining two relatively minor wounds. Years later he reflected on the horrors he endured: "Pictures of battlefields may be vivid, but what is the reality? Many a gallant command swept forward only to destruction. When the pall of night came to close the bloody scene the army, though unsuccessful, was not defeated. The heroic spirit, the confidence was still unimpaired."[36]

Kershaw, meanwhile, was already compiling his initial casualty lists after posting his pickets well out in front of his position that night. "I commenced the melancholy task of looking up my numerous dead and wounded," he noted. "It was a sad list." De Saussure's death was a severe blow, as was the fall of the Eighth South Carolina's Maj. Donald McLeod, "a gallant and estimable officer." Col. John Kennedy of the Second was wounded for the third time in the war but would survive. Lt. Col. Franklin Gaillard led Kennedy's regiment during the rest of the battle. Other notable casualties were Lt. Col. Elbert Bland of the Seventh South Carolina, shot in the thigh while leading the right wing of the regiment "with his usual courage and ability," Kershaw noted, and Maj. D.B. Miller of Rice's battalion, also wounded. "A long list of brave and efficient officers sealed their devotion to the glorious cause with their blood," Kershaw wrote. "All of the officers and men of the command behaved most admirably, and are entitled to the gratitude of the country." The general knew his brigade had been wrecked, but that night he still had no idea as to the extent of his losses. Surgeon Welch of the Thirteenth South Carolina in Perrin's command also would learn at some point about the fate of his back-home friends in Kershaw's ranks, including the lighthearted soldier killed by shellfire. Treating the wounded and dying behind the battle lines, his ears told him that the combat greatly intensified around noon or shortly thereafter, "from which time it raged with great fury." In at least one letter to his wife, written in the coming weeks, Welch mentioned the deaths of Capt. D.M.H. Langston and several other men in the Third South Carolina Regiment whose blood soaked the hills, ravines and fields of Gettysburg.[37]

Another officer lost to the Second South Carolina was Capt. George W. McDowell of Company F. He had been with the company since it was organized as the Secession Guards and paraded proudly through the streets of Greenwood, South Carolina, when the world was young and war was a grand adventure. He died of his wounds on July 3 at the Black Horse Tavern.[38]

Despite his heavy losses, Longstreet had nothing but the highest praise for his corps' achievements this day, writing that it was "the best three hours fighting ever done by any troops on any battle field." David McIntosh, the South Carolina artillerist, added, "The veterans of the first corps were not wanting in their old time spirit, and they added renewed lustre to the splendid record which they had already borne."[39]

At his headquarters that night, Robert E. Lee pondered the sanguine events of the day, the losses, the gains, and how he would proceed on Friday, July 3. Longstreet, after "a severe struggle" had taken ground that could give the Confederate artillery an advantage in bombarding the "more elevated ground beyond, and thus enable us to reach the crest of the ridge." Ewell also had "carried some of the strong positions which he assailed (mainly in the vicinity of Culp's Hill) and the result was such as to lead to the belief that he would ultimately be able to dislodge the enemy." To Lee, these "partial successes determined me to continue the assault next day."[40]

Longstreet had a much different view of the day's outcome, later criticizing Hill and Ewell for being tardy in joining the battle. Yet Lee had pronounced the day "a success, as we were in possession of ground from which we had driven the Federals" and captured several fieldpieces, the Carolinian related. He was proud of the accomplishments of his two divisions against greater numbers. "The conflict had been fierce and bloody, and my troops had driven back heavy columns and had encountered a force three or four times their number," Longstreet recalled.[41]

Into this haunted night Longstreet sent scouts around the extreme right of the Confederate line, past the area where the Carolinian Evander Law toiled to regroup and bind the wounds of Hood's tough fighters, who had lost so many comrades hours earlier. The day's vicious combat "had accomplished little toward victorious results," Longstreet recalled, but he remained optimistic in still "thinking General Lee might yet conclude to move around the Federal left." The fate of thousands raced through the minds of these two Confederate generals and many other soldiers as funereal blackness shrouded the merciful end of Gettysburg's second day.[42]

On the Rose farm, the exhausted Lt. Col. Gaillard of the Second South Carolina tried to get some rest among others of Kershaw's command, his mind numbed by the day's horrors. With Col. Kennedy wounded, Gaillard led the regiment, which sustained appalling losses. He had seen "about half of our men killed or wounded" in some ten minutes or so of the worst combat he had yet endured. "It was the most shocking battle I have ever witnessed," he wrote home weeks later.[43]

At some point over the next few days, Union Lt. Frank A. Haskell walked the battleground, hideous sights abounding at every step. The blue and gray litter of the armies was everywhere, ripped uniforms, hats, muskets, canteens—most everything sprinkled or soaked in red—dead and mangled horses, splintered wagons and caissons and the miscellaneous personal effects of so many fallen soldiers. What moved Haskell most, however, was the human carnage: "and last but not least numerous, many thousands of men—and there was no rebellion here now—the men of South Carolina were quiet by the side of those of Massachusetts, some composed, with upturned faces, sleeping the last sleep, some mutilated and frightful, some wretched, fallen, bathed in blood, survivors still and unwilling witnesses of the rage of Gettysburg."[44]

7

"Carnival of Hell"

Friday, July 3

"The sun rose clear and bright over the field of blood," one of Kershaw's veterans recalled of that fateful Friday. The sultry heat was in its third day of baking hundreds of corpses and many more bloating carcasses of horses and mules, all contorted across a tortured landscape that had been so pastoral and pristine only 48 hours earlier.

The most famous South Carolinian on the field, however, had some monumental decisions to make or oppose that morning. It was the day of reckoning for not only his career but for his life.

With Stonewall Jackson dead, Lt. Gen. James Longstreet was Robert E. Lee's new right arm, a grim, stout and calculating Viking of a warrior who had already served in that capacity on several occasions. Some of Kershaw's rebs called Longstreet the "Wild Hun" or "bulldog" for his hard-hitting tactics, tirelessness and fierceness, while Lee referred to him as his "war horse." The nickname "Old Pete" was also heard in talk around the soldiers' campfires and on the march. At age 42, Longstreet's combat record already had spanned more than two decades well before the Confederacy was born. Of Dutch blood, his ancestors had moved south from New Jersey years earlier. A native of Edgefield District, South Carolina, Longstreet and his mother had moved to Alabama in 1831 when Longstreet was 10, his father dying during this period. Longstreet was appointed to West Point from that state and graduated 54th in the class of 1842. One of his oldest friends from his Academy days was Ulysses S. Grant, who later married Longstreet's cousin. Other future Confederate generals in the Class of '42 were another South Carolinian, Richard H. Anderson, Lafayette McLaws, A.P. Stewart, Earl Van Dorn, Daniel Harvey Hill, and G.W. Smith. Assigned to the U.S. Fourth Infantry Longstreet fought in the Mexican War and was severely wounded in the thigh while carrying the regimental flag during the storming of Chapultepec in September 1847. Twice he won brevets for gallantry in that conflict and also saw action in various Indian campaigns. He resigned from the army in May 1861, was appointed a Confederate brigadier shortly afterward and fought at First Bull Run in July. By October 1861 he was promoted to major general. He was "a powerful figure, nearly six feet tall, broad of shoulder, with cold gray-blue eyes, thin sandy-brown hair, and a heavy beard that almost concealed his mouth," Douglas S. Freeman related. Longstreet was "a thickset, determined-looking man," the British army observer, Lt. Col. Arthur Fremantle of the Coldstream Guards, wrote of him a few days before Gettysburg. "He is never far from General Lee, who relies very much upon his judgment…. By the soldiers he is invariably spoken of as 'the best fighter in the whole army.'" Longstreet would forever be haunted by the events of January–February 1862. His wife, Louise, spending the winter in Richmond, had sent a desperate call for him to return to the capital in late January. Scarlet fever was ravaging the city and devastated the Longstreets, like many other families. Two of their four children, one-year-old Mary Anne and four-year-old James died from it on consecutive days, January 25 and 26, and were buried together; a third child, 13-year-old Augustus, succumbed on February 1. Compounding their unfathomable grief, the Longstreets already had suffered through the loss of two children, one-year-old William D. in July 1854 and infant Harriett in August 1856. Despite his mourning, the war churned on and Longstreet soon returned to duty. His combat record was distinguished in the Peninsula campaign, Second Bull Run and Antietam, resulting in his rise to lieutenant general in October 1862. At Fredericksburg in December 1862, his First Corps held one of the strongest defensive positions of the war on Marye's Heights, mowing down ranks of Union infantry who tried to seize it.[1]

There was much for "Old Pete" to ponder as the eastern sky lightened over Cemetery Ridge, where Meade's army awaited. "The position of the Federals was quite strong, and the battle of the 2d had concentrated them so that I considered an attack from the front more hazardous" than the previous day, the Carolinian noted of conditions that Friday. "However, General Lee hoped to break through the Federal line and drive them off." By then the Federals had emplaced batteries on Round Top to rake any Confederate assault made against Meade's front. When Lee met with Longstreet that morning, the latter still hoped to persuade Lee to move against the enemy left, telling the commander of his reconnaissance effort overnight. But Lee remained firm: "No, I am going to take them where they are on Cemetery Hill," he told Longstreet. The Carolinian was to renew his attack against "probably the strongest point of the Federal line"—the center—with three infantry divisions, the assault preceded by a massive artillery bombardment to try to silence the Union guns. Longstreet later wrote he was "disappointed" by Lee's mandate, but he had yet to rest his case in his conference with Lee. "That will give me fifteen thousand men," he estimated of his assault force, "and I think I can safely say there never was a body of fifteen thousand men who could make that attack successfully." When Lee appeared to be "a little impatient" at these remarks, Longstreet said nothing more.[2]

To the north the early morning was violated by voluminous rolls of musketry and artillery as Ewell's Confederates resumed their clash against the Union right flank amid the rocky slopes of Culp's Hill and Cemetery Hill. Ewell's troops fought well but were driven back with heavy losses by mid-morning, losing the costly ground they had gained on July 2. After the repulse and some six hours of combat, Ewell's corps would be little help, if any, in supporting Lee's grand assault.[3]

While Longstreet mulled over his epic orders, tens of thousands of other men on both sides wondered what the day would bring and whether they would live to see the sun slip behind the western Pennsylvania hills. "What next? Who knew?" recalled South Carolina Pvt. J. Merrick Reid of Garden's battery. "Doubtless councils of war were held on both ridges and reconnoitering parties and field glasses were busy while the royally irresponsible rank and file loitered away the welcome calm in restful repose…. Many, very many, who while away those moments enjoyed their last smile on earth." Reid's assessment was an epitaph for "very many" by sundown. "Scores of thousands of American soldiers were ready to lay down their lives for the cause they believed to be right," one South Carolinian noted years later of both armies.[4]

Kershaw

The soldiers of Kershaw's brigade roused "as the sun rose bright and clear," the Palmettos and the rest of the army sensing the day would bring a decisive end to the battle, Augustus Dickert of the Third South Carolina related. "No one could conjecture what the next move would be, but the army felt a certainty that Lee would not yield to a drawn battle without, at least, another attempt to break Meade's front." "We bivouacked on the battlefield and expected an early attack from the enemy, but no advance was made by either side," the Eighth South Carolina's William Shumate wrote of forenoon. All were wondering how the day would unfold—would the Yankees try to take advantage of their successes on the 2nd and take the offensive to crack the Confederate lines, or would Lee be able to build on the momentum the rebels had seized on the battle's first day?[5]

"After the heavy battle of yesterday [the 2nd] and the all night's march preceding, the soldiers felt little like renewing the fight … still there was no despondency, no lack or ardor, or morale, each and every soldier feeling, while he had done his best the day before, still he was equal to that before him." The Eighth South Carolina in particular had little firepower to add to any action this day. Henagan's regiment had only 59 men out of the 170 who had gone into combat on the 2nd.[6]

"The morning hours were spent by both armies in looking after dead and wounded comrades wherever they could be reached, while some letters were written to loved ones at home," remembered Pvt. Daniel Hargrove, one of the Eighth's survivors. "A grim, earnest look, silence and determination characterized the whole scene of carnage. Americans slain by Americans." Hargrove lived through Kershaw's fight on July 2, but was far from unscathed, suffering a "fearful wound by a canister shot." Some comrades placed him at the base of an apple tree, "which was my resting place for several days."[7]

Earlier that morning McLaws had tightened up his division's line, including Kershaw's men, in the Peach Orchard/Wheatfield sector, "all concealed by the woods from the batteries on the hills," he recalled. "We lay undisturbed by the enemy," McLaws continued. "The exertion of the previous day had been tremendous, and excepting burying parties, those engaged in attending to the wounded and collecting and stacking arms, my division was resting." Not resting were Pvt. John Coxe and his comrades in the Second South Carolina, who were still burying the dead and getting the wounded to the rear, despite being in "close proximity" to the Union positions. Among the fallen was Sgt. R.W. Pool of Company B, who was retrieved from the battlefield Thursday night, in agony from a grapeshot in the stomach. "Death relieved him" about 4 a.m. on Friday, Coxe noted.[8]

The exhausted Lt. W.E. James of the Eighth South Carolina's Company F awoke to the stirrings all around him at Kershaw's brigade hospital at Black Horse Tavern. James had brought in two wounded Carolinians hours earlier. He bedded down at the hospital, meaning to return to his regiment early on Friday to join in the expected battle on the 3rd. "But when I awoke … I found that more than half of Company F had been brought in during the night, some of them mortally wounded and all in need of attention, so I could do more good there," he wrote. James was helping lift men onto a table to receive treatment when an orderly approached, telling him that Lt. George Bozeman had been brought in with a head wound and needed a doctor's immediate attention. James went to the "kind and skillful surgeon" Dr. James F. Pearce who, along with Dr. James Evans, "had been hard at work … amputating limbs and relieving the sufferings of the wounded." Based on James's account, Pearce told him that Bozeman was mortally wounded and would likely die that day. "'We can't help him. We are trying to save those who may live,'" Pearce said.[9]

Perrin

A short distance from Kershaw's battle line position, Abner Perrin's Carolinians were still posted overnight between the brigades of Ramseur (Ewell's corps) and Thomas (Hill's corps) in front of Cemetery Hill, but the day had begun ominously. The early morning was shattered by "the heaviest skirmishing I have ever witnessed," Perrin noted of his sector, "kept up during the greater part of the day." This is not surprising, since Ewell's troops and the Federals defending nearby Culp's Hill renewed their combat about 4:30 a.m. Union artillerists on Cemetery Hill were within close range of Perrin's skirmishers, and the Federals "made desperate efforts" to dislodge them and recapture the position seized by the Confederates the previous night. Perrin's troops "repulsed every assault," holding their ground until ordered "back to the main line at Gettysburg," he stated. At one point that morning there was a particularly heavy attack as "the enemy poured down a perfect torrent of light troops from the hill," shoving the rebel skirmishers back to the main line. To meet this menace—from elements of Union Brig. Gen. Adolph von Steinwehr's division of the XI Corps—Perrin ordered his decimated Fourteenth South Carolina, under Lt. Col. Joseph N. Brown, to deploy and charge. The counterattack was launched "in the most gallant style," blunting the enemy threat, but Brown and Major Edward Croft were seriously wounded in the effort. Brown was shot in the left shoulder while Croft, struck in the chest and right hand, was not expected to live. A picket slain was the Carolina infantryman who captured a Union flag on July 1, tucking it inside his shirt.[10]

Among others wounded was Pvt. J.C. Buzzard of the Fourteenth's Company K. Buzzard was in action on the first day's battle, hit by a bullet that tore through his knapsack, blankets and clothes before flattening out and barely breaking the skin. "I thought I was killed," he remembered. In the combat on the 3rd, Buzzard wasn't as lucky, being hit twice in the arm. "It was so hot and I had lost so much blood that when I reached a North Carolina regiment I fainted and the litter-bearers carried me to their hospital," he related.[11]

At some point on Friday, the wounded Maj. Gen. Dorsey Pender, whose division included Perrin's troops, tried to mount his horse but was unsuccessful. Pender had been hit in the thigh by a shell fragment on July 2, the injury not believed to be life-threatening. After all, Pender had been wounded three other times in combat from Seven Pines to Chancellorsville and survived. Unknown to him, or anyone else that day, he would never take the saddle again. Perrin's brigade was strengthened on the 3rd by the return of Hadden's First South Carolina (Orr's) Rifles, which had been on wagon train guard duty. They were not involved in the battle, but one of these Carolinians helped a fallen Union soldier he happened upon. The wounded Federal was lying helpless in the sun, a leg broken and a piece of his lip shot off, the unidentified rebel recalled years later: "He was craving water. I had nearly a canteenful and I put it in his canteen."[12]

"Fighting Dick" Anderson's division of Hill's corps held the same ground after its repulse the previous day. The Carolinian noted "nothing of consequence" occurring in his portion of the line that morning and early afternoon. Anderson, however, had orders "to hold his division ready to take advantage of any success which might be gained by the assaulting column, or to support it, if necessary," Hill related in his battle report. To prepare for action, Wilcox's and Lang's brigades "were moved forward to eligible positions." In addition to Anderson's troops, Hill was to "hold my line" with Perrin's Carolinians and Edward Thomas's Georgia brigade. The grand assault by about 12,000 rebel infantry would be anchored by Maj. Gen. George E. Pickett's division of Longstreet's corps, which had reached Gettysburg on the afternoon of the 2nd. Now they were the bayonet point of the attack. The assault troops also included Henry Heth's division—led by Brig. Gen. Pettigrew since Heth was wounded on the first day—and the two other brigades of Pender's division, Scales's and Lane's. Pender's wounding had resulted in a confusing situation in his division's command. Lane initially led the division after Pender fell, but Maj. Gen. Isaac Trimble rejoined the army on July 3 after almost a year of recovery from a severe leg wound at Second Bull Run. Trimble reported to Hill as "the troops were filing off to their positions" and Lee ordered Trimble to lead Scales's and Lane's brigades in the assault.[13]

Pickett accompanied Longstreet to the crest of Seminary Ridge, the Carolinian explaining Lee's orders, showing him the Federal positions and pointing out the area of the enemy line which was the objective of the assault. Longstreet noted that Pickett "seemed to appreciate the severity of the contest upon which he was about to enter, but was quite hopeful of success." Longstreet did not share his optimism, although he did not voice it. The rolling, open ground over which the attack would be launched was, for the most part, within range of a lethal array of enemy sharpshooters, infantry, and artillery, the latter posted to sweep the approaches to Cemetery Ridge. "With my knowledge of the situation," Longstreet wrote, "I could see the desperate and hopeless nature of the charge and the cruel slaughter it would cause. My heart was heavy when I left Pickett." Gilbert Moxley Sorrel of Longstreet's staff added, "While Longstreet by no means approved the movement, his soldierly eye watched every feature of it. He neglected nothing that could help it and his anxiety for Pickett and the men was very apparent." As in many instances on the Confederate side in this battle, Pickett was attacking over terrain he was seeing for the first time against an enemy of unknown strength. Here the story of South Carolina at Gettysburg must also include a mention of perhaps a crucial absence of Carolinians in Pickett's command who were left behind in Virginia. Brig. Gen. Micah Jenkins of Edisto Island was a rising star in Confederate military circles, but he and his South Carolina brigade were not with the army in Pennsylvania, having been assigned to bolster the Richmond-Petersburg defenses. Frustrated, Jenkins tried every avenue he could to be allowed to participate in the offensive, but his efforts were in vain. This left Pickett with three Virginia brigades, those of Brig. Gen. R.B. Garnett, Brig. Gen. J.L. Kemper and Brig. Gen. Lewis Armistead.[14]

Artillery

The South Carolinians of Lt. William E. Zimmerman's Pee Dee Artillery in Pegram's Battalion, and their other comrades in the Artillery Reserve of Hill's corps, were posted in the same position they held on July 2, about a mile to the right of the Chambersburg Pike. The battalion's combat on the 2nd, primarily an artillery duel, had cost two men killed, seven wounded and 25 horses dead, its captain, E.B. Brunson, noted. About noon these gunners received orders to open fire on the Federal batteries in their front.[15]

The battalion, including Zimmerman's cannoneers, were to be part of one of the greatest barrages of the war, the Confederates assembling some 150 guns to hammer the Union positions on Cemetery Ridge, softening them up before the massive infantry assault. Brunson's orders were that once the enemy artillery in his front was "silenced" and "the batteries on our right advanced, we were … to advance our batteries to the crest then occupied by the Yankee guns." In other words, the Confederates expected to soon drive the Union army off the heights and into the morass of another complete defeat like Chancellorsville, a mere eight weeks earlier. Zimmerman's artillery would support the Virginia infantry of Col. J.M. Brockenbrough's brigade in Heth's division of Hill's corps, one of the three divisions in the upcoming attack. Brockenbrough's troops were posted behind the artillery and would pass through the gun stations as they began the charge. The Fifty-fifth and Forty-seventh Virginia regiments would advance from behind Zimmerman's guns.[16]

Other Carolina batteries were also in positions to join in the earth-quaking bombardment. The Palmetto Light Artillery of Capt. Hugh Garden went into line about a mile north of their position on the 2nd and targeted the Union lines within their range on Big Round Top. During the night, the Palmettos had carried off four rifled guns captured during Hood's attack. Garden's battery, along with Capt. A.C. Latham's North Carolina battery, both of Hood's division artillery battalion, were sent to Col. E.P. Alexander early that morning to join in the cannonade. By dawn on the 3rd, what was left of the Brooks Artillery unlimbered with other Confederate guns aligned on a ridge running north from the Peach Orchard—ready for action, but bloodied, beat up and totaling its losses from the fierce fighting on the 2nd. Its commander, Lt. Stephen C. Gilbert, was down with two wounds, more than half of its men were dead or wounded, two of its four twelve-pound howitzers were disabled and a multitude of horses had been killed. The Brooks Artillery were posted east of the Emmitsburg Road, about two hundred yards northeast of the John Sherfy farm and in front of the right flank of Brig. Gen. Cadmus M. Wilcox's brigade of Alabamians in Dick Anderson's division.[17]

Alexander, who would command the overall artillery barrage, slept on the field overnight, helping his battalion replenish its ammunition by dawn and posting it, including the survivors of the Brooks Artillery, in position "for the attack upon the enemy's new line." As he had the day before, Maj. Frank Huger commanded the battalion on the 3rd, as Alexander focused on his greater duties. Based on Hill's orders, two Whitworths from Maj. David McIntosh's artillery battalion moved from McIntosh's position on the 2nd to "a commanding point north of the railroad cut, to enable them to enfilade the enemy's position," the Carolinian reported. "They fired, it is believed, with effect from this point."[18]

The main drama of the day—indeed the entire war—was to yet to come. "The rays of the midsummer sun beat down fiercely upon the long and silent battle lines on ridge and heights and upon the intervening slopes of orchard and wheat fields," related Pvt. J. Merrick Reid of Garden's battery. "The very air seemed to hold its breath." "The armies seemed like mighty wild beasts growling at each other and preparing for a death struggle," Longstreet recalled. Union Brig. Gen. Henry J. Hunt, Meade's artillery chief, had ridden to check on the fighting in the Culp's Hill sector on the Federals' right and returned to Cemetery Ridge between 10 a.m. and 11 a.m. Scanning the Confederate positions, he quickly took in a sight he would recall to the rest of his days. "Here a magnificent display greeted my eyes. Our whole front for two miles was covered by [rebel] batteries already in line or going into position. They stretched—apparently in one unbroken mass—from opposite the town to the Peach Orchard … the ridges of which were planted thick with cannon. Never before had such a sight been witnessed on this continent, and rarely, if ever, abroad."[19]

The curtain rose with unprecedented man-made thunder. Lee's cannon erupted about 1 p.m., punishing the enemy defenses on the ridge for some two hours in preparation for the infantry assault. Union artillery replied, but not with the same intensity. From the Confederate right flank, Brig. Gen. Evander M. Law, the Carolinian now commanding Hood's division, watched the terrible spectacle: "The cannonade … presented one of the most magnificent battle-scenes witnessed during the war. Looking up the valley toward Gettysburg, the hills on either side were capped with crowns of flame and smoke, as 300 guns, about equally divided between the two ridges, vomited their iron hail upon each other. Dense clouds of smoke settled over the valley, through which the shells went hissing and screaming on their errand of death. Numbers of these from opposite directions exploded midway over the valley, apparently with venomous impatience, as they met each other in mid-air, lighting up the clouds with their snake-like flashes." To Capt. William S. Dunlop of the Twelfth South Carolina, the artillery spectacle was "like a deafening echo from the caverns of Hades.… Thunder and fire and smoke issued from the opposing hilltops in roaring volumes that rent the air and shook the earth, while shot and shell swept across the valley, hissing and screaming and crashing." General Dick Anderson recalled the "equal force and fury" of the foes.[20]

Col. D. Wyatt Aiken of the Seventh South Carolina added, "Such a battle of artillery the world never heard or saw before. Sebastopal was nowhere." "The artillery fight was one of the most terrific on record," the Carolinian Capt. Brunson related, "and never were guns served more splendidly, and never did men behave more heroically, than the artillerymen did in that memorable battle," he wrote of the army's entire artillery arm. The Carolinian Maj. McIntosh recalled in a postwar account, "The air became thick with flying missiles and bursting shells. Rifts of smoke floated over the landscape amidst which the occasional explosion of a caisson or limber chest lit up the scene, and added to the terror of battle. No such cannonade had been experienced before by either Army, and it required all the staying qualities of those under fire to resist its effects." In his report after the battle, McIntosh stated: "Previous to the charge of our men, a general fire of artillery commenced on the right, and extended along the left. The bombardment was replied to with equal spirit by the enemy, but their fire in time slackened, and, when the charge was made by our men, had almost entirely ceased."[21]

"The roar of the guns was awful," added Pvt. W.M. Reid, a cannoneer from St. Charles, South Carolina, who was in Garden's battery. "The very earth seemed to tremble under the concussion." Another of Garden's Palmettos, Pvt. J. Merrick Reid, noted that when the order to commence fire was given, "the next instant the earth trembled as a mighty roar from 150 cannon's mouths belched flame and smoke and murderous metal toward the frowning heights with deadly accuracy. But this defiant challenge was quickly answered and the long range of hills became an undulating line of flame, under heavy, hanging palls of smoke issuing from the muzzles of Meade's bronze war dogs, as they fiercely roared 'Come on!' While Lee's guns from the ridge thundered grimly, 'We are coming!'"[22]

"One piece after another took" up the firing "until all along our entire line, a hundred and fifty cannon poured their missiles against the opposite line," noted Lt. James Caldwell of the First South Carolina in Perrin's brigade. "Their batteries replied with equal will, so that soon at least three hundred pieces of artillery raged in the grandest conflict witnessed during this war." Only a few of Perrin's men were hit by Union rounds, "for the enemy fired clear over our heads, at the Confederate batteries behind us," Caldwell wrote. "But it was a most unpleasant position, between the horrible, hissing, bursting missiles these Titans hurled against each other."[23]

Zimmerman's Pee Dee artillerists and the rest of A.P. Hill's artillery "kept up an incessant fire from about 1 p.m. to the time of the advance of the infantry," noted Col. Walker, Hill's reserve artillery chief. "This fire having been continued so long and with such rapidity, the ammunition was almost exhausted." One of Kershaw's Confederates added, "For a time it looked as if the Heavens above had opened her vaults of thunder bolts, and was letting them fall in showers upon the heads of mortals below." From his position under the apple tree, the wounded Pvt. Daniel Hargrove of the Eighth South Carolina later noted, "The most fearful cannonade ever recorded continued for more than an hour, the combatants being often hidden by smoke, but they knew where to shoot … shells shrieked and exploded everywhere; it did not seem that anything could live."[24]

The cannon "opened their fiery mouths, sending their shrieking missil[e]s of death across the valley," a rebel in the Second South Carolina wrote years later, adding that both sides soon "poured their iron hail through the heated air. Language cannot express the intensity of this blood curdling, sullen thunder, of these war dogs of destruction."[25]

"All their batteries were soon covered with smoke, through which the flashes were incessant, whilst the air seemed filled with shells, whose sharp explosions, with the hurtling of their fragments, forming a running accompaniment to the deep roar of the guns," added Gen. Henry Hunt, Meade's artillery commander. The accuracy of Hunt's long arm, however, was exacting a toll in the Confederate lines, including Kershaw's troops and others nearby. Pvt. Hargrove recalled that a "color-bearer with palmetto buttons on his coat lay a little way off … [his] dying desire was that his flag be kept." The soldier died and an officer from Hargrove's Company K of the Eighth South Carolina soon arrived and found his dead brother. "With sobs in his throat he did what he could for me, then, with two friends, took his brother off for burial." Also in his immediate vicinity was a boyish Georgian "shot entirely through the body … calling the names of comrades and sending messages to loved ones at home…. He grew weaker and weaker in voice and strength, till his eyes closed in death."[26]

With the artillery fire winding down about 3 p.m.—primarily because the Confederate cannoneers were running low on ammunition—Pickett rode to Longstreet and asked if the time for his infantry assault had come. "I was convinced that he would be leading his troops to needless slaughter, and did not speak," Longstreet recalled. Pickett "repeated the question and without opening my lips I bowed in answer. In a determined voice Pickett said: 'Sir, I will lead my division forward.'" The Virginian then rode away to rejoin his men, Longstreet heading to a nearby point where he could observe the advance. "Old Pete" would later describe what he saw as "one of the grandest, most desperate assaults recorded in the annals of war." Longstreet watched the gray ranks of Pickett's division move over Seminary Ridge and down the slight east slope. Looking into the Virginians' faces, "lighted with hope," he may have recognized some of the soldiers in Kemper's brigade, which Longstreet had led into battle at First Bull Run almost two long and bloody years earlier. Abner Perrin's Palmettos also had a front seat for the panorama, Pettigrew leading Heth's division, moving past them toward Cemetery Ridge.[27]

As the sprawling Confederate lines advanced, their artillery, including Garden's Palmettos, tried to provide covering fire for the infantry. Garden's gunners, now posted in the Peach Orchard, concentrated their shelling against Union artillery on Little Round Top, but their rounds had little effect on the cannon there, which were already shredding the rebel ranks. Maj. McIntosh, still holding the line with the bulk of his artillery battalion northwest of Gettysburg, received word that one of the two Whitworths engaged in the bombardment from its position near the railroad cut, was disabled again "from its own firing." This gun had sustained a broken axle in the July 2 combat but had been repaired and returned to service. Amid the height of battle, the frustrated major again sent the gun to the rear to be fixed. Still the Carolinian was able to watch while the infantry moved over the open fields. The gray wave "presented a spectacle, and one which no beholder can ever forget," he remembered. "The ranks were beautifully dressed and the battle-flags told of the different commands. Many a brave heart in the Federal ranks must have blanched at the prospect which loomed so terribly before them."[28]

With the Pickett-Pettigrew-Trimble Charge underway, the Confederate artillery that still had ammunition was ordered to limber up and follow the infantry as support. The problem was that a great number of the guns were down to their last rounds. Garden's Carolinians had only enough shells for one gun, and all the rounds were put into the limber of the piece commanded by Lt. William A. McQueen, a Baptist minister's son from Sumter, South Carolina. The young, clean-cut lieutenant and his ten-man crew started forward out of the orchard, four other guns also trundling ahead out of the splintered peach trees. McQueen's little band advanced about one hundred yards before unlimbering. Pickett's long gray ranks were already enduring enemy fire, but the Palmettos were as yet unscathed as they readied their piece. This was about to change, however. "Not a shot was fired at us until the first shell left the muzzle of our gun and then there was a hail of shot and shell in reply," noted one of McQueen's men, Pvt. W.M. Reid. "Then hell broke loose!" added Pvt. J. Merrick Reid, also assigned to McQueen's gun. "No sooner had flame and smoke gushed after the hurtling shell than Round Top … became a veritable seething volcano of destruction, emitting dense volumes of smoke, lurid tongues of flame and hurling metal missiles that hissed or shrieked, or wailed through space, or burst with deafening peals as they scattered their jagged, death ladened fragments around." In less than five minutes the Union rounds had mortally wounded two artillerists, wounded several others and fatally ripped through five of the gun's six horses. McQueen "then called to us to leave, which we did without a second summons," recalled W.M. Reid, who had rammed home the one shot fired from their exposed position. His comrade J. Merrick Reid related, "Man after man went down with his death-hurt or disabling wound from deadly aim or fatal chance."[29]

Seeing his men in lethal trouble, Garden went to their aid. "I took volunteers and fresh horses in to remove my men and gun," he remembered. "There for the first and only time during the entire war I felt compelled to encourage my men by personal example." In addition to Garden, the rescuers were Sgt. J. Henry Wilson, Cpl. John J. Green and Pvt. James D. Wilder, all from Sumter County, and Pvt. Lawrence W. Scarborough from Darlington County. Twice Garden and his volunteers were driven back by "the same concentrated, terrible fire," worsened by exploding caissons and outgoing rounds screeching overhead from the rebel artillery in front of Seminary Ridge. Despite this "carnival of hell," as Garden described it, the captain, his fresh men and horses succeeded on their third attempt to reach McQueen's position. The gun was brought off and the Palmettos beat a hasty retreat.

Garden and another soldier were carrying a wounded comrade across an open field to safety when they happened upon an injured Union officer who told them he had lain on the field since the fighting on the previous day. Garden unslung his canteen and gave it to the Federal, saying "I would help you, but I cannot get my own men out of this fire."[30]

Among McQueen's casualties were "two splendid boys," Pvt. Thomas R. McIntosh of Lynchburg, South Carolina, and Cpl. Robert F. "Bob" Small of Charleston. Both were "cut almost in twain by the same shell," W.M. Reid related. McIntosh was killed outright, while Small was carried to the rear, struggling to live despite his ghastly injuries. "Some of my best men fell there," Garden recalled of Gettysburg. J. Merrick Reid had been very close to Small and McIntosh when they were hit but had escaped unharmed. He described his "closest call" and "most amazing, miraculous escape." The three men were momentarily in line one behind the other when a solid shot struck the first two. Reid was "untouched, save by a gob of warm, quivering flesh from one of the victims, which was hurled against my shoulder and stuck tenaciously for some time and the stain for days. Where did the line shot go? Eternity may answer."[31]

Longstreet watched some of the combat while sitting on a rail fence near Seminary Ridge, giving his horse some relief from his bulky frame. Shortly after taking his perch, he was joined by Lt. Col. Fremantle, the British army observer. "I wouldn't have missed this for any thing," Fremantle remarked. Longstreet, "looking perfectly calm," replied, "'The devil you wouldn't! I would like to have missed it very much; we've attacked and been repulsed.'"[32]

The Carolinian had just watched some 2,000 Confederates be killed or wounded in a half hour or so of desperate combat. Now the exhausted and bloodied survivors, individually and in small groups, were streaming out of the gun smoke back to Seminary Ridge. As these rebels limped toward the supposed safety of their lines, Longstreet scanned the enemy positions for signs of a Union counterattack. "I fully expected to see Meade ride to the front and lead his forces to a tremendous counter-charge," he recalled. In a different account of this time frame, Longstreet claimed that he almost wished or even prayed for death to sweep him from this terrible day: "Looking confidently for [the] advance of the enemy through our open field, I rode to the line of batteries, resolved to hold it until the last gun was lost," he wrote. "As I rode, the shells screaming over my head and ploughing the ground under my horse, an involuntary appeal went up that one of them might take me from scenes of such awful responsibility; but the storm to be met left no time to think of one's self."[33]

Some bluecoat skirmishers did venture forward, but they were quickly driven off by Confederate artillery. There would be no massive riposte from Meade. Yet Fremantle never forgot his impression of Longstreet in this situation of crisis and high drama: "No person could have been more calm or self-possessed than General Longstreet under these trying circumstances, aggravated as they now were by the movements of the enemy, who began to show a strong disposition to advance. I could now thoroughly appreciate the term bulldog, which I had heard applied to him by the soldiers. Difficulties seem to make no other impression upon him [other] than to make him a little more savage."[34]

Anderson

Dick Anderson's division of Hill's corps, meanwhile, had steeled for battle to sustain the expected success of the great charge. The Carolinian had orders "to hold my division in readiness to move up in support if it should become necessary." Hill noted: "Anderson had been directed to hold his division ready to take advantage of any success which might be gained by the assaulting column, or to support it, if necessary." With Lang's Floridians and Cadmus Wilcox's Alabamians already posted in a forward position, Anderson, at what he "supposed to be the proper time," was about to advance Wright's and Posey's brigades when Longstreet directed him "to stop the movement, adding that it would be useless, and would only involve unnecessary loss, the assault having failed," "Fighting Dick" noted. He then pulled his troops back into their original line "to afford a rallying point to those retiring and to oppose the enemy should he follow our retreating forces." Each of Anderson's brigades suffered casualties due to the Union shelling, Wilcox's troops taking the most losses.[35]

The South Carolina artillery captain Ervin Brunson described the monumental cataclysm of July 3 thus: "Had the result of that day's fight on the luckless heights around Gettysburg been dependent upon the heroic conduct of the artillery, we might now read upon the resplendent roll of victories that have heretofore marked the career of the Army of Northern Virginia the battle of Gettysburg." Lt. Col. Joseph Brown of the Fourteenth South Carolina, however, had a much more succinct take on the monumental impact of that afternoon's events: The "great, world renowned assaults were made on the iron-crested and rock-bound heights … resulting in disaster, and then the star of the Southern Confederacy began first to wane."[36]

8

The Cavalry Fights and
Monumental Decisions—July 3

With the Confederates preparing for their all-or-nothing assault on Cemetery Ridge, a separate battle—one of three involving South Carolinians—was about to erupt as the blue and gray cavalry took the stage. When Jeb Stuart reunited with Lee on the afternoon of July 2, there were no heated words about Stuart's absence from the army or his lack of communications, which most certainly had handcuffed Lee's offensive on enemy soil. Immersed in what he probably recognized as possibly the most decisive battle of the war, Lee instead focused on how he could employ and incorporate the cavalry arm into his tactical plans. Stuart's horsemen would bolster the Confederates' left flank.

After caring for the dead and wounded from the cavalry scrap the previous day, Wade Hampton's brigade left the Hunterstown area that Friday morning, arriving in the Gettysburg vicinity about noon and rejoining Stuart's main force. Stuart deployed his four brigades, including Hampton's, in woods on Cress's Ridge about three miles east of Gettysburg. The ridge overlooked fields of John Rummel's farm north of the Hanover Road. Stuart was intent on driving west across this open land with his 6,000 or so troopers and striking the right flank and rear of the Union army. Opposing the Confederates were two brigades of Brig. Gen. David M. Gregg's Second Division and Brig. Gen. George A. Custer's Second Brigade of Brig. Gen. Judson Kilpatrick's Third Division—some 4,500 Union troopers in all—posted mainly along the Hanover Road. Kilpatrick and the other brigade in his division, that of Brig. Gen. Elon Farnsworth, were sent to the south end of the battlefield earlier in the day. They were involved in combat with South Carolinians, which will be covered later.[1]

Surveying the blue ranks partially visible in the distance, Hampton rode a horse named Butler, in honor of Col. M.C. Butler of the Second South Carolina Cavalry, who lost a foot to an artillery round at Brandy Station. Meanwhile, the cacophony of the momentous artillery clash underway along Cemetery Ridge filled the senses of troopers and horses on both sides. "There was one incessant roar of artillery and the ground was shaken," Trooper Peter J. Malone of the First South Carolina Cavalry recalled, "while to the northwest [actually the southwest] cumulous clouds of smoke rose above the unbroken thunder" of the massed guns. "We were in ignorance of the juxtaposition of the enemy's cavalry, but anyone without risking his dexterity might have ventured to predict that the quietude of this part of the field was soon to be broken by the clash of sabres, the shout of triumph and the agonizing cry of death." Malone, 19, had been on the staff of the *Charleston* (S.C.) *Courier* before the war and was known for his poetry. On this day he was in the First's color guard as they and the rest of Hampton's men were "calmly awaiting orders for the engagement." Hampton, meanwhile, was everywhere on Butler, galloping about with his blood boiling for battle. "The quick eye of our stalwart leader, his rapid movements from regiment to regiment, his hurried, yet confident, tone of command, and above all his frequent anxious glances towards a certain dense oak forest one mile away, were indications" that action was imminent, Malone related. In the fields in the intermediate distance, blue and gray skirmishers were already embraced in their lethal sniping. In the color guard, Malone was to the right of J.H. Koger, the standard bearer, while to Malone's right was Sgt. T.P. Brandenburg, "a peerless soldier and truly imperial spirit."[2]

A Union battery opened fire about 3 p.m., its rounds shrieking over, into and just short of the Confederate horsemen. "They [the Federal gunners] managed their guns with admirable precision, and although branches of trees were rifted from their trunks and shells exploded in our very ranks, little damage was done," Mahone related. "The battle had opened." Hampton's command was in line next to Col. John R. Chambliss Jr.'s brigade of Virginians and North Carolinians. Brig. Gen. Fitzhugh Lee's Virginia brigade was to Hampton's left. Hampton quickly sent out sharpshooters to contest a possible Union advance. The rebel sharpshooters soon were firing rapidly and "succeeded perfectly in keeping the enemy back, while the three brigades were held ready to meet any charge made," Hampton wrote. A major concern was that the Confederates had only a few artillery pieces on the field while the Federals appeared to have at least two batteries in position, Hampton noted.[3]

"The Federal cavalry kept us quite busy," noted John Esten Cooke, one of Stuart's staff officers. "It was handled here with skill and gallantry—the heavy lines were seen to form, the officers galloping up and down; three measured cheers were given by the men … then the bugle sounded." Stuart, meanwhile, sent the First Virginia Cavalry of Fitzhugh Lee's brigade charging down the ridge and across the fields, but Gregg hurled the Seventh Michigan forward in a counterthrust, blunting the attack. The Union horsemen "came on, shaking the ground with their hoofs," Cooke related. Seeing this, Stuart ordered the rest of Lee's command and Hampton's troopers to the assault, moving forward in a narrow column of squadrons with swords flashing. "In the van floated a stand of colors," a Michigan officer recalled. "It was the battle-flag of Wade Hampton, who with Fitzhugh Lee was leading the assaulting column. In superb form, with sabers glistening, they advanced. The men on foot gave way to let them pass. It was an inspiring and an imposing spectacle, that brought a thrill to the hearts of the spectators on the opposite slope."[4]

Capt. William Brooke-Rawle and Pvt. John C. Hunterson, both of the Third Pennsylvania Cavalry, recalled seeing the force of Confederate troopers emerge from woods near Daniel Stallsmith's farm about 3 p.m. It was a "large mass of cavalry," Rawle related, adding, "Everyone saw at once that unless this, the grandest attack of all was checked, the fate of the day would be decided against the Army of the Potomac." "They advanced in close columns … with sabres drawn, glistening in the bright sunlight," Hunterson noted. "It was a sight which awakened a murmur of admiration, although it made many of our hearts flutter within us, and our breathing to quicken nervously lest we should be crushed by these superior numbers." Rawle continued that the enemy brigades readied for the attack "'as if in review,' the spectacle … indeed a memorable one." "They were formed in close column of squadrons and directed their course [south] toward" the Hanover Road,

William E. Miller, another officer in the Third Pennsylvania, added of Hampton's and Fitz Lee's horsemen. "A grander spectacle than their advance has rarely been beheld. They marched with well-aligned fronts and steady reins. Their polished saber-blades dazzled in the sun. All eyes turned upon them."[5]

The Federals' admiration was soon punctuated by artillery canister and shell hurtling into the packed body of gray riders, shearing bloody holes in their ranks. In the distance the Confederates could see more Union cavalry forming in the afternoon shadows of the woods. "We started out in fine style, and one continued shout arose from the charging column," Malone said. "The enemy now appeared in a black compact line, and at a casual view appeared rather a continuation of the forest. The intervening ground over which we were passing was so crossed and seamed with fences and ditches as to greatly impede our progress, and the [Union] sharpshooters, concealed wherever concealment was possible, found in the moving mass of beings an excellent mark for their rifles." "Hampton's battle-flag floated in the van of his brigade," Capt. Rawle remembered as the rebel horsemen closed in. "The orders of the Confederate officers could be heard, 'Keep to your sabres, men, keep to your sabres!'" Gregg quickly sent Col. Charles H. Town's First Michigan Cavalry in Custer's brigade storming toward Stuart's column, Custer leading the charge and shouting, "Come on, you Wolverines!" Capt. Rawle added, "As the charge was ordered speed increased, every horse on the jump, every man yelling like a demon."[6]

A Union bullet pierced Malone's right side, about two hundred yards into the regiment's attack from the trees where the Carolinians and the others had begun their charge. The ball ripped through his abdomen and lodged near his kidneys, but he rode on, believing that he had been hit by a shell fragment that had not broken the skin. The fact that Union artillery rounds were exploding among the gray-clad force strengthened this belief, as Twiggs's horsemen closed with the bluecoats coming toward them. "We were soon at the sabre-point and fighting desperately," he recalled. Now the blue and gray lines melded in a roiling mass of yelling men, swords clanging, horses colliding or toppling onto their riders while the sharp bang of carbines and revolvers rent the dust-choked air. Slashing, stabbing and firing as their mounts wheeled and reared, the rival troopers clawed at each other at point-blank range, many of the curses and battle cries now replaced by the screams of the wounded and dying, both soldiers and horses. "The struggle was bitter and determined, but brief," Cooke recalled. "For a moment the air was full of flashing sabres and pistol smoke, and a wild uproar deafened the ears…. We lost many good men."[7]

Wade Hampton was in the midst of this melee near the Rummel barn where some of his troopers were fighting on foot. "Hampton came into view at the head of his column," recalled Lt. George W. Beale of the Ninth Virginia in Chambliss's ranks. "For a time as he dashed toward the barn, he held the colors in his right hand, and his men responded to his intrepid actions with a mighty yell. Just as he closed in on the foe, he passed the flag back to its bearer at his side, and his bloody work began." At one point, a Yankee private charged directly at Maj. Lipscomb of the Second South Carolina, yelling, "Oh damn you, I've got you now." Lipscomb "coolly leveled his Colt's revolver and sent a bullet crashing through his brain," stated one Southern account. The First South Carolina's color guard had become separated from the rest of the regiment and found itself meeting Yankee horsemen at the small opening of a fence. Other rebels soon crowded into the opening, blocking it and preventing assistance to Malone, Koger, Brandenburg and others battling for their lives on the opposite side of the barrier. Suddenly, Malone was overwhelmed by the effects of his wound. "At this critical juncture, my right side and arm became paralyzed, the sabre fell from my hand, and large cold drops of sweat collected upon my face," he remembered. No longer able to sit up, Malone slumped forward onto his blankets, rolled up and fastened to the front of his saddle. Seeing his plight, surgeon Joseph Yates of the First South Carolina Cavalry rode into the midst of the combat and assisted Malone over the fence. His mount, meanwhile, "infuriated by the crash of cannon, the explosion of shells, and sight of blood, rushed desperately to the rear." Making his way back toward a field hospital, Malone encountered Pvt. W.D. Shirer of the First South Carolina's Company E. The young trooper from Orangeburg District, South Carolina, had been severely wounded in the right arm and "was in the very acme of pain," but Malone could do nothing for him as he continued to the rear.[8]

Custer's Michiganders were obviously outnumbered, but help was not long in coming from Gregg. He rocked Stuart's force with flank attacks on both sides, while a squadron of the Third Pennsylvania Cavalry speared through a gap and separated the main body from the rear of the rebel column. Assailed on three sides and still being battered by Union artillery, Stuart's horsemen retreated to the safety of their line on Cress's Ridge. Despite some sporadic firing, the three-hour battle was essentially over, neither side losing any ground. The engagement ended with the Confederates blunted in their apparent goal of reaching the right flank and rear of the Union army. Wade Hampton, meanwhile, had been seriously wounded, suffering two saber cuts to the head and shrapnel in his hip. Lt. Beale of the Ninth Virginia had seen Hampton's glorious gallop into battle and also watched him borne from the field. "A few minutes later he was brought back bleeding in limb and face, with an ugly gash across his brow," Beale noted. "But he had saved the day on that part of the field."[9]

John Hunterson, the Pennsylvania cavalryman, credited a squadron of the First New Jersey Cavalry under Capt. James H. Hart for striking down the giant Carolinian. Hart's troopers "came charging across the field, and headed for a passing general and his staff," Hunterson claimed. "This proved to be Wade Hampton, and in the melee he was wounded." Capt. Rawle, also of the Third Pennsylvania, agreed that Hart's troopers had injured Hampton. In the combat "near the [enemy] colors was an officer of high rank, and the two [Hart and a Capt. Thomas] headed the squadron for that part of the fight. They came within reach of him with their sabres, and then it was that Wade Hampton was wounded."[10]

At least one account—written by a Charlestonian who knew Hampton and had access to his personal papers and documents—possibly offers more insight into the general's personal combat that day. Hampton tried to fire his revolver, but the trigger merely snapped on five of six chambers, the pistol having been much exposed to rainy conditions the previous night. Taking advantage of this, a Union trooper sabered him on the forehead and the side of the head, but Hampton's sixth shot "did its work" in dropping his assailant. Moments later the general saw one of his men being "hard-pressed" by another Federal and rode to his assistance. The beleaguered Confederate made his escape, however, and the Yankee turned his attention to this new menace. Somewhat blinded by his own blood, Hampton and his foe crossed swords, the Federal whipping under a missed parry to slash the general across the head again. It would be the Yank's last action, "for Hampton's sabre cleft his head down to the chin, a feat which novels and newspapers airily ascribe to their heroes, but which is rarely performed, and never, except by a stalwart arm and skillful hand." As the brigadier bled and swayed in the saddle, shrapnel ripped into his right thigh.[11]

John Esten Cooke was shocked by the suddenness of Hampton's fall. "General Hampton was shot in the side, and nearly cut out of the saddle by a sabre stroke," he wrote. "Ten minutes before I had conversed with the noble South Carolinian, and he was full of life, strength and animation. Now he was slowly being borne to the rear in his ambulance, bleeding from his dangerous wounds." After his combat injuries, Hampton was replaced in brigade command by Col. Laurence S. Baker of the First North Carolina Cavalry, a trooper in the Second South Carolina Cavalry describing Baker as "a very good officer" in a letter home.[12]

Still making his way off the field, Peter Malone weakened, "sinking into a state of insensibility," and was carried the rest of the way to the hospital by stretcher bearers. When he regained consciousness he was among "hundreds of others, friends and foes, receiving medical attention." Nearby were several wounded cavalrymen of the First South Carolina, including Cpl. H.J. Culler of Company E, and Pvt. Charles Franklin of Company B. His last recollection of surgeon Yates that day was of the doctor "at the head of the regiment, cheering it on with the most gallant bearing." Malone would add of Yates: "Temperate, humane, untiring in his energy, unflagging in his zeal, he was still as brave as Julius Caesar."[13]

Hampton's cavalry sustained losses of 17 killed, 57 wounded and 16 missing for a total of 90, basically half of Stuart's 181 total casualties. Union losses in this clash were 254, including 30 killed, 149 wounded and 75 missing. Among Hampton's slain was Sgt. Thomas L. Butler, younger brother of the maimed Col. M.C. Butler of the Second South Carolina. The 21-year-old sergeant was among troopers in the Second who were dismounted and sent forward to challenge the enemy's sharpshooters, stated at least one account. With ammunition dwindling, Butler continued to fight with his pistol and "maintained his position until he fell pierced by a Minnie ball." Another account, however, states that the sergeant was "struck by a minie ball" and "fell lifeless from his horse without speaking a word or uttering a groan." Whatever the case, "In battle no one was more cool and self-possessed," one newspaper said of the younger Butler.[14]

Of Hampton's casualties among his two home-state regiments, the First South Carolina had one dead, nine wounded and four missing, while the Second South Carolina's Sgt. Butler was its only fatality, along with six wounded. Certainly the most significant casualty was Hampton, singled out by Stuart in his overall campaign report: "That brave and distinguished officer, Brigadier-General Wade Hampton, was seriously wounded … in this engagement." Possibly not included in Hampton's casualty tally was Cpl. H.L. Culler of Company E, First S.C. Cavalry, seriously wounded at Gettysburg. He died there on July 9. Another trooper in the Second, William A. Black of Company A, emerged unscathed from the bloodletting. At age 24, he was a seasoned cavalryman who had been in a number of engagements. He had been a freight office clerk for the South Carolina Railroad in peacetime. Black likely considered himself fortunate to ride out of the combat uninjured, but his Gettysburg ordeal was yet to begin and will be described later.[15]

On the extreme right of the Confederate line—south and west of the Round Tops—Hood's exhausted division under the Carolinian Evander Law was vigilant, but they were not expecting major action as the battle raged in the near distance to the north.

Posted with Hood's infantry was a crazy-quilt force of cavalry and artillery led by Col. John Logan Black of the First South Carolina Cavalry, who was trying to reunite with his regiment even as it fought along Cress's Ridge that afternoon. Black's journey to Gettysburg had been roundabout and adventurous by his arrival on the battlefield on July 2, a few days before his 33rd birthday. Born in York, South Carolina, his family had been prominent landowners and active in mining enterprises in the north-central part of the state for decades. Black was a large man, known for his aggressive nature. He had been accepted to West Point but did not graduate, for reasons that are unclear.[16]

When war came, the First South Carolina was formed with men from Spartanburg, Laurens, Abbeville, Chester, Edgefield, Orangeburg and Colleton. Black led his regiment at Brandy Station and suffered a head wound from a shell fragment in the battle of Upperville on June 21. He spent several days resting and recuperating, but he was still suffering from dizziness due to his injuries when he rode out alone to rejoin his regiment and the rest of the army somewhere to the north. Near Williamsport, Maryland, he linked up with almost an entire company of his own regiment, a group of troopers from the Second South Carolina, some men of the First North Carolina Cavalry, under a Lieutenant Maxwell, also from Hampton's brigade, and the South Carolinians of Hart's Battery, led by Capt. James F. Hart in the Stuart Horse Artillery. These soldiers had all been separated from Stuart's main column in advancing through the unfamiliar and mountainous terrain. "I took command of these detachments and moved on," Black recalled, estimating that his patchwork force consisted of 80 to 100 men. Reaching Gettysburg, Black met with Lee and later Longstreet, the latter assigning him to Law that morning. Black's command was apparently augmented by about 100 "medical train personnel and ambulatory convalescents" sent by Longstreet. The addition of some other soldiers separated from their commands raised his strength to between 200 and 300.[17]

Under their 26-year-old captain, Hart's cannoneers were considered among the best of the horse artillery due to their efficiency and consistent combat performance. The battery had previously been known as the Washington Light Artillery Volunteers under Capt. Stephen Dill Lee, a Charlestonian who, at age 30 in 1864, would become the youngest lieutenant general in the Confederate service. It "was composed of some of the best men of the State, representing nearly every branch of the literary professions as well as a sharp sprinkling of the military," a battery veteran related a decade after the war, describing Capt. Lee as being "notorious as a rigid but intrepid disciplinarian."[18]

Hart himself was a native of Union County, South Carolina, the youngest of eight children. He was an 1857 graduate of the state military college and taught school for a year before studying law and being admitted to practice in 1860. In December of that year, after U.S. troops had occupied Fort Sumter in Charleston Harbor, he had been involved in one of the earliest prewar covert operations when South Carolina governor Francis Pickens sent him to "make a secret examination of the harbor." Based on Hart's recommendations, Pickens sent state troops to occupy Sullivan's Island, one of the first steps in isolating the Sumter garrison. Hart took part in organizing the Washington Artillery Volunteers for Confederate service (evolving from the Washington Artillery of Charleston, also known as the Washington Mounted Artillery) in June 1861 when it was attached to the Hampton Legion, soon heading to Virginia. When Lee was promoted to major, Hart rose to captain and command of the battery. In August 1862, Hampton was assigned to lead a cavalry brigade, Hart's battery being converted to horse artillery as part of that command. The Carolina gunners had seen action from First Bull Run to Savage Station to Malvern Hill and beyond. Hart's Battery as it came to be known, fought under Stuart and Hampton in the Maryland campaign at

Chancellorsville and Brandy Station. "Throughout almost the entire [conflict] Captain Hart was in command, and his gallant and intrepid leadership was a ruling factor in the brilliant record of his battery," former Confederate Brig. Gen. Ellison Capers wrote of these cannoneers after the war. In the June clash at Upperville, the battery was temporarily put out of action, all of its guns dismounted. But Hart was able to repair his fieldpieces at the abandoned railroad shops at Martinsburg before Stuart's horsemen speared further north.[19]

Among Hart's soldiers was Louis Sherfesee, who would turn 21 on July 4 amid the carnage of Gettysburg. Sherfesee, born in Prussia in 1842, immigrated with his parents to America and settled in Charleston, South Carolina, that same year. Sherfesee was raised and educated in Charleston and was in the Washington Artillery amid the war's opening chapter at Fort Sumter. When the battery left Charleston for Columbia on June 11, 1861, to join Hampton's Legion, the belles of Charleston presented the soldiers with a guidon, and Sherfesee was chosen as the color-bearer. "From that date … he carried the colors of his company through more battles, it is believed, than any other flag ever passed in all the history of wars," stated one Confederate account. Sherfesee had been in combat at Yorktown, Williamsburg, Savage Station, Second Bull Run, Antietam, Fredericksburg, Chancellorsville, Brandy Station and many lesser clashes leading up to Gettysburg. The key question for him: Would his uncanny luck again bring him through the latest bloodbath? His charmed survival would likely need a cat's nine lives and then some to come home from Gettysburg.[20]

Another noteworthy artillerist was 25-year-old Lt. Francis Marion Bamberg, born in an area of Barnwell County, South Carolina, that would later become Bamberg County, South Carolina. He had enlisted in early 1861 as a private in the light artillery commanded by Lee. The battery "was in more engagements than any other in the service," and Bamberg was in all of them before and after Gettysburg.[21]

A major problem for Hart, however, was that his command had only two serviceable Blakely rifles, according to Black, two others being disabled. Some accounts state that the Carolinians had three Blakelys in action; whatever the case, Hart was not at full strength. On the afternoon of July 3, Law's division artillery was minus two batteries—the South Carolinians of Hugh Garden's Palmetto Light Artillery and the Branch Artillery of North Carolina—the latter of which, along with the First Corps artillery reserve under Alexander, was involved in the bombardment of Cemetery Ridge. This left Law with the Charlestonians of Capt. Bachman's German Artillery and the Rowan (North Carolina) Artillery under Capt. James Reilly—a total of ten guns between them. Toiling amid Bachman's fieldpieces was Lt. Rudolph Siegling, who had rejoined the battery shortly before Gettysburg after barely returning from the grave. Siegling had been desperately wounded at Second Bull Run in August 1862. His injuries were believed to be mortal and soldiers had ripped boards from a fence to build a coffin, since he was expected to die within a few hours. Siegling rallied, however, and the crude casket eventually held the corpse of a Confederate colonel killed in action. After almost a year of recuperation, the lieutenant was back with his comrades.[22]

The other troops of Hood's division posted in this vicinity were elements of three infantry brigades: Law's Alabamians, now led by Col. James Sheffield since Law now commanded the division after Hood's wounding; Brig. Gen. George T. Anderson's Georgians (who fought alongside Kershaw's Carolinians on July 2); and the Arkansas and Texas troops of Brig. Gen. J.B. Robertson's brigade. (Sheffield had been colonel of the

Forty-eighth Alabama and assumed command of Law's brigade when Law took over the division's reins.)

As mentioned earlier, Union cavalry general Kilpatrick, with Elon Farnsworth's brigade, was detached from the main Federal cavalry force bracing to meet Stuart's expected attack. Kilpatrick and Farnsworth reached the vicinity of Law's division before noon but remained basically inactive for a few hours, awaiting Brig. Gen. Wesley Merritt's Reserve Brigade, which arrived from Emmitsburg about 3 p.m. The Federals planned to attack this extreme end of the Confederate line, possibly reaching around Law's position to the enemy's rear. Kilpatrick posted Merritt's men about 300 yards west of Farnsworth's position and just east of the Emmitsburg Road. Skirmishing between Merritt's troopers and the Confederates in their front—including Black's men—erupted almost immediately and lasted more than an hour. Merritt then launched an attack about 4:30 p.m., his troopers advancing mounted and on foot, supported by artillery.[23]

"A considerable body of Yankee Cavalry came out of a piece of woods and commenced to form in a field to my front," Col. Black related. "I ordered Hart's Battery to open on them, which was done effectually & the formation broken up, so accurate was Hart's fire." Merritt's U.S. Fifth Cavalry charged on horseback, piercing Black's line, but also quickly came under a torrid fire from Bachman's and Reilly's batteries, as well as the muskets of Anderson's Georgians. The combat swirled a few more minutes before Merritt's troopers retreated about 5 p.m.[24]

Kilpatrick then ordered Farnsworth, who commanded the First Brigade in Kilpatrick's Third Division of the Cavalry Corps, to attack. Farnsworth, 25, had been promoted to brigadier on June 29. His troopers—New York, Pennsylvania, Vermont and West Virginia regiments—had tussled with Stuart's cavalry at Hanover and Hunterstown on July 1 and 2 respectively, the latter engagement involving Wade Hampton's horsemen. On the Gettysburg field, Kilpatrick and Farnsworth realized the Confederates in their front were posted behind stone walls and hidden in woods. The mounted attack would be made over uneven ground broken by fences and laced with boulders. Farnsworth made his thrust about 5:30 p.m., but it would not be without controversy. Farnsworth and his officers opposed the effort, seeing the strength of the rebel positions and the sanguine results of Merritt's assault. He and Kilpatrick engaged in a heated discussion about the situation, Kilpatrick pressing the new brigadier to follow his order.[25]

Shortly thereafter, Farnsworth sent his brigade—about three hundred horsemen with drawn sabers—in a three-pronged but uncoordinated charge against the enemy line. The First West Virginia thundered toward the Confederates, a spray of canister from the rebel guns and the Texans' musketry dropping some of the horsemen. Still they rode on, reaching the gray line, where hand-to-hand fighting flared before the outgunned bluecoats scampered back to their positions. The left prong of Farnsworth's assault—the Eighteenth Pennsylvania Cavalry—went in now, but also was promptly ripped by artillery rounds from Bachman's cannoneers, Reilly's battery and the infantry volleys of the Ninth Georgia. The Pennsylvanians quickly pulled back to their lines, their portion of the charge already thwarted.[26]

Farnsworth himself then entered the fray, leading the third prong of the assault. His saber drawn, he rode to the front of his First Vermont, heading them in a furious charge by three separate battalions. Bachman's men quickly shifted their Napoleons to bear on the oncoming cavalry while Reilly's gunners remained in place, both batteries unleashing a hell of canister at the mass of enemy horsemen. Despite this carnage, Farnsworth and some of his troopers smashed through the Confederate line in a wild ride that soon saw them wheeling about in a virtual circle of fire from the rebels. The end result was that Farnsworth was killed; the surviving Vermonters galloped back to their lines. Longstreet later singled out Bachman's gunners for praise, writing that the enemy "were met by a counter-move ... by the Ninth, Eleventh and 59th Georgia regiments [Anderson's brigade]" and "the well-directed fire of Captain Bachman's battery and driven back."[27]

Kershaw

From their positions on the combat-torn ground east of the Emmitsburg Road, Joe Kershaw's soldiers had watched the concentration of artillery for the grand assault and listened to the loudest and most violent, earth-shaking bombardment humankind had yet experienced. With the rest of McLaws's division, the Carolinians saw nearby Confederate batteries belching fire, the ground trembling under their feet. "The shot and shell ... poured over my command, those of the enemy crossing ours, going in opposite directions, but all bent on the same mission of destruction," McLaws remembered.[28]

About 2 p.m. soldiers of the Second South Carolina were called to attention and told to be prepared for any "emergency," basically meaning any Union threat, in their front. After the great charge and the doomed foray by Farnsworth, a silence swept over all, a fitting solemnity for the tens of thousands of souls lost there. Pvt. John Coxe of the Second's Company B described the "absolute quietness [that] prevailed on our part of the field." Kershaw himself noted that the brigade "remained unemployed" on July 3.[29]

Kershaw's Third South Carolina Regiment received a much needed boost late that afternoon when Col. James D. Nance reached the field to assume command of his battered regiment. Nance had been wounded at Fredericksburg, some seven months earlier and, after recuperation, had "returned from my home [in Newberry, S.C.], where I had been for some time." He replaced Maj. Robert Maffett, who led the regiment through the three-day battle. Nance, 25, was described as "the best all round soldier in Kershaw's Brigade, none excepted," by a brigade historian. A graduate of the Citadel Military Academy, Nance was practicing law in Newberry when the war erupted. While he missed most of the action at Gettysburg, his combat resume already included First and Second Bull Run, the Peninsula campaign, Antietam and Fredericksburg. It was Maffett, however, who had experienced how the command had performed—and paid dearly—in the battle. "The regiment went into the fight in as good spirits as ever before observed," he reported, "and stood their ground gallantly, none leaving the field unless disabled. Our line was not broken during the engagement." The day would not be without more pain and spilled blood for the Carolinians, regardless of who led them. Two infantrymen were maimed by the Union cannonade that afternoon.[30]

Earlier in the day, soldiers in Kershaw's Fifteenth South Carolina were still finding and burying their dead, including their beloved Col. William De Saussure, killed on July 2. In tallying his losses from the combat that day, Kershaw first lamented his second in command: "First among the dead was the brave and able officer ... De Saussure, the senior colonel of the brigade, whom I had been pleased to regard as my successor in command should any casualty create a vacancy," the general noted in his battle report. "His loss to his regiment is irreparable; to his State and the country not to be estimated." He was laid to rest in a private cemetery near Black Horse Tavern, and his remains were removed to the family's burial ground after the war. At least one account states that paperwork for De Saussure's promotion to brigadier was in the hands of Confederate Secretary of War James Seddon when the colonel was slain. Elsewhere, the survivors of the Eighth South Carolina went about collecting and burying 28 of their comrades killed. "We lost many gallant officers, among whom were Captains Thomas E. Powe (Company C) and John K. McIver, (Company F)" related Capt. S.G. Malloy of Company C. Powe and McIver were severely wounded, as was Major Donald M. McLeod, who had been hit by an artillery round.[31]

The Seventh South Carolina's Col. D. Wyatt Aiken had been awed by the massive bombardment and infantry assault. He admired the gallantry of Pickett's troops and the other Confederates who participated in the attack, but he held no such esteem for the grandiose Virginian himself, instead leveling incendiary criticism at Pickett. "That Div[ision] fought well, but Pickett was *drunk*, forced his men too often, they became demoralized, and could not be rallied," he wrote in a letter a week or so after the battle. Pickett "got great credit for the conduct of his Div. He should be cashiered in my opinion." Aiken added that at least one man in his command was "close enough to see he was beastly drunk."[32]

Near the Black Horse Tavern, the many wounded Carolinians of Kershaw's command and those attending them listened to the thunderclaps of battle as Lee's great assault unfolded. Lt. W.E. James of the Eighth South Carolina spent much of the day caring for the soldiers of Company F who had been injured in the fighting the previous day. Among those beyond help was Cpl. Leonard B. Harrell, a "gallant and handsome boy," who died and was buried by James and others that afternoon. Meanwhile, Company F's Lt. George Bozeman, pronounced "mortally wounded" by a surgeon that morning, still clung to life, despite the grapeshot lodged in his head.[33]

Neither Kershaw nor his troops knew that the highest-ranking casualty they had inflicted on the Federals in the Stony Hill clash the previous day was in the last clutches of death on July 3. Brig. Gen. Samuel Zook was gravely wounded but fought for his life into late afternoon at a Union field hospital in a home along the Baltimore Pike. Fed chicken soup and whiskey, Zook inquired about the battle's progress and was told of the repulse of the Confederates' massive charge. "Then I am satisfied and ready to die," the brigadier replied. Zook did just that about 5 p.m., as the bullet from a Palmetto in the Third or Seventh South Carolina finally worked its fatal efficiency.[34]

At another Confederate field hospital a few miles from the Black Horse Tavern, cavalrymen from both sides were being treated after the Cress's Ridge combat. P.J. Malone of the First South Carolina Cavalry's color guard asked a physician about the probability of surviving from a bullet in the right side fired by a Union sharpshooter. Malone recalled that he "was candidly but kindly informed that the 'chances were against me.' The medical opinion was opposed to the performance of an operation, as such would render the 'chances' of recovery still more precarious," he related. "I was utterly prostrate, and sank from sheer exhaustion if any effort was made to raise me up."[35]

As if to surpass the monumental artillery tempest of the afternoon, nature assailed both armies with a tremendous and vicious thunderstorm about 6 p.m. John Coxe of the Second South Carolina watched while "the heavens were suddenly darkened by an angry black cloud. Soon the thunder and lightning became terrific, and I heard a cool-looking officer say, 'Now for heaven's thunder and lightning.'" The Second, along with the rest of Kershaw's brigade, were among Longstreet's troops ordered to pull back to the

Emmitsburg Road shortly before the skies darkened. "The storm broke and great Jupiter Pluvius, how the rain did pour down upon us!" Coxe recalled. "Soon all the streams were out of their banks and the low places covered with sheets of water." The deluge and nature's aerial circus abated before dark, allowing the Carolinians to kindle campfires. With this small comfort, Coxe and his comrades, "under the circumstances, passed the night comfortably."[36]

Soldiers of the First South Carolina (Orr's) Rifles, who returned to the army that day after guarding the wagon trains, were ordered to watch over a group of Union prisoners, including some Pennsylvania "Bucktails," recognized by the deer tails attached to their caps. When relieved of this duty, the Carolinians rejoined the rest of Perrin's troops. "We were ordered to dig rifle pits and I dug all night with my bayonet and threw the dirt out with my tin plate," recalled Pvt. George W. Speer of Company A.[37]

Riding to the rear about 7:30 p.m., the British Lt. Col. Fremantle was met by many wounded rebels anxiously inquiring about Longstreet, who had reportedly been killed. Fremantle wrote that when he "assured them he [Longstreet] was quite well, they seemed to forget their own pain in the evident pleasure they felt in the safety of their chief. No words that I can use will adequately express the extraordinary patience and fortitude with which the wounded Confederates bore their sufferings." Still, rumors of Longstreet's death persisted, even spreading through the Union army, as will be seen. "Old Pete" was alive, but for a man who had weathered so many personal tragedies and seen so much violent carnage and death as a professional soldier, July 3, 1863, ranked high among the nightmarish days of his scarred years. "That day at Gettysburg was one of the saddest of my life," he confided after the war. "I foresaw what my men would meet and would gladly have given up my position rather than share in the responsibilities of that day."[38]

9

"Death Freed Many from Their Sufferings"

As if emerging from the netherworld, the sun rose over a mutilated and Hadean scene on Saturday, July 4, illuminating the battleground. It was Independence Day, a holiday no longer recognized in the states of the Confederacy, but the observance by Meade's soldiers on the heights was muted as well. It was as if nothing in American history mattered anymore to either fought-out army unless they decided to scrawl another—fourth—chapter in gore that day. If so, all the fireworks would be violent, lethal and maiming—but this was not to be. "On the 4th not many more guns were fired than I have seen celebrate the day in a small town," noted Lt. James Caldwell of the First South Carolina.[1]

The "two hostile armies sullenly faced each other, with only here and there a random gun, or an occasional rattling fire from the picket lines," the Carolina artillerist Capt. James Hart recalled. "The ghastly battlefield was apparently in repose." Hart went on to describe what he saw:

> Under the alternating July sun and showers, the fetid odors from decaying corpses of men and animals had become almost insufferable to men accustomed to such scenes. The dead lay in shallow graves under the low mounds that flecked the hillsides and plains below, as far as the eyes could reach, but the carcasses of artillery and other horses by the hundred, and even the carcasses of cattle that had been grazing in the peaceful valley when the first shock of battle came, lay in swollen heaps far and near. Broken gun-carriages, small arms of every description, some shattered by bullets, canteens, soldiers' blankets and jackets lay near the little mounds where those who had used them had fallen.
>
> The plain was ploughed at places in great furrows, torn open by shell from the enemy's batteries in the terrific combat of the previous day, when three hundred pieces of artillery blazed at each other.... Altogether it was a typical battlefield—one that neither pen nor pencil can paint, and that happily few are ever the eyewitnesses of.[2]

"A flag of truce now waves over both armies," noted Augustus Dickert of Kershaw's brigade, "granting a respite to bury the dead and care for the wounded.... There is no systematic work, time being too precious, and the dead are buried where they fell. Where the battle was fierce and furious, and the dead lay thick, they were buried in groups." He added that shallow pits were dug for the corpses, usually wrapped in a blanket "and sufficient dirt thrown upon it to protect it from the vultures." "Men were detailed to bury the dead, which was of great importance, to give our dead comrades a decent burial as far as circumstances admitted," recalled a soldier in the Second South Carolina. "Poor fellows, they were … laid away at rest; awaiting the resurrection morn." It may have been during this lull that Union Lt. Col. Freeman McGilvery, whose artillery at the Peach Orchard had so devastated Kershaw's troops at the Rose farm, saw the human carnage wrought by his guns. "After the battle, I visited the position where this column in its confusion massed up around the house and barn … and found 120 odd dead, belonging to three South Carolina regiments," he wrote in his battle report. "This mortality was no doubt from the effect of the artillery fire."[3]

"Not a gun was to be heard today," D.J. Carter of the Twelfth South Carolina wrote in his diary. "Both parties engaged in burying their dead, sending off all the wounded that can bear transportation." Capt. William Dunlop, also of the Twelfth, added, "Both armies bivouacked for the night [July 3] in their respective original positions and all the next day stood silently gazing at each other across the bloody chasm." Years later, Longstreet was eloquent in describing the day, writing: "The armies rested on the 'Fourth,'—one under the bright laurels secured by the brave work of the day before, but in profound sorrow over the silent form of the host of comrades who had fallen during those three fateful days … the other, with broken spirits, turned from fallen comrades to find safety away from the fields that had been so promising of ennobling fruits."[4]

Lt. Col. Fremantle was walking to the Confederate front line about 8 a.m. when he met Longstreet, "who was in a high state of amusement and good humor." A truce flag had just arrived from the Federals, its bearer announcing, among other things, that Longstreet was wounded, a prisoner, and was being cared for. Longstreet "sent back word that he was extremely grateful, but that being neither wounded nor a prisoner, he was quite able to take care of himself," Fremantle related. The colonel continued to be in awe of the Carolinian's infinite stamina, even as he saw some of the general's staff officers dismount from their horses and collapse, fast asleep: "The iron endurance of … Longstreet is most extraordinary; he seems to require neither food nor sleep." A heavy rainstorm wept from the heavens about 1 p.m., washing much of the blood from the grass, fields and boulders of the shattered landscape as the earth began its struggle to regain its natural order. The deluge subsided about an hour later, but more rain was on the way near dark. Surgeon Spencer Welch of the Thirteenth South Carolina recorded his thoughts in a letter to his wife. "On the 4th our army remained in line of battle, earnestly desiring the advance of the Yankees, but they did not come," he wrote. "During this day the rain fell in torrents, completely drenching the troops."[5]

Lee, however, had already reached a momentous decision. Overnight on July 3–4, he decided to retreat from Gettysburg. "Owing to the strength of the enemy's position and the reduction of our ammunition, a renewal of the engagement could not be hazarded," he related in a July 31 report, "and the difficulty of procuring supplies rendered it impossible to continue longer where we were." At some point on Saturday he proposed a prisoner exchange, but Meade declined. Longstreet acknowledged defeat, noting in his memoir: "The enemy had cast his lines on grounds too strong for lead and steel, and there was nothing left for the vanquished but to march for distant homeward lines."[6]

The Carolinians of the Brooks Artillery held their ground the rest of the day on the 3rd, pulling back after dark. On the 4th, Lt. Gilbert's men returned to a position near where they had been posted in the Confederate line on the 2nd. They remained there until about 4 p.m., when they withdrew toward Marsh Creek on the Fairfield Road. Reaching the Black Horse Tavern a few yards from the creek, the Carolinians and the rest of their battalion prepared to take their place in the retreating column. Gilbert himself was in a field hospital, being treated for the serious wounds suffered on the 2nd. More than thirty of his men were either dead or wounded, many seriously. Garden's Palmetto Light Artillery, meanwhile, had been posted a short distance to the west of their position the previous day. They held this position until about 6 p.m., when they withdrew from the field, heading south with the main column. Somewhere to the rear, one of Garden's cannoneers, Cpl. Robert F. Small, was still fighting for his life after being mangled by a Union round during the artillery dueling the previous afternoon. Small was only 19 but had been in the army since the war began. He was serving Lt. W.A. McQueen's gun advancing in support of Pickett's Charge when he was mortally wounded. "When being borne from the field under a very heavy fire, he seemed to feel more concern for his litter-bearers than himself," the *Camden* (S.C.) *Confederate* later reported, "thus exhibiting that magnanimous feeling which always characterized him…. The country mourns the loss of such young patriots." Small lingered until his death on July 7 "after four days of intense suffering. Thus ended the life of our Christian soldier," noted the *Charleston Courier*. "Mother, and other relatives of the deceased, your loved one has left you a precious legacy, far richer than earth's treasures."[7]

The Pee Dee Artillery of Lt. William E. Zimmerman, along with the rest of Pegram's Battalion in the Third Corps reserve artillery, remained on the battleground most of the day on the 4th, then withdrew near sundown and took its place behind A.P. Hill's infantry on the road south. Capt. E.B. Brunson of Pegram's command reported battle loss totals in the five batteries as 10 men killed, 37 wounded, 38 horses killed, three guns and a caisson disabled, and two caissons destroyed. The battalion's five batteries expended 3,800 rounds of ammunition in the three-day combat.[8]

Maj. David McIntosh's artillery battalion, also in the Third Corps, stood its ground that Saturday. The Carolinian was proud of the Virginians and Alabamians in his command; he noted the "general good conduct of officers and men," adding, "Not a single case came under my notice where any one flinched from the post of danger." The battalion launched 1,395 rounds at Gettysburg. On the 4th, "with but little firing," McIntosh received orders from Hill that afternoon to pull back, and marched toward the village of Fairfield—some eight miles distant—with the rest of Hill's corps.[9]

Abner Perrin's bloodied infantrymen were not engaged the rest of the 3rd after the Fourteenth South Carolina's costly counterattack. They remained in position near Gettysburg overnight and retreated with the remainder of Pender's division in Hill's corps on the night of the 4th, marching toward Hagerstown. "We left the battle ground on the night of the 4th & a most disagreeable march through the mud & rain we had of it," Perrin wrote a few weeks later. "The enemy made no pursuit." George W. Speer of the First South Carolina Rifles recalled the "whispered order" to withdraw and how "with muffled cannon, through rain and mud, we marched." Learning of the army's retreat, Pvt. J.C. Buzzard of the Fourteenth tried to leave the field hospital where he was being treated and rejoin his comrades. A doctor earlier had tried to secure a place in one of the ambulances for him but without success. "When the boys began to leave … I told them I was going to try and go," he said. "They told me I was too weak to go but I tried it anyway. When I got about fifteen steps away from the tent I fainted. They picked me up and carried me back and said I told you you couldn't go and soon I realized that they were right and that I really couldn't go." Isaac Trimble's tenure as division commander after Pender's wounding lasted only a few hours. As bad luck would have it, he again suffered a serious wound in the left leg on July 3, and the limb was amputated. Unable to retreat with Lee's army, he was captured. Brig. Gen. James Lane was again elevated to temporary division command.[10]

Somewhere within the Union lines, the Carter brothers from Darlington District lay among the thousands of other wounded, in all likelihood not in the same one of many makeshift hospitals. Both men, in the Fourteenth's Company A, were shot down during the assault of Perrin's brigade on the first day and captured. Lt. Sidney Carter was struggling to live while Pvt. Giles Carter was recovering from a leg injury. The Rev. W.B. Carson, chaplain of the Fourteenth South Carolina, stayed behind with the wounded, including ninety from his regiment too badly hurt to be moved. At some point during the battle, Carson ventured "into the heavily shelled woods for blankets for his wounded men and remained to administer to their wants until death freed many from their sufferings," related Lt. Col. Brown of the Fourteenth. Still recuperating from his leg amputation, Lt. J.R. Boyles of the Twelfth South Carolina remained in his bed of straw at another field hospital on the 4th. A good friend, Edgar Powell of the First South Carolina Volunteers, brought him some "nourishment," which allowed him to gain "a little strength." Boyles was told of the army's retreat and "that we were left to the tender mercies of five or six well men of our regiment left to nurse and dress our wounds until the enemy should take charge of us."[11]

Amid a continuous heavy downpour, the main Confederate wagon train began its withdrawal about 4 p.m. Most of the army's wagons and ambulances, all brimming with wounded, trundled slowly west on the Cashtown Pike. The "very windows of heaven seemed to have opened," recalled Brig. Gen. John D. Imboden, a Virginia cavalryman whom Lee placed in charge of the column. "The rain fell in blinding sheets; the meadows were soon overflowed, and fences gave way before the raging streams.... Canvas was no protection against its fury, and the wounded men lying upon the naked boards of the wagon-bodies were drenched." Mules and horses were "blinded and maddened by the wind and water, and became almost unmanageable. The deafening roar of the mingled sounds of heaven and earth all around us made it almost impossible to communicate orders, and equally difficult to execute them."[12]

In the column were rebels in the "hundreds with arms off, or otherwise wounded as not to prevent locomotion [who] 'hit the dust' as the soldiers used to say, on their long march of one hundred and fifty miles to Staunton, Va.," one of Kershaw's veterans recalled. The wagon train, stretching some fifteen to seventeen miles long, took a route through Cashtown, Greenwood, Greencastle and Hagerstown to reach the Potomac crossing near Williamsport. Imboden had about 2,100 cavalry, including the brigades of Hampton and Chambliss, to guard the flanks and rear of the column. Hampton's cavalry, now commanded by Col. Pierce M.B. Young, covered the rear of Imboden's convoy, assisted by Capt. Hart's South Carolina battery. All told, Imboden had twenty-three artillery pieces to defend the train, which was later joined by Brig. Gen. W.E. "Grumble" Jones's cavalry brigade. Young, 26, was born in Spartanburg, South Carolina, but he and his family moved to Georgia when he was a child.[13]

"As dark set in that evening long lines of wagons, disabled artillery and ambulances with the wounded, moved out by.... Cashtown and on the turnpike through South Mountain towards Chambersburg," Capt. Hart recalled. "The rain fell all night in drenching sluices, softening the roads until they soon became impassable." Generals Hampton and Hood shared an ambulance in the "vast procession of misery," as Imboden described it. Hood recalled how he was "suffering very much from the wound received in my arm," while Hampton was "so badly wounded that he was unable to sit up, whereas I could not lie down." Hampton was semi-conscious in the early stages of the journey due to his wounds and the opiates administered to ease his pain.[14]

Also among the multitude was Carolinian Lt. Gilbert of the Brooks Artillery, twice wounded on July 2, and Maj. Edward Croft of the Fourteenth South Carolina. Severely wounded on the 3rd, Croft—supposedly the first rebel to enter Gettysburg on the first day—was placed in an ambulance, where he was attended by his "servant" Henry Deas. Shot in both legs on July 1, Lt. William H. Brunson of the Fourteenth's Company D also was apparently somewhere in the procession of agony, as was Lt. Robert Briggs Watson of Company B. With a gunshot in the thigh he sustained on the battle's first day, Watson was put in a wagon with three other wounded men. He had only a hat, an old blue shirt and a blanket to cover himself for the next three arduous weeks.[15]

Wounded on July 2, J.W. Lokay of the Fifteenth South Carolina reached a Confederate field hospital the next day and listened to the titanic artillery bombardment preceding the great charge. "I served through the Virginia campaign and was in many hard fought battles, but I never heard such cannonading as was at that field hospital," he noted. More important to him at that time was his immediate fate: "I had never been a prisoner and had a horror of a Yankee prison. I saw no chance of getting back to Virginia." He watched as every ambulance and empty wagon was loaded with wounded men. In one of the last wagons were four men lying on the bed. The driver or a corpsman—it's unclear who—told Lokay there was room for him if he could sit up. Lokay climbed aboard. "I could stand no pressure on my wound so rode holding my wounded leg with both hands that were locked together, below the knee, then I let my left leg dangle out of the wagon." Imboden, Hampton, Hood and every other rebel in the column had no way of knowing that Union cavalry was slushing through the mud, rain and waning daylight to try to destroy or capture as much of Lee's wagon train as possible.[16]

Indeed, none of the Gettysburg warriors—regardless of uniform color—sensed the startling news of events unfolding a thousand miles to the south, deep in the snaky backwaters and swamps of Mississippi. Vicksburg, the Confederate Troy on the Mississippi River, had fallen to Union forces under Maj. Gen. Ulysses S. Grant after a lengthy campaign and siege. On July 4 morning, the rebel defenders, some 29,000 starving and exhausted troops, marched out of the city's fortifications and stacked arms. The Confederacy would never recover from this pair of monumental defeats.[17]

With Imboden's wagons and ambulances embarking on a head start, the rest of Lee's army prepared to limp away from Gettysburg after dark on July 4. This main column took a shorter, more direct route to the Potomac crossing, following roads on the east side of South Mountain through Emmitsburg toward Hagerstown and Williamsport. Lee was unaware, at least initially, that Union cavalry had struck at Williamsport that day and destroyed his pontoon bridge at Falling Waters. With the heavy rain resuming—about 9 p.m.—the river would rise, possibly making it difficult or impossible to cross.[18]

Hill's corps led the main column, followed by Longstreet's troops—including Kershaw's brigade—charged with guarding about 4,000 Union prisoners, and Ewell's corps bringing up the rear. Artillery accompanied the respective corps, and the rest of Stuart's cavalry was divided to precede and follow the army. The Confederates paroled some 2,000 captives before the withdrawal and left behind "the enemy's numerous wounded that had fallen into our hands" after the first two days of the battle, Lee noted. "The commanding general earnestly exhorts each corps commander to see that every officer exerts the utmost vigilance, steadiness, and boldness during the whole march."[19]

Kershaw's troops pulled out of line shortly after midnight on July 5, marching via Franklin toward Monterey. Col. Nance of the Third South Carolina had gotten his first taste of the Gettysburg fighting on the 4th: "The day was marked by considerable skirmishing, and once or twice an attack seemed probable, but none occurred." "At daylight … the remnant of that once grand army turned its face southward," Augustus Dickert recalled. "I say remnant, for with the loss of near one-third its number … the pride, prestige of victory, the feelings of invincibility, were lost to the remainder, and the army was in rather ill condition when it took up the retreat." Another Carolinian, Pvt. Robert R. Hemphill of Company G, First South Carolina Rifles in Perrin's command, also never forgot this part of the campaign. "The storm spirit held high carnival, rain was pouring down in torrents, the streams of the country were flooded and the roads were cut to pieces by the artillery and wagon trains," he related years later. "Mud was everywhere over the ankles and in some places above the knee." In the pitch black, the drenched soldiers "kept our places guided by the splashes of the footsteps of the men in advance." On the 6th, the Carolinians marched through Waterloo and Hagerstown. "Along down the mountain sides, through gorges and over hills, the army slowly made its way," Dickert remembered. "No haste, no confusion…. The rain fell in torrents, night and day. The roads were soon greatly cut up, which in a measure was to Lee's advantage, preventing the enemy from following too closely." Kershaw's troops were among Confederate units that encamped near Funkstown on the night of July 6.[20]

Somewhere in the Confederate retreat was G.A. White of the Third S.C. Battalion's Company F, who had helped armor the ironclad CSS *Virginia*. White was wounded at Gettysburg, likely in Kershaw's thrust on July 2, but it was unclear if he was with Imboden's column or on the move with the main army. Spencer Welch, the surgeon in Perrin's brigade, was with the infantry column, and described the route as "very rough and not macadamized … the passing of wagons and artillery over it cut it up horribly and made it almost impassable. Yet over this road our large army had to pass." Welch continued that he was "lucky enough to get into a medical wagon and rode until the next morning [the 5th]. It rained nearly all night, and such a sight as our troops were the next day! They were all wet and many of them muddy all over from having fallen down during the night." At some point on the 5th, the surgeon saw his brother, Pvt. William E. "Billie" Welch of the Thirteenth South Carolina's Company D, in the column. "Billie looked as if he had been wallowing in a mud hole, but was in a perfectly good humor," the doctor later wrote.[21]

The artillery battalion of Maj. David McIntosh reached Fairfield with the rest of Hill's corps. There on July 5, McIntosh was ordered to attach two of his batteries to Dick Anderson's division. Most of Anderson's infantry and McIntosh's attached guns reached the village of Monterey and crossed South Mountain before dark. Another battery was assigned to support a Mississippi regiment in Anderson's command posted on a hill overlooking Waynesboro, Pennsylvania, and protecting the army's flank. Additionally, two other guns were to guard the Emmitsburg Road.[22]

The Foe

At Gettysburg, Meade spent much of July 4 resting and regrouping his battered but victorious army, not expecting Lee to mount another attack. By late afternoon he received word that enemy movements indicated a Confederate retreat, apparently toward the Potomac River. Meade held a council of war that night with his corps commanders, most of whom favored a pursuit by the cavalry with infantry following on other roads. Still, Meade wanted confirmation of Lee's whereabouts before he committed to such a move. He ordered a cavalry reconnaissance for the next day to find the rebels. Also on the 4th, Meade ordered a Union force under Maj. Gen. W.H. French to move from its post at Frederick, Maryland, and try to block Lee's retreat. To that end, French's most notable achievement was destroying the Confederates' pontoon bridge at Falling Waters on July 5.[23]

In the hours after the Confederate withdrawal, some Union soldiers ventured out to explore the ghastly ground contested by giants over the last three days. One of these Federals was Robert Carter, a young Massachusetts infantryman who walked the terrain where Kershaw and Wofford had attacked on July 2. The gruesomely efficient work of the Union artillery posted in and around the Peach Orchard and Wheatfield was very much on display. "Masses of Kershaw's and Woffords's [sic] brigades had been swept from the muzzles of the guns, which had been loaded either with double-shotted, or spherical case, with fuses cut to one second, to explode near the muzzles," Carter recalled. "They were literally blown to atoms. Corpses strewed the ground at every step. Arms, heads, legs and parts of dismembered bodies were scattered all about, and sticking among the rocks and against the trunks of trees, hair, brains, entrails and shreds of human flesh still hung, a disgusting, sickening, heart-rending spectacle to our young minds."[24]

J. Howard Wert, a Gettysburg native who fought in the battle as a militiaman, walked the ravaged ground of the July 1 combat, west of Seminary Ridge, a day or so after Lee's retreat. The ground over which Pender's division—including Perrin's Carolinians—and Heth's troops had advanced was dotted with corpses from both armies. "The dead were buried wherever they fell—right in the pike with teams driving over them—in the fields and through the woods on either side," he wrote. Most of the Union slain remained unburied during the Confederates' three-day possession of this area of the battleground, he stated, adding, "The dead on this part of the field were much decomposed." Proceeding west from Willoughby Run toward Marsh Creek, Wert noted the increased numbers of Confederate bodies. These men, who without doubt included Palmetto soldiers, "were more numerous, many [wounded] having, after the battle of the 1st, been removed to the rear and dying there. Nearly all were most scantily buried, if you may dignify the few shovels-full of earth thrown over them.... In some cases where numbers were thus slightly intered [sic] swine were found reveling in the remains in a manner horrible to contemplate." On the gory acreage of the Rose farm, where so many of Kershaw's Carolinians fell, the heavy rain created an equally gruesome situation shortly after the battle. A "small, marshy stream" ran between some of the Rose buildings, including the spring house, before cutting into the nearby woods. After the July 2 fighting, the stream was "clogged with the dead bodies of Confederates" to such a degree that "in this valley so much was the course of the stream obstructed that great ponds were formed where the waters were dammed up by the swollen corpses of the Southern soldiery," Wert recalled.[25]

Near nightfall on the 4th, elements of Kilpatrick's cavalry located the rear of the rebel wagon column at Monterey Pass, and attacked. It was a miserably surreal fight over several hours. Carbine and musket flashes ripped the night as the foes struggled along the muddy, hilly road, rain drenching all. The Carolina artillerist James Hart recalled how "every now and then a marauding squadron of Federal cavalry would dash in at some cross-road and attack the helpless train, generally with temporary success, until driven off" by the escort.[26]

"Language would fail me if I tried to tell all these poor men suffered on the trip," the wounded J.W. Lokay of the Fifteenth South Carolina noted of the hundreds of wounded soldiers in the wagon train. During the night Lokay told the men with him, "I would have to get out, even if the Yankees got me." He climbed out of the wagon and made his way to an old schoolhouse for shelter. After resting awhile, he returned to the road, the caravan still passing, but every teamster told him their wagons were full. "After hobbling along two or three miles in the rain and mud," Lokay said, he was finally picked up by a wagon belonging to the Virginia cavalry. In this way he made it to the Potomac River. Maj. Donald McLeod of the Eighth South Carolina, mangled by artillery fire on July 2, also was in the melancholy caravan. At some point on the route, perhaps on July 5 or 6, the Marlboro native lost his fight for life. "Borne away by his comrades on their retreat, to prevent his falling into the hands of the enemy, he breathed his last on the road … and now sleeps where they laid him by the way side, a board with his name carved upon it marking the spot of his resting place," stated one account.[27]

Most of Imboden's massive convoy reached Williamsport, the crossing point on the Potomac, during the afternoon of July 5 after "a great deal of desultory fighting and harassments along the road…. We took possession of the town to convert it into a great hospital for the thousands of wounded we had brought from Gettysburg," Imboden recalled. The rainfall, meanwhile, had raised the Potomac to some ten feet above the level where the army could ford it, forcing the Confederates to stay in the Williamsport vicinity until the waters subsided. Imboden seized two small ferry boats to cross the river with wounded who, "after being fed and having their wounds dressed, thought they could walk to Winchester." The craft were kept in continuous use, taking a "large number" of rebels to the opposite shore. "Our situation was frightful," Imboden recalled. "We had probably ten thousand animals and nearly all the wagons of … Lee's army under our charge, and all the wounded, to the number of several thousand, that could be brought from Gettysburg." His supplies consisted of a "few wagon-loads of flour" from his own brigade train, "a small lot of fine fat cattle which I had collected in Pennsylvania … and some sugar and coffee."[28]

Well to the rear, General Young with Hampton's cavalry, along with Hart's South Carolina battery, were repelling enemy thrusts against the rest of the convoy and guarding the roads from the north and west. During one of these clashes, Trooper William A. Black of Company A, Second South Carolina Cavalry, was captured. Black, a railroad freight clerk before the war, had evaded injury in many major battles, including Gettysburg, but now found himself a prisoner of war. Jacob W. Cagle, an officer in Company B of Kershaw's Second South Carolina, found himself in nearly the same circumstances. The 30 year old, wounded in the leg, was in an ambulance when it was seized by the Federals. This portion of the wagon train was soon retaken by the Confederates. In the combat confusion, Cagle's servant managed to snare a riderless horse from the Yankees. The pair and their mount managed to get across the Potomac.[29]

The last wagons of Imboden's column, accompanied by Hart's artillerists, reached Williamsport about noon on July 6, leaving Hampton's cavalry posted some 10 miles behind to picket the roads. Hart, his battery mates and many other Confederates "stopped to wait and sleep." Within an hour or so, their respite was disturbed by reports of enemy cavalry heading their way from the direction of Hagerstown. Imboden had received word earlier that day that a large force of Union cavalry with artillery were approaching Williamsport. He immediately posted his guns, including Hart's cannoneers, on a low range of hills north of the town, dismounting the troopers of his own brigade to support them. "Our little force of organized companies was hastily strung out over the hills, in a thin skirmish line, to oppose them," Hart related.[30]

Desperate for more fighters, Imboden armed his teamsters with guns from the wagons. The weapons, along with ammunition, had been collected earlier from the army's dead and wounded. In this endeavor, he was "greatly aided" by Hart and Col. John Black of the First South Carolina Cavalry, whom he singled out for praise by name. Wounded officers and soldiers also joined in the effort and by early afternoon some 700 teamsters and walking wounded had been organized into makeshift companies. Black, still suffering from his Upperville head wound, commanded about 250 of these men on the left of the Confederates' defensive line. Among this force were some fifty Carolinians from Abner Perrin's brigade, led by Capt. R.E.B. Hewetson, quartermaster of the First South Carolina. Hewetson "was a veteran and stood high for gallantry as a line-officer, before being appointed quartermaster, and most of his teamsters had been under fire before," noted a fellow officer in the First.[31]

The Federal cavalry, about 4,000 troopers led by John Buford and Wesley Merritt, appeared about 1:30 p.m. on both the Hagerstown and Boonsboro roads, and the battle erupted with an artillery duel. "Every man under my command understood that if we did not repulse the enemy we should all be captured and General Lee's army be ruined by the loss of its transportation, which at that period could not have been replaced in the Confederacy," Imboden recalled. The enemy was "now gazing down on the richest prize a cavalry leader could aspire to—the wagon and ordnance trains of a whole army," Hart related.[32]

The Union attack "was met with firmness but it was perfectly evident that our little force, on open ground as it was, would soon melt away under the terrible fire that began to pour into it," Hart noted. Sgt. John Newton was in charge of the wagon train for Hart's Battery. As the first shots of the clash echoed through the hills, Newton, who was with the wagons at the time, hurried to join the fight. Unable to locate Hart's command, he assisted a Louisiana battery, taking charge of one of its guns. For half an hour he helped man the fieldpiece "until he fell, cut in two by a shell," Hart recalled. Also amid the fight, Hart was approached by an officer he did not know wearing a captain's insignia. The captain asked to be posted in the battle line and Hart put him in charge of a squad of Confederates who had just arrived on the scene. During the combat, Hart especially noticed the captain's bravery and handling of his men. "His coolness, self-possession and daring soon attracted attention and his command was rapidly enlarged," Hart recalled. Hart later approached the officer and asked his name. The man replied that he was the Rev. Manning Brown, chaplain of the Second South Carolina Cavalry.[33]

The clash resulted in the bluecoats being repelled, Hewetson and his men among many performing admirably. "The detail from this brigade [Perrin's] charged the line opposed to them, drove them back, and held the ground until relieved at night," stated one account. The action cost Hewetson's Palmettos two men killed and five or six wounded. Sgt. Newton's bravery and aid touched the Louisiana gunners, who buried him near where he fell. Hart's Carolinians also earned more accolades from Imboden: "Hart, seeing how hard we were pressed … charged the enemy's right with his little command."[34]

Neither Wade Hampton nor General Hood were able to participate in the Confederates' patchwork defense that day due to the seriousness of their injuries. Hampton had endured the inhumane trip aided by doses of laudanum. The Brit Sir Arthur Fremantle encountered these generals on the sixth. "I saw General Hood in his carriage; he looked rather bad, and has been suffering a great deal; the doctors seem to doubt whether they will be able to save his arm," he noted. "I also saw General Hampton, of the cavalry, who has been shot in the hip, and has two sabre-cuts on the head, but he was in very good spirits."[35]

Col. Black, at some point before or after the July 6 clash, visited a Williamsport church, being used as a temporary hospital, and happened upon Capt. John K. McIver of Company F, Eighth South Carolina Infantry in Kershaw's brigade. McIver, of Society Hill, South Carolina, had had both eyes shot out and was "in a dying condition and suffering untold agony," Black was told. The surgeon wanted to find a quiet place where the captain could die in peace. Shortly afterward a man named Simmons approached Black, who had earlier helped prevent the man's home from being plundered by unruly soldiers. Simmons thanked the colonel for his effort and Black was quick to ask a return favor, requesting that McIver be taken to Simmons's home to spend his remaining time. Simmons, a pro–Union man, replied that he had "noisy children" but that his two unmarried sisters lived in a nearby cottage and would take in the officer. Arrangement were made and McIver was soon "placed on a very neat bed in a nice Ladies' chamber," Black recalled. "Goodbye, I leave you in good hands," he told the captain. The captain "held my hand and asked my name. I gave it to him & he thanked me kindly." Leaving the cottage, Black expressed his appreciation to the sisters, recalling their compassion despite the war. "These people were our enemies but they were truly noble," he wrote. "They recognized the fact that the grave should cover all earthly strife."[36]

Believed to be mortally wounded on July 2, Lt. George Bozeman of the Eighth South Carolina's Company F endured the nightmarish retreat and reached Williamsport. There a doctor who had more time than the harried surgeons at the Black Horse Tavern examined and treated his wound. According to the account by Bozeman's comrade, Lt. W.E. James, in the same company, an unidentified physician probed Bozeman's skull, trying to locate the ball lodged within. The surgeon made several efforts with his forceps before finding the projectile, "lodged under the bones of his head." Minutes later the doctor extricated "a grape shot weighing ten ounces" near Bozeman's ear.[37]

Lt. James Armstrong of McCreary's First South Carolina also was among the wounded in Imboden's column. Sharing the wagon with Armstrong was Lt. James R. Hamilton, also in the First, and another unidentified soldier whose "leg was shattered." Years later, Armstrong recalled of Hamilton "how patient he was under severe suffering and how he cheered by his lively words another noble comrade." Despite Hamilton's encouragement, the other soldier died shortly afterwards. Armstrong penned a letter from "Near Williamsport, Md," on July 6, after arriving that morning: "We left the hospital on Saturday afternoon [July 4] in a wagon…. We did not stop even at night. On the route, a body of Yankee cavalry attacked our trains, among them our baggage wagon. We had the good fortune to escape unmolested…. My wound [in the left arm] is not as bad as I thought; it is very painful." Armstrong then noted the death of Capt. W.T. Haskell, who led the brigade sharpshooters: "His loss is irreparable. He was a model of an officer, and a most refined gentleman." Armstrong also wrote that Perrin had "behaved in an admirable manner" in leading the brigade at Gettysburg and mentioned that Pvt. Michael McGinnis of the First's Company I had died of injuries he sustained from a grapeshot wound to the head.[38]

10

"Locked in the Embrace of Morpheus"

Lee himself arrived at the Potomac on July 7, finding the river flooded and his pontoon bridge destroyed by French's Union raiders two days earlier. Realizing the gravity of his situation, Lee quickly set his troops to constructing defensive works stretching from Conococheague Creek near Hagerstown to the Potomac. Work on a replacement bridge was also begun. From this position Lee would await either an assault by Meade or for the river to recede. Other than the cavalry thrusts, however, Meade did not launch a mass assault against the wounded Confederate lion; the Union tiger was bloodied as well, and likely just as exhausted. Years later, one of Hampton's men, Trooper David H. Russell of the First South Carolina Cavalry, noted defiantly, "Meade did not care to repeat the dose he had at Gettysburg."[1]

On July 6, Maj. David McIntosh's reserve artillery battalion in Hill's corps moved with the army's main column to Hagerstown. There McIntosh dispatched two of his batteries for picket duty with the divisions of Anderson and Lane. "We were told at that point to go into camp, that rations would be issued and the men would have an opportunity to do some cooking," the Carolinian recalled. "The sight of a nearby grove arrested our attention, and the battalion at once took possession. Worn out with fatigue, I dismounted and threw myself on the soft grass in the grateful shade, and was soon locked in the embrace of Morpheus."[2]

McIntosh soon had an awakening he would remember forever. "My sleep was of short duration," he related. "I was aroused by my colored servant and told that General Lee wanted to see me. Making my way to where he was, I awoke to the fact that a long row of camp-fires were blazing brightly in full view, piled high with fence rails, and I became dimly conscious that something was going wrong. Lee received me with great austerity of manner, and pointing to the fence, inquired if I had received general orders No. 72. I replied that I had, and that the orders had been duly published. Looking at me for a moment, he said, 'Then, sir, you must not only have them published, but you must see that they are obeyed,' and with a bow and majestic wave ... he turned and rode away, leaving me decidedly crest-fallen."[3]

The Pee Dee Artillery and the other batteries of Pegram's Battalion, also in Hill's reserve artillery, reached the Hagerstown vicinity on July 7 or 8, depending on the source, "without anything of interest transpiring," the battalion's Capt. Brunson noted. On the night of the 10th, the South Carolinians and Virginians were sent to Maj. Gen. Heth at Funkstown, just outside Hagerstown, where they posted their guns in line with Heth's

118

infantry near the College of Saint James (the present-day Saint James School) the next morning.[4]

Kershaw's troops were nearby, encamped near Funkstown since July 6, but ordered into action on the 10th. Kershaw was to move into defensive position at a bridge over nearby Antietam Creek, where a strong Union force had been seen on the opposite side. The Carolinians were accompanied by Paul Semmes's brigade—now led by Col. Goode Bryan—and a few artillery pieces. Semmes's Georgians had no way of knowing that their brigadier, who had been wounded on July 2, would die that day in Martinsburg, West Virginia (West Virginia had gained statehood in June 1863), some thirty miles to the south. There was some "unimportant skirmishing" along the creek, Kershaw noted. His troops rejoined the rest of McLaws's division near the college the next morning. Col. Nance of the Third South Carolina Regiment reported one casualty, Pvt. G.L. Beasley, who was killed when he and the rest of the regiment's Company I advanced beyond the bridge, serving as sharpshooters.[5]

Pvt. Edwin Kerrison of the Second South Carolina found a few minutes on July 7 to write home regarding his well-being and that of his brother, Charles, also in the Second. "Dear Sister—I now write in great haste to let you know where we are. On the … 2nd we fought a desperate battle at Gettysburg in Pa. in which we suffered terribly[,] being compelled to stand the fire of artillery within one hundred & fifty yards of said battery," he noted in fine cursive. "Our Reg. acted gloriously but has lost many a brave man—[Pvt.] Charley [Kerrison] I am sorry to say was wounded not by any means dangerously. He was shot in the thigh with a piece of shell & in the face by a buck shot. He was in fine spirits when I last saw him & doing finely." After listing several other comrades who were casualties, Edwin continued: "Since we left [the 5th] our wounded have been all captured by the Yankees…. They will receive more attention & be more comfortable than if they were with us…. We have only 8 or 9 men for duty in the company now. Our Regt has but two captains left…. Col. Kennedy was shot in the arm."[6]

That same day near Hagerstown, Capt. James McCutchen of the Fifteenth South Carolina wrote to the mother of one of his slain soldiers, Pvt. Gabriel G. Gist, who had been mortally wounded on July 2:

> Mrs. Gist—Dear Madam: I am exceedingly sorry to inform you of the death of your son…. No better soldier has entered the Confederate service than your worthy son. He was a man that I esteemed very highly for the excellence of his character, and deeply regret his death…. I wish I could comfort you in your affliction. A lofty patriotism and a reliance upon the wisdom of God in all the events of Providence will go far to make you submissive to this heavy stroke, which has taken from you a noble son. I beg to offer you my sincere sympathy.[7]

Another of Kershaw's men, an unidentified soldier in the Third South Carolina, remembered the hunger the troops endured during this time and the temporary remedy that revived them. "At Williamsport, rations got scarce and we were allowed to kill the hogs and cattle that came in our reach," he noted. Augustus Dickert recalled that he and the rest of Kershaw's men were without bread for two days and had "only a few beef cattle" with them. The Confederates demolished some houses for the planking needed to build the pontoon bridge, but the lack of provisions was a much more immediate concern. Their luck soon turned, however. Pvt. Jim George in Company C found a cache of flour-filled barrels hidden in a stack of straw near some old outbuildings. The contents of the eight or ten barrels were quickly distributed among the regiment, and George got "an extra portion for himself," Dickert wrote.[8]

One of Kershaw's wounded officers was 31-year-old Capt. Chesley W. Herbert of the Third South Carolina's Company C. The Newberry County native was shot on July 2. During the withdrawal he was captured by Union cavalry but was freed, apparently in the confusion of combat. Furloughed, he was sent home to recuperate. Tragedy would soon savage this Carolinian and his family.[9]

"By one means & another Genl Lee has got his tattered, half starved, ragged, but high spirited army this near the Potomac all around Hagerstown," Col. Aiken of the Seventh South Carolina wrote during this period. "Report says he will fight the enemy again before he crosses. I hope not." Aiken also addressed the casualties in his regiment: "I lost 133 men, 20 of whom are now in camp with a simple flesh wound, loss of a finger, &c. 18 were killed on the field, several died since, and 16 amputations. The Brig lost 630 men now absent from the command. Barksdale lost about as many." Aiken added: "The Pot[o-mac] is swimming, & we are thrashing … wheat and grinding flour to feed the army upon. Beef plentiful." He also noted that the Union prisoners with the army were "helping to make our rations shorter still."[10]

As previously mentioned, the Confederates did succeed in getting some of the wounded south of the Potomac in the first few days of the retreat. Lt. S.C. Gilbert of the Brooks Artillery was in Winchester by July 9, where he was treated for his severe wounds. That day he composed a letter to the editor of the *Charleston Mercury* detailing his battery's casualties at Gettysburg, although it is unclear if those who survived were safely across the Potomac, still with the army at Hagerstown or in Union custody. The list was published in the *Mercury* on July 18. Killed were corporals R.W. Ackis and Andrew Martin, privates W.P. Casey, William Eason, D.H. Mitchell, Edward Street and D.T. Williams. In addition to Gilbert, the other losses were Cpl. Thomas Hayes, privates J. Allgood and W. Watts, all mortally wounded; Lt. E.F. O'Neill; sergeants W.L. Calvitt, Martin Murphey, and O.H.C. Smith; corporals H. Braun and H. Bruning; privates George Antibus, M. Carolan, A.A. Kimmey, E. Maher J. Nichlas, J.C. Hagans, P.H. Williams, H. Woodworth, and a soldier identified only as Noll, all severely wounded; Cpl. H.R. Kennedy and Pvt. J.S. Ackis, seriously wounded; and Lt. W.W. Fickling, privates A. Buckner, J.C. Farrell, G.T. Jones, A.C. Meyers, Joseph Kennedy, J. Youngblood and J. Doran, slightly wounded.[11]

After several days of rest and inaction, Maj. David McIntosh's reserve artillery battalion moved with Dick Anderson's division on July 11, taking positions in battle line at the College of St. James, near their comrades in the Pee Dee Artillery. "Fighting Dick," meanwhile, kept an eye on Union forces on the hills behind the army and made defensive preparations: "Skirmishers were advanced at once, and the troops were diligently employed in strengthening the position."[12]

That same day at Hagerstown, Trooper William Hayne Perry of the Second S.C. Cavalry penned some thoughts to his father, Benjamin Franklin Perry, at home in Greenville:

Dear Pa

For the first time in nearly a month I have an opportunity of writing to you. For the past four weeks we have been on a constant go. We crossed the Potomac just two weeks ago to-night, and have had a busy time of it ever since, and there is a prospect of it lasting some time yet. But I am quite well … one of my horses is a little lame but not much. You have no doubt heard of the battle of Gettysburg which I think was about a drawn one. We all thought we were going to go back into Virginia a few days ago, but now I expect we will remain, and there will in all probability be another great battle in a day or so…. Our loss in the Gettysburg battle was heavy, but the men are in good spirits and ready to meet the enemy again.

Perry also wrote that the regiment had been in "over a dozen fights and skirmishes" in the campaign and that various elements of the cavalry corps had been engaged daily "for the past 34 days." He then gave a brief description of the cavalry clash on July 3: "In the Gettysburg fight we were on the left and had a big Cavalry fight. Gen. Hampton was pretty severely wounded…. Our regiment did good service." He also mentioned the death of Sgt. Thomas Butler and others who were wounded. "But ours has been a lucky Reg. so far," he penned. "We have been shelled over and over and suffered very little. Gen. Hampton I suppose has gone home by this time."[13]

Perrin's brigade reached the vicinity of Hagerstown by July 7 and "lay in line of battle" with other elements of Hill's Third Corps. With Pender's fall, Harry Heth led his own division and that of Pender during this phase of the campaign. "The Potomac in impetuous majesty, lay in our way," noted Robert Hemphill of the First South Carolina Rifles. "There we halted and faced the oncoming hosts who were crowding upon us. There was nothing to eat, neither bread nor meat. So we sat down without rations and with little ammunition." Infantryman D.J. Carter of the Twelfth South Carolina had little time to write his diary entries during this frenetic period of Lee's retreat. He made one journal entry for those three days, briefly describing the terrible night march in heavy rain over thick mud on tar-black mountain roads. What registered most to Carter, however, was the sight of slain Union soldiers at Hagerstown. "Our cavalry had had a fight here the day before we arrived," he wrote, "and some of the yankee dead lay along the streets unburied."[14]

Also in the Twelfth, assistant surgeon Willis W. Keith wrote a July 9 letter to his mother, Anna Bell Keith, hoping that it would reach her back home in Anderson Court House, South Carolina. He had written several recent letters but had gotten no response and was worried and unsure about this only link to his loved ones. "I suppose you have heard of our battle," he wrote from camp near Williamsport. "It was the least successful one that we ever fought. We failed to take the heights on which the enemy entrenched themselves and lost many valuable men. The first two days of the fighting we whipped them badly, and slaughtered them terribly…. I think it more than probable that we will have another fight before we cross the river." Keith wrote home again on July 10:

> My Dear Mama,
>
> I wrote to you from Pennsylvania and also a few hurried lines day before yesterday. But I am afraid that there is not much chance of them reaching you. I am trying again in hopes that you may receive one out of them all. I am quite well, but heartily tired of this life. It is truly a dog['s] life. When will this war end[?] I do so long to see you again. It is now nearly seven months since we parted. We have been lying for several days near the Potomac. None of us know whether we will recross the river, or only send off the wounded, and then strike out for some other portion of the enemies territory. I do hope the former…. I have not seen a paper and do not know whether Vicksburg has fallen or not…. We lost a great many men in the late battle. Our division suffered more severely than any other in the army. Our Regt. had twenty five men killed and a large number wounded…. Our Brigade Postmaster was captured the other day. He was along with the wagon train…. All most everything that I have, a change of clothing, and two blankets, I carry with me on my horse. Love to all…. W.[15]

In their Hagerstown defenses on July 11, the Carolinians again tasted combat when threatened by a Union force. Perrin's skirmishers were engaged, and the Confederates sustained a few more killed and wounded. Among the dead was Capt. John W. Chambers of the First South Carolina, who fell leading his company into action. Perrin described him as "a most gallant and worthy officer." They would continue to be held up near Hagerstown because the Potomac River was swollen by the rains, and the army would have to wait to cross the river at Falling Waters near Martinsburg. At some point on July 13, Robert Hemphill and some of his famished comrades in the First South Carolina Rifles managed to capture some sheep, which they promptly slaughtered and prepared to eat. Their excitement was quickly quelled because the mutton "afforded only unsavory and indigestible rations," he recalled. "We had no salt and no bread, and in a drenching rain, cooked the repulsive meat upon our ramrods. We managed, however, to eat enough 'to keep soul and body together.'"[16]

Meanwhile, the Potomac's water had slowly receded enough by the night of the 13th that most of Lee's army was able to cross on the rickety pontoon bridge at Falling Waters after sunup the next day. Ewell's corps forded the river at Williamsport. Perrin's Carolinians marched from their Hagerstown camps on the night of the 13th, but it was tough going. "The road was everywhere shoe-deep in mud and in many places almost to the knees," recalled Lt. James Caldwell of the First South Carolina Volunteers. "The rain fell in torrents…. The men straggled, of course. Many of them, in attempting to make short cuts, lost their way and were captured. No one could recognize another in the storm and darkness." "The rain continued … and the blackened heavens hung over us unrelieved by the light of a single star," added Pvt. Hemphill. Soon after daybreak on July 14, Perrin's troops, along with the rest of Pender's division and Heth's command, were halted to rest on a ridge about two miles from the bridge. They would remain on that side of the river as rearguard for the rest of the army.[17]

The Carolinians were "hungry, worn and exhausted, but still undaunted, for every man held his place in line as only a veteran could," said Hemphill, who was "barefooted, for my shoes had been worn out by the rain and mud and hard marching of the campaign." Amid the overnight storm some Southerners lay down by the wayside to rest. In the rain and dark, officers sent back for them searched in vain; many of these stragglers had been captured. Heth was ordered to place his division in battle line on either side of the road and along the ridge crest, facing Hagerstown. Pender's troops were posted to the rear of this position "in column of brigades," Heth noted. With the river in sight, Perrin's troops passed the area where the remnants of Brig Gen. Pettigrew's decimated North Carolina brigade were resting in line. Likewise, Perrin's men were ordered to the side of the road for a much-needed break. "Almost everyone soon fell asleep by the stacks of arms," Caldwell related. The rearguard remained there for "several hours" while wagons and artillery crossed the span.[18]

Lt. Zimmerman's Pee Dee Artillery and the rest of Pegram's Battalion in Hill's artillery held their position at Funkstown without firing a shot until pulling out on the night of the 13th, heading toward the pontoon bridge. The march from Gettysburg added six or eight men captured to the battalion's campaign losses, and a howitzer caisson had to be abandoned. Maj. McIntosh's cannoneers, also in Hill's artillery, withdrew that night as well "without battle." His men struggled through the darkness and muck to haul their guns, "moving to Williamsport, and thence to Falling Waters, over the worst road and during the worst night of the season." McIntosh continued: "It was still raining, the road was next to impassable, and the night was blackness itself." At the bridge McIntosh ordered a lieutenant to go over with the battalion's caissons. The guns were to remain on the north bank until all of the troops, other than the cavalry, were safely over the pontoons. McIntosh's men fired 1,249 rounds at Gettysburg, with losses of one officer and six men killed, seven officers and eighteen men wounded. His command had thirty-five horses killed in action, thirteen captured and twenty abandoned. One caisson was lost and another disabled. Dick Anderson's division of Hill's corps also marched after dark on the 13th, crossing at Falling Waters the next morning.[19]

Kershaw's brigade also withdrew on the 13th, heading to Falling Waters. "An hour after dark we took up the line of march, and from our camp to the river, a distance of one mile or less, beat anything in the way of marching that human nature ever experienced," related Augustus Dickert. "The dust that had accumulated by the armies passing over on their march to Gettysburg was now a perfect bog, while the horses and vehicles sinking in the soft earth made the road appear bottomless. We would march two or three steps, then halt for a moment or two; then a few steps more, and again the few minutes' wait. The men had to keep their hands on the backs of their file leaders to tell them when to move and when to halt. The night being so dark and rainy, we could not see farther than 'the noses on our faces' while at every step we went nearly up to our knees in slash and mud. Men would stand and sleep—would march (if this could be called marching) and sleep. The soldiers could not fall out of ranks for fear of being hopelessly lost, as troops of different corps and divisions would at times be mingled together." The Carolinians began recrossing the Potomac early on the 14th. "Just as the sun began to peep up over the eastern hills, we came in sight of the rude pontoon bridge, lined from one end to the other with hurrying wagons and artillery—the troops at opened ranks on either side," Dickert remembered. "If it had been fatiguing on the troops, what must it have been on the poor horses and mules that had fasted for days and now drawing great trains, with roads almost bottomless?" Dickert and the other soldiers of James Nance's Third South Carolina crossed the bridge near midday, after what the colonel characterized as a nightmarish overnight ordeal. "This night's march deserves to be characterized as the severest which I have ever witnessed," Nance, the cool-headed, young combat veteran, said in his August 6 campaign report. "Its trials were too great for 2 of my men, who fell by the way-side, exhausted, and they have never been heard from since."[20]

Capt. William C. Coker (also identified as William C. Cohen by another source) of Company M in Kershaw's Eighth South Carolina would not be making the crossing, despite being within a short distance of the Potomac. Coker, 24, was wounded in the foot at Gettysburg and endured the rigors of the ambulance train retreat. He was a teacher in his hometown of Society Hill before the war and also had been wounded by a shell fragment at Malvern Hill. Coker was in one of the many makeshift hospitals in Williamsport and was taken prisoner by the Federals.[21]

There still was blood to be spilled this day. About 11 a.m., Heth received orders from Hill to ready Pender's division to go over the span, following Anderson's troops who "crossed without molestation." Pender's troops were "in the act of crossing when the enemy made their appearance," Hill noted. Earlier, about 10 a.m., the rearguard had been surprised by a small group of Federal cavalry, elements of Brig. Gen. Judson Kilpatrick's division leading the way. The brief battle was soon over, the enemy troopers being killed or repelled, but General Pettigrew was mortally wounded in the process.[22]

Now a larger force of Union horsemen, supported by artillery, assailed Heth's line. More Federals were coming up, as well. The rebels scrambled to fend off these bluecoats as rival skirmishers blazed away at each other. "Seeing the attack was becoming serious," Heth ordered Pender's brigades, including Perrin's, still north of the Potomac, to return and join the fight. Hill, however, wanted Heth's and Pender's divisions to withdraw "as speedily as possible and cross the river." Perrin's Carolinians, meanwhile, hustled to rejoin and reinforce Heth, but were soon retracing their tracks toward the Potomac. "As soon as I got in position and was prepared to receive the enemy's attack, I was ordered to fall back toward the bridge at Falling Waters," Perrin noted. Heth engaged in a fighting withdrawal, having his brigades pull back "simultaneously" and leapfrog their positions along the road toward the Potomac.[23]

Perrin's "brigade fell back in perfect order, and gained the road, and formed in line of battle across it," the colonel reported. His Carolinians then retreated toward the span "in rear of the whole corps." Hemphill remembered how he and his comrades held their ground with their "Springfield" rifles despite the rapid fire of the Federals "with their seven-shooters." The action cost Perrin about thirty men captured after they were sent ahead to strengthen the skirmish line. From the time the brigade left Gettysburg to its crossing at Falling Waters, Perrin lost an additional sixty soldiers, "from men breaking down, sick, barefoot, straggling." For the Gettysburg odyssey, Perrin tallied a total of 654 killed or wounded and 90 missing.[24]

The crossing by the portion of the army using the bridge was not completed until 1 p.m. on the 14th when "the bridge was removed," Lee reported. "The enemy offered no serious interruption, and the movement was attended with no loss of materiel excepting a few disabled wagons and two pieces of artillery" stuck in the deep mud, he added. Perrin's Carolinians covered the army's retreat for a second time across the Potomac, meaning at Gettysburg and Antietam. "You see our Brigade was the rear guard of the Army—so it was after the battle of Sharpsburg last summer," Perrin wrote to Gov. Bonham. Lt. James Caldwell added, "The division was marched across the pontoon. McGowan's Brigade covered, for the second time, the retreat across the Potomac!"[25]

11

Carolinians Left Behind: The Gettysburg Wounded

When Kershaw's regiments left Gettysburg, they had to leave 176 comrades behind, men too severely wounded to be moved. Of these soldiers, 70 belonged to the Second South Carolina, 36 to De Saussure's Fifteenth, 35 to Rice's battalion, 19 to Henagan's Eighth and 16 to Aiken's Seventh. Of the four infantry brigades and artillery battalion that formed McLaws's division, 576 badly injured soldiers remained under supervision by surgeon F.W. Patterson of the Seventeenth Mississippi in Barksdale's command.[1]

At least one of Maffett's men unfit to travel was Sgt. William Hood of the Third's Company E, who suffered a serious wound to his left knee. Hood, 30, was from Chester County, South Carolina, an Erskine College graduate and a principal and teacher in Newberry, South Carolina, before the war. He fought through virtually every major battle unharmed until reaching the Peach Orchard and Wheatfield, where he fell on July 2. Despite the torturous pain and lying on the field as bullets and shells screeched by, Hood likely thought of his wife, Martha, and their children back home in Newberry. He was eventually removed to a field hospital.[2]

Kershaw's total casualties at Gettysburg were 630, including 115 killed, 483 wounded and 32 missing. The Second South Carolina was hit hardest, with 27 dead, 125 wounded and two missing for a total of 154 casualties, followed by the Fifteenth South Carolina with 21 slain (its Col. De Saussure among them), 98 wounded and 18 missing, a total of 137. Aiken's Seventh counted losses of 110 including 18 killed, 85 wounded and seven missing, while Henagan's Eighth lost 100 men, 21 dead and 79 wounded. The Third South Carolina Regiment had 18 slain, 63 wounded and two missing, for a total of 83, while Rice's Third Battalion lost 10 killed, 33 wounded and three missing—46 total.[3]

Each of McLaws's brigades detailed medical personnel, including surgeons and nurses, along with cooks, to stay with the men who could not be moved, all under the supervision of Dr. Patterson. Kershaw's contingent included surgeon J.F. Pearce of the Eighth South Carolina, assistant surgeon H.J. Nott of the Second and assistant surgeon Simon Baruch of the Third S.C. Battalion, along with a total of 25 nurses and cooks.[4]

One of many Carolinians unable to travel was 19-year-old Charles O. Wheeler of Kennedy's regiment, recovering from a thigh wound sustained on the 2nd. Wheeler was transferred from a field hospital to Kershaw's brigade hospital at the Black Horse Tavern on the Fairfield Road, about two miles southwest of Gettysburg. He watched as assistant surgeons Baruch, Nott and others attended to the many injured soldiers, some of whom were put into the wagons and ambulances on July 4. Baruch himself had labored nearly nonstop for 36 hours, as a seemingly endless line of bloodied and maimed men— gray and blue—were laid before him. Near sunset on the 4th, he collapsed into a hay pile, quickly lapsing into an exhausted sleep. Waking the next morning, Baruch was told that he, Pearce and Nott were to stay with the immobile wounded. One of these was Color Sgt. Elisha Adams of the Eighth South Carolina, the flag bearer still clinging to life despite his July 2 wounds.[5]

The three doctors' most immediate need, however, was a long-overdue meal, and the hospital cook prepared what was available. The main course was a peacock that had ventured too close to the tavern, along with some stale biscuits, coffee and sugar found in the kitchen. The famished physicians were just sitting down to eat in one of the orchards north and west of the tavern when a Union artillery round exploded in a nearby field, followed by more shells. Wheeler noted that at least one projectile smashed into a barn being used by the surgeons. The rebels had neglected to hoist a yellow hospital flag, which would have been generally honored by both sides. The "flag" was soon flying, after Baruch and his colleagues scurried to the top of the barn and attached a piece of yellow cloth to the lightning rod. Six or so rounds fell in the tavern's vicinity before the artillery fire stopped and the three doctors returned to their breakfast. Shortly afterward, the Confederates saw a small force of Union cavalry approaching. Baruch went out to meet them and surrender on behalf of the medical personnel and the wounded. After a brief conversation with a Federal captain about the presence of other rebels in the area, the horsemen clattered away. About an hour later the cavalry returned, this time accompanied by a large contingent of Yankee infantry, elements of the U.S. Sixth Corps, Baruch related. The Carolinian soon approached a Union adjutant general and complained of the shelling of the hospital. The officer was courteous and replied that the Federals had not seen the yellow flag until after they began bombarding a hill where they suspected Confederates were sheltered on the opposite ridge.[6]

Pvt. W.H.H. Bevil of the Fifteenth South Carolina also recalled the visit of the Union cavalry captain, along with the Federal infantry and artillery passing nearby. Bevil had been slightly wounded and on July 4 had set out from the hospital to see some of his buddies in the Fifteenth's Company H. After his visit, he returned to the Black Horse, realizing it might be some time before he saw his comrades again. After the army's overnight retreat, Bevil decided to strike out on his own for Virginia, but a physician he identified only as "Dr. James" ordered him to stay with the wounded and assist Baruch, Pearce and Nott. Bevil recalled that he and another soldier "nurse," Pvt. William Addis, also of the Fifteenth's Company H, soon found themselves on a regular but grim detail. Bevil wrote, "When any one of our fellows would die, he [Addis] and I would bury him … and I would mark their name on a plank or board with a pencil and…. Addis would cut it out with his pocket knife."[7]

Almost immediately the dearth of rations and medical supplies became an issue for these Carolinians left behind as well as for the thousands of other wounded from both armies who were suffering in houses, barns, churches and other buildings all over the Gettysburg area. Some of Kershaw's men were able to augment their meager fare with a quantity of apple butter discovered on the premises, the wounded C.O. Wheeler remembered. Wheeler would spend about three weeks healing at the tavern before being shipped north in Union custody. Another of Kershaw's troops unable to travel was Pvt. E.J. Lake of the Third South Carolina, badly wounded on July 2 and taken to a field hospital, in all likelihood the tavern. When the army retreated, "a detail of surgeons and men were left to care for us," he recalled.

Trying to alleviate the food and medical shortages, Simon Baruch encountered a kindly Federal officer who suggested that he go to the depot of an organization called the Christian Commission set up in town to distribute supplies to the various makeshift hospitals. Baruch did so, getting several bags of provisions. He also made a stop at a U.S. Sanitary Commission warehouse brimming with food including lemons, eggs, butter and even ice. Baruch also was able to fill some of his medical needs through the Federal military authorities.[8]

The humanitarian effort was also boosted by civilian physicians from Baltimore and other locales as well as ladies from Baltimore—many Southern sympathizers—who came to aid the injured. Baruch befriended a "Dr. F." who greatly helped in caring for the soldiers and who presented the Carolinian with a fine set of surgical instruments. He also noted the care, compassion and hard work of two ladies from the Howard family of Baltimore, along with their English nurse. Pvt. Lake also praised the care he received from some of the Baltimore ladies as well as the Union medical personnel. Like many other Confederate wounded, Lake was eventually transferred to a prison hospital compound on Davids' Island in Long Island Sound near New York City. Despite gangrene setting in, his health improved there, and he was eventually exchanged.[9]

Trooper Peter Malone of the First South Carolina Cavalry's color guard and other wounded from the July 3 cavalry combat were told of the army's retreat on the 4th, "and that, as we could not be removed, our capture was certain." Surgeon Joseph Yates of the First South Carolina Cavalry remained behind with the Confederate wounded, all of whom were soon in Union hands. Malone and others were promptly transferred from the field hospital to a Union medical facility in Gettysburg. Malone recalled, "Our treatment, though kind, was rendered repugnant by the flippancy of some of the United States surgeons." In one instance, Malone noted how a Union doctor passed the area where he and a comrade, Cpl. H.J. Culler, were lying. The doctor remarked "that we 'must die in any event,'" Malone remembered. Culler was "shot in the body and, though expecting this announcement, his spirits sank and he groaned heavily when he heard it," Malone recalled. "In three days he was a corpse."[10]

The amputee Lt. J.R. Boyles of the Twelfth South Carolina was one of Perrin's wounded; he had been captured on July 5 or July 6 in a field hospital. A group of Union cavalrymen entered the camp with sabers drawn, one proclaiming that the Confederates were prisoners in the name of the United States. It would be some time before they saw any Federals again, and the wounded lay "nearly naked and starved," Boyles recalled. Someone gathered blankets from the battlefield for Boyles and his comrades, but the covers were so lice infested that the blankets seemed to almost move on their own, he wrote. Shortly after they were taken prisoner, two wounded soldiers whom Boyles knew, Pvt. Wylie P. Wyrick of the Twelfth's Company C and a man he identified as R.K. Moses, died of their injuries. To pass the time and keep up their morale, the survivors sang hymns and "all who were able joined in," the lieutenant recalled, and "the little camp resounded with strains of sacred music, [and] praise to the great Creator." One of the medical personnel remaining behind to attend to Perrin's fallen was Thomas McCoy, a 31-year-old doctor from Laurens County, South Carolina. McCoy was in charge of the First South Carolina's sick and wounded, but his Gettysburg story would last for months after the battle.[11]

The Yankees began moving some Confederate wounded, including Boyles, into

Gettysburg early on July 17. Boyles was put in an ambulance which trundled out over a rough road toward town. The Carolinian noted, however, that the Yank at the reins was careful not to jostle him on the ride and wrote, "If I suffered, it was not the fault of the driver, for he used the utmost care to keep me from jolting; good, kind-hearted soul, I hope the Lord blessed him for it." In town Boyles and others were transferred to box-cars bound for Elmira, Fort Delaware, Camp Chase and other Union prisoner-of-war compounds. Before Boyles's train chuffed away, members of Baltimore's Sisters of Mercy moved along the line, distributing "milk punch" and other refreshments to the apprecia-tive Southerners. Earlier, Boyles had learned that the Confederate surgeon who ampu-tated his right leg was drunk when he performed the operation, leaving him with an "imperfect stump." As the train trundled away from Cemetery Ridge, Devil's Den and other instantly famous sites around the town, Boyles must have wondered about his fate and whether he could survive imprisonment with only one leg.[12]

His injured ankle healing, Pvt. John Bagwell of the Fourteenth South Carolina was also among rebel wounded transferred into town on July 18. There "we spent two weeks, burying our dead," he recalled. His wounded comrades Lt. N. Austin, also of the Four-teenth, and Sgt. John Pool of the First South Carolina were sent to one or more hospitals in Chester, Pennsylvania. Both died there as a result of their injuries.[13]

One of the more touching stories of the wounded Carolinians still at Gettysburg involved Lt. Henry J. Rauch of the Fourteenth's Company B and an unidentified brother, also wounded. Georgeanna Woolsey recounted the episode after she and her mother traveled from Baltimore to volunteer at the U.S. Sanitary Commission's Relief Lodge on the battlefield. Woolsey labored there for some three weeks, helping treat hundreds of soldiers from both sides. Among them was Rauch, in a group of more than one hundred injured rebels who arrived at the facility one afternoon. Rauch had been shot through both thighs and was lying on a blanket spread over some straw after being brought in. Woolsey was immediately taken by the handsome Southerner, later describing him as "a fair-haired, blue-eyed young lieutenant" with "a face innocent enough for one of our own New England boys. I could not think of him as a rebel, he was too near heaven for that," she noted of his serious injuries. Rauch had not eaten for days and even refused nourish-ment, but Woolsey coaxed him to try some "milk gruel" mixed with lemon and brandy, for which he thanked her profusely. "Poor creature, he had had no care, and it was a sur-prise and pleasure to find himself thought of," she wrote. Despite his decline, Rauch sang hymns "in a clear, sweet voice," and Woolsey learned from another Confederate that the lieutenant's father was a Lutheran minister back home. "Lord have mercy upon me!" he sang.[14]

Rauch survived into the next day, singing and refighting battles in his delirium. At some point a rebel prisoner poked his head into the tent, looking over its occupants, and recognized Rauch, lying nearby. "Henry! Henry!" the prisoner called, but Rauch didn't respond. The soldier explained that the officer's brother was also wounded and was on a nearby train about to leave Gettysburg. Attendants allowed two or three men to carry the brother into the tent, where he "threw himself down by his [Rauch's] side on the straw" although Rauch did not recognize him, Woolsey wrote. The brother "for the rest of the day lay in a sort of apathy, without speaking, except to assure himself that he could stay with" his dying sibling. "In a strong clear voice" Rauch kept singing "Lord have mercy upon me" before there was silence. "The Lord *had* mercy, and at sunset I put my hand on the lieutenant's heart, to find it still," Woolsey noted. "All night the brother lay close against the coffin." By morning the brother prepared to head north with other prisoners. He graciously thanked Woolsey and others for their kindness and care, offering them a palmetto tree ornament from the lieutenant's cap and a button from his uniform. Henry Rauch, meanwhile, was buried that morning with his name and regiment etched on a small headboard. Weeks later and hundreds of miles away on August 5, readers of the *Edgefield* (S.C.) *Advertiser* noted a list of casualties in the Fourteenth South Carolina's Company B which were contained in a letter home from Jesse Black, a soldier in the company. Lt. Rauch was listed as being wounded in "both thighs" while another Carolinian, S.N. Rauch, had a severe gunshot in a leg. The latter apparently was the lieutenant's brother.[15]

Another pair of Carolina brothers in the Fourteenth were fated to similar circumstances. Lt. Sidney Carter of Company A succumbed to his July 1 injuries about a week later. Pvt. Giles Carter, also a prisoner, was eventually transferred to the Union hospital facility at Davids' Island, where he was treated for his leg wound. Giles was released in September during a prisoner exchange. Wounded in both legs, Pvt. James Harvey of the Twelfth South Carolina remained in a Gettysburg hospital, beset by a fever that "clung to him for months." During this time he was attended by a young woman he later identified as Miss Ella McClelland, a cousin of the Union Maj. Gen. George McClellan. She "tried in vain to procure a permit for his removal to her own residence" and was "assiduous in her attentions to the wounded boy as long as he was" in Gettysburg. Harvey was eventually sent to Davids' Island.[16]

The Rev. R. Fuller of Baltimore came to Gettysburg sometime in the week or so after the battle and gave a grim description of what he found. "From the condition of many lying dead on the fields and in the woods, it is plain that hundreds of lives might have been saved if they could have received immediate attention," he wrote in a letter published in the Baltimore *American*. "And now, in the field hospitals, some are dying and more must die unless speedily supplied." In these facilities "a large number still lie, not only in the open air, (which is better really than a house in this hot weather,) but in the mud and water. In one field hospital a soldier literally lay in the water with no clothes at all. He had received no attention for three days, except from God, to whom he turned in this hour of anguish, for he was reading a Testament." The Lutheran seminary was being used primarily as a Confederate hospital, Fuller related. "Dr. Frazer, of South Carolina, well known to me as a noble specimen of a medical gentleman, remained with the wounded and has charge."[17]

An unidentified soldier from Kershaw's brigade was a prisoner and assisted in the burial of three wounded Carolinians from the Second South Carolina who died a few days after the fighting. "It was [a] sad privilege of mine to share in the burial," he remembered. "We buried them in one grave, wrapped in their blankets." Other "sad sights" from the hospitals still gripped his memories more than four decades after the battle: "One poor fellow who had his lower jaw torn from its socket, did not live long. Another with a leg amputated, arteries broke in some way, and could not be taken up. Poor young soldier, he bled his life away."[18]

Within days of the battle, the first curiosity seekers—actually the first tourists of the millions who would visit this suddenly sacred ground—began arriving. Among them was Lt. John B. Linn of the 51st Pennsylvania, wounded in March and recuperating at Lewisburg, Pennsylvania. He came to Gettysburg on July 7 and began visiting the various battle sites. He and some companions continued their tour the next day, looking for the Union

First Corps hospital off the Emmitsburg Road. "We soon came to marks of a fearful contest," he wrote, "hats with holes in them, rebel canteens, overcoats and torn clothing, dead horses, broken gun cartridges, letters, torn knapsacks and haversacks strewed the road." Soon they came upon the Rose farm, whose main structures, the family's house and large stone barn, had been the epicenter of Kershaw's attack on July 2. Days later the once bucolic farmland had been savaged by combat, the soil barely cloaking the corpses of scores of South Carolinians and others. North of the barn, Linn and the others happened upon a hastily filled mass grave of Palmettos from the brigades of Perrin and Kershaw. Linn counted thirty-three graves of soldiers from Miller's Twelfth South Carolina in Perrin's command. "They were only slightly covered with earth and you could feel the body by pressing the earth with your foot." The lieutenant also took notice of the resting place of one of Kershaw's men, a corporal in the Eighth South Carolina: "One man's left hand stuck out of the grave looking like an old parched well worn buck-skin glove." Under a pear tree across a lane and on the other side of the barn was the grave of Capt. T.J. Warren of the Fifteenth South Carolina in Kershaw's brigade. Rose also told Linn that ten "superior officers, colonels, majors, etc.," had been buried in his garden but that he had removed them that morning for fear that the bodies would contaminate his well. He had taken the corpses to a ravine about a half-mile east of his farm, where he left them with their headboards beside them, "not having the strength or means to bury them," Linn wrote. That night, Linn and some of his fellow travelers stayed for a second night at the home of the Rev. T.P. Bucher, a Gettysburg minister who was assisting with the wounded. Bucher told them of baptizing a South Carolina cavalryman in a hospital earlier that day. The trooper, John Cullen from Columbia, South Carolina, had "so earnestly requested it, so after reading over the Creed to which he gave solemn assent," he baptized him. Cullen died shortly afterward.[19]

If Linn's account is accurate regarding the graves of the Twelfth South Carolina soldiers in Perrin's brigade, these men had to have been brought to the Rose farm sometime after the July 2 fighting to rest with their slain brothers in arms in Kershaw's brigade. There was no doubt, however, that the Rose property had become a makeshift Confederate cemetery, mainly for Kershaw's dead, although a number of Semmes's Georgians also shared the acreage. Returning to their home shortly after the combat, members of the Rose family were shocked by the odors and sights of the macabre carnage as well as the battle damage to the property. "A much disgusted man was Rose when he returned," noted J. Howard Wert, who visited the farm at the time. "His stock was gone, his furniture was gone. His house was filled with vermin, his supply of drinking water polluted with dead bodies; nothing left of his farm but the rocks and some of the soil. Nearly 100 Confederates were buried in his garden, some 175 behind the barn and around the wagon shed; the half of a body sent asunder by spherical case shot was in his spring whence came the drinking water. Graves were everywhere, one Confederate Colonel being buried within a yard of the kitchen door." Some historians have called the Rose place "the bloodiest farm in America," according to a modern-day guidebook. The 230-acre property is indeed enriched by the blood of a great many Palmetto State soldiers.[20]

In preparing an 1886 tour book about the Gettysburg monuments, Wert gave another account of his post-battle walks over the land where 6,000 to 7,000 soldiers—blue and gray—and including so many South Carolinians, were casualties. "The vivid impression of the horrible sights there beheld can never be effaced from the memory," he wrote.

"Death in its ghastliest and most abhorrent forms, everywhere. Festering corpses at every step; some still unburied…. All the fields and woods from the Emmitsburg road to the base of Round Top were one vast, hideous charnel house. The dead were everywhere. In some cases nothing but a few mutilated fragments and pieces of flesh were left of what had been so late a human being following his flag to death or victory were buried." Wert also continued his descriptions of the dozens of "scantily buried followers of the Confederate cause" hastily interred all about the Rose farm. "No pen can paint the awful picture of desolation, devastation and death." Other than the human carnage, this part of the Gettysburg field, like all the others from Culp's Hill to Big Round Top, was adorned by the macabre and massive litter of war, Wert describing it as "broken muskets and soiled bayonets, shattered caissons and blood defiled clothing, trodden cartridge-boxes and splintered swords, rifled knapsacks and battered canteens."[21]

South of the Potomac, many Confederates began to reflect on the historic campaign and what the future held for their struggle. Augustus Dickert opined that the army did not blame Lee for what happened at Gettysburg, even amid this ignoble retreat: "It was with a mingled feeling of delight and relief that the soldiers reached the Virginia side of the river—but not a murmur or harsh word for our beloved commander—all felt that he had done what was best for our country, and it was more in sorrow and sympathy that we beheld his bowed head and grief-stricken face as he rode at times past the moving troops." Kershaw's command continued its march the next day to Bunker Hill, Virginia, where the men would rest until July 18.[22]

Another of Kershaw's more fortunate soldiers, Tally Simpson of the Third South Carolina, wrote to his cousin, Caroline Virginia Miller, on the 18th about the events that had befallen the army during the past few weeks:

> Ere this reaches its destination you will have heard of the terrible battle of Gettysburg and the fate of a portion of our noble Army…. I am … extremely hopeful. But I must confess that this is a gloomy period for the Confederacy. One month ago our prospects were as bright as could well be conceived. Gallant Vicksburg, the Gibraltar of the West and the pride of the South, has fallen…. Port Hudson has surrendered…. A few weeks ago Genl Lee had the finest Army that ever was raised in ancient or modern times—and commanded by as patriotic and heroic officers as ever drew a sword in defence of liberty. But in an unfortunate hour and under disadvantageous circumstances, he attacked the enemy, and tho' he gained the advantage and held possession of the battlefield and even destroyed more of the foe than he lost himself, still the Army … lost heavily and is now in a poor condition for offensive operations.

Simpson went on to note that about one third of the army was barefooted or "almost destitute of necessary clothing." The war news from other fronts also was wearing on the soldiers. "Charleston is closely beset, and I think must surely fall sooner or later," he wrote. "The fall of Vicksburg has caused me to lose confidence in something or somebody, I can't say exactly which. And now that the gunboats from the Mississippi can be transferred to Charleston and that a portion of Morris Island has been taken and can be used to advantage by the enemy, I fear greatly the result of the attack." If Charleston fell, followed by Savannah, Mobile and Richmond, it "is certainly calculated to cast a gloom over our entire land. But we profess to be a Christian people, and we should put our trust in God. He holds the destiny of our nation, as it were, in the palm of his hand."[23]

Still in the same wagon after crossing the river, the wounded generals Hampton and Hood "journeyed together in this manner" to Staunton, Virginia, a distance of about 200 miles. From there, the generals and some of the other wounded were taken by train to military hospitals in Charlottesville. Hampton, by now, was conscious and alert, but still in a great deal of pain.[24]

Lt. William Zimmerman's Pee Dee Artillery and the rest of Pegram's Battalion in A.P. Hill's reserve artillery clattered through the Virginia countryside, no doubt relieved to be back in Southern territory. Their relief was short-lived. Reaching Gaines's Crossroads, the battalion received orders to move on a dirt road toward Culpeper Court House, in line behind Heth's infantry division. After covering several miles, the battalion's Capt. E.B. Brunson noted the presence of Union cavalry, supported by artillery, "posted to harass our advance." Zimmerman's men were rushed into position to quell this threat, unlimbering and tangling with the enemy cannoneers. The Carolinians "soon succeeded in silencing the Yankee battery" of four guns, Brunson related, two guns from the Purcell Artillery of Virginia punishing the enemy cavalry. Three of Zimmerman's gunners were wounded, and the lieutenant himself was knocked down by a shell fragment but escaped serious injury. Later reports about the Gettysburg campaign showed that Pegram's gunners expended 3,800 rounds of ammunition, with casualties of two officers and three men killed, 11 officers and 26 men wounded, and one officer missing. The battalion lost 89 horses killed in action, 11 captured and 50 abandoned. One gun was lost, and another disabled, along with five caissons lost or disabled. Specific numbers for the Pee Dee Artillery are not known.[25]

"You will see by this letter that we have gotten back into 'Old Virginia,'" surgeon Spencer Welch of the Thirteenth South Carolina penned to his wife, Cordelia, on July 17 near Bunker Hill, Virginia. "It seems that our invasion of the North did not prove successful. We fought a dreadful battle at Gettysburg, Pa. It was the greatest battle of the war." Welch then told her about some of the young soldiers who would never see their loved ones again. "Milton Bossard, Captain Cromer, Buford Wallace, Mr. Daniel's two sons [James and William, both of Kershaw's brigade and mentioned earlier] and many others from Newberry were killed, but it is better for us all to be killed than conquered." Kershaw's troops resumed their march on the 18th, passing through Millwood, Front Royal, Chester Gap and Gaines's Crossroads, reaching their destination, Culpeper Court House, about 10 a.m. on July 24.[26]

Lt. Col. Franklin Gaillard of the Second South Carolina also was at Culpeper by then and ready to finish a letter he had begun to his sister-in-law, Maria, during the retreat. Putting thoughts to pen on July 27, he reflected on Gettysburg's outcome and what it meant for the army as well as the Confederacy: "The battle was an unfortunate one. Our army went into it in magnificent style and I never saw it fight better, but the position defeated us. For this I blame our Generals. In a day by our injudicious attack they defeated the most brilliant prospects we have ever had. It was caused by their overconfidence. The greatest misfortune is that it destroyed the unbounded confidence reposed in Gen. Lee. Before, the army believed he could not err. They now see that he can, once in a while. Viewed in a political aspect, it was a disaster to us, in my judgment." Gaillard added that the battle "was, I think, the most sanguinary of the war and was as clear a defeat as our army ever met with. Our Brigade suffered very severely."[27]

In a Charlottesville hospital, Wade Hampton was feeling well enough to pen a letter to his sister, Mary Fisher Hampton, on July 16. The general complained about not receiving any letters from home but wrote that he was "steadily improving" and hoped to be "well enough to start home" within a few days. "If I stay here much longer my wound will get well and then there will be no excuse for me to go home," he wrote. "My head is well externally but very tender inside; perhaps it is only weak." He also joked about his unbecoming haircut due to his wounds: "The penitentiary style in which my hair is cut, half the head being shaven, is striking, if not beautiful. It suits all kinds of weather, as one side of my head is sure to be just right, whether for cool or for hot weather. But the flies play the mischief, as they wander over the bald side. When I get home I will shave my whole head to be uniform at least." Hampton again showed his wit in telling Mary about how he was wounded: "Don't you feel mortified that any Yankee should be able on horse back, to split my head open? It shows how old I am growing, and how worthless." The Carolinian turned serious near the end of the letter, writing of his worries about his oldest son, Wade Hampton IV, who was on army duty in Richmond. "My heart is full of anxiety about Wade," he penned. "May God in mercy spare him. God bless you all," he closed. A few days later Hampton was moved to Richmond. "General Wade Hampton reached this city last evening," the *Richmond Examiner* said. "He is wounded by a bullet and sabre cut, though not dangerously." Hampton earlier had written to his friend Senator Louis T. Wigfall about his injuries: "I have been handled pretty badly, having received two sabre cuts on the head—one of which cut through to the tables of my skull—and a shrapnel shot in my body, which is there yet. But I am doing well & in a few days I hope to be able to go home."[28]

A number of other sick or wounded Carolinians were among Confederates being treated at Winchester, some in private homes. Col. John L. Black of the First South Carolina Cavalry was one of them, still recovering from his head wound, the campaign's rigors and a touch of typhoid fever. Feeling stronger after a week or so of rest and treatment, Black tried to determine if any troopers from his regiment were recuperating in the vicinity. He soon learned that Pvt. Wash Wilkes, of the First's Company D, was nearby and very ill. "He was very corpulent, but a good soldier & I had a great fancy for Wilkes," Black noted. "I sent and had all I could done for Wilkes ... but, poor fellow, his last day of soldier life had come and he was taking his discharge from trouble to peace." Black purchased a burial plot in a cemetery and watched from a window the next day as some of Winchester's ladies helped lay Wilkes to rest. The cavalryman also learned that a friend, Capt. William Z. "Zack" Leitner, a company commander in Kershaw's Second South Carolina, was also in dire straits. Leitner, from Camden, South Carolina, was seriously wounded on July 2 and was rescued from the battlefield by the brigade surgeon T.W. Salmond. Now he lay in a Winchester family's home, one of his legs having been amputated. Black did all he could for Leitner, but the captain's chances of survival appeared slim. "He was one of the cases of bad wounds that ought, by all rules, to have been left behind."[29]

Well enough to leave Winchester, Black soon traveled south with an army column for about two days when he was approached by Arno Niles, another soldier from Camden. Based on Black's account, Niles told him that the wounded Col. John D. Kennedy of Kershaw's Second South Carolina had been "abandoned on the wayside." Black went to investigate and found Kennedy lying "on the ground by a broken down vehicle and badly wounded he was. I told him I would see him out." Black related that Jeb Stuart's "private property" ambulance with two horses was somewhere in the rear of the column. He "waited for it to come up and pressed it into service & had Kennedy put into it."[30]

"My wound is healing rapidly," an unidentified South Carolina officer wrote home from "Midway" hospital, somewhere in Virginia. "One of the muscles was severed, which annoys me at times." He complimented his surgeon, "Dr. McIntosh," for his fine work and noted the facility's collection of "choice books" to help "relieve the tedium of hospital life.

There is a large supply of ice in this place. I wish part of it was in Charleston; the wounded and sick require it, as the water is very warm in summer at home."[31]

From "Camp near Winchester" on July 19, assistant surgeon Willis Keith of the Twelfth South Carolina composed yet another letter to his mother and was nervous about not hearing from her since almost a month earlier: "I am quite uneasy…. Did you get my letters from Pennsylvania and Maryland…. Our reverse in Pennsylvania and then the far greater blow, the loss of Vicksburg and Port Hudson look gloomy for the Confederacy." In the same letter under the date July 20, Keith continued: "The only pair of pants that I have, I captured on the battlefield. My own were … so I stripped them off, and [put] these on. I have one of the flannel shirts I brought with me and one striped cotton shirt that I captured, and change from one to the other. So you see my wardrobe is small." Keith at one point also seemed to be suffering from the campaign's hardships: "I am quite weak, and we are very quiet," he scrawled. "I wish that we would commence a move for the other side of the mountain."[32]

In one of the Confederate camps, Pvt. J.A. Walker of the Forty-fifth Georgia began to write a very personal letter to a South Carolina woman he had never met. Leading a burial detail on July 1, Walker found a piece of pink paper with the woman's name and address on it among torn-up letters and a destroyed daguerreotype near the corpse of one of Perrin's soldiers. He kept the pink paper until his return to Virginia when he "wrote the young woman, inclosing the slip of paper and describing the body." Walker added: "She replied in due time, giving me the sad information of her betrothal to the young man. It was her photograph he had destroyed."[33]

More than a month after the sanguine drama in the hills and valleys around Gettysburg, the valor and deeds of many of his officers remained with Abner Perrin as he compiled his after-action report. The wounded Maj. Edward Croft of the Fourteenth South Carolina, Maj. Isaac F. Hunt of the Thirteenth, and Maj. E.F. Bookter of the Twelfth, "proved themselves fully worthy of their positions throughout the engagements around Gettysburg," Perrin noted on August 13. "I remarked particularly the cool and gallant bearing of Major Bookter, and the force and judgment with which he managed the men under his control." Perrin continued in his compliments, praising captains W.P. Shooter, T.P. Alston and A.P. Butler of the First South Carolina, captains James Boatwright and E. Cowen of the Fourteenth and Capt. T. Frank Clyburn of the Twelfth for being "distinguished for uncommonly good conduct in the action, as I can testify from my personal observation." Clyburn, it will be remembered, led two companies of the Twelfth in a foray along the picket lines on July 2. Perrin did not mention Capt. John Dewberry of the Thirteenth South Carolina and at the time may not have known the captain's whereabouts or fate. Recuperating from his amputated arm, Dewberry spent seventeen days in a Union hospital at Gettysburg before being transferred to a medical facility in Chester, Pennsylvania. He stayed there until September, when he was well enough to be sent to the Union POW compound at Johnson's Island, Ohio.[34]

Perrin remained frustrated about the Confederates' missed chances and mistakes at Gettysburg, most notably the days leading up to the battle and the events of July 1. As mentioned earlier, he was critical of fellow Carolinian R.H. Anderson's perceived failure to reach the field with his division on the 1st, but there was a bigger picture for Perrin: just as Lee had experienced at Antietam the previous September, the Confederates again had their forces scattered before facing a concentration of the enemy. Against the elements of two Union corps present at Gettysburg on July 1, Perrin wrote, "We soon eat these up," if Lee's entire army had been in the nearby vicinity. "Had our force been where it could have united rapidly the 20,000 Yankees that were there in the morning would have been devoured in twenty minutes," he wrote to Gov. Bonham. "The balance would have been an easy task." Yet "the gravest mistake of all … was the absence of our Cavalry after we crossed the Potomac," Perrin noted. Instead of reconnoitering ahead of the army, Jeb Stuart's horsemen were "off on one of these fruitless raids … which resulted in the capture of a few hundred wagons." Without Stuart, Lee blundered into an unexpected clash at Gettysburg: "Hence you see he [Lee] was ignorant of the approach and presence of Meade's Army. His cavalry was miles away, and of course he was deprived of the only means he had of getting a knowledge of the enemies movements in an enemies country. He was thus also deprived of their services on the battle field which would have been of incalculable advantage."[35]

Still, Perrin was extremely proud of his brigade, telling Bonham that it "never fought as well" as it did on July 1. "It has always done its duty true enough, but in this instance it showed more dash and fought more desperately and more effectually than ever before. It now stands second to no Brigade in this Army. I am proud to say as far as I can learn that South Carolina troops generally in this Army stand at the very top of the list." Perrin also lamented his heavy casualties. "It is painful to think of the many brave men we have lost in the campaign," he wrote. "Some of the Regts lost three or four color bearers one after another. The 14th my own Regt out of 28 officers who went into the fight all were killed or wounded but seven. 225 men received surgical treatment out of about 325 who were engaged in the fight. But this is no worse than the loss in many other Regiments."[36]

Perrin's casualties for the campaign totaled 577, including 100 dead and 477 wounded. By far, the Fourteenth South Carolina was hardest hit, with 27 killed and 182 wounded (209); followed by the Twelfth with 20 slain and 112 wounded (132). With 31 dead, the Thirteenth South Carolina had the most fatalities, along with 99 wounded (130); followed by the First South Carolina (Provisional Army) with 20 slain and 75 wounded (95). The First S.C. Rifles, which had served primarily as guard for the wagon train, had two killed, nine wounded (11).[37]

There were still some other wounded Confederates in Gettysburg that month, including Sgt. James T. Wells of Company A, Second South Carolina, who was severely wounded in Kershaw's assault. Captured shortly afterward, he remained in a field hospital there until mid–September, when he was transferred to a Baltimore hospital. There Wells received everything he needed thanks to "the kind and noble ladies of Baltimore," he recalled. Later he was sent to Fort McHenry, serving as a temporary prison, and then transferred to the notorious POW compound at Point Lookout, Maryland, where he suffered many cruelties, he said.[38]

Among the Carolinians captured at Falling Waters was Pvt. Robert Hemphill, who had fought barefooted along with his eighteen comrades in Company G of the First South Carolina Rifles. These soldiers battled to the last until outflanked and overwhelmed by enemy artillery, dismounted cavalry and infantry. Their effort aided the last units of Lee's army to cross the Potomac in safety. Four of the Confederates were wounded, but as Hemphill and the other prisoners were marched to the rear, Union soldiers shared their rations with them. Hemphill recalled details of the Gettysburg campaign in a small diary he hid in his clothing.[39]

The approximate loss of Lee's army at Gettysburg was 2,592 killed, 12,709 wounded and 5,150 captured or missing—a total of 20,451. The statistics are based on reports of brigade commanders and/or subordinate commanders, and the reports indicated that many of the "missing" were killed or wounded. Meade's medical director reported 6,802 wounded Confederates as prisoners. South Carolina had a combat strength of 4,930 at Gettysburg with losses of 1,310, a casualty rate of 27 percent.[40]

12

The Grieving Home Front

Within days of the battle, word began to filter south of the epic struggle in Pennsylvania and the outcome. Like those of almost every other state in the Confederacy, families and friends across South Carolina anxiously awaited word as to the fate of those loved ones who fought at this faraway place called Gettysburg.

Like they had since the war flared, residents of Chester and Yorkville—probably along with others in the state—got some semblance of war news from the whistle blasts of the daily train running between the towns. Short, rapid shrills meant good tidings, possibly a Confederate victory. Long, mournful blasts signaled grim tidings, like a defeat or lengthy casualty lists to come.[1]

The dispatches from correspondents with the army were the first reports of what had happened, although the initial claims were grossly inaccurate in this case. "Glorious News" was a headline in the *Abbeville Press* on July 10: "Last Wednesday brought the cheering intelligence of a great victory by Confederate arms in Pennsylvania," the article began, adding that New Orleans also had been recaptured. The *Charleston Courier* on July 8 featured page 1 headlines "Confederates Victorious," "General Lee's Victory," and "Thrilling And Glorious News."[2]

In the coming days, however, came word that the Confederates had withdrawn, although the army's whereabouts and Lee's intent were still unknown. Then came the letters home from soldiers writing to assure their families that they were safe and to share their views of the events, or what had happened to comrades or relatives in the ranks. There also were letters from soldiers who had survived the battle but were writing to another man's family with the shattering news that he had been killed or seriously wounded. All of this was true of every state in the Union or Confederacy, and every Yankee or rebel. "There will be published in the papers a list of casualties," Lt. Col. Franklin Gaillard of Kershaw's Second South Carolina wrote to a relative on July 27. "I took a great deal of care in the preparation."[3]

On July 22, the weekly *Edgefield (S.C.) Advertiser* ran the first of several letters from local boys in the army who gave the names of casualties, primarily from the Seventh South Carolina in Kershaw's brigade and the Fourteenth South Carolina in Perrin's command. More letters and casualties were printed in the *Advertiser* on the 29th. The *Yorkville Enquirer* on the 22nd published a piece headlined "From the 12th Regiment" with a list of killed and wounded of "three York companies"—A, B and H—in Col. John L. Miller's Twelfth South Carolina in Perrin's brigade. At Miller's request, a soldier named William J. Kimbell submitted the list from Winchester, Virginia, on July 12 "for the anxiety of our friends at home." A particularly graphic extract was from a letter written by Lt. E.H. Covar of the Seventh's Company A to his wife, Sarah. The letter regarded casualties from the Edgefield companies of the Seventh and Fourteenth regiments. "N.L. Bartley was one who fell to rise no more," Covar wrote. "Sergt. Charles I. Durisoe was wounded through the right knee, and I saw his leg cut off about four inches above the knee. I also saw Corp'l James Youngblood's right arm cut off just below the elbow. Lieut. Harvey Crooker was wounded in the left breast, and died on the morning of [the] 3rd. Sergt. [Buford] Wallace was also severely wounded, and died the same day.... Milledge Bartley was severely wounded through the mouth and neck." Covar's weary despair was apparent as he continued: "I hav'ent [sp] time to give all the names, in fact I do not know all the casualties. But you may rest assured the loss of the 14th was very heavy." The lieutenant then focused on the Edgefield soldiers of the Seventh South Carolina who had been killed or wounded in Kershaw's combat on July 2. "When both parties evacuated the field, our whole Brigade ... was found to have suffered severely—especially the old 7th," he penned. Lt. A.W. Burt was wounded in three places, including the ankle, which caused his leg to be amputated. Lt. P.E. Walker was mortally wounded "through the breast" and John Elsmore "had his finger shot off." In Company E, lieutenants J.M. Daniel and W.A. Rutland were both slain, as was Lt. J.F. Hodges of Company B. A separate note in the July 22 *Advertiser* mentioned that Durisoe was "in hands of enemy, doing well at last accounts," while Burt, Youngblood, Lt. B.F. Sharpton of Company I and others of the Seventh were also prisoners. Some other slightly wounded men of the Seventh were recuperating at Howard Grove Hospital near Richmond, "all doing well," claimed the writer, identified only as "D.R.D."[4]

In another section was a casualty report from Lt. Jiles M. Berry about the soldiers in his Company K of the Seventh. Berry submitted the information himself despite being slightly wounded in the arm and leg. Company K had fared better than others, emerging with one dead, Pvt. M.B. Gentry, and Pvt. John T. Henderson having a leg amputated below the knee. The July 24 issue of the *Abbeville Press* included a list sent by Lt. W.R. White from Winchester on July 8. White, commanding the Fourteenth's Company I, named fifteen wounded Carolinians in his dispatch. White himself was on the list, recovering and writing despite a "severe contusion, right arm, from grapeshot," the piece noted.[5]

Also on the 22nd, the *Lancaster Ledger* published a list of casualties in Companies I and E of Perrin's Twelfth South Carolina. Company I was composed primarily of men from the "Lancaster Hornets," while Company E had soldiers belonging to the "Blair Guards" before the war. A correspondent identified only as "Local" sent the dispatch from near Hagerstown on July 8. *The Ledger* on July 29 ran a casualty report for Company H in Kennedy's Second South Carolina under Kershaw.[6]

The Abbeville paper also contained a casualty list of Company H, First South Carolina; the company was so decimated that Sgt. George C. Mackey was commanding. Among the dead listed was Capt. W.T. Haskell of the sharpshooters. Another piece listed casualties from Company G, Orr's Rifles, based on the July 14 fighting as the army crossed the Potomac; these Carolinians were among the rear guard. The losses included three men "wounded and left on the field," along with seventeen soldiers who were missing. Yet another article detailed the casualties of the Seventh South Carolina's Company C—Kershaw's brigade—in the July 2 firefight. Highest ranking in the slain was Lt. Albert Thomas Traylor, according to the dispatch compiled by Cpl. John F. Lyon. In a separate account written years later, soldier T.P. Quarles of Traylor's company noted that the lieutenant was mortally wounded and "died in my arms, after intense suffering," at Cashtown, Pennsylvania, during the army's retreat.[7]

"No mail came without bringing sad news to some home, and the telegraph wires would flash the report of the deaths of hundreds and thousands of loved ones who had lost their lives for the 'Cause,'" Margaret Crawford Adams of Congaree, South Carolina, recalled of the war years, especially after a colossal battle such as Gettysburg. The July 17 issue of the *Camden Confederate* devoted almost a full column to the death of native son Capt. Thomas J. Warren, the longtime newspaperman who was among Kershaw's slain in the Fifteenth South Carolina. "We feel that we only give utterance to the universal sentiment of the community, when we express the profound grief with which we make this announcement," the *Confederate* stated.[8]

In Bluffton, South Carolina, Charles M. Furman, an officer in the Sixteenth South Carolina Volunteers was at the regiment's headquarters on July 22 when he penned a note about the Gettysburg losses to his sweetheart, Frances Emma Garden. Both had strong and emotional interests in the fighting in Pennsylvania—Miss Garden's brother, Hugh, led his battery in the battle, while Furman had been in the Second South Carolina of Kershaw's brigade earlier in the war and still had close friends in that regiment. Furman had read a copy of the *Charleston Mercury* from the previous day which identified some of Kershaw's casualties. He wrote:

> Dearest Love
>
> The sad details of the battle of Gettysburg have come in. The Mercury of yesterday contained a list of the casualties in Kershaw's Brigade. The losses are terrible, five of my former comrades are reported among the killed, viz. Lt. [William L.] Daniel, [Sgt.] LaBruce Mortimer, Thos. Gadsden, S.[C.] Miles and E. Mills—William Lawton has lost an arm, Charlie Colcock a hand, some one else a leg. There are as many more who are wounded more or less seriously. I do not know the number carried in by my company, but from my knowledge of its reduced condition I would judge that the greater part of those engaged were killed or wounded. It is probable that had I been there I would have been among the number.... Your Cousin—I believe—[Lt.] DeSaussure Edwards is also named among the slain.
>
> When we look over the long lists of killed & wounded and think of the noble fellows lying there on that bloody battle-field—some dead, others gasping out their last breath, some moaning in pain, others dying silently—who an hour or two before were in high health, were looking forward to a triumphant victory, were thinking of home and of friends, were making plans for the future and talking of "after the war"—we must then feel that our country is grievously afflicted & we should pray to God to withdraw his hand from afflicting us.... I have seen a list of the casualties in the "Brooks Arty," but none of Hugh's Company [Garden's Battery].[9]

Gadsden, 21, left college to join the Palmetto Guard as a private and an original member "to do battle for his country," his obituary stated. "He passed unscathed through all the great battles of the army of Virginia until he fought his last fight" somewhere in the bloodshed of Kershaw's July 2 attack. Capt. R.E. Elliott, who led the Second South Carolina's Company I, witnessed Gadsden's death: "I saw the ball hit him. He was fighting by my side *as coolly* and *bravely* as *usual*."[10]

Lt. DeSaussure Edwards belonged to the Second South Carolina's Company K when he died at Gettysburg, "fighting with his usual and hereditary courage," said one account. A South Carolina College graduate and prewar lawyer, Edwards had "a patriotism of the most exalted character." "Green be the turf above thee, noble friend and gallant soldier," stated his death notice in the *Charleston Mercury*.[11]

"Almost every mail brings the sad tidings of the death of some brave young hero, formerly the hope and delight not only of the family circle but of numerous friends," the

Mercury stated on July 22, in a prelude to news of the death of Pvt. S.C. Miles. Company I, Second South Carolina, in Kershaw's command. Miles was "almost instantly killed" on July 2 "while in close combat with the enemy." This notice contained a July 8 letter written by Capt. R.E. Elliott, Miles's company commander. Elliott was still in the Confederate lines near Hagerstown when he wrote to one of the young soldier's relatives:

> We all regret his loss exceedingly. He was the life of the company, and there is no one to supply his place. He was cool and brave in battle, and died like a good soldier doing his duty. We were unable to bury the body. I had a headboard prepared, with his name and company marked, and placed it on his body, but before the implements could be procured to dig the grave our whole line was ordered to retire, and his body was left in the hands of the enemy. With deep sympathy for you in your bereavement.[12]

A Charlestonian, Sgt. Mortimer, 21, had been a medical student when war was imminent and joined the Rutledge Mounted Riflemen before Fort Sumter's bombardment. Craving action, he was granted permission to enlist in Kershaw's regiment as a private in the Palmetto Guard embarking for Virginia in 1861. His right hand was shattered by enemy fire at Antietam and some urged him to seek a discharge from the army due to his wound, but he refused, replying, "If my arm or leg were shot off, I would not leave it." His hand was still healing when he rejoined his company and marched toward Gettysburg. Desperately wounded on July 2 "while charging one of the enemy's batteries," he died at the Black Horse Tavern two days later "in perfect resignation and calmness, having an abiding hope in the merits of his Saviour." The *Mercury* also that day announced the death of Edmund James Mills, 21, another Palmetto Guard and in the Second South Carolina's Company I. He was yet another Carolinian to fall victim to the Union artillery on July 2. "A precious sacrifice has been offered up by his parents upon the altar of their country."[13]

The *Southern Enterprise* (Greenville, S.C.) on July 23 noted the death of Capt. R.C. Pulliam of Company B, Second South Carolina Infantry, who fell in Kershaw's July 2 attack. Pulliam was in the "Butler Guards" militia unit before the war. His loss "is a severe and heavy blow upon the corps and one that will be hard to sustain," the article stated, based on a letter from one of Pulliam's fellow officers, Lt. William Holland, the company's temporary commander, due to losses. "A nobler spirit has not wielded the sword or sacrificed his life in defence of his country." Holland stated that he assisted Pulliam off the field and to a hospital, making him "comfortable as possible. I did not regard his a mortal wound, and was surprised the next day when I heard he was sinking"; Pulliam died soon afterward. Holland also offered solace to the father of Company B's Sgt. R.W. Pool, whose life was ended by a grapeshot in the stomach. "Tell Mr. Poole [*sic*] his son was well cared for and is buried beside Capt. Pulliam. Some of his mess[mates] will write to him and give him particulars." Pulliam and Pool died on July 3 at the Black Horse Tavern. Holland added that two other Carolinians, Cpl. J.A. Jennings and Pvt. Charles A. Markley, also of Company B, "were struck in vital parts and died instantly." Both were buried on the field with "headings marked."[14]

One of the more tragic home-front stories involved the Columbia family of Pvt. James H. Casson, Company A, Second South Carolina, in Kershaw's command. The private's father, Maj. William H. Casson, had led this company early in the war, and in May 1862 was transferred to the South Carolina coast as commander of the Eighth South Carolina Volunteers. James was badly wounded at Savage Station but recovered enough to accompany his regiment into Pennsylvania. An only son, he was killed at Gettysburg.

News of his death gradually filtered back to the family and James's only sister, Sara, died on the day they received the sad tidings.[15]

In Laurens County, the dark wave of grief soon washed down from Gettysburg to the family of Alsey and Anna Jane Fuller, who had five sons in the Confederate army. The Fullers already had experienced the deep sorrow of one death, that of John C. Fuller, mortally wounded at South Mountain. A member of Company B, Third South Carolina Battalion, John had supposedly been captured and died in a hospital, "as nothing more was ever heard from him," said one account. Two of the others, Adolphus A. and Edwin P. Fuller, were also in the same Third Battalion company when Kershaw's troops reached Gettysburg. Both were killed there.[16]

News of Col. De Saussure's death also trickled south. "We deeply regret to learn that private dispatches confirm the report of Col. W.D. De Saussure's death," the *Columbia Guardian* noted; "a gallant spirit and every inch a soldier." "Private telegrams have been received which leave no doubt of the death of the brave … De Saussure … in the battle of Gettysburg," the *Charleston Mercury* added on July 18. The colonel "had much energy of character, and as a disciplinarian exacted strict obedience and a faithful performance of duty on the part of both officers and men," an unidentified friend and college mate, recalled. "At the same time through tact a genial disposition, he preserved his popularity with his" men. "He wore his heart upon his sleeve, and all could see that it was brave and tender."[17]

The *Mercury* on July 25 also contained a lengthy list of Carolinians wounded at Gettysburg who were being treated at Howard's Grove Hospital near Richmond. The sixty-one soldiers were from Perrin's and Kershaw's brigades, the majority of the injuries being described as a "flesh wound" or "not serious." Among the worst was Pvt. Y.P. Reagan of the Seventh South Carolina's Company C, with "three fingers shot off on right hand," Lt. R.L. Simmons of the Twelfth South Carolina's Company B, "wounded in left arm—serious," and Sgt. S.O. Cusack of Company I, Eighth South Carolina, "wounded in arm—bone fractured."[18]

By this time, some wounded Carolinians had already returned home to heal and recuperate. One of them was Lt. W.H. Brunson of Co. D, Fourteenth South Carolina, shot in both thighs, the "pleasant punctures he received from the hands of the Yankees at Gettysburg," the *Edgefield Advertiser* stated on July 29 in a grim attempt at humor. It will be recalled that Brunson had fallen on an injured Union officer on Gettysburg's first day and shared his canteen with the Yankee. "The friends of this intrepid soldier [Brunson] will be glad to hear that his wounds are doing well, and that he is already getting about a little on his crutches." For Brunson, it was an anniversary of sorts, since he had been wounded in combat around Richmond about a year earlier. Separately, the paper ran a list of the other casualties in the Fourteenth's Company D, submitted by Lt. E.S. Mims, the company commander. That same day, the *Advertiser* also ran an obituary for Col. Matthew C. Butler's brother Thomas, of the Second S.C. Cavalry, and a list of casualties in Kershaw's Seventh South Carolina, including Cpl. Thomas Harling, killed while carrying the regimental colors on July 2. Under a melancholy headline, "The Tomb," the *Southern Enterprise* printed a tribute to Sgt. Butler on August 27, mentioning that he had earned posthumous praise from General Hampton. "Amiable, conscientious and brave, he won the hearts of all who knew him," the paper said of Butler, slain in the July 3 cavalry clash.[19]

Col. J.L. Black of the First S.C. Cavalry was with his command near Hagerstown on July 11 when he compiled a casualty list that was published in the *Mercury* sixteen days later. Most of the killed and wounded occurred at Gettysburg, but the headline stated casualties were "Since Crossing The Potomac Up To Date." The piece also mentioned "Dr. Joseph Yates, left in Gettysburg in charge of wounded." Black's list also detailed the type of injuries suffered in Civil War cavalry combat: "Lieutenant and Adjutant Ragsdale, injured in leg by fall of horse.... Captain M T Owen, foot, pistol ball, sent to Staunton.... Corporal McClinton, head; sabre cut.... Privates C E Franklin, shoulder, severely, missing; J F Wells, thigh, severely, missing.... [Private] J W Forman, head, dangerously."[20]

Readers of the *Yorkville Enquirer* on the 29th saw a short list of some losses sustained by the First South Carolina Cavalry, along with a note that Wade Hampton had reached his home in Columbia "on Friday last" (July 24) and that "his wounds have proven severe and painful, but it is trusted the danger of them has passed off." One doctor told Hampton that his wounds were serious enough to incapacitate him from military service for at least a month and possibly much longer. The general's wife, Mary, and the family's physician gave him the best care they could, but it would be almost four months before he could even consider returning to his brigade. An army surgeon examined Hampton about every three weeks, each time requesting an extension of his leave, which was always granted. The general sometimes became discouraged about his slow recovery, but his outlook brightened when he thought of the much longer, ongoing and more painful recuperation of his friend, the cavalryman Col. Butler, who lost his right foot at the battle of Brandy Station.[21]

News of the death of Pvt. Gabriel G. Gist of the Fifteenth South Carolina was published in the *Mercury* on July 31, along with the July 7 letter to his mother from Gist's company commander, Capt. James McCutchen. "He was a hero of many a hard fought field," his obituary stated. "He was a robust man ... and his fond parent had hoped that he at least would be one to return home ... but alas! for human hopes—her fondest expectations have been blasted."[22]

The death notice of Capt. Joseph P. Cunningham, Company G, Second South Carolina Volunteers, ran in the August 7 *Camden Confederate*. Cunningham, 28, was a planter and member of the "Flat Rock Guards," from the Kershaw district before the war. He had fought from First Bull Run to the fields of Gettysburg unscathed, until the afternoon of July 2 when he fell, four days short of his 29th birthday. "Alas! That so much rich experience, so much usefulness should perish, with so much yet to do," the paper lamented. In an earlier report of Cunningham's death, the paper expressed a sentiment which could have described thousands of the slain from blue or gray. "Day by day we are called upon to chronicle the death of those whom the community can ill afford to spare," the *Confederate* eulogized on July 17. "The State has lost in this case a valuable and effective officer, and a large circle of friends mourn the untimely loss of one whose place can never be supplied." The same edition also mentioned "the painful intelligence" regarding the leg amputation of Capt. W.Z. Leitner and said "fears were entertained" that Col. John D. Kennedy, both of the Second South Carolina, might lose his seriously wounded hand. The July 24 issue of the *Confederate* contained a preliminary list of casualties from the Second South Carolina and the Fifteenth South Carolina, the latter also in Kershaw's brigade.[23]

A list of Gettysburg casualties in the First South Carolina Volunteers was in the *Charleston Mercury* on July 18. The killed and wounded were identified by companies, the regimental tally reaching 105, including 19 dead and 86 wounded. As were other such lists during the period, this one would be ever-changing for weeks and even longer, as some of the wounded died or initial reports were gradually updated. Nevertheless, Charlestonians and other people across the state anxiously scanned the newspaper that day for any morsel of news about their soldiers. "Company A ... B.C. Matthews, killed; T.F. Dunn, killed.... J.B. Weathersbee, left arm—amputated above elbow.... Company G ... Serg't John C. Mays, killed, J.C. Schafer, killed.... J.L. Turner, right leg, amputated at knee joint.... Company H ... Color Serg't Jas Larkin, right lung—mortal.... Company I ... Corporal M McInnis, killed...."[24]

On July 20, a much longer and detailed list took up an entire page of the *Charleston Courier*, under the headline, "Casualties in South Carolina Regiments at the Battle of Gettysburg." The tally actually contained casualties in Kershaw's brigade only. Still, it must have been a shocking jolt to anyone who viewed the hundreds of Carolinians' names identifying the killed, wounded and missing from one brigade in one battle.[25]

The *Mercury* on July 20 contained a melancholy article, basically an epitaph of the Eighth South Carolina. "This glorious old regiment may, with truth be said to be extinct" after Gettysburg, wrote a Carolinian identified only as "Pee Dee." The Eighth's previous major battles "all attest [to] her courage, her mettle and her glory," he noted. "The field of Gettysburg was pre eminently the field of her glory and her grave. She went into battle one hundred and seventy strong, and now, along the borders of Pennsylvania, their cool and gallant Colonel Henagan, has left him but forty men to rally around the old Palmetto flag.... When the long roll of your lost is read around the hearths of your friends, every home in the swamps of the Pee Dee will find itself desolate—sadness will cover the land." The article contained a partial list of casualties "as far as they have reached us with certainty." The list included Maj. D.M. McLeod, Lt. H.R. Adams, Company G, Pvt. Samuel Dixon, Company C, and Pvt. J.K. Easterling, Company G, among the slain.[26]

The extended family of the Rev. William Ayres of Marion County, South Carolina, learned that one of the reverend's three sons, Pvt. D. Dwight Ayres of the Eighth South Carolina's Company I, had been killed at Gettysburg, while his brother, Enoch, also in the Eighth, was unharmed. Six Ayres men marched off to war—and only two, Enoch and the third brother Thomas W., returned. Additionally, five brothers-in-law, married to Ayres women, donned the gray, four never to return. On his deathbed some years after the war, the reverend, in his nineties, was still haunted by the loss of his son and the other kinsmen, crying out in delirium, "I must go back to Virginia and get my boys." At least one Ayres fought in the Spanish-American War, while a number of descendants served in World War I. The latter included Kiffin Rockwell, who volunteered as a pilot with the French Escadrille. He was shot down and killed in September 1916.[27]

More than a month after the battle, information about loved ones in the army was still slowly reaching those at home. The August 5 *Edgefield Advertiser* contained a letter from Jesse Black, a soldier in Company B of the Fourteenth South Carolina, about casualties in his company. Another letter was from Lt. J.H. Allen, commander of the Fourteenth's Company K, detailing the company's 37 losses, including six killed, 29 wounded and two missing. The paper also had a brief notice about the death of Capt. W.E. McCaslan of Abbeville, "a noble and a gallant spirit" who "was well known and esteemed in this vicinity, having taught school in the Village for several years." The August 7 *Abbeville Press* noted the passing of Capt. M.T. Owen of Company A, First South Carolina Cavalry, who had been wounded in Pennsylvania. Owen had been recuperating at home for about two weeks but died on August 3. The *Charleston Mercury* on August 13 ran an August 6 letter from Capt. William A. Kelly of the First South Carolina's Volunteers'

Company L regarding four of his soldiers left behind at Gettysburg. From the regiment's camp near Orange Court House, Virginia, Kelly identified them as Cpl. James Steedman, who was ill, and privates George E.L. Duffus, J.A. McKethian and H.R. Wiecking, who were wounded. The four, "not being able to travel themselves, and the means of transportation not being sufficient to convey them," were among the thousands unable to return south with the army. Kelly asked that the letter be published "for the information of anxious relatives and friends" of these Carolinians.[28]

The *Charleston Courier* on August 14 had a notice republished from the Baltimore *American* about wounded Confederate prisoners from South Carolina who had died at the Chester Hospital in recent weeks. The Carolinians were W.S. Berry, Seventh South Carolina; A.C. Bowen, First S.C. Rifles; and J.S. Hendricks, Twelfth South Carolina.[29]

Also on August 14, members of the Aetna Fire Engine Company in Charleston gathered at the Mills House Hall to honor a comrade, William Eason of the Brooks Artillery, killed at Gettysburg. Eason "died in manhood's early morn, but he leaves a name without a stain, a memory that will be to his bereaved widow and aged parents in coming years an inheritance of beauty and honor," read part of the preamble and resolution in his memory. A few days earlier, the *Charleston Courier* noted that Eason's death resulted in his widow and one child dependent on "the care of a grateful country." The artilleryman had been ill when the army marched north, but "insisted upon sharing, as he had previously done, all the privations and dangers of his gallant comrades." Meanwhile, the loved ones of another Brooks Artillery soldier, Pvt. E. Carew Newton of Charleston, were anxiously awaiting any news about him. It is unclear what the family knew, if anything, about the 23-year-old Newton in August, but he had been wounded and captured. Newton had been a Charleston firefighter before joining the artillery unit in the war's early days. It would be a long, torturous time before the family learned about his whereabouts and fate.[30]

The August 17 *Mercury* contained a lengthy article on the slain Capt. W.T. Haskell of the First South Carolina. "Fortunate indeed were those who had such an example before them—the example of a Christian soldier," it stated. "A courteous gentleman, a rigid disciplinarian, a careful observer, constantly attending to the wants and comforts of his men; a brave and heroic leader in battle.... He had no rule for his men which did not apply to himself.... That life, which he had freely offered on so many battlefields, was at last taken in the bloody battle of Gettysburg. The loss is his friends,' his fellow soldiers, his country's—the gain his own. Few have served their country so well—none, we trust, rest more happily from their labors."[31]

The *Mercury* on August 18 published the obituary for Maj. Donald McLeod of the Eighth South Carolina. "The report of his death was heard with profound sorrow by the people of his District, and fell with crushing weight upon his family," it stated. "The members of his church will not soon forget him ... and to whom, on Sabbath mornings, the recitations of their Bible-class were usually made." A comrade in arms, Augustus Dickert, added, "Thus ended the life of one of the noblest and most devoted of Carolina's sons." McLeod left behind his widow and three young children.[32]

More weeks passed and the newspapers still had briefs and notices about the soldiers slain at Gettysburg. The death of Pvt. Thomas Pressley Jacobs of Company E, Fourteenth South Carolina, was mentioned in the *Yorkville Enquirer* on August 26. Jacobs, "in the 20th year of his age," had been born in Yorkville and was the son of the Rev. Ferdinand Jacobs, who lived in Laurensville, South Carolina. For the private, Gettysburg was the sixteenth battle "in which he had fought in his country's defence," the paper stated. Nineteen-year-old James S. Johnson of Company A, Seventh South Carolina, had been killed in Kershaw's fighting on July 2, the *Edgefield Advertiser* related on October 7. A letter to his mother, written by his captain and an orderly sergeant, said Johnson "fell while nobly battling for his country's rights on the bloody field of battle. Your son was a brave boy and a good soldier, always ready and willing to do his duty wherever it called him." "But he cannot be startled now from his sweet slumbers by the roll of the drum to face the bellowing cannon or roaring muskets," the article added. "He is gone!—gone to that land from whence no traveller ever returns. So we must bid him farewell."[33]

News of the August 30 death of Pvt. George E.L. Duffus at Davids' Island, New York, was published in the *Charleston Mercury* on September 12. Duffus, 21, had served in the Sumter Guards and the Carolina Light Infantry before entering Confederate service in the First South Carolina Volunteers. At Gettysburg he was severely wounded by a "ball entering the left shoulder, and passing out of the middle of the back, on the left side of the spine." Captured, he was sent to Davids' Island, where "lingering for nearly two months, declining gradually in strength, he came gently to his end." The *Mercury* on August 13 had published a letter from Duffus's company commander stating that he and three others from Company L had been left behind at Gettysburg.[34]

Duffus's death was not mentioned in a September 8 *Mercury* piece about Carolinians still at Davids' Island or those soldiers by then known to have been killed at Gettysburg. Information for the article was based on "returned prisoners" who arrived by boat in Virginia on August 28. Duffus died two days later. Still, the list published on the 8th was succor or the bitterest of concoctions for loved ones and friends of Carolina Confederates who had had no news of their soldiers for almost two months. In Rice's Third Battalion, F.O. Sims, A. Davis and G. Hasel were surviving "flesh" wounds, as were Sgt. J.B. Wilson and John McClure, of the First South Carolina, and the Second's F.E. Gaillard. Cpl. J.R. Wessinger of the Thirteenth was still being treated for a "slight" leg wound. Amputees were detailed by which limb was lost. W. Elkins, J.R. Smith, and H. Jennings, of the Fourteenth South Carolina, and L. Turner of the First and Thomas Hayes of the Brooks Artillery were among wounded who lost a leg. Another man identified only as "Watts" in the Brooks Artillery had an arm amputated, as did an infantryman named "Pevis" in the Seventh's Company I and T.L. Garden of the Twelfth. C.J. Colcock of the Second had a hand sawed off but apparently survived. Others endured what was bluntly described as "thigh amputated," apparently meaning that the entire leg was taken off. These included Capt. J. Hinant of the Twelfth's Company O and a Lt. "Blass[?]" of the Twelfth's Company C. Then came the dead, marching onto the printed pages by regiment. In the First were those who died at Davids' Island, including J.F. Sprawls, E. Mathewes, J.B. Weatherly and A. Owens. The Twelfth's J.H. Smith, F.M. Gardner, James Wherry, and P.P. Hall succumbed there as well, as did the Fourteenth's C. (or O.) Dursoe and the Fifteenth's S. Oswald. This newsprint procession was followed by some Carolinians who never left Gettysburg but whose fate may not have been known until the *Mercury* article. A. Wooly and A. Lewis of the First died within days of the battle, as did J.H. Casson and L. Oranva of the Second and W.N. Ashly of the Seventh. The Thirteenth's G.A. Keisler struggled to live until July 29, and the Fifteenth's Sgt. (F.M.) Lenerieux (spelled "Lennereax" in the article) took his last breath a day later. The Fourteenth's J.W. Owens died four days after the battle. Of those men on the list, two of them, Cpl. Thomas Hayes and M. Carolan, who had a shoulder wound, were mentioned in a July 9 letter sent to the *Mercury* from Lt. S.C. Gilbert of the

Brooks Artillery. Gilbert was recuperating in Virginia from his own wounds at that time. Gilbert's casualty list was published in the paper on July 18.[35]

The September 18 *Mercury* included a combined obituary for four soldiers of the Eighth South Carolina's Company G. Lt. H.R. Adams and privates Alex McIntosh and J.K. Easterling were slain on July 2, as previously mentioned. Color Sgt. Elisha Adams meanwhile survived at the Black Horse Tavern until July 17, when he died of his leg injuries. The latter's death was not the first public notification of his passing; Adams was included in Baruch's casualty list published in the *Mercury* on August 28.[36]

On October 5, the *Mercury* published an October 1 report from Richmond regarding "still other South Carolinians who have died" and some "still in the hands of the enemy whose names have never been published for information of their friends." The piece identified thirty soldiers, many of whom had died or were still being treated at Davids' Island—erroneously called "Davis Island"—while most of the rest remained in Gettysburg, either in hospitals or graves. One Carolinian was hospitalized in Harrisburg, while another—both of Kershaw's Seventh South Carolina—was recuperating in Hagerstown. At Gettysburg, Lt. S.W. Bissel of the Second South Carolina was still recovering from a leg wound. J. Ross, also of the Second, had had a leg amputated and was "doing well." In the Third S.C. Battalion, J.D. Brown also was healing from a leg wound, while W.J. Hanvy was "well" with no wound disclosed. S. Ataway of the First South Carolina's Company G died on August 12. W. Adkins of the First South Carolina Cavalry and W. Adis of the Fifteenth South Carolina were "well" at Davids' Island, but E.E. Murphy of the Fifteenth died in September.[37]

The October 14 issue of the Edgefield paper noted the death of another local soldier, Thomas Alton, 21, of Company G, Seventh South Carolina. His parents, Joseph and Mary Alton of the Edgefield District, already had endured the loss of another son to the war. Robert Alton died at Manchester, Virginia, in May 1862 from "disease aggravated by camp life," the *Advertiser* stated. Prior to Gettysburg, Thomas Alton had "proved himself gallant and brave" enough to be assigned to the color guard, his captain had written to the family. On July 2, "he fell at his post under the folds of the battle flag of his country.… A truer, braver, or better young man never stood by that flag." The paper added an epitaph for the two Altons, but it also was a fitting tribute to all Confederates who had fallen on fields so far from their homes: "These brave boys lie buried in strange lands (with many others of our sunny south) but angels watch them till God shall bid them rise."[38]

On November 19, 1863, President Abraham Lincoln delivered his famous Gettysburg Address in dedicating the national cemetery there. Among the hundreds of Union soldiers' graves was the resting place of Lt. Sidney Carter of the Fourteenth South Carolina's Company A. Mortally wounded and captured on July 1, Carter died about a week after the battle. A Union burial detail erroneously recorded him as a member of a Connecticut infantry regiment and Carter was interred in Row A, Grave 5 of the Connecticut section of the National Soldiers' Cemetery.[39]

Not until about the first week of January 1864 did J.A. and Mary Shirer of St. Matthews Parish near Orangeburg apparently learn of the death of their son at Gettysburg. Pvt. W.D. Shirer of the First South Carolina Cavalry's Company E was mortally wounded during the July 3 cavalry battle, lingering until sometime in August. In his early twenties when he died, Shirer was in school at the war's outset and "nobly closed his books, and rushed to the defence of his native land," the *Charleston Courier* related. "He survived his wound long enough to write to his parents, to whom his last words were, 'Should I not see you again on earth, I will meet you in heaven.'"[40]

Weeks after the battle, the Black Horse Tavern remained a hospital for Kershaw's wounded. The numbers were gradually diminishing; some Carolinians recovered enough to be transferred as prisoners to other medical facilities or POW camps in the North, while others were fated to sleep in shallow graves across the Gettysburg countryside.

Doctors Simon Baruch, J.F. Pearce and H.J. Nott were still there in early August, tending to their patients, some of whom were unable to rise from their crude straw pallets in the orchards or barn on the premises. As if the carnage of cannon and musketry weren't enough, a tetanus outbreak had smothered the lives of a few Confederates too weak to withstand its onslaught. Still, Baruch had enjoyed the six weeks or so he spent at Gettysburg, gaining much experience and associating with the civilian and Union physicians with whom he came in contact. He observed his 23rd birthday at Gettysburg in late July, while thousands of other young men at the same place never reached that personal landmark. By sometime in mid–August, Baruch, Pearce and Nott were among about one hundred Confederate surgeons and some chaplains who received orders from Union authorities to leave Gettysburg and go to Baltimore, apparently to be paroled and sent South. The Baltimore ladies still in Gettysburg offered a roll of money to the three Carolina doctors, graciously telling them to take as much cash as they needed for the trip. Believing that he would be quickly exchanged, Baruch accepted only $5.[41]

The medical contingent soon boarded a train for Baltimore, the cars filled with convalescent soldiers of both sides. On reaching the city, the doctors' reception was ominous. Baruch and the other surgeons were separated from the other passengers and escorted by Union guards to a downtown hotel being used by the Federals as a temporary prison. The Southerners were issued meager rations and a few hours later were marched to Fort McHenry, a distance of about three miles on the city streets which the men covered in the August heat. At the fort, the physicians were quartered in a barracks with wooden bunks and no mattresses. This would be their home for several weeks. For a time, other than sparse rations, confinement at McHenry was not without its privileges. Baruch and the others were permitted to roam the grounds, play ball, visit the sutler's store and even swim in the waters of the inner harbor. Some prisoners, supported by Southern sympathizers in Baltimore, bribed Federals to be allowed to attend social functions in the city, even to the point of overnight stays outside the fort. All of this changed abruptly when one of the physicians abused the privilege and lax security and didn't return to McHenry. The other surgeons, including Baruch, were told to pack their baggage and were marched to a brick stable where deserters also were held. The physicians occupied a dreary loft, and their outside liberties were drastically curtailed. This punishment lasted about two weeks before their regular activities were renewed.[42]

While confined at McHenry, Baruch compiled a list of Confederates who died at the Black Horse Tavern from July 4 through August 8. He managed to send the list south, and it was published in the *Charleston Mercury* on August 28 under the headline "List of Deaths at Kershaw's Brigade Hospital, Near Gettysburg, Pa." Of the forty-seven soldiers on the list, forty-five were South Carolinians, with a Virginian and a Georgian completing the tally.

"July 4—Private W C Horton, Company H, 2d S C Regiment—Wound of abdomen." "July 14—Private C W Bell, Company K, 2d S C. Regiment—Severe chest wound by grape." "July 23—Private J M Cannady, Company I, 3d S C Regiment—Irritative fever after amputation." "July 6—Sergeant W Y Robinson, Company E, 15th S C Regiment—Wound of bowels." "July 17—Corporal J J Golding, Company A, James' Battalion—Amputation of thigh." Baruch's list also was apparently the first public mention of the fate of Capt. Thomas E. Powe of the Eighth South Carolina. The young officer lost a leg in the July 2 fighting, but lived until July 22, finally succumbing to "Tetanus," he noted. The *Mercury* ran a brief notice a few days later further confirming Powe's demise. "We are pained to learn that letters have been received by flag of truce, which announce the death of this gallant young officer," it stated.[43]

The calendar flipped into late September before Baruch and his colleagues boarded a ship in Chesapeake Bay. They were taken to Fortress Monroe, where they were finally exchanged. A Confederate vessel took them up the James River to Richmond. Despite all that he had endured, however, Simon Baruch's war was far from over, as will be seen. W.H.H. Bevil of the Fifteenth South Carolina was apparently among the hospital contingent with Baruch that was sent to Baltimore. Like Baruch, he also recalled the kindness and generosity of the Baltimore ladies, as well as members of the U.S. Christian Commission, in helping ease the suffering of the wounded before they left Gettysburg. Reaching Baltimore, however, Bevil was separated from the doctors, finding himself with other Confederates confined in the city jail. Months of imprisonment awaited him.[44]

The prison train carrying Lt. J.R. Boyles of the Twelfth South Carolina huffed through the Pennsylvania countryside, making several stops after leaving Gettysburg on or about July 17. The Confederates' destination was unknown to them, but at each stop throngs of people gathered to get a glimpse of the rebel prisoners. Boyles, minus his right leg, eventually ended up at Davids' Island in Long Island Sound, where he was surprised by the great care he received. He marveled at the "new and soft mattresses," clean sheets and clean clothing issued to the prisoners. "We had every attention and privilege that we could expect," he wrote. A number of New York ladies with Southern sympathies were permitted to visit the captive rebs, bringing clothes, money and other items to ease their imprisonment. If Boyles's account is to be believed, however, there was at least one incident of his Davids' Island experience that can only be described as barbaric and fiendish. A Virginia lieutenant identified only as Goode had his leg amputated there and died a few days later. Boyles claimed that "so eager were the Yankees for Confederate trophies that they actually made finger rings of the [leg] bones." Boyles spent three months on Davids' Island and was later transferred to Johnson's Island. He suffered through the cold there before being exchanged in March 1864 among 300 or so Confederate "cripples." He was a prisoner for nine months or so after being wounded and captured at Gettysburg.[45]

In and around the town of Orange Court House, Virginia, Lee's army healed, rested, regrouped and reorganized into late August. The South Carolinians there were all affected by the changes, whether by the loss of a comrade or officer in their companies, reassignment of regiments or shifts in command.

Lee's most critical single loss was Maj. Gen. Dorsey Pender, the division commander mortally wounded on July 2. "No man fell during this bloody battle of Gettysburg more regretted than he, nor around whose youthful brow were clustered brighter rays of glory," Pender's corps commander, A.P. Hill, noted in his battle report. The South Carolinians in Pender's division had varying opinions about the late general. "Previous to the battle [Gettysburg], he had not been very popular with our brigade," noted an officer in Perrin's command, "but after seeing his management there, we learned to admire and love him while living, and to regret him with all our hearts when dead." Lt. Col. Joseph Brown of the Fourteenth related, "Our army lost in him another of our great generals." Perrin himself mourned the loss of his commander: "His death is a grievous misfortune to me personally," he wrote to Governor Bonham in late July. "In my humble judgement, he was the best Major General in the Army. He was a most thorough officer. He was brave, energetic, a thorough disciplinarian & in fact everything that a soldier should be. His place will be hard to fill in this Army." Pender was replaced by Maj. Gen. Wilcox.[46]

The officers of Pender's division met on August 15 to "draft resolutions" expressing the "sentiments" of the command about the slain Tarheel general. A committee of five officers, including Perrin, composed the resolutions, which were unanimously adopted. In summary, they expressed the "mingled feelings of pride and sorrow" regarding his "untimely death," which had resulted in "an irreparable loss" to the army.[47]

Another significant event was the return of Brig. Gen. Samuel McGowan—at least in name though still not present—to the head of his brigade, which had taken high casualties under Perrin's gallant leadership at Gettysburg. With this development, Perrin resumed command of the brigade's Fourteenth South Carolina, whose Lt. Col. Brown was still recuperating from wounds. Additionally, Col. D.H. Hamilton of the First South Carolina returned to duty after having left the brigade in early June due to illness. As senior colonel, and with McGowan still absent, Hamilton assumed brigade command from Perrin. Col. F.E. Harrison took command of the First (Orr's) South Carolina Rifles, replacing Capt. William Hadden, who had led the First at Gettysburg. The brigade's leadership shifted again a few weeks later when Perrin was promoted brigadier general and Hamilton was assigned to duty in South Carolina.[48]

"Too much credit cannot be awarded to Colonel Perrin and the splendid brigade under his command for the manner and spirit with which this attack was conducted," Maj. Joseph A. Engelhard, assistant adjutant general of Pender's division, wrote in the Gettysburg battle report, Pender having been mortally wounded. "To the former, the Government has recognized his valuable services in a manner the most grateful to the true soldier, by a prompt promotion [Perrin rose to brigadier on September 10, 1863]. Of the latter, all who are acquainted with their gallantry on this occasion unite in their commendation to both." Pender "was most enthusiastic in their praise" before his July 18 death.[49]

With De Saussure's death, leadership of the Fifteenth South Carolina in Kershaw's brigade went to Lt. Col. Joseph F. Gist. Maj. William M. Gist had led the regiment in the battle after De Saussure fell. All told, the Army of Northern Virginia had an effective total of 56,326 troops of all arms as of August 31, records showed.[50]

The Carolinians of Brooks Artillery of Alexander's battalion in Longstreet's First Corps had a new leader in Capt. W.W. Fickling, replacing the wounded Lt. Stephen Gilbert. Fickling, newly promoted and slightly wounded at Gettysburg, needed a number of replacements, based on Gilbert's casualty list sent from Winchester on July 9. Regarding the condition of the four South and North Carolina batteries that comprised Henry's Battalion in the First Corps, the "horses for [the] most part [were] in good condition," an organizational note stated. "Transportation good and sufficient." The diagnosis for Bachman's German Artillery and Hugh Garden's Palmetto Light Artillery was much worse: "Men ... greatly deficient in Bachman's and Garden's.... Needs a number of men ... and 26 horses."[51]

A correspondent with the *Columbia Guardian* was in the Virginia camp of the Pee Dee Artillery in the first week or so of September when he filed a report headlined "The

South Carolinians Under Gen. A.P. Hill." The reporter wrote that Zimmerman's gunners and the Carolinians of McGowan's Brigade "are the only representatives of the 'Old Palmetto' State in Hill's corps … but have shared with that distinguished chieftain the hardships and perils, both of the march and of battle…. The brigade has won for itself on many hard fought fields an enviable reputation for courage and gallantry…. In the late battles it fought with its accustomed obstinacy and firmness—worthy of their former leader—the brave and chivalric [Brig. Gen. Maxcy] Gregg," killed at Fredericksburg.[52]

Wade Hampton, meanwhile, continued to recuperate late into October, but was feeling stronger by the day. The terrible headaches were manageable now and his hip wound was healed, so he left his home before the month was out and caught a train for Virginia. By November 5 or so, he reported to army headquarters near Culpeper Court House, receiving a warm welcome from Lee and many other officers and comrades. "The country will be gratified to learn of the return to command of Maj. Gen. Wade Hampton, now commanding a division of cavalry in the army," the *Charleston Mercury* briefly noted. "Gen. H. was wounded at Gettysburg."[53]

Already, however, the second-guessing and finger-pointing about Gettysburg was underway. Surgeon Spencer Welch of the Thirteenth South Carolina criticized his corps commander A.P. Hill and, as did many Confederates, lamented the absence of "Stonewall" Jackson at Gettysburg. Welch envisioned that they would have had a "victory completely won" if Hill had hurried Dick Anderson's relatively fresh division into action on the first day, to relieve the fought-out troops of Pender's and Heth's commands and push the Federals off Cemetery Hill and nearby heights before they were organized and reinforced. "If 'Old Stonewall' had been alive and there, it no doubt would have been done," Welch wrote to Cordelia. "Hill was a good division commander, but he is not a superior corps commander. He lacks the mind and sagacity of Jackson."[54]

13

Sunset Years

In mid–December 1864, a year and five months after Gettysburg, the family of Pvt. E. Carew Newton of the Brooks Artillery learned of his death. Newton was wounded in the battle, taken prisoner and sent to Fort Delaware. The Charlestonian turned 24 during his imprisonment. His obituary, published in the *Charleston Courier*, stated that he had been a prisoner for about six months when he succumbed to chronic bronchitis on January 7, 1864. "In the time of God's severe chastisement of a nation where there is scarce a house in which there is not one dead … we wish to make the record of another victim on the altar of his country," the obituary stated of Newton, adding that he was "one of the many thousand martyrs to the cause of independence and constitutional rights…. A widowed mother mourns this her last son."[1]

Pvt. Thomas Jefferson Young of Company B, Fifteenth South Carolina, was wounded in the wrist and captured at Gettysburg. He healed but remained a prisoner of war until the Confederacy's collapse, being released in June 1865 at Fort Delaware. He came home to his wife and children and resumed his farming, living into the 1920s.[2]

Pvt. John B. Bagwell of the Fourteenth South Carolina was sent from a Union hospital in Gettysburg to Baltimore, where he was confined for about three weeks. Recovering from his injured ankle, he was transferred to the prison camp at Point Lookout, Maryland. Bagwell remained there until his release in early March 1865, when he returned to his home in Laurens County, South Carolina. Forty years after the battle, he wrote a letter to the *Laurens Advertiser* describing his experiences at Gettysburg and beyond.[3]

W.H.H. Bevil of the Fifteenth South Carolina was transferred from the Baltimore jail and shipped by transport to Point Lookout. He survived the hardships there, noting that three New Hampshire regiments—the Second, Fifth and Twelfth—were assigned guard duty there after having been "torn up" at Gettysburg. Bevil was held until February 1865, when he was released.[4]

Pvt. J.C. Buzzard of the Fourteenth fell into Union hands when he was too weak from his wounds to join his comrades in the retreat from Gettysburg. He eventually ended up in the prison hospital complex at Davids' Island near New York City. His experience was unlike the horror stories associated with prisoner of war compounds on both sides; Buzzard described the fine care he received while in confinement: "I was treated well there, had good doctors, and they did all they could for us," he wrote of Davids' Island. "We had plenty of food, good beds to sleep on, and our clothes were changed every Sunday morning also our bed clothes." When he was healthy enough, Buzzard states, he was sent home on parole and finally exchanged. He spent the rest of the war serving in a home guard unit near Edgefield, South Carolina. Charles O. Wheeler of the 2nd South Carolina's Company

D also was sent to Davids' Island, adding his praise about his time there: "We were well treated, each man had a nice iron bunk and a mattress and clean sheets." Wheeler eventually recovered enough to also be exchanged. The Darlington, South Carolina, native was wounded a third time at the Wilderness, but he survived the conflict.[5]

Pvt. James R. Harvey of the Twelfth South Carolina was still at Davids' Island in November; then he was transferred to a hospital facility on Bedloe's Island, also near New York City. He remained there until the following June, still recuperating from the wounds to his legs. "His extreme youth and patience in suffering won for him other devoted friends," noted a postwar account. Foremost among them were a Miss Julia Granberry and her mother. The ladies "became so much attached to him as to offer bond for his release that they might take him to their house in New York till convalescent." This was not to be; Union authorities soon deemed him healthy enough to be imprisoned at Fort Delaware. He lost touch with "the gentle Miss Julia" other than receiving the occasional boxes of food she sent him. Harvey later claimed he would have starved without them. Eventually exchanged, he tried to "keep up the acquaintance" with her. It was not until after the war ended, however, that he learned she had died "in the West." Harvey thereupon resolved to "embalm her memory in his heart and live and die a bachelor." When a Georgia newspaperman interviewed him in Winnsboro in late June 1886, Harvey was "40 years of age, a handsome, respected planter, whose influence is always exerted for the good of others."[6]

Captured at Gettysburg, Pvt. William B. Parson of the Fourteenth South Carolina was still recovering from his thigh wound received there when he was exchanged after two months in Union confinement. Before the year was out, he and his family would be mourning the death of his brother, Richmond, also of the Fourteenth, who succumbed to fever sometime in 1863. William healed enough to rejoin the army, but was again wounded, shot in the right shoulder in combat near the old battlefield at Frayser's Farm. He was recuperating at home when the war ended.[7]

Lt. William Alexander McQueen of the Palmetto Light Artillery survived Gettysburg but not the war. McQueen, the Baptist minister's son from Sumter, was home on furlough in April 1865 when a force of Union raiders under Brig. Gen. Edward E. Potter moved through the central portion of the state. Facing these Yankees, McQueen was killed in the battle of Dingle's Mill—a few miles from his family's home—on April 9, 1865. About the time of McQueen's death, his comrades in the Palmetto Light Artillery were surrendering with Lee and the rest of the Army of Northern Virginia at Appomattox.[8]

Trooper William A. Black of the Second South Carolina Cavalry was captured on the retreat and taken to the POW compound at Camp Chase, near Columbus, Ohio. He was confined there for seven months before being transferred to Fort Delaware. Black was held there until early April 1865, when he was exchanged. He had been imprisoned for nineteen months and twenty-three days. Black had used a clever—and perhaps morbid—bit of deception to effect his release. The exchange process involved rebels from the Western army and none from the east, based on a Southern account. Black got the names of several Arkansas soldiers who had died in prison, and when the surviving Arkansans were called out, he stepped into their ranks "and awaited events." Aided by another Arkansas prisoner, Black posed as Jesse J. Treaderway, who hadn't survived imprisonment, and secured his exchange. "The trip on the prison ship was full of apprehension and misgivings, but he [Black] finally reached home all right as an exchanged prisoner." Black farmed after the war and then spent nineteen years in Columbia in the insurance business. He later became superintendent of a rice milling company in Georgetown, South Carolina.[9]

Pvt. G.A. White, of the Third S.C. Battalion, recuperated quickly enough from his Gettysburg injury to accompany Kershaw's brigade and the rest of Longstreet's Corps to Georgia and Tennessee in late 1863. Wounded again during the fighting at Knoxville, White was captured and sent to a U.S. POW camp at Rock Island, Illinois. Despite brutal conditions there, where he and other starving prisoners ate rats and dogs, White endured a 17-month confinement and was released in late March 1865. Returning to Columbia after the war, he married, and the couple had three children. White and his family relocated to Fairfield County, South Carolina, in 1870, living in the Eau Claire section. White celebrated his 80th birthday in 1916.[10]

Captured at Falling Waters on July 14, Pvt. Robert Hemphill of the First South Carolina Rifles and his fellow prisoners camped that night under guard after leaving the battlefield. They drew rations of crackers, pork and coffee from the Federal troops. "This was our first square meal for days," Hemphill wrote in his diary. By train he and other POWs were sent to Baltimore, arriving on July 16. Hemphill's experience in imprisonment is vague, but he survived the war. Based on his diary, he wrote of his Gettysburg and Falling Waters recollections for the *Charleston Weekly News* in 1882, and his chronicle was reprinted in at least one other newspaper.[11]

Sgt. William Hood of Kershaw's Third South Carolina was captured and also taken to Davids' Island, his wounded knee still far from healing. Paroled in September, he reached home on crutches and was assigned desk duties in the army. Elected treasurer of South Carolina in 1864, Hood later served as a professor at Erskine College, his alma mater, for almost a quarter century, and was also a state legislator.[12]

Still nursing his thigh wound, J.W. Lokay of the Fifteenth South Carolina in Kershaw's ranks crossed the Potomac, but the wagon train ended there. Lokay and many other Confederates still had to walk many miles to the Virginia Central rail line at Staunton. "The road was lined with wounded soldiers," he recalled. Lokay survived the war but noted, "None but the 'old vets' know what we suffered."[13]

Pvt. John Coxe of the Second South Carolina was an old man living in Groveland, California, when he wrote to *Confederate Veteran* magazine in 1913 about his Gettysburg experiences, including his encounter with the wounded Union officer he helped. "I shall never forget his profuse thanks for the little service I was able to render to him," Coxe recalled, half a century later. Joel Hough, 22, of the Second South Carolina's Company G, was severely wounded at the Peach Orchard, captured and imprisoned for three months. After the war he returned to Kershaw County, farming and teaching. He also served in the state legislature.[14]

Trooper Peter J. Malone of the First South Carolina Cavalry's color guard was among Confederate wounded sent from Gettysburg to New York for treatment, where he "received the most considerate attention," he recalled. "Here I made the acquaintance of many excellent ladies and gentlemen from the Southern States," who used their resources and influence to aid him and thousands of other wounded rebels at the mercy of the foe. "True they were among our enemies, but from this very circumstance they were [able] to render us most important services.... Never shall I forget them." Malone slowly regained some semblance of his health, endured captivity and returned to South Carolina after the conflict. He was living in Orangeburg District, South Carolina, in January 1867, when he responded to a written request from his former regimental commander, Col. John L.

Black, asking for a description of the First South Carolina's July 3 charge at Gettysburg. Black had sustained a head wound at Upperville in June 1863 and was returning to the army when the Gettysburg battle unfolded. He fought in the battle but didn't reach his command in time to lead it. Malone, however, still suffered almost daily from the gunshot and resulting internal injuries he sustained in the July 3 cavalry clash. He was 29 when he died in 1873 "after ten years of suffering," said one newspaper account. "His early death was directly due to the wound that he received at Gettysburg."[15]

Lt. William S. Bissell of Company I, Second South Carolina, in Kershaw's brigade, recovered from his serious wounds at Gettysburg, remaining in Union custody. He returned to South Carolina, but it was not a joyous homecoming since he and other rebels were placed in a Union stockade on Morris Island outside Charleston. The stockade was in range of Confederate cannon, retaliation by the Yankees for Union prisoners in Charleston being housed where they could possibly be injured or killed by the Federals' shell fire. Bissell was eventually released and returned to army duty in South Carolina before being captured again and held until the war's end. He and his four brothers all returned home.[16]

Lt. James Armstrong of the First South Carolina's Company K survived his third wound of the war while carrying the regiment's flag at Gettysburg, but his bad luck continued. Armstrong, the transplanted Pennsylvanian, was shot again at Spotsylvania, but his fifth wound of the conflict, sustained in the last stages of the Petersburg fighting in April 1865, was the worst. In action at Sutherland Station on the Southside Railroad, Capt. Armstrong (promoted in 1864) had his right leg shattered and was captured. Armstrong spent eleven months recuperating in a Union hospital, returning to Charleston "when the surgeon felt it safe for him to be moved," well after the war's end. He continued to suffer from this last wound until it finally healed in 1871. Armstrong later served on the staff of South Carolina governor Wade Hampton. Armstrong was 87 when he died in August 1930. Lt. James F. Caldwell, also of the First South Carolina, was wounded at Gettysburg and again later in combat at Fussell's Mill and Deep Bottom. His history of McGowan's Brigade was published in 1866. After the war he was a lawyer in Newberry and also on the board of trustees for the University of South Carolina for eight years. He also served as director of the national bank of Newberry and was a longtime counsel for the Southern Railway.[17]

Almost two months after Capt. Thomas Powe's death was published in the *Charleston Mercury* on August 28, along with another notice on September 1, his obituary ran in that paper's October 17 edition. Powe, who led the Eighth South Carolina's Company C, was among the fatalities noted by Dr. Simon Baruch. "So died, as he preferred to die, this gallant young man at the head of his company—the Chevalier BAYARD of his regiment—loved, respected and honored by his comrades.... The noble boy, he is gone, and who can fill the void left at home?"[18]

Capt. James F. Hart and his battery fought through the rest of the war, adding to their stellar combat record. These Carolinians were in some 140 engagements during the conflict "and everywhere was distinguished for valor and effectiveness," former Confederate general Ellison Capers wrote. Hart, however, was not to emerge unscathed. After being with Hampton during the Petersburg campaign, the captain, now 27, was wounded at Burgess's Mill on October 27, 1864, losing his leg as a result. He returned home to recover, his service bringing a promotion to major. Crippled but undefeated, Hart began his journey to rejoin the army in spring 1865, but the Confederacy was finished. In Yorkville,

South Carolina, he resumed his law practice in 1866, later being elected to the state legislature. He and his wife, M.J., raised six children.[19]

Unlike Hart, the seemingly bulletproof color bearer Louis Sherfesee of Hart's Battery continued his run of luck and divine intervention by surviving the rest of the war without being wounded. In four years of war, Sherfesee bore his flag in more than 140 engagements, including virtually every major battle fought by the Army of Northern Virginia. During that time he was absent one week due to illness and had three weeks of furlough. After surrendering with the army in North Carolina (where he apparently hid the colors to prevent their capture), Sherfesee returned to Charleston and was successful in the insurance business for several years. He also dabbled in politics during this period, becoming a member of the state convention that helped his old general, Wade Hampton, be elected governor. Sherfesee moved to North Carolina in 1877, where he engaged in farming for a decade or so before settling in Rock Hill, South Carolina, and establishing a "machine works." By 1895, he had returned to the insurance business, and he and his family were again living in Charleston. Sherfesee and the rest of Hart's Battery were immortalized in an untitled poem from that period whose writer is unknown:

> High rolled the tide of battle through the years
> And ever on its crest Hart's battery moved,
> While women, bowed in grief, shed bitter tears
> For many who by death their fealty proved
> To State and Cause. Still led Guidon on!
> Still Sherfesee upheld it in the fight—
> While through the smoke its pure white crescent shone
> And staunch Palmetto said: "Right shall be Might!"[20]

Capt. William Bachman and his cannoneers were sent to South Carolina in fall 1863 to recruit and try to fill the battery's depleted ranks. The battery served between Charleston and Savannah until winter 1865, when it moved north and surrendered with Joe Johnston in North Carolina. Returning to civilian life, Bachman was a state legislator in 1865–1866, later serving as state assistant attorney general from 1880 to 1890.[21]

In Bachman's ranks, Louis Jacobs and his battery mate Anton William Jager also survived Gettysburg and the rest of the war, excelling in their return to peacetime. Jacobs relocated to Kingstree, South Carolina, where he became a successful businessman. He was elected to a probate judgeship in 1870 and later served as Williamsburg County sheriff for several years before being appointed chief inspector of customs for the port of Charleston. Jacobs returned to Kingstree in 1895, where he resumed his mercantile career and also served as postmaster. Married in 1870, he and his wife, Mary, had eleven children. Jager bore the battery's colors throughout the war and "had the good fortune to escape with slight wounds," stated one account. He returned to Charleston after the guns fell silent and decades later was described as "for many years a prosperous merchant" in the city. "Jager among the veterans enjoys the reputation of being a gallant and devoted soldier, nobly earned in a brave and unselfish career," said one contemporary account.[22]

Blinded and believed to be dying, Capt. John K. McIver of the Eighth South Carolina's Company F was nursed by the Simmons sisters in their Williamsport cottage and regained some degree of health. His ongoing recovery, however, would ultimately doom him, because Union authorities sent him to Point Lookout. McIver died of exposure either en route to the prison complex or after arriving there, based on different accounts, and was buried in a nearby cemetery. "Such was the sad end of many gallant officers &

many more breathed their last far, far away from the dearly loved ones at home," related the South Carolina cavalryman Col. John L. Black, who tried to assist McIver at Williamsport. Despite a grapeshot wound to the head, Lt. George Bozeman, also of the Eighth's Company F, recovered from his supposedly mortal injury at Gettysburg and rejoined the army. He survived the war, raised a large family and kept the grapeshot —scratched by the surgeon's forceps during its extrication—as a souvenir.[23]

Capt. Romulus Bowden, of the Thirteenth South Carolina's Company A, lived despite his two Gettysburg wounds but was forced to retire from active duty in 1864. He carried a bullet in his left arm for fifteen years after the war, and the missing index finger on his left hand was evidence of his other wound. He resumed his mercantile career as a civilian in Greenville and Spartanburg counties, later becoming vice president of the Spartanburg Savings Bank. Bowden and his wartime bride, Mary, had six children.[24]

The wounded Lt. Robert Briggs Watson of the Fourteenth South Carolina endured the retreat, crossing the Potomac and being taken by wagon to Winchester, Virginia. He spent a week in bed there, amid rat-infested conditions, before being moved to Staunton, Virginia, and later to Richmond. From the Confederate capital Watson made his way toward home in a boxcar, with stops in Florence and Society Hill, South Carolina, before reaching Columbia, where his wife met him in a carriage to take him home.[25]

Due to his Gettysburg wounds, Lt. Stephen Gilbert of the Brooks Artillery was disabled for more than three months—107 days to be precise—before he recovered enough to rejoin the army. Gilbert was in combat at Spotsylvania and in the Petersburg siege before he was among the Confederates captured at Sailor's Creek, a few days before Lee's surrender at Appomattox. Gilbert was held at Johnson's Island until his release in July 1865. He then returned to his prewar job as a conductor on the South Carolina & Georgia Railroad and was active in Confederate veterans' affairs. Gilbert had not yet arrived at Johnson's Island when another Carolina soldier was leaving after surviving a seventeen-month incarceration there. One-armed Capt. John Dewberry of the Thirteenth South Carolina in Perrin's brigade was sent to Virginia in late February 1865 to be exchanged and was furloughed in March. The long road from Gettysburg was finally leading him home to Spartanburg County. His war was over. Dewberry's later years were devoted to various county positions, including nine years as sheriff and also three years as a state legislator. He died at his home near Spartanburg in January 1909. A newspaper account stated that in Dewberry's passing, the county "loses one of her most highly esteemed citizens…. He was a man of high Christian character."[26]

Jacob W. Cagle, the officer in Kershaw's Second South Carolina who, with his unidentified servant, escaped across the Potomac on a captured horse, recovered from his leg wound and rejoined his company. He fought to the end, surrendering his command with Johnston's army in North Carolina. In the postwar era, Cagle was a successful builder and contractor in Greenville, South Carolina.[27]

Still pained by his foot wound, Capt. William C. Coker—or Cohen, depending on the source—of Kershaw's Eighth South Carolina, was taken from the Williamsport hospital, where he was captured, and was sent to Johnson's Island. He was imprisoned there until March 1864, when he was sent to Fort Delaware, paroled in February 1865. In peacetime, he farmed in Darlington County and married Mary E. McIver of Darlington, the couple having seven children. Coker also went into manufacturing and served as a state senator.[28]

The Third South Carolina's Capt. Chesley W. Herbert healed from his Gettysburg injuries in time to fight at the Wilderness in May 1864. There he was shot in the left knee; the wound plagued him for the rest of his short life. Herbert was carried by litter from Virginia to his Newberry home to convalesce yet again under the care of his wife, Elizabeth. Herbert was well enough to return to the army shortly before the war's end. On March 8, 1866, he was returning home from a trip in the Lexington County vicinity when a man stole his horse, states one account from a Newberry County historian. Though lame, Herbert managed to apprehend the thief and then shared food with the man by the roadside. Suddenly, the man attacked, clubbing Herbert with a "heavy stick." With Herbert lying insensible, his assailant snatched a pistol from his pocket and shot Herbert in the head, killing him instantly. The man was later arrested and escaped but was recaptured. He eventually confessed and was convicted and hanged for the slaying.[29]

The severely wounded Maj. Edward Croft of the Fourteenth South Carolina, still attended by his servant Henry Deas, made it to Winchester, where he was nursed in the home of a "Mrs. Williams." Union forces soon swept through the town, which changed hands repeatedly during the war, but Federal doctors still did not expect him to survive. Croft proved them wrong, living to be exchanged and sent home to Greenville to continue his recovery over several months. Despite losing "the use of his sword arm," he returned to the army and fought with the Fourteenth in the Richmond-Petersburg battles and was promoted to lieutenant colonel in the war's waning months. Wounded again, he refused to leave his regiment, remaining with Lee's forces until the surrender at Appomattox.[30]

Maj. William Wallace of the Second South Carolina, who led Kershaw's sharpshooters in the July 2 fighting, was wounded in the arm at Gettysburg. At least two South Carolina newspapers reported that Wallace by mid–July was "on his way home" to Columbia to recuperate. He recovered and fought through the rest of the war, being promoted colonel after the battle of Bentonville in North Carolina. Wallace came home after the conflict, resuming his life as a planter, serving as a state senator and being appointed postmaster of Columbia in 1894 by President Grover Cleveland. He was 78 when he died in November 1902. "No truer soldier drew sword for the southern States in that great war," one account stated.[31]

The rigors of the long marches to and from Gettysburg, not to mention the titanic battle itself and the severity of his Antietam wound, were too much to bear for Col. D. Wyatt Aiken of the Seventh South Carolina in Kershaw's brigade. Deemed unfit for further active duty in the field, he spent much of the rest of the war as post commander at Macon, Georgia, before being discharged due to his disabilities. He was active in politics and a Democratic Party leader for many years before his death in April 1887. Aiken was "a fine officer, rigid in discipline and brave to a fa[u]lt," one of his old soldiers remembered.[32]

N. Scott Allen of Company K, Fourteenth South Carolina, escaped being wounded or killed at Gettysburg, although his uniform was riddled and the stock of his musket splintered. His good fortune there would soon turn bad again, like it had at Gaines' Mill and Chancellorsville, where he was wounded on both fields. In action at Spotsylvania in 1864, he was shot in the face, the bullet entering one cheek and passing out the other. His mouth was open and he was yelling at the time, thus saving his tongue, but his speech was impaired for the rest of his days. The ghastly injury caused him to be sent home to recover, but his gallantry at Spotsylvania resulted in a promotion to captain. Allen returned to service during the Petersburg campaign. By the time of the surrender at Appomattox, the Fourteenth had been so decimated that Allen commanded six companies, a total of

35 men in all, according to one account. During Reconstruction, Allen organized a rifle company that helped keep the peace during this turbulent time. John Robert Smith of the Fourteenth's Company C was wounded in both legs at Gettysburg. Left on the field, he was captured and eventually had his right leg amputated. Observing his 20th birthday in Union custody, Smith was sent to Davids' Island and later Fort Delaware before being exchanged in 1864. Smith graduated S.C. Medical College in 1867 and settled in his native Laurens County, serving as a doctor and a state representative. Harrison P. Griffith of the Fourteenth's Company E was shot in the leg at Gettysburg but returned to duty in time to fight at the Wilderness in May 1864. A more severe wound disabled him there. The war then being over for him, he returned to civilian life with his wife, Amanda, and in 1902 was still working as a professor of English at Limestone College.[33]

In the ranks of the Seventh South Carolina of Kershaw's command, Lt. Col. Elbert Bland, 40, recovered from his thigh wound at Gettysburg, but his life's hourglass was running short. Bland had served as an assistant surgeon of the Palmetto Regiment in the Mexican War and was a principal organizer of the Seventh after the guns blazed at Fort Sumter. He was still healing from a serious arm wound he sustained at Savage's Station in June 1862 when he fell at Gettysburg. He recuperated enough to accompany the regiment to Chickamauga, but was mortally wounded on September 20, 1863, living only about two hours. Bland was beloved by his troops, one old "hell cat" recalling, "He had the ear of a tiger and the eye of an eagle and was as straight and slender as the mountain pine." Bland's remains were returned to his native Edgefield County, South Carolina, for burial. Years later, when his widow, Rebecca Griffin Bland, was on her deathbed in 1891, she asked that her husband's grave and casket be opened so that she could be placed there with him in their eternal sleep.[34]

After Gettysburg, Lt. Col. Franklin Gaillard of the Second South Carolina continued to lead the regiment until its commander, Col. John D. Kennedy, recovered from the wound he had received there. Gaillard continued in service with the Second until his death at the Wilderness on May 6, 1864. In that drawn-out battle, Kennedy was again wounded, and Gaillard took over. "He assumed his duties cheerfully and with a smile, but fell immediately after, pierced by a rifle ball in the forehead." He was 35.[35]

Col. J.W. Henagan of the Eighth South Carolina in Kershaw's brigade survived Gettysburg, which had so decimated his regiment. But war ripped him away from his family and Marlboro County farm. Captured near Winchester in fall 1864 and sent to Johnson's Island, he died there on April 22, 1865, the war's end in sight. "There was little or no fear in him," Dickert wrote of Henagan, adding that he was "as generous as brave. His purse was open to the needs of the poor."[36]

Col. James D. Nance of the Third South Carolina in Kershaw's ranks returned to his regiment on July 3 after recuperating from his Fredericksburg wound. Known for his coolness in combat, "the well being of his men seemed to be his ruling aim and ambition," one Carolinian wrote. Nance led the Third South Carolina at Chickamauga and Knoxville. He was killed at the Wilderness on May 6, 1864, and his body was brought home to Newberry for burial "with honors befitting a brilliant and brave officer," said one account. Nance "was as consistent a Christian as he was a brave soldier and a brilliant man." Maj. Robert C. Maffett of the Third South Carolina was promoted to colonel in the months after Gettysburg, his rise based not only on his leadership and gallantry but also on the fatal attrition of officers above him. Maffett was captured in a skirmish near Charlestown, West Virginia, in August 1864. Described as "being a perfect type of an ideal soldier," he died of "brain fever" in prison shortly before the war's end, leaving behind his wife and young daughter.[37]

Col. W.G. Rice and his Third S.C. Battalion fought under Longstreet in the 1863 Knoxville campaign. It was there that Rice suffered his second severe wound of the war; this time he was incapacitated from further service. He returned to his home state and eventually settled near Abbeville, where he resumed farming. Rice and his wife, Sarah, had eleven children.[38]

Maj. William M. Gist, who led the Fifteenth South Carolina after Col. De Saussure's fall on July 2, "had no opportunity to display his great qualities as a civilian, but as a soldier, he was all that the most exacting could desire," wrote another Carolinian. Gist did not survive the year. At Knoxville, he was killed on November 18, 1863, while leading his troops, casting "aside all prudence and care, recklessly" dashing in front of his column against the city's defenses. "Leadership placed himself [*sic*] where danger was greatest, bullets falling thick and fast; thus by the inspiration of his own individual courage, he hoped to carry his men with him to success, or to meet a fate like his own."[39]

Maj. Thomas J. Lipscomb, who led the Second South Carolina Cavalry at Gettysburg, was promoted to colonel in September 1863 and survived the war. He would serve as mayor of Columbia, South Carolina, and was superintendent of the state penitentiary for several years. At age 75, he died on November 4, 1908, after a "lengthy and severe illness," and was buried in Newberry, South Carolina.[40]

Maj. David G. McIntosh, of A.P. Hill's artillery reserve, fought through the rest of the war, suffering a slight wound in the fighting at the Crater. In peacetime, he settled in Towson, Maryland, where he continued in the legal profession. Dr. T.W. Salmond, Kershaw's brigade surgeon, had seen action with the South Carolina troops from Fort Sumter to Gettysburg to Chickamauga and beyond. In ill health, he left the army and returned home in spring 1864. Salmond resumed his medical practice in Camden until his death on August 31, 1869, his 44th birthday.[41]

In December 1863, several weeks after his prisoner exchange, one of Salmond's colleagues, Dr. Simon Baruch, was assigned to the military hospitals at Newnan, Georgia, near Atlanta. Baruch was there a few months before returning to the medical corps of the Army of Northern Virginia in spring 1864. He endured the horrors of the meat-grinding battles of the Wilderness and Spotsylvania. His bravery and medical deeds earned him a promotion from assistant surgeon to full surgeon in July; this also resulted in his rise from captain to major. Baruch, however, was having eye problems which were ongoing and was granted a leave of absence in December. He spent Christmas 1864 in Camden and weeks later requested assignment for hospital duty behind the lines. Baruch served in Confederate hospitals in North Carolina in the spring—hearing of Lee's surrender at Appomattox—but soon developed a severe case of typhoid fever which left him fighting for survival. He slowly improved over a two-week period and learned that the war was over. Baruch set up his medical practice in Camden, later relocating to New York City before returning to Camden in March 1866. He spent the next fifteen or so years there, practicing and developing new medical techniques, also serving as president of the South Carolina Medical Association.[42]

Returning to New York in 1881, Baruch "became a consulting physician of wide repute" while studying and redefining surgery for appendicitis. He also spearheaded efforts to establish free public baths in the city by 1901, believing this would help sanitary conditions and thus curtail many health issues. During World War I, Baruch visited and lectured at various army and navy camps and installations, promoting the "vital importance of water, rest, air, food and exercise in battling with disease." He and his wife, Isabel, celebrated their golden wedding anniversary in 1917 with their four sons and eight of their grandchildren. By 1921, however, the 80-year-old Baruch was engaged in a months-long struggle with lung problems complicated by heart disease. He lost this battle on June 4, 1921, dying at his home on West 70th Street. *The New York Times* described him as "the pioneer of scientific hydrotherapy in America," but the physician was also well known as the father of the famous financier Bernard M. Baruch.[43]

Dr. Thomas McCoy, who tended to the First South Carolina's sick and wounded left at Gettysburg, was eventually taken into Union custody and imprisoned at Fort Delaware for fourteen months before his release. McCoy eventually returned to his medical practice in Laurens, South Carolina.[44]

Some two weeks after Gettysburg, General Wade Hampton was still recuperating in Charlottesville, Virginia, and was optimistic about his recovery. His head was healing nicely, but the fragment in his hip had not yet been extracted and was troublesome. A promotion to major general in early August bolstered his spirits, but by late that month his progress had slowed and shortly thereafter he suffered a relapse, which lengthened his return to duty. Hampton was finally able to return to command in early November 1863. When Jeb Stuart was mortally wounded at Yellow Tavern on May 11, 1864, Hampton rose to command of the Army of Northern Virginia's cavalry corps. He did a stellar job of leading the cavalry through the rest of that year in the combat around Richmond and Petersburg, despite the ever-weakening condition of the Confederate military. As always, his personal bravery was beyond question, the major unknown being the number of Yankees he had personally slain. "It is said that Major General Hampton has killed twenty-two men in hand to hand fights," stated the *Richmond Enquirer* on June 13, 1864. "He always goes into battle in advance of his troops, generally has the first blow, and does yeoman's share of the conflict."[45]

A small note about Hampton, appearing in several newspapers in South Carolina and Virginia in October 1864, illustrated that the war flame still burned fiercely within him despite his wounds and the South's decline. Hampton had ordered a new sword from "Messrs. Kraft, Goldsmith & Kraft, of the sword factory in the vicinity of Columbia," the *Richmond Sentinel* reported on October 21. A correspondent for the Columbia *South Carolinian* was shown the blade, "destined to flash, ere long, in the hand of" the general. "A polished black sheath, a richly guilt hilt, handsomely wrought with the figures of St. George and the dragon, and a long, straight, heavy, but well balanced blade, of the truest temper, make it a weapon worthy of a leader who is said to unite the qualities of a *pruex chevalier* with those of a wise and skillful strategist."[46]

In January 1865, Hampton and some of his command were assigned to Joseph E. Johnston, fighting in the Carolinas, and he was promoted to lieutenant general in February. Hampton was with Johnston's army when it surrendered to Sherman in late April. Returning to South Carolina politics after the war, Hampton was a key figure in opposing Reconstruction and was elected governor in 1876. Reelected two years later, he also served as a U.S. senator from 1879 to 1891. In November 1878, shortly before heading to Washington, Hampton was thrown from a mule while hunting and sustained a compound fracture of the right leg. The limb had to be amputated a few weeks later, in early December. Hampton's many supporters kept a close eye on the state of his health during this period. In late January or early February 1879, there were rumors that he had suffered a setback "and was again dangerously sick." A report in the *Charleston News and Courier* quieted these fears, stating there was "no foundation" that the ex-governor had relapsed, although his Gettysburg injuries still tormented him. "The wound he received at Gettysburg [it is unclear which one] gives him intense pain, his nervous system is sadly shattered, and he makes little progress in regaining the bodily strength he sorely needs."[47]

Hampton recovered enough to take his seat in the U.S. Senate. A New York newsman offered an interesting account of Hampton in the Senate, including a pair of incredible—if true—Gettysburg-related encounters one day in Washington. "It is rather mournful to look at Wade Hampton in the Senate, nursing his stump of a leg and subjecting his splendid physique to the disgrace of crutches," the unidentified reporter with the *Brooklyn Eagle Ledger* wrote in spring 1880. "The General, in the hope of picking up some views about cut legs, has a way of stopping people similarly afflicted." One day Hampton was standing on his crutches near the Senate chamber entrance when he saw a large man minus a leg who was using a contraption "like a framework, light and portable" to help him get around. Hampton approached the stranger, inquired about the device and was told that the man had invented it himself.

"May I ask where you lost your leg?" Hampton continued.

"Yes certainly, it went off when Hampton charged our battery at Gettysburg."

"Indeed; I am grieved to hear it," said the general very sincerely. "My name is Hampton."

"They shook hands over the bloody chasm," and Hampton learned the stranger was a House representative from Wisconsin. Later that day Hampton took a streetcar for the ride to his Washington residence. A one-armed man boarded the car and Hampton "invited him to a seat and managed the payment of his fare." Asking where the man lost his limb, the stranger replied, "'Well sir, it was at Gettysburg when Hampton made that terrific charge with his cavalry.' Whereupon those two shook hands and made up."[48]

Finally leaving the political realm, Hampton was a railroad commissioner for five years before exiting that post in 1899. He was 84 when he died in Columbia in April 1902. An estimated 20,000 people lined the streets as his hearse made its way to the Trinity Church cemetery. Hampton held the distinction of being one of three civilians with no formal military training to attain the rank of lieutenant general in the Confederate armies (the other two were Richard Taylor and Nathan Bedford Forrest). His last words were reported to be: "God bless all my people, black and white."[49]

Brig. Gen. Joseph Kershaw fought through the rest of the war, and was promoted to major general in May 1864. He and his troops accompanied Lee's army on the retreat from Richmond and Petersburg. He was captured in the battle of Sailor's Creek on April 6, 1865, and was imprisoned until July. In peacetime he returned to his law practice and was elected to the South Carolina Senate in 1865. Kershaw was elected a circuit judge in 1877, holding this post until ill health forced him to resign in 1893. He was the Camden postmaster in the following months, dying there on April 12, 1894. He was buried in the town's Quaker Cemetery. "The widespread grief at the death of Gen. Kershaw is the natural expression of the love and devotion of each and every one to that noble son of South Carolina," the Fairfield *News and Herald* noted on April 18. "Pure as a soldier, pure as a judge, pure as a citizen and a man, pure in every walk of life, he could not but possess the esteem and honor, the love and affection of each and all of his fellow citizens…. None of South Carolina's many soldiers did better service, [or] saw more of hard and desperate fighting." The *State* added: "No man was more closely identified with South Carolina in the different stages of her history in the past half century—no man was more generally loved by her people…. The death of such a man is a loss to the State—to the country— which would be all the greater but for the example he has left—an example which all the people of South Carolina will do well to follow."[50]

Years after the conflict, Kershaw reflected on Gettysburg and the causes of the Confederate debacle there. He boiled it down to eleven words: "the want of simultaneous movement and cooperation between the troops employed." Of the "eventful series of battles" over the three days, "this was the cause of all the failures. Every attack was magnificent and successful, but failed in the end for the want of cooperation between corps, divisions, brigades, and, in some instances, regiments of the same brigade," he wrote. "The want of cooperation … caused the loss of Gettysburg to the Confederates." Kershaw also defended himself, McLaws and their troops for their promptness throughout the campaign: "It will be seen, too, that there was no loss of time on the part of McLaws's division, from the day it left Culpeper to that of its arrival at Gettysburg. If any ensued after that, it was due to circumstances wholly unknown to the writer. Certainly, the loss of time, if any, would not have lost the fight, if there had been perfect cooperation of all the troops. But, except to vindicate the truth, it is vain to inquire into the causes of our failure."[51]

After Gettysburg, Maj. Gen. Richard Anderson continued his division command through the rest of the combat trials of 1863 and into the bloodbath of the 1864 spring campaigns. When Longstreet was wounded at the Wilderness, Anderson, then 42, was promoted lieutenant general to lead Longstreet's corps. Upon Longstreet's return, Anderson commanded a portion of the Richmond defenses. When Lee evacuated Richmond in early April 1865, Anderson led troops in the retreat. The battle of Sailor's Creek resulted in a large portion of the army being captured. Anderson escaped to rejoin Lee's remaining forces, but his military career was over. He was relieved and authorized to return home the day before Lee's surrender at Appomattox. His postwar life was uneventful, although he struggled to make ends meet. He was the state phosphate inspector when he died at Beaufort, South Carolina, in 1879. Anderson was buried at Beaufort in the Episcopal Cemetery of St. Helena's Church.[52]

Brig. Gen. Evander Law fought at Chickamauga in September 1863 and assumed command of Hood's division when the latter was again felled by a severe wound. Law fought at the Wilderness and Spotsylvania before being wounded in the head at Cold Harbor, a bullet injuring his left eye. After months of recovery, Law asked to be relieved so that he could command a force of cavalry. Sent to North Carolina in the war's closing weeks, Law served under Joe Johnston until the surrender. Despite his wartime injuries, Law lived for more than half a century; he moved to Florida, where he was a key figure in establishing the state's public education system. He also was a journalist until his last years, serving as editor of the *Bartow* (Fla.) *Courier-Informant*, one of the oldest and best newspapers in the state. In an interview with the *Tampa Daily Times* in May 1920, the aging general spoke about his physical condition. "We old folks get a little too smart occasionally … and suffer as a result," he said, adding that he had bought a new hoe a few days earlier. He used the hoe too much and was beset by rheumatism, which "doesn't exactly agree with a man of 83. It's a mighty poor bed fellow." Asked about his career, Law replied, "For a long time I thought … that the most effective work of my life was done while I was fighting Yankees. In recent years, however, I have concluded that my best work has been for the school children … and in loving the men I fought. There's no room in our country for factionalism and hatred—there's room for nothing but unity and love." Law turned 84 in August and died at Bartow on Halloween, 1920, after being ill for about a week. At the time, he was the ranking surviving officer of the Confederate army. "Thousands of South Carolinians will be grieved to hear" of Law's passing, the *State* reported on November 1. "He had many relatives and friends here and was a frequent visitor." The article also noted Law's strong ties to York, South Carolina, where he taught school and met his future wife.[53]

Col. Abner Perrin, whose South Carolina brigade distinguished itself at such a high cost on Gettysburg's first day, was promoted brigadier general in September 1863. He continued his fine combat record in the coming months before the armies clashed at Spotsylvania Courthouse on May 12, 1864. "I shall come out of this fight a live major general or a dead brigadier," Perrin is reported to have remarked before going into that battle. Much as he had done at Seminary Ridge some ten months earlier, Perrin rode into the fray, waving his sword to encourage an attack by his troops. Moments later he was riddled by seven bullets, toppling dead from the saddle. That night, Robert E. Lee mentioned the death of the "brave General Perrin" in a dispatch to Confederate secretary of war James A. Seddon. Perrin was buried in Fredericksburg's City Cemetery. "All Edgefield [Perrin's home district] is saddened to learn that this high-toned gentleman has fallen," the *Edgefield Advertiser* said on May 25. "Here where we have known him long and loved him well, this sad announcement brings a sigh and a tear, and in sorrow we mourn, for one of nature's noblemen has been taken from us forever.... At home he was the upright man and the true gentleman; in the army the brave soldier and courteous officer. Ever bright and glorious will be the memory of Gen. Abner Perrin."[54]

Two of Perrin's regimental commanders at Gettysburg also never saw the Palmetto State again before the war's end. Col. John L. Miller of the Twelfth South Carolina was mortally wounded at the Wilderness. Shot in the throat, Miller "only survived a few hours," a news account stated. Days later at Spotsylvania, Lt. Col. Benjamin T. Brockman of the Thirteenth was desperately wounded in the head and right arm. The arm was amputated, and Brockman lingered until June 8, when he died in a Richmond hospital. Maj. Charles Wick McCreary of the First South Carolina was promoted colonel of the regiment in May 1864. On March 31, 1865, less than two weeks before Lee's surrender at Appomattox Courthouse, McCreary was killed in action near Hatcher's Run, Virginia.[55]

Col. John D. Kennedy overcame his Gettysburg injuries only to be seriously wounded again at the Wilderness; he was incapacitated for about five months. He was able to continue in Kershaw's command in fall 1864 when he and his troops were detached and sent to help oppose Sherman's march through Georgia and the Carolinas. Kennedy was promoted brigadier in December 1864, serving with Johnston's army until the war's end. His service showed he was either very lucky or very unlucky, based on one's point of view: Kennedy was wounded six times, but survived, and also was struck fifteen times by spent balls. The general was primarily engaged in planting until 1877, when he returned to his law practice in Camden. Becoming active in Democratic Party politics, he served in the legislature and as lieutenant governor before being appointed consul general at Shanghai by President Grover Cleveland in 1886. Kennedy died of a sudden stroke at Camden on April 14, 1896, two years and a day after the passing of his friend and comrade General Joseph Kershaw. Like Kershaw, Kennedy rests in Camden's Quaker Cemetery.[56]

Col. John L. Black of the First South Carolina Cavalry returned to his hometown of

York, South Carolina, after the war and settled in the nearby community of Blacksburg, where his family had property and mining interests. The village, in fact, was named for Black's uncle, William Black. The ex-colonel was vice president of an iron and steel ore company in that area in the 1880s. In Columbia, South Carolina, on a December night in 1881, Black had a chance encounter with William "Zack" Leitner, the wounded captain in Kershaw's brigade whom Black had tried to aid when both were recuperating in Winchester, Virginia, some eighteen years earlier. Still hobbled by the amputation of his leg, Leitner told Black about how he had reached Williamsport during the Confederate retreat. The ambulance conveying him and others was forced to stop by a broken doubletree, and Leitner had sent the driver about a mile to the rear to retrieve a replacement from another wrecked wagon. The ambulance made it to Williamsport despite enduring shellfire from Union guns. After crossing the Potomac, both Carolinians ended up in Winchester, never forgetting the ladies of that town who had aided them and so many other wounded. "They were ministering Angels, and more to us," Black recalled. "They worked night and day, placing the bleeding forms of our wounded on their beds and gave us all they had to give." Black likely also saved the life of Col. J.D. Kennedy, mentioned above, commandeering Jeb Stuart's personal ambulance to rescue his fellow Carolinian, who was abandoned by a Virginia roadside. According to Black, he and Kennedy enjoyed "a very warm, personal relationship" after the war. Black was 71 when he died of a heart attack in March 1902, being laid to rest at Aimwell Cemetery in Ridgeway, South Carolina.[57]

Gettysburg took its painful toll among South Carolinians for years, even decades, after the battle. William E. Murphy was a teenager when he marched north with Company E of the Fifteenth South Carolina in Kershaw's command. A terrible wound at Gettysburg "disabled him for life" and he died in Winnsboro in April 1869 "after a long and painful illness of disease of the heart." He was 22 when the gravediggers covered him. M.C. Brewer, "a prominent resident" of Florence, South Carolina, died in October 1882 "from the effects of a wound which he had received in the leg at … Gettysburg," the *Yorkville Enquirer* noted. "It had never healed, and about two weeks ago brought on an attack of paralysis from which he did not rally."[58]

Some thirteen years after Gettysburg, James M. Davis of Camden was still living with a shell fragment in his body. Davis was a lieutenant in the Fifteenth South Carolina's Company D and was the regimental adjutant. He was wounded in the thigh by a shell which exploded over his head. With the metal still lodged in his leg, he came home and resumed his law practice, becoming a community leader. Davis "recovered from the wound, which gave him no uneasiness until a few months back, when an abscess formed on his thigh," an 1876 news account noted. Dr. L.H. Deas examined the leg and, cutting into the abscess, extracted the shell fragment "that had been imbedded in the muscles" since July 1863. Still suffering from the effects of the wound and extraction, Davis was 43 when he succumbed "after a painful and protracted illness" at his home in January 1878, his mother, widow and six children mourning his loss. "Tidings of the death of this estimable gentleman will be received with the profoundest regret wherever he was known," the *Camden Journal* stated. S. Hamilton Fellers had lost an arm and was also wounded in the knee in Kershaw's July 2 attack. He was 59 when he died at his Newberry home in May 1892. "He had been suffering for some time with an old wound received at Gettysburg during the late war," a newspaper death notice said.[59]

"A Good Man Gone" was the headline on the death notice for Col. Edward Croft, credited with being the first Confederate officer to enter Gettysburg on July 1. Despite his severe wounds, Croft survived the war, returned to his civilian life as a planter in Edge-field County, and was on the Board of Visitors at the Citadel (formerly the S.C. Military Academy). Croft, 56, died at his home in Greenville on May 9, 1892, after a months-long struggle against heart disease. His right arm remained useless to the end of his days due to his Gettysburg injuries. "In the death of Col. Croft the State loses one of her truest cit-izens—his wife a devoted husband and his children a fond and loving father," the *State* said of Croft. "Peace to his ashes and green be his memory!"[60]

Other Palmetto soldiers who came home from the war were already rejoining their comrades lost at Gettysburg. B.R. Clyburn was 37 when he died near Yorkville, South Carolina, in March 1877, his body wracked by combat injuries. As captain of the Second South Carolina's Company H, Clyburn was twice wounded at Antietam, was hit in the face and leg at Gettysburg and lost a leg at Cedar Creek.[61]

One-legged William "Zack" Leitner, mentioned earlier in this chapter, served his state for more than two decades after the war. His record included two terms as state rep-resentative from Kershaw district, a district judgeship, serving as state senator, and being elected the South Carolina secretary of state in 1886. All of his civilian accomplishments seem worlds away from that July day when then–Capt. Leitner led his company in the Second South Carolina into the jaws of perdition at the Peach Orchard and Wheatfield. Leitner's demise was much less eventful. At his Columbia home on Sunday, April 15, 1888, the 60-year-old veteran dressed for church, collapsed and died of natural causes. "He was one of the most popular men in the State; and he was a true friend to all who sought his friendship," the *Yorkville Enquirer* eulogized three days later.[62]

John O.H. Clarkson, 57, died in Columbia, South Carolina, in September 1895, a survivor in the ranks of the Second South Carolina. Clarkson "participated in at least 20 battles, [including Gettysburg] and what is remarkable never received a wound or obtained a furlough," stated an obituary. Clarkson was invalided for the last ten years of his life "doubtless from the effects of his unremitting exposure in the service of his coun-try." Eight pallbearers, all fellow veterans, laid him to rest. Among Clarkson's mourners was his "old body servant," identified only as "Manda," who was with him throughout the war. Hearing of Clarkson's illness, Manda came twenty miles to aid and comfort Clarkson in the month before his death. The former slave "mingled his tears with those of the fam-ily" as the old soldier took his last breath.[63]

Jacob Rentiers was a child when his family immigrated to America from Heidelberg, Germany, and settled in Charleston. He enlisted in the Richardson Guards and eventu-ally joined Kershaw's Second South Carolina. Wounded three times in the conflict, he was captured at Gettysburg and imprisoned at Point Lookout for seven months. "Mr. Rentiers was intensely Southern in his views and was interested in all matters pertaining to the Confederacy," a news account stated. He spent many of his postwar years supervis-ing or working in local sawmills. "It was his wish, often expressed during his recent ill-ness, that he would be spared to see the coming reunion, being then content to die." It was not to be. Rentiers was 58 when he passed away in his Charleston home on the morning of March 21, 1899. Lancaster resident Lewis Parker, in his mid–60s, died of "dropsy" in early September 1899 after being ill for several months. Shot in the face at Gettysburg, he "bore the scar to his grave."[64]

One of the more bizarre endings came to William J. Germany, a former private in the Twelfth South Carolina's Company F, who lived through the war despite wounds and hardships. Germany was unscathed in combat until Gettysburg, where he was shot in the thigh and captured. Sent to Davids' Island, he recovered and was exchanged in time to fight at Spotsylvania, where he was again taken prisoner. Freed again, he returned to the army and was captured a third time. After the war he worked in a sawmill and as a railroad engineer. The latter job resulted in his death in a "deplorable railroad accident" on June 9, 1893. Surviving veterans of the old Company F called a meeting for July 6 at the Fairfield County courthouse in Winnsboro, South Carolina. The meeting was "for the purpose of offering a tribute of respect" to their late comrade, "Bro. Jack." Each veteran "spoke feelingly and appropriately of his meritorious character," the Fairfield *News and Herald* said of Germany, who left behind a widow and three children.[65]

John A. Montgomery, a veteran of Company I, in the Twelfth South Carolina, survived the war, but also met his doom under violent and tragic circumstances. Montgomery, a native of Lancaster County, South Carolina, was a corporal, fought at Gettysburg and was wounded three times during the conflict. After the surrender, Montgomery and his parents moved to Mississippi, where Montgomery married and settled in Oxford. In December 1901, Montgomery was a lawman, possibly a sheriff's deputy, when he and another officer tried to arrest an "outlaw by the name of Will Mathis," a newspaper account stated. There was a bloody confrontation at Mathis's home, some twelve miles from Oxford, and both officers were killed, their bodies found in the burning house. Mathis and two others were caught and sentenced to hang for the murders. W.G.A. Porter, a comrade in the Twelfth and a childhood friend of Montgomery, remembered their early days before they went to war: "Many were the days we played together and swung on the grape vine swing when little boys, and when the cruel war began we were still in our teens."[66]

There were other Gettysburg victims from South Carolina who had never been there but were haunted by tragic personal losses in Pennsylvania. Among them was Lucinda H. Mays, who left behind her husband George and three daughters when she died of "paralysis" three days before Christmas in 1871. On the evening before her passing at her Edgefield home, Mrs. Mays, a devout Baptist, asked one of her daughters to sing a hymn about "a heavenly rest which she rejoiced in as fast approaching." She looked forward to joining her two small children "long since taken to the spirit land" and her son, John C. Mays, "who fell on the battlefield of Gettysburg." Mrs. Polly M. Cromer, 90, of Newberry, was a widow who raised eleven children before her demise in fall 1909. She was preceded in death by two sons, Capt. W.P. Cromer, killed at Gettysburg, and Thomas A. Cromer, who also died in the war.[67]

Then there were many other Carolinians, veterans who also went about their daily lives despite the ghastly injuries they had suffered in the battle. J.R. Boyles the Twelfth South Carolina lieutenant, who lost a leg at Gettysburg, was a probate judge in Winnsboro in the 1880s. After being exchanged in March 1864, Boyles was unfit for further active military service and returned to his home near Ridgeway. He learned telegraphy and obtained a job with the railroad and telegraph offices there, working the lines during Sherman's fiery advance through the Palmetto State. Boyles would be reminded of Gettysburg for the rest of his days as he hobbled about on his crutches. The drunken Confederate surgeon who amputated his leg had done such a horrific job that Boyles was never able to wear an artificial limb.[68]

In the 1882 county commission race in Fairfield County (of which Winnsboro is the county seat), three candidates were ex–Confederates maimed in the war, including

Capt. John A. Hinnant, also of the Twelfth, a farmer "having frequently to follow the plow on his wooden leg," his real limb having been left behind in July 1863. Nine years before the election, Hinnant was lauded as "a model citizen" of Fairfield County who set "an example of industry that our people would do well to follow." Leading the Twelfth's Company C at Gettysburg, he weathered an amputation that left "a stump of only nine inches." The 1873 newspapers noted that despite his disability, Hinnant was "a successful farmer and this year he has himself done all the plowing of twenty acres of land." G.W. Lott was among those vying for school commissioner in Edgefield in 1882, "many friends and ex-Confederate soldiers" supporting him. "Having lost a leg at ... Gettysburg, and having a large family to support, he has special claims upon the voters of Edgefield County," a local paper stated. "He is fully competent to fill the office." E.Y. Sheppard, 43, of Ninety-Six, South Carolina, ran for county commissioner in Abbeville in 1884 and was one of the area's most prosperous farmers. His prosperity came despite being wounded twice in the war, including injuries at Gettysburg that "disabled him for life."[69]

Mike R. Sharp of the Bamberg, South Carolina, area, went to Gettysburg as a lieutenant in the Twelfth South Carolina's Company D. He lost his left arm in the fighting and returned home with nothing after the war. Sharp, who also had been wounded at Antietam, was 75 and destitute when he died in Columbia in mid–April 1900, survived by "an aged widow and an afflicted son," the *Bamberg Herald* noted. Friends saw to it that Sharp received a proper burial, while his former comrades in gray vowed to help the widow and son. "The old Confederates here will do what they can for the family—too brave to let their poverty be known till revealed in death and they invite all citizens to contribute to so worthy a cause."[70]

On a July day in 1900, Gilmer C. Greer walked into the offices of the *Union Times* in Union, South Carolina, carrying a package. It was not uncommon for old Confederates to bring in their war relics to show, but Greer's would be one of the most unique. Unwrapping the package and opening the box inside, he showed the newsmen its contents: a Minié bullet with its nose blunted, and a two-and-a-half-inch-long bone with a socket at one end. Greer was a private in the Twelfth South Carolina's Company A in Perrin's brigade at Gettysburg. He was assigned as a sharpshooter and skirmisher, fighting on July 1 and escaping injury. He wasn't as lucky on July 2, when he and his fellow marksmen engaged in heavy skirmishing that at times was hand-to-hand combat. Greer found himself confronted by two Union infantrymen who turned their muskets toward him. Greer triggered his rifle and dropped one of the Yanks, planning to hit the ground himself and take cover before the other bluecoat fired. He was too late—the second Federal's bullet tore into his right arm, through the bone and lodged under the skin. The Minié was extracted by a Confederate surgeon, but that was all that could be done for Greer before the army retreated. Captured, Greer was sent to Davids' Island, where a doctor wanted to amputate, but Greer would not consent to the operation. The wound was dressed but the arm remained in a shattered condition when Greer was paroled some two months later. His family in South Carolina, meanwhile, believed he had been killed in battle, but Greer, unable to write, got another rebel prisoner to send a letter to his loved ones, saying that he was alive. Hospitalized in Richmond, Greer was finally persuaded to have surgery, more than two inches of bone removed from the arm, including the shoulder socket. Weeks later, another inch or so of bone was taken out. Greer spent about four months recuperating in Richmond before being furloughed home in January 1864. Thirty-seven years after being wounded, he still kept the bullet and the larger bone removed from his right arm.[71]

T. Ben Leitzsey was a member of the first company to leave Newberry, South Carolina, when the conflict began. He and his buddies in the Rhett Guards were organized as Company B in the First South Carolina Volunteers. Leitzsey was shot in the knee at Gaines' Mill and wounded in the left ankle with Perrin at Gettysburg, fighting with the regimental color guard. Leitzsey was hit again, this time in the right thigh, at Fussell's Mill in 1864, but was with the army to share the agony of Appomattox. He was 64 when he died at Newberry in early September 1908. Leitzsey "returned home as many others and started life anew and by hard work and honesty of purpose accumulated a competency," a local paper noted. "Leitzsey oversaw the 'county home' for twelve years."

Young John Pope of Newberry was a sergeant in the Third South Carolina's Company E and was wounded in two places by a shell in Kershaw's July 2 assault. Altogether, Pope sustained seven wounds in the war, including the loss of his left eye at Cedar Creek in 1864, but returned home to thrive in peacetime. He was Newberry mayor and a state legislator, eventually rising to chief justice of the South Carolina Supreme Court in 1903. Forced to resign due to health reasons in 1909, Pope was 68 when he died in March 1911.[72]

James Longstreet, who, along with Lee, still remains one of the most controversial figures of Gettysburg, died in Gainesville, Georgia, on January 2, 1904, six days short of his 83rd birthday. News reports described the cause of death as "acute pneumonia," rather than the Yankee lead which had failed to kill him during the war. Indeed the closest Longstreet came to death was when he was seriously wounded by friendly fire at the Wilderness. The aged warrior "was a sufferer from cancer of the eye, but his general health had been good until ... he was seized with a sudden cold, developing later into pneumonia of [a] violent nature." After the war he was a businessman in New Orleans and later was appointed by his personal friend, General Grant, to the position of surveyor of customs at that port. He also later commanded the metropolitan police force and then was appointed the city's postmaster.[73]

In early 1871 a *Chicago Tribune* reporter, identified only as "Gath," interviewed Longstreet, apparently in Georgia, describing him as "one of the most perfect types of a professional soldier.... He wears plain dress, and his whole presence has a nameless self-possession and self-respect which is not unfrequently amongst Southern men." The account continued: "Longstreet discusses with calmness and good judgment the military ability of his old associates, and it is not palpable that he has lost any of the zest and heartiness which used to distinguish him as a member of the 'Lost Cause.' He says nothing which indicates his regret at the part he took, but, on the contrary, seemed to have a docile sort of fondness for his military life and prominence during the rebellion." Gath related that Longstreet "evidently considers Joe Johnston to be the first military reputation of the South" and "speaks of all the Federal Generals with respect." Questions about Gettysburg eventually arose, leading Longstreet to discuss his conversations with Lee about turning the Union left flank and possibly forcing Meade to retreat from Cemetery Ridge. When asked what he would have done if Lee had allowed him to sweep around the Round Tops, Longstreet "replied that he should have moved by forced marches directly upon Washington City."[74]

Longstreet served as U.S. minister to Turkey in 1880 on an appointment by President Rutherford B. Hayes, was President James Garfield's choice as U.S. marshal for Georgia, and also was a commissioner of Pacific railroads under presidents William McKinley and Theodore Roosevelt from 1897 to 1904. Longstreet's war memoir, *From Manassas to Appomattox: Memoirs of the Civil War in America*, was published in 1896. By then, however, he had become a virtual pariah to many ex–Confederates for his friendship with Grant and other Union generals, and his political views as a Republican at a time when a majority of white Southerners favored the Democratic Party. A *New York Times* reporter journeyed to Gainesville to see Longstreet in spring 1888 and offered a rare look at the old soldier: "Gen. Longstreet seldom comes to town. Somewhere in his country place, clad in a long duster and a broad-brimmed hat, you will find him clipping his fruit trees or trailing up the vines in his grape orchard. He will show you his turkeys with pride and, like Cincinnatus, revels in his rustic surroundings and farm duties."[75]

Even in death, however, Longstreet was remembered more for the Gettysburg upheaval and his criticism of Lee than he was for being one of the best Confederate generals. In reporting his passing, the newspapers reflected on the command questions of the battle and Longstreet's role in the defeat. He "denied that he was responsible for the loss of the battle claiming that he was never ordered or expected to attack the enemy's left early in the morning of the 2d," the *Newberry Herald and News* railed three days after Longstreet's passing. "Had he been content with attempting to defend himself without assailing Lee, the storm of indignation that has been pouring upon him would never have broken, and those who might have criticized him on the bare issue whether he was responsible for the Gettysburg disaster would have materially failed of sympathy." Former Confederate Maj. Gen Thomas L. Rosser offered this eulogy, apparently as an olive branch to both sides of the Gettysburg issue: "Now that Longstreet is laid away to rest, all old and true soldiers of the Southern Confederacy will kneel around his tomb and pray that [they] may stand at the great reville with Lee, Jackson and Longstreet."[76]

14

Reunions: "One God, One Flag, One Country"

By 1869 there was a movement afoot to gather blue and gray veterans at Gettysburg to discuss the positions of both armies so that battlefield monuments might someday be erected. The project was met with enthusiasm from former Union officers, but the rawness of defeat still salted the attitudes of many of their Confederate counterparts. The gathering took place, but only one rebel attended—Col. Walter Harrison of Richmond, who served on Gen. Pickett's staff. Robert E. Lee, upon receiving his invitation from the Battlefield Memorial Association, replied on August 5: "My engagements will not permit me to be present.... I think it wisest, moreover, not to keep open the sores of war, but to follow the example of those nations who endeavored to obliterate the marks of civil strife, and to commit to oblivion the feelings it engendered." Lee's nephew, former Maj. Gen. Fitzhugh Lee, added his rejection, stating, "If the nation is to continue as a whole, it is better to forget and forgive rather than perpetuate in granite proofs of its civil wars." The *Charleston Daily News* expressed the view of a likely majority of South Carolina's ex–Confederates: "The Gettysburg gathering, as a national affair, is poor business," adding, "Our old foes may glorify themselves without the help of men who do not love them much better today than they did in 1863. The day for writing the history of our battles has not yet come."[1]

In South Carolina, a much more somber and less traditional "reunion" was in the works. On May 10, 1871, about 6,000 people gathered in Charleston's Magnolia Cemetery for the reburial of 84 Palmetto soldiers killed at Gettysburg. The men had been buried on the battlefield and were finally coming back to their state through the efforts and funds of the Ladies' Memorial Association of Charleston. The remains were conveyed from Gettysburg to Baltimore, where they were put aboard a steamer bound for Charleston. Former Confederate Lt. Gen. Richard H. Anderson, who led his troops at Gettysburg, presided at the 4:30 p.m. ceremony. Many of Charleston's businesses were closed for the day, and trains offered round-trip fares of 25 cents for adults and ten cents for children to the cemetery. Notes accompanying the shipment of remains detailed where some of these soldiers had been buried on the battlefield. Five were found "under a cherry tree back of the barn at Rose's farm." Two sergeants were "from McMillan's apple orchard" on Seminary Ridge. Six other men came from "Rose's meadow peach orchard" and a captain from "under a peach tree northwest of Rose's barn." Nineteen others were disinterred from "north of Black Horse tavern by a graveyard near the creek." The remains of Lt. M.B. McCowan of the Third South Carolina's Company K and six other Carolinians were located "west of Rose's barn under a large cherry tree (the grave was deep with a board cover, all lay side by side and were undoubtedly buried by their comrades)." Nine others returned to Charleston also were exhumed from the Rose farm.[2]

The body of Capt. Thomas J. Warren was returned from Gettysburg to Camden in May as well. The journalist and much-loved son of the community fell while leading his company of the Fifteenth South Carolina in the July 2 attack. More than a year later, in June 1872, another group of remains was brought from Gettysburg and reburied at Hollywood Cemetery in Richmond. Most, if not all, of these soldiers belonged to the Second, Seventh and Eighth South Carolina in Kershaw's brigade, all having died or having been mortally wounded within a few violent hours on July 2, 1863.[3]

Meanwhile, gatherings of veterans on both sides, including those of South Carolina, were being held irregularly as the years passed. In August 1891, sixteen survivors of Hart's Battery joined 500 to 600 other Confederate veterans of York County, South Carolina, for a two-day reunion. Speeches and the aroma of barbecue flavored the summer air. Former general Evander Law presided over the event. Eighteen veterans of the Fourteenth South Carolina's Company F gathered on August 19, 1902, for the seventh consecutive reunion of the company. The date was the forty-first anniversary of the day in 1861 when the company, then known as the "Carolina Bees," marched off to war, commanded by Capt. R.S. Owens of Clinton, South Carolina. The company saw service on the Carolina coast and in Virginia before heading toward Gettysburg with the rest of the army. Its new commander, Capt. J.P. Sloan, was wounded and left on the field there, spending the rest of the war in captivity. The 1902 gathering, held at Yarborough's Mill near Clinton, was the largest ever for the grizzled soldiers of old Company F.[4]

Gettysburg's fiftieth anniversary in 1913 was a major national event, drawing aging veterans from across the country, and billed as the "Peace Reunion." There had been several smaller Gettysburg reunions up to that time, but none compared to this observance. South Carolina was represented by sixty-six men who had fought there, an official with the South Carolina division of the U.S. Confederate Veterans told the press. The event was spread over July 1–4, with a total of about 50,000 former Yanks and rebels attending. For the observance, the Southern Railway offered round-trip tickets from several South Carolina cities and towns—and many other locales in the old Confederacy—in late June and early July. A fare from Charleston to Gettysburg cost $16.90, the highest ticket in the state being from Allendale to Gettysburg for $17.15. The railroad also featured a "special through train" with no changing cars for "the accommodation of Confederate Veterans and their friends."[5]

Of special interest to the Southerners were fifty-nine handsome granite markers with bronze tablets placed on Confederate avenues at Gettysburg, showing the positions of Lee's brigades and artillery batteries. The markers cost $500 each. Obviously, this was years after the early spring of 1901 when 225 mounted cannons were in place, and 310 markers and about 500 monuments had been already erected in Gettysburg National Park, most, if not all, honoring the Union side.[6]

In 1913 the old soldiers from both armies were sheltered in "a vast sea of tents"— about 5,000—spread over the battlefield, the men feasting on mutton, beef, eggs, chicken "and every conceivable delicacy," one Carolina veteran recalled. The South Carolinians were late in arriving, however, and did not get settled in their tents until late night. When they arose the next morning, they took in the tent city, but "it was not until we saw old Round Top, silent, sullen, defiant, that we could get our bearings," noted Augustus

Dickert of Kershaw's brigade. Dickert and his comrades were camped between Louisiana and Texas veterans and at a point along Seminary Ridge just to the left of where George Pickett's troops had formed for their part in the ill-fated charge. Across a temporary street in the encampment were their former foes, "Federals of every hue, from Maine to the Dakotas," Dickert related. Another Carolinian recalled that throughout the reunion the Union men warmly greeted the old rebels with "hats off and outstretched hands, as brothers should meet brothers." Veteran David H. Russell from Anderson, who fought in the First S.C. Cavalry, remembered the camaraderie of "men who fifty years before were clutching at each other's throats in the death grapple of battle. It was wonderful, and the feeling of brotherhood exhibited by the men who wore the Blue and the Gray was something special to witness."[7]

J. Russell Wright of Kershaw's brigade made the trip north with the faded battle flag of the Seventh South Carolina Volunteers. Wright lost three brothers in the war, and three others had been twice wounded. The banner had been carried at Gettysburg by color bearer John Clark, who was wounded there and killed at Chickamauga with the flag still in his grasp. "So I am going to take it back and let the [Union] boys see what they run from so hurriedly across the meadow, and the wheat field," Wright said of the combat five decades earlier on July 2. "But then our breasts were full of daggers, now the white dove of peace will spread her silver wings over that once bloody plain; and united we will stand. The blue and the gray." The nation was one again and had been healing for many years, but Wright's heart still harbored the deep loyalty of a soldier who had endured great suffering and hardship while fighting under a cherished banner. "I love this flag, as a mother loves her first born," he noted. "While I stand ready to strike down to the death any foe" of the U.S. flag, "there never was, nor never will be a flag that floats on land or sea that I can love as I do this."[8]

In a later account, Wright related how he met and shook hands with retired Union Maj. Gen. Daniel Sickles at the reunion. Sickles had commanded the U.S. III Corps in the July 2 struggle in the Peach Orchard, where Kershaw's command was heavily engaged and Sickles lost his right leg. Wright claimed that Sickles asked if he was at Gettysburg, Wright telling him that he was there and fought in the Wheatfield and Peach Orchard. Wright continued: "'Well,' said the general, 'I expect it was you who shot off my foot.' No general, I was aiming above the feet that day, I was to get the heads."[9]

A Carolinian from Kingstree, South Carolina, who identified himself only as "Poor Conrad," attended the event with W.M. Reid, a cannoneer in Hugh Garden's Palmetto Light Artillery. The two were exploring the battlefield when they were approached by a number of old Federals from Philadelphia who were camped nearby and had set up a makeshift table with food and drink under a shade tree. "They recognized us at sight to be Confederate veterans, and nothing seemingly could have given them more pleasure," Conrad wrote. Amid embraces and friendly banter, the former enemies drank together and recalled their unforgettable experiences there. "We drank many toasts to the governor and good people of Pennsylvania," Conrad noted. "What a pity, my friends, all South Carolina was not present. All certainly was genuine friendliness. There were bearded men and hoary heads in that group, but you could see a swelling in the throat, an almost choking sensation, words sometimes half uttered." The encounter "was not the only spot where good fellowship and the outpouring of hearts were felt and seen."[10]

The cavalryman David Russell spent the greater part of one day in the Pennsylvania camp, attracting groups of Northerners who wanted to shake hands and talk. "There was not a harsh word uttered anywhere so far as I heard, but we met as American soldiers who had illustrated American valor and manhood in the fiery ordeal of battle," he recalled. Russell passed through the New York camp and was called into a tent where a group of old Yanks wanted to visit with him. The men reminisced for about two hours, one of the boys in blue presenting Russell with a handsome pair of gloves before he departed. Augustus Dickert basically echoed Russell's sentiments regarding the fraternal nature of the reunion. "Old scores of hatred, engendered by the war, seemed to have been entirely wiped from the slate and instead of 'Yanks' and 'Johnny Rebs' you heard on all sides, 'Hail brother' [or] 'Ho comrade.'"[11]

One of the many highlights of the reunion was President Woodrow Wilson's address, "interrupted by frequent cheers." "I need not tell you what the battle of Gettysburg meant," Wilson said in his opening remarks to the veterans:

> These gallant men in blue and gray sit all about us here. Many of them met here upon this ground in grim and deadly struggle. Upon these famous fields and hillsides their comrades died about them.... But fifty years have gone by since then.... What have they meant? They have meant peace and union and vigor and the maturity and might of a great nation. How wholesome and healing the peace has been! We have found one another again as brothers and comrades in arms, enemies no longer, generous friends rather, our battles long past ... except that we shall never forget the splendid valor, the manly devotion, of the men then arrayed against one another, now grasping hands and smiling into each other's eyes."[12]

With the reunion over, the veterans returned to their homes at all points of the American compass, many of them never to return to Gettysburg. "Poor Conrad," who had toasted the Pennsylvania governor with his new Philadelphia friends, traveled back to the Palmetto State, but he was not empty-handed. In his bags were a cannonball fragment he picked up on ground contested by Longstreet's corps, a rock from the infamous Devil's Den, and some cigars given to him by a Union veteran. These items, including the cigars—since Conrad didn't smoke—were soon on display in a window of the Kingstree Hardware Company for all to see.[13]

The gathering was far from a flawless success, however. A "torrid sun" and the "discomforts of camp life" melted away some 6,000 of the veterans by July 2, with another 1,000 expected to leave that day. "Most of them have looked over the battlefield, shaken hands with comrades they knew in other regiments, got another glimpse of their friends and left for home," said one news account. The camp was "crowded beyond capacity and hundreds of old men were being quartered in tents that were made for circuses, but not for sleeping purposes. Scores slept on the ground and although the cooks made continuous efforts, the mess tables did not groan with food."[14]

One Carolina veteran who didn't make the reunion trip was Louis Jacobs of Bachman's German Artillery, which had helped repel Farnsworth's doomed cavalry charge on July 3. A successful merchant and prominent citizen of Kingstree, Jacobs's health was failing by summer and fall 1913. He died on October 13, a few days short of his 71st birthday. Mary, his wife, had preceded him in death, but their eleven adult children were all there as a rabbi presided over the funeral. "About the casket was draped the old company flag of Bachman's battery," a newspaper account stated. "Although many times rent with shot and shell, and discolored by time, Mr. Jacobs cherished this old emblem of the past." The tattered banner was brought to Kingstree by Anton W. Jager, Jacobs's old friend and battery mate who had borne the flag throughout the war and now owned it. Jager, also in his early 70s by now, wanted to honor Jacobs and had the banner "to place upon the bier of his departed comrade."[15]

A few weeks before the 1913 reunion, A.S. Salley, Jr., secretary of the South Carolina Historical Commission, received a letter from Union veteran J.R. Dunlap of Lansing, Michigan. Dunlap explained that he had been a member of the Pennsylvania volunteers in the war and had fought at Gettysburg. Captured there, he was swept up in the Confederates' exodus and aided Capt. Harrison Weir of the Third S.C. Battalion, who was wounded in the battle. Dunlap wrote that he was contemplating going to the reunion and hoped to meet Weir there fifty years after their encounter. Salley sifted through records and found that Weir had been killed at Deep Bottom, Virginia, in 1864. Still, Dunlap's inquiry was an interesting story and the facts were published in the *State* newspaper in Columbia shortly afterward. The article prompted a response from Mrs. Mattie W. Glenn of Clinton, South Carolina, Weir's sister. She noted that the captain "was badly wounded at Gettysburg" and "had to use crutches for two or three months or perhaps longer" while recuperating at home. "I often heard him speak of the kindness of the Union soldier assisting him off the battlefield." She requested Dunlap's address so that she could contact him. Letters passed back and forth, Mrs. Watts Davis of Clinton, a niece of Weir, informing Dunlap of the captain's death. She added in one letter that the family "was truly glad to hear of one who had rendered such good service in time of suffering." The "correspondence was continued and developed a strong friendship" such that in October 1915, Dunlap journeyed to Clinton after attending a Grand Army of the Republic reunion in Washington, D.C. The Union veteran was the honored guest in a party at the Davis home, with Mrs. Glenn also in attendance, and "the occasion marking an interesting combination of circumstances," said one account. Weir's relatives invited a dozen former Confederates to meet Dunlap, but only nine were able to be there. A "day long to be remembered was enjoyed," the account continued. "Mr. Dunlap and the nine former enemies spent the day in fighting their battles over in a friendly manner."[16]

In May 1914, an estimated 800 or more Carolina veterans gathered for the state's Confederate Reunion held in Anderson. The event "was in many ways the happiest gathering of these good men since Appomattox," noted the local newspaper. The reunion was highlighted by a grand reception and a parade, some 300 or so of the spryest and strongest old soldiers marching "between ranks of wildly cheering children waving Confederate flags." The gathering was marred by the death of a 73-year-old veteran from Abbeville who succumbed to a "stroke by paralysis" after arriving in Anderson by train. Still, the event was deemed a grand success, and plans were made to hold the next reunion in Columbia.[17]

With World War I raging, more than 4,000 Confederate veterans from across the South assembled in Washington, D.C., in June 1917, the first reunion of the surviving rebels held north of the Potomac River. It also marked the first time Union veterans marched with their old foes from more than half a century earlier. J. Russell Wright, who had fought in Kershaw's ranks at Gettysburg, was on hand for the historic and moving event. "Along Pennsylvania Avenue, where marched the armies of Grant and Sherman in 1865, what is left of the army of Lee and the Confederacy paraded to-day," he wrote. "No Southern city could have given the survivors of the Confederate armies a more touching greeting than they received…. The Flag of the United States fluttered beside the 'Stars and Bars' and told the story of what was and what is—one flag, one country, one people; that's all." As President Wilson watched the procession from a reviewing stand, two former foes, one a Texas veteran, the other from Maine, passed by, dipping their battle flags in his honor. Together they shouted: "We are weaving the two flags together, President Wilson! We are reunited; it is now one God, one Flag, one Country; together let us sweetly live, together let us die." There were other cries as the veterans marched past Wilson: "We will go to France or anywhere you want to send us." And, "Call on us if the boys can't do it," Wright recalled.[18]

At 77, L.D. Robertson was "in feeble health," unable to make the Washington trip, but still feisty when a newspaperman interviewed him in Pageland, South Carolina, on a spring day in 1917. Robertson was a veteran of Company G, Second South Carolina, and fought under Kershaw from First Bull Run to Gettysburg, where he was wounded in the leg. Bleeding and lying in a ditch, the combat swirled over him. Finally captured, he was "carried to prison near New York [probably Davids' Island] and kept for a while" before being released. When asked about the ongoing war in Europe and American intervention being a strong possibility, "Mr. Robertson's eyes began to sparkle, and he said, 'If I was a young man I expect I would go with the boys. Not that I love it, but I like to see our side win.'"[19]

The Pee Dee Artillery held annual reunions of its survivors every July 21 until "they numbered too few and feeble to attend." The battery's last living veteran, Elihu Muldrow, passed away on July 21, 1934, at the age of 102. An unidentified "daughter of the famous battery" wrote that Muldrow had joined his comrades in answering the last "Long Roll Call—thus the reunion was held as was their custom on the usual date, and we doubt not but that the attendance was full."[20]

In late June 1938, nineteen or so old Confederates from South Carolina headed north to Gettysburg for a reunion to mark the battle's seventy-fifth anniversary. They were among 300 to 500 former rebels who traveled for the event, most by train. They represented "the remnants of that gray host [which] moved again toward the Pennsylvania hamlet." Trains were scheduled to reach Gettysburg on June 29, "giving the visitors time to rest" before ceremonies opened on July 1. The Eternal Light Peace Memorial was dedicated on the 3rd, highlighted by a speech by President Franklin D. Roosevelt. Based on train reservations, Georgia had the most veterans, at sixty-three; Arkansas the least, with nine. Some sources state that a total of only twenty-five Gettysburg veterans—Union and Confederate—attended the reunion. The other participants, about 1,300 Federals and 480 Confederates, had not fought at Gettysburg.[21]

15

"Taps" for the Last
Gettysburg Carolinians

The funerals and newspaper obituaries became more common as time marched ahead, the aging Carolina Confederates dwindling in ranks the calendars would never allow them to refill. Capt. Alex A. King of Kershaw's Third S.C. Battalion had fallen with a mangled arm on July 2, the limb amputated at a field hospital two days later. Captured and sent to Johnson's Island, the Abbeville, South Carolina, native came home and lived many years on his farm. In his early eighties, by 1902, King was described as a "very prominent old Confederate veteran" who had lived in the same house for 42 years. He was better known for girth and strength, cutting "all his wood with one hand." King was 86 when he succumbed to "paralysis" on August 6, 1908.[1]

R.B. Hutchinson of the Seventh South Carolina had lived through the nightmare of the Peach Orchard and Wheatfield with some of the rest of Kershaw's boys, losing a leg in the process. He survived the war and was 68 when he died at his home near Lowndesville, South Carolina, in March 1906, leaving behind a wife and nine children.[2]

Despite his severe leg wound, Sgt. G.M. Langston of the Third South Carolina had escaped the war alive and returned to Laurens, South Carolina. He and his family mourned the loss of his brother, Capt. Mason Langston, killed on July 2 near the point where the sergeant was wounded. Langston lived the quiet civilian life for more than 35 years after Gettysburg, finally overwhelmed by "weak health" on April 20, 1898. Six Carolinian comrades who also wore the gray served as pallbearers at his funeral. J.A. Derrick, 70, drew his last breath at his family's home in Springfield, Illinois, on April 8, 1908. A captain in Kershaw's Fifteenth South Carolina, he had been captured at Gettysburg, imprisoned at Johnson's Island and returned to civilian life.[3]

Wounded at least six times in battle, including in both legs on Gettysburg's first day, William H. Brunson had ended the war as a captain and returned to his family in Edgefield District. Three brothers, also in the Confederate service, also came home. Brunson served as the Edgefield postmaster for some twenty-five years afterward. He relished discussions about the war, no doubt telling of his experiences at Gettysburg when Perrin's Carolinians charged into the jaws of death on Seminary Ridge. His health began to fail in 1910 and declined over the coming months before his passing on August 20, 1911. "Capt. Brunson was a gentleman of the old school," one obituary read. "His loyalty and love for the old South and the principles for which her people stood were unabated to the day of his death." George B. Lake, who served as a private in Brunson's company in the war, wrote of him before Brunson's death: "No man ever had a truer friend, no community a courtlier gentleman, no country a better soldier."[4]

One of Hampton's old troopers, Simon M. Mills, 84, died quietly at his home on Confederate Street in Fort Mill, South Carolina, in November 1911. He had been wounded twice at Gettysburg, fighting with the First South Carolina Cavalry, and was ill for about six weeks before his life flickered away. Mourners remembered his 50 years as a devoted Presbyterian, merchant and one of the town's oldest and "most highly esteemed" residents. J.M. Berry, 71, passed away quietly and suddenly in the bedroom of his Augusta, Georgia, home on a December night in 1911. He was a native of the Liberty Hill section of Edgefield County. His wife, Sarah, preceded him in death in October after some thirty-nine years together. Berry had fought at Gettysburg with the Seventh South Carolina. Despite an arm wound at Chickamauga that perpetually troubled him, Berry was described as a "golf enthusiast and played many a game that taxed the best skill of his competitors," a news account stated. Playing at a country club on the afternoon before his death hours later, "he drove the ball with the best of them over the links."[5]

William H. Hobbs had lost an arm at Gettysburg and served as a county magistrate and commissioner in the Sumter and Timmonsville areas after the war. His last days, however, were a sad chapter, as he was living in an old soldiers' home and collecting a $72 pension from the state when he died at age 73 in December 1913. "I trust that he had a triumphant entry into the Promised Land through his faith in the Lord Jesus Christ, where he will rest under the shade of the trees with Lee and Jackson," one of his old comrades, D.J. Bradham, wrote of Hobbs. Jacob L. Fellers, 73, in March 1914, had made the rush up Seminary Ridge on July 1, 1863, in Company C of the Thirteenth South Carolina with the rest of Perrin's Carolinians. He died at his home in Newberry County, survived by his wife of 43 years, Mary, five children and a grandson.[6]

John Eskew's end in September 1914 was due to a nine-week illness from "softening of the brain." The Anderson resident was 73 and one of four brothers who had served in the Confederate military. He was a member of Company D in the First South Carolina Rifles (Orr's Rifles) in Perrin's brigade, fighting in the Gettysburg campaign after recovering from a serious wound at Second Bull Run. Eskew was among the Carolinians who attended the fiftieth anniversary reunion at Gettysburg. In January 1915, J.M. Riddle, "one of Lancaster's oldest and most highly esteemed citizens," purchased a silver loving cup in a unique tribute to his old comrades in the Second South Carolina's Company E of Kershaw's command. Riddle, 74, wanted the cup presented to the last of six still-living survivors of his company. The "unusually pretty" cup was put on display at a Lancaster jewelry store and was inscribed, "J.M. Riddle to Last Surviving Member of Company E, Second Regiment, S.C.V., C.S.A., 1861–1865." Riddle fought in many of the major battles, including Gettysburg, was wounded several times "and yet wears upon his body several battle scars," a news account said. The reporter speculated that since Riddle "is exceedingly active and energetic" and "probably the best gardener in Lancaster," doing his own work, "it very likely has never occurred to him that he himself may possibly be the last survivor of brave Company E, thus falling heir to his own cup."[7]

"'Thirty' Sounds for Capt. Charles Petty" read the headline over the death announcement for the longtime Spartanburg journalist and Confederate soldier in February 1915. Petty, 80, had fought throughout the war, including Gettysburg, as a member of Company C of the Thirteenth South Carolina. He was editor of the *Carolina Spartan* for years after the conflict and also was associate editor of the *Spartanburg Journal* and a state legislator. Within a few days of Petty's passing, 72-year-old Samuel Boykin died at his rural home between Camden and Sumter. Boykin had been a private in the Second South Carolina Cavalry's Company A. He left behind his studies at South Carolina College to fight for the South. Boykin was captured during the retreat from Gettysburg, imprisoned at Camp Chase and later at Fort Delaware. The widower and Presbyterian was survived by seven children.[8]

Alexander M. Black was scarred by wounds at Gettysburg and Cold Harbor as an officer in the Twelfth South Carolina's Company H. Enduring the sorrow of Appomattox, he lived a long life during peacetime, dying in Rock Hill at age 78 in April 1915. A widower, he was survived by five grown children. His body was borne to the gravesite by an escort of local Confederate veterans.[9]

One-armed R.H. Jennings of Winnsboro, South Carolina, was 76 when he died in late May 1915. The former state treasurer had fought in most of the major battles of Lee's army as an officer in Kershaw's Second South Carolina. He was wounded by shrapnel at Gettysburg and lost his arm to amputation after he was injured in combat at New Market Heights in 1864. Jennings was also remembered as a prominent Methodist, a trustee of Columbia Female College (later Columbia College) and for holding various municipal offices in his native Fairfield County.[10]

Joel L. Minick was "one of Saluda's [S.C.] oldest and most honored citizens" when he succumbed to a "lingering illness" at his home in late December 1915. Minick, 74, left behind his widow, Laura, and eight grown children. He was a good Baptist and one of the area's most successful farmers after the war. Wounded at Port Royal, Pvt. Minick had recuperated to fight at Gettysburg in the ranks of the Fourteenth South Carolina's Company B in Perrin's brigade, where he was again a casualty. Still, his injuries did not keep him from further service, and he was with Lee's army at the surrender. When he died more than fifty years after Appomattox, his pallbearers were former comrades in arms. The June 1916 passing of Samuel A. Byrd, "one of Walhalla's oldest and most highly respected citizens, cast a deep gloom over the people of the town," said one news account. Byrd was 80 and had lost a leg at Gettysburg as a member of the Twelfth South Carolina's Company G in Perrin's command. He lost his last battle, waging a longtime fight against cancer.[11]

"Another old Confederate has crossed over the river of death," the *Union* (S.C.) *Times* noted three days before Christmas, 1916. "A few more years and the last one of the heroes of the Civil war will be gone." Pvt. F.R. Cudd had been in Company H of Kershaw's Fifteenth South Carolina. He lived through the war and returned home to the Kelton community of Union County to become "an industrious and good citizen." The Presbyterian had been "in bad health for many months" before his death. Reuben Patterson of the Second South Carolina was 80 when he died on Easter Sunday, 1916. He had never been able to play his flute again after losing his fingers on one hand during Kershaw's July 2 attack. In addition to his injuries at Gettysburg and Savage's Station, Patterson had also been shot in the face at Appomattox Court House, hours before Lee's surrender. He lived a long life before "throat paralysis" accomplished what the aim of many a Yankee couldn't do.[12]

In an issue spotlighting some of its prominent citizens that same year, the *Union Times* noted the achievements and toughness of 72-year-old Gilmer C. Greer, still running a small farm near the town. He had enlisted in the Confederate army at age 17 and was slightly wounded in the Seven Days battles in 1862. Recovered enough to fight at

Fredericksburg, he was severely wounded in the right shoulder at Gettysburg and captured. A Federal surgeon removed a portion of his arm, and he was held at Davids' Island for two months before being exchanged. He was sent to a Confederate hospital in Richmond, where a doctor cut away another four inches of bone in the arm. After four months of recovery, Greer returned to Union County in January 1864, 20 years old, disabled but determined to create a better life for himself. "This man came home, and although maimed for life, set about building up his broken fortune," the *Times* stated. "He is one of Union county's most worthy sons." The paper earlier in the article noted of Greer: "No braver, more loyal son of South Carolina is anywhere to be found." At age 78, William R. Smith of Sumter had survived the war despite wounds at Gettysburg and Chickamauga. Fate, however, caught up to him in late December 1916, when he was thrown from his buggy on his way to his business—a local marble works—and critically injured. He lingered for two weeks before dying, survived by four children and nine grandchildren.[13]

Professor William Hood, a longtime member of the Erskine College faculty, was living in Bartow, Florida, when he died in February 1917. The former sergeant in Kershaw's Third South Carolina was wounded and captured at Gettysburg. To the end of his days, Hood was appreciative of the care and comfort he had received while recuperating at Davids' Island. "He has borne testimony of many kindnesses at the hands of strangers during his imprisonment," his obituary noted. Described by a fellow veteran as "a faithful soldier of the 'Lost Cause,'" Robert S. Rutledge passed away in late January 1918 in upstate South Carolina. Rutledge had been in Orr's Rifles' Company C and fought in almost every major battle in the East, including Gettysburg. While serving as a sharpshooter in September 1864, he lost a leg in combat, hobbling about for more than five decades before his death. "There was not a braver man in the Sharpshooters than Bob Rutledge," an old comrade, W.T. McGill, wrote a few days after his passing. "Peace to his ashes!"[14]

The United States was in the last days of World War I when word reached South Carolina about the deaths of two doughboys whose fathers had Gettysburg connections. *The Abbeville Press and Banner* carried the grievous news about these casualties and a few others on November 8, 1918, three days before the Armistice was signed, effectively ending the European conflict. Pvt. Claude E. Hughes of the 316th Field Artillery, 81st Division, had died of pneumonia while serving in France. The 26-year-old Abbeville native was survived by his mother, Elizabeth, four sisters and two brothers. "He gave his life for his country and for humanity," the account said of him. Hughes's late father, George, had been in the Confederate army and was wounded at Gettysburg. On the same page was a brief notice about the death of Lt. William A. Hudgens of Honea Path, South Carolina, killed in action. Hudgens was a battalion adjutant in the 118th Infantry Division when a shell fragment pierced his heart. In addition to his wife and three children, Hudgens was survived by his father, who was a veteran of the First South Carolina (Orr's) Rifles, which fought in the Gettysburg campaign. The "old soldier will hear with regret of the death of his son," the article stated.[15]

Described as a scout for R.E. Lee, 87-year-old John S. Wilbanks may have been in one of the two cavalry regiments when he was captured at Gettysburg. The private later escaped, but the Laurens County native couldn't evade death in May 1922. The news briefs about his death state that he belonged to the Third S.C. Cavalry, which was not in the battle, fought almost sixty years earlier. Wilbanks's status remains unclear. A. Noah Sease of Chapin, South Carolina, was 80 when cancer claimed him in May 1920. Survived by his widow, nine children and several grandchildren, Sease was "a gallant ex-Confederate" private and artilleryman who was wounded in the arm at Gettysburg. Part of the arm bone was removed, but "the wound healed so perfectly that the arm was about as strong as ever," said a newspaper account about his passing.[16]

In Anderson, South Carolina, on January 24, 1921, another Gettysburg milestone was passed forever. Col. Joseph N. Brown, who had led his Fourteenth South Carolina up the west slope of Seminary Ridge with the rest of Perrin's brigade on July 1, died at his home. Brown had survived the war, being captured on April 2, 1865, when the Confederate lines collapsed around Petersburg. He was imprisoned until July, when he was permitted to return home. In Anderson, he soon became a community leader, lawyer, businessman, banker and member of the state House of Representatives. Brown was the highest ranking South Carolina veteran of the Confederate army when he died at age 89. Of Gettysburg, Brown wrote in his memoir of the rebel dead there: "Hundreds of brave men fell, most of them young, and on the threshold of life, whose names were not recorded in the official reports of the battle. But they still live in the memories of loved ones at home."[17]

In January 1922, Robert Briggs Watson, an 86-year-old veteran of Perrin's infantry, made newspapers across the state for his winter equestrian exploits. Watson had been wounded in the thigh and captured at Gettysburg as a lieutenant in the Fourteenth South Carolina. He lived to return home and more than five decades later was still going strong. Walking with a limp due to his Gettysburg injury, Watson embarked on a 100-mile horseback ride from his home at Ridge Springs in Saluda County, South Carolina, to visit his son in Greenville. The old soldier refused to travel by train, preferring to take his favorite horse, Dolly, on the rigorous trip. "As agile as a youth in the saddle … Watson doesn't walk … if Dolly can get there," said one account. "He does not want to be bothered with waiting for street cars and automobiles when he reaches his destination, he says, so he rides horseback." Watson left Ridge Springs on a Monday morning, spent the night at a friend's home in the Cambridge community and arrived in Greenwood, South Carolina, the halfway point of the trip, early on Tuesday, despite bitter cold and snow threatening. He was to stay there a few days with another relative before resuming the journey to Greenville. Watson and Dolly had made the trip two years earlier, reaching Greenwood "in a blinding snow storm." They stayed there until the snow ceased and rode into Greenville on schedule.[18]

Evander McIver Ervin breathed his last at his rural Florence County home on an August morning in 1925 after being "stricken with paralysis" some ten days earlier. Ervin, 79, was a private in the Eighth South Carolina and a Gettysburg veteran. Due to his "courage, physique and horsemanship," he also served as a courier on the staffs of several generals and "frequently carried important despatches from General [E.M.] Law and General [William F.] Perry to General Longstreet and General Lee," a news account stated. Wounded at Spotsylvania, Ervin recovered and was present for the Appomattox surrender. "Perhaps no one in this [Florence-Darlington] community ever had a larger number of relatives and admiring friends and no one has ever been more respected or beloved," the account continued. "He was a gentleman of the old school."[19]

Sgt. Hugh G. Bullock, who led the First South Carolina's Company F over the Union breastworks at the Lutheran Seminary on July 1, died at his Horry County home in September 1925. At eighty-four, still bearing his war scars, his health had already been failing for several years when a "stroke of paralysis" proved too much for him to overcome. After Gettysburg, Bullock fought in the Wilderness, where he was captured and imprisoned at

Fort Delaware until the war's end. Freed, he went by boat to Charleston and walked home to resume life as a civilian and farmer. Soon thereafter, he married Mary Ann Anderson. Their bond lasted some fifty-nine years, until his death, and resulted in two sons. Bullock "was known and honored as an upright and honest man, a loyal friend, and peacemaker" in the Loris, South Carolina, community, his obituary stated.[20]

Described as the "man who carried the Palmetto flag of the First South Carolina" at Gettysburg, William W. Williams was eighty-four when he died of bronchial pneumonia at Aiken in May 1929. Williams was captured "nine months before Appomattox" and was held at the infamous Union prison complex at Elmira, N.Y, until after the war ended. He later served as a probate judge and editor of the *Aiken* (S.C.) *Times* before his passing. At the time of his death, Williams was described as Aiken's oldest citizen. He was survived by his wife, Martha, a son, two daughters and six grandchildren.[21]

Two old soldiers of the Twelfth South Carolina Volunteers were the last of that regiment still living; then both passed away within weeks of each other in 1930 at age 87. Cadwallader Jones died in Greensboro, Alabama, on or about August 13. At Gettysburg on July 1, he was captain of the regiment's color company; three men were shot down while carrying the Twelfth's colors. After the third soldier fell, Jones took up the colors himself and "told the remaining men of his outfit that he would call for no more volunteers for the dangerous task, but would carry the standard himself," his obituary related. "This he did during the remainder of the battle." Jones survived the battle with only eight of thirty-two men in his company unscathed. The other Confederate veteran, Robert J. Moore, died at his daughter's home in Columbia's Eau Claire neighborhood on September 7, 1930. Moore had been a sharpshooter in the Twelfth and was wounded at Gettysburg and in the Wilderness. Five Moore brothers went to war in the 1860s, but Robert and his sibling David were the only survivors. David died about five years before Robert's passing, the latter's obituary related. Six grandsons, from Moore's thirty-five grandchildren and twenty-two great-grandchildren, served as pallbearers. Moore was the last surviving member of the Twelfth South Carolina.[22]

The July 12, 1930, death of Richard O'Neale was page one news in Columbia's *The State*. O'Neale served as mayor of the South Carolina capital in 1880–1881 and had been ill for about five weeks prior to his passing. At eighty-nine, he was "known … as Columbia's oldest native citizen" and had been active during Reconstruction and in business after the war. He served in the Fifteenth South Carolina of Kershaw's brigade throughout the war and surrendered at Appomattox. "With his passing Columbia has lost one of its outstanding and most beloved citizens," the *State* noted. "He had a strong love for humanity and his many fine characteristics made him loved and honored by all." Four months earlier, O'Neale was featured in an article celebrating his last birthday and delving into his military and civic accomplishments and background. The piece included his account of Colonel De Saussure's premonition about his own death at Gettysburg and O'Neale's views about the long-lost opportunities of the battle. "It was our last chance and a desperate one," he said. "If we had won that battle we could probably have taken Washington and won the war, but we were fast weakening and were forced to take the tremendous chance!"[23]

The sixty-eighth anniversary of Gettysburg came and went in July 1931. A few days later, an old soldier who had hobbled about on one leg all that time finally gave up the ghost. Jacob C. Copeland was in the ranks of the First South Carolina's Company G when Perrin's brigade attacked on July 1, 1863. He lost a leg in the battle but survived the war and returned to his home in the Bamberg-Ehrhardt area of the state. Copeland was a magistrate in Ehrhardt for many years before his death at age 86 on July 9, 1931. A widower, he was survived by five grown children, sixteen grandchildren and eight great-grandchildren.[24]

One of the state's few remaining Gettysburg veterans marched into the endless night in August 1932. J. Belton Shealy, 92, died suddenly at his home in White Rock, South Carolina. He had served in the Thirteenth South Carolina's Company H in Perrin's brigade and was severely wounded in the battle. Recovering from his injuries, he returned to the regiment and served until the war's end. Shealy was a farmer and later a merchant. He retired when he was eighty. Twice widowed, he was survived by seven grown children, forty-one grandchildren and twenty-five great-grandchildren. "Mr. Shealy was a highly respected citizen who went to his grave with the love and affection of all who knew him," his obituary said.[25]

Ninety-five-year-old James Dudley Fooshe died quietly on the morning of January 11, 1940, at his home near Augusta, Georgia. Fooshe was one of the area's "most beloved and respected citizens" and left only one surviving Confederate veteran in the county. Fooshe was born in what is now Greenwood County, South Carolina, on March 29, 1844, and served as a private in the Third S.C. Battalion. Wounded in the 1862 fighting around Richmond, he recuperated and returned to the army in the Hospital Corps, serving as a hospital orderly with Dr. Simon Baruch, the battalion's assistant surgeon. There is no mention of Fooshe at Gettysburg, but he attended the festivities for the seventy-fifth anniversary of the battle in 1938. Based on that, it is likely that the nineteen-year-old orderly was at Baruch's side aiding Kershaw's myriad casualties at the Black Horse Tavern. Fooshe was captured by Federals at some point in the war, but escaped, his obituary stated. He was about sixty years old when he moved to Georgia, and prided himself on his orchards and other gardening endeavors.[26]

On a sunny Tuesday, July 2, 1963, in the same area where Kershaw's Carolinians had steeled for their assault one hundred years earlier, the South Carolina Memorial was unveiled at Gettysburg. Governor Donald S. Russell was among several speakers at the dedication and took the opportunity not only to honor the soldiers but also to mention the menace of communism, one of the main global issues of the time. "I hope that on this historic occasion, we may resolve to pay tribute to those honored dead, not merely with words but a reviving of our spirit by a rearming of America's strength with a new dedication of principle that, too, will not hesitate to hazard home or life in the cause to which we have given allegiance and which demands of us uncompromising devotion…. We shall not counter the fanaticism of communism … with faint hearted dedication, with expedient compromise of principle, or with sugar-coated words that seek to patch over the incompatability of freedom and communism."[27]

A few hundred miles to the south, in Columbia, South Carolina, demolition of the Confederate Soldiers' Home was in its final stages during this time. The two-story frame building was completed in January 1909 as a refuge for the state's aging Confederate veterans. It contained 18 bedrooms—each accommodating four men—a dining room, kitchen, game room, library, smoking room and two bathrooms. The facility, called the Confederate Dispensary in the early days, opened in June 1909. The home had a capacity for 82 residents but rarely had more than 70 occupants as "time was fast thinning the ranks of the men who had survived Union shot and shell." By 1925 there was room enough for wives and widows of the veterans, sisters soon being welcomed as well. In

1931, the facility housed 24 veterans, two widows and 12 sisters. The old soldiers were allowed $10 annually for tobacco and drew a $50 yearly pension from the state. The last veteran there, 97-year-old D.W. Seigler of Aiken, died in 1944, and for the 13 years before the home's closure in 1957, it housed only women—the widows, sisters and daughters— the latter allowed entry in 1935. As a wrecking crew completed the destruction in summer 1963, a reporter noted its passing: "Now the voices [of the old soldiers] have fallen silent on the wide veranda where the wisteria grew and the lemon scent of magnolia blossoms hung in the peaceful evening air."[28]

A few months before his death in 1930, Richard O'Neale, a veteran of the Fifteenth South Carolina who had fought in the inferno around the Rose farm on a July day so many years earlier, was hesitant to speak about his war experiences. "I don't like to talk about them, but the line of gray grows thinner and in three or four more years there will be none left to tell about what hardships and sacrifices the Confederate soldiers went through. A few are still left but many are passing away and many more were swept away by the conflict."[29]

His words were a fitting epitaph for the South Carolina ghosts of Gettysburg, and hundreds of other fields, who still march amid the thunder and lightning of the guns.

Appendix: Odds and Ends

Battlefield Relics

A brief Gettysburg note in the Yorkville paper, and likely other newspapers across the country in 1896, would have piqued the interest of the South Carolina veterans and many more who fought there. Some slight repairs were being made to the stone wall at the "bloody angle" where the Pettigrew-Pickett-Trimble Charge crested on July 3. The rocks yielded over 100 bullets, shell fragments, gun parts and other battle artifacts.[1]

The Long Journey of Pvt. John Robert Smith

A few weeks after Gettysburg, a Confederate captain in Perrin's brigade wrote a letter to Mr. and Mrs. Joel A. Smith of Laurens County, South Carolina, about the apparent death of their son, who was in the captain's company.

Pvt. John Robert Smith of the Fourteenth South Carolina's Company C was "fighting in the forefront of battle" and was believed to have been killed at Gettysburg, although his body was not recovered, the letter said. The family grieved, but held out hope that John was still alive, but passing time dimmed that candle as days and weeks turned into months and years with no other word about his fate. Lee's surrender at Appomattox in April 1865 basically ended the war, although a Confederate army was still fighting in North Carolina and scattered rebel forces remained in action. Still the Smiths heard nothing more about John.

Shortly thereafter, Joel Smith was at a railroad station in the Laurens area when a train hissed to a halt there. Smith must have thought his eyes were deceiving him when a familiar figure emerged from a car. "Out of it, hobbling on crutches and on a 'peg leg' was the son, who had been mourned as dead," a newspaper account said of the unlikely reunion.

Finally the long mystery was unraveled. John was wounded in the leg in the July 1 battle and carried to the rear by a comrade, B.L. Henderson. The limb was amputated, but he was captured. In Union custody it was determined that "a second amputation was necessary," and another portion of the leg was removed. "He was lying in the federal prison the years that his family and comrades believed him dead," the news report said.

Smith made the most of his charmed life. He earned his degree from the South Carolina Medical College in Charleston and set up practice in Laurens, marrying and raising a family. Locals affectionately called him Dr. "Peg Leg" Smith, and he was elected to at least one term in the state House of Representatives. Almost forty years after Gettysburg, Smith was still alive, but his days were running out at age 64. His health having been failing for some time, he left behind his wife and seven children when he died in late March 1903. "His community sustains a heartfelt loss in the death of Dr. Smith," a neighboring newspaper stated.[2]

A Light Moment During Kershaw's Attack

Years after the battle, Pvt. William Shumate of the Second South Carolina in Kershaw's brigade recalled an incident on July 2 "which brought a smile to my face" amid the mayhem. Based on Shumate's account, the regiment's adjutant—whom he did not identify—was in line beside him when the man was hit on the foot by an enemy projectile and was "painfully, but not dangerously wounded." The private tried to aid him, asking what he could do, the adjutant replying, "'Please cut off my boot.'" Shumate quickly complied, and the wounded Carolinian "took one swift, eager look at the [enemy] battery, turned his back to the foe and made the best time on record until he reached a place of safety. 'I can, in my mind's eye, see him running now, with one foot naked, bleeding and mangled, and the other encased in a long cavalry boot,'" Shumate wrote. The "gallant fellow survived the war" and was honored with a position in "public office," he continued. "I have met him once since the unpleasantness, and when I jestingly reminded him of the great speed he made through the oat field he did not seem to relish being reminded of the race with grape and canister."[3]

Painful Reminders of Gettysburg

W.B. Franklin, of the First South Carolina's Company B, was wounded in the right hand amid the combat of Perrin's troops on July 1. The stonecutter from Newberry went home after the war and resumed his civilian life. In January 1872, more than eight years after Gettysburg, "a slight rising exhibited itself" in Franklin's right hand, "which on being lanced showed signs of some hard substance underneath." The next day a doctor removed a "flattened bullet" lodged between the bones of his third and fourth fingers. Franklin had "carried the memento in his hand without his knowledge," a newspaper account stated. "It is needless to say that Mr. F. cherishes the piece of flattened lead with affection." Franklin was still going strong in 1905 as a delegate to Confederate reunions. "He is a quiet, an unassuming gentleman and a good citizen," said a news story at the time. "May it be a long time before his familiar figure is missed from the streets of Newberry."[4]

In the days after Thanksgiving in 1884, Confederate veteran Henry Southern of Greenville, South Carolina, was annoyed by pain in his neck near the collarbone. Southern had fought at Gettysburg and been severely wounded in the neck area there. He survived, but the bullet was still in him more than twenty years later. Suspecting that the round was the cause of his discomfort, Southern summoned a doctor named Wallace who "soon saw that the long imprisoned lead could be released successfully with a little care," a news account said. Wallace "after considerable effort extracted a large sized rifle ball from beneath the collarbone," the newspaper stated, adding that the projectile "has just made its appearance in a rather remarkable way." The operation was "quite an extraordinary one and relieves Mr. Southern of a very unpleasant companion. The bullet is not at all disfigured and looks as new as it was on the day it was discharged in the decisive struggle."[5]

Wade Hampton's Battle Horses and Other Cavalry Notes

What was the name of the horse Wade Hampton rode in the cavalry clash at Gettysburg? This is a great Civil War trivia question, but one that may not have a definitive answer.

At least one account states Hampton rode "Beauregard" at Gettysburg, the mount described as the "handsomest horse in the Confederate army" and 16½ hands high. The animal was wounded in the July 3 cavalry battle shortly after Hampton himself was cut down and borne from the field. Beauregard followed the general's ambulance to a field hospital where soldiers unsaddled him. "Then throwing himself down outside the hospital tent, he died," one account said of Beauregard.[6]

After the war, then–Senator Hampton said that he took three thoroughbred stallions to war, all "worth a prince's ransom." "I rode the chesnut sorrel at the great cavalry fight" at Gettysburg, rode the black at First Bull Run and the dark chestnut at Brandy Station. "All of them were wounded three or four times, but they pulled through." Former Confederate cavalryman and historian U.R. Brooks claimed that Hampton's mount at Gettysburg was "Butler," as mentioned earlier, but offered no description of the steed. Brooks was not at Gettysburg.[7]

The Boykin Rangers formed Co. A of the Second S.C. Cavalry and fought at Gettysburg. "Among the first sabres drawn and the last to be sheathed in defence of the South…. They were gay and gallant troopers, the Boykins," said one account. They served as Jeb Stuart's advance guard going into Pennsylvania. After the war two of the former Rangers, W.A. Ancrum and Charles J. McDowell, settled in Camden. McDowell became a "silent partner" in the business of W.A. Ancrum & Co., "grocers and commission merchants."[8]

A Fictitious Cavalry Fight and a Séance?

Could an 1894 article in the Atlanta *Constitution* and later the *Southern Historical Society Papers* about Wade Hampton's combat exploits in the Gettysburg campaign have been a massive fabrication that duped modern-day authors and historians?

Yes.

A piece titled "Hampton's Duel on the Battle-Field at Gettysburg with a Federal Soldier" was published in the June 1, 1894, edition of the *Constitution*. Written by Thomas J. Mackey, the story depicts a one-on-one clash between Hampton and a Union cavalryman on July 2, 1863, near the Pennsylvania village of Hunterstown, a few miles from Gettysburg.[9]

At one point Hampton waited, not triggering his revolver, as the trooper from the Sixth Michigan Cavalry tried to clear his fouled carbine, the story goes. While Hampton was thus distracted, a Union lieutenant identified in postwar only as "Major S.," also of the Sixth Michigan, surprised the general from behind, and sabered Hampton across the head, inflicting injuries, Mackey claimed.

Neither Hampton nor his immediate superior, Maj. Gen. Jeb Stuart, mention the Carolinian being engaged in or wounded in any personal combat at Hunterstown that day. Hampton fared much worse on July 3 in the major cavalry clash around the Rummel Farm. There he was in the midst of the melee and sustained two saber wounds to the head and shrapnel ripping into his leg. Stuart reported that Hampton "was seriously wounded twice in this engagement" while Hampton noted merely that "I was wounded and had to leave the field."[10]

For years after the war nothing was written about the supposed duel until Mackey, a South Carolinian himself, penned the article. He had been a judge of dubious character and shifting loyalties during Reconstruction, based on accounts from the period, and he and Hampton had worked in some of the same political circles. Mackey later began writing articles for various newspapers to make ends meet, his stories often featuring "well-known South Carolinians" as "heroes," such as Hampton. By the early 1890s, Hampton had served two terms as the state governor and as a U.S. senator from 1879 to 1891.[11]

The flies in this literary ointment were questions about Mackey's integrity and truthfulness shortly after his story was published. There were no other accounts— Union or Confederate—to support his tale. "Hampton was of course a gallant man; but the whole story sounded so much like the fool-hardy doings of the days of the crusaders, that nobody would believe it could be true of a sensible man," noted the *Yorkville Enquirer* on June 20, 1894, days after "Duel" appeared in the Atlanta paper. "In a recent card, General Hampton robs it of all further interest by politely saying that it is not altogether true. Anyone who knew Tom Mackey should have been aware of that fact all the time."[12]

Possibly the most outrageous part of "Duel" is the mention of Hampton's brother, Frank, conversing with "Major S.," in a meeting in Mobile, Alabama, some ten years after the war. The outlandish problem with this is that Frank Hampton had been in the grave since 1863, having been mortally wounded at Brandy Station about three weeks before Gettysburg. Mackey's piece makes no mention of a séance. Mackey also claimed that Hampton corresponded with "Major S." and also with the Union trooper, whom Mackey identified as Frank Pearson, "a successful farmer living near Kalamazoo, Mich."[13]

Hampton himself addressed Mackey's story after it also ran in the *State* newspaper in Columbia, South Carolina, sometime in early June. Hampton was in Washington when he wrote a June 13 letter to the editor published in the paper three days later. "Same Old Tom Mackey—He is Making Money Out of Pleasant Fictions About the War," read the headlines over Hampton's letter. The old general admitted that the article was "complimentary to me" but said it was "erroneous in many particulars." He continued: "So I am impelled to say that Judge Mackey is mistaken in stating that any such 'duel' as he mentions happened. I was severely wounded at Gettysburg, and like many of my gallant command on that bloody field, I had some personal [combat] encounters, but none such as were described as occurring with the sharpshooter, nor have I ever had any communication with my antagonists of that day."[14]

At least one modern-day Hampton biographer and Civil War historians through recent decades have used Mackey's account as unquestioned fact. Some identify "Major

S." as Lt. Charles E. Storrs, who led a company of the Sixth Michigan in the Hunterstown fight. Storrs had risen to the rank of major by the war's end. Oddly, Storrs, in at least one work, is referred to as a major at the time of the battle, adding a blatant error to an untrue story, if that is possible!

Chapter Notes

State abbreviations for most newspaper locations are given only on first reference.

Prologue

1. *Edgefield* (S.C.) *Advertiser*, July 29, 1863.
2. *Lancaster* (S.C.) *Ledger*, September 2, 1863.
3. *Charleston* (S.C.) *Weekly News*, n.d., reprinted in the *Anderson* (S.C.) *Intelligencer*, May 1, 1884. Miss Rhett was a member of the infamous Rhett family, many of whom were "fire-eaters," or extreme secessionists, later blamed for helping push the South into war.
4. *Confederate Veteran* 23: 343.
5. *Confederate Veteran* 18: 520; *U.S. National Park Service Soldier Search* (www.nps.gov/civilwar/search-soldiers). Of the 106 men, including Varner, who went to war, only 11 came back "and they all bore the scars of war," Varner wrote years later.
6. *Lancaster* (S.C.) *News*, May 9, 1916.
7. *Anderson Intelligencer*, June 29, 1882; *Newberry* (S.C.) *Herald*, January 24, 1872; *Newberry* (S.C.) *Herald and News*, October 3, 1905.
8. Winnsboro (S.C.) *News and Herald*, February 24, 1916.
9. *Charleston* (S.C.) *Courier*, September 11, 1861; *Charleston* (S.C.) *Mercury*, June 3, 1862.
10. Fremantle, *Three Months in the Southern States: April–June, 1863* (Mobile, AL: S.H. Goetzel, 1864), 114–115.
11. *Ibid.*
12. Mrs. Thomas Smythe Taylor, Mrs. A.T. Kohn, Mrs. August Poppinheim, and Miss Martha B. Washington, *South Carolina Women in the Confederacy* (Columbia, SC: State, 1903), 212–213. Mrs. Adams's husband, James, was a cavalry major but was not at Gettysburg.
13. J.R. Boyles, *Reminiscences of the Civil War* (Columbia, SC: n.p., 1890), 39; Augustus Dickert, *History of Kershaw's Brigade* (Newberry, SC: Elbert H. Hull, 1899), 148; Frances H. Kennedy, ed. *The Civil War Battlefield Guide* (Boston: Houghton Mifflin, 1990), 119.
14. *Keowee* (Pickens, S.C.) *Courier*, February 3, 1909.
15. J.F.J. Caldwell, *The History of a Brigade of South Carolinians, Known First as "Gregg's" and Subsequently as "McGowan's Brigade"* (Philadelphia:

King and Baird, 1866), 95–96; Dickert, *History of Kershaw's Brigade*, 146.
16. Boyles, *Reminiscences*, 39–40.
17. James I. Robertson, Jr., *General A.P. Hill: The Story of a Confederate Warrior* (New York: Random House, 1987), 192–193; Ezra J. Warner, *Generals in Gray: Lives of the Confederate Commanders* (Baton Rouge: Louisiana State University Press, 1959), 84–85, 134–135.
18. Guy R. Everson and Edward W. Simpson, Jr., eds., *"Far, Far from Home":The Wartime Letters of Dick and Tally Simpson, Third South Carolina Volunteers* (Oxford: Oxford University Press, 1994), 263. Tally Simpson to his sister Anna, written from Culpeper Courthouse, Virginia, July 27, 1863.
19. Spencer Glasgow Welch, *A Confederate Surgeon's Letters to His Wife* (New York: Neale, 1911), 57; Dickert, *History of Kershaw's Brigade*, 149.
20. Jeffrey D. Wert, "Gettysburg: The Special Issue," *Civil War Times Illustrated* (hereafter cited as *CWTI*) 27, no. 4 (Summer 1988): 26; Dickert, *History of Kershaw's Brigade*, 148.
21. William H. Perry to Benjamin F. Perry, July 11, 1863; University of South Carolina Libraries.
22. *Lancaster News*, August 4, 1906–July 30, 1863; letter owned by John Steele's daughter, Mrs. C.M. Hardin. It is unclear if Steele was a private or corporal at the time of Gettysburg. The letter was written by Steele "near Culpeper Court House" Virginia.
23. Everson and Simpson, 250–251. Tally Simpson stated that these Georgians belonged to Brig. Gen. W.T. Wofford's brigade.
24. Everson and Simpson, 261–262.
25. U.S. War Department, *The War of the Rebellion: A Compilation of the Official Records of the Union and Confederate Armies*, 128 vols. (Washington, D.C.: U.S. Government Printing Office, 1880–1901) (hereafter cited as *OR*), pt. 2, 616. Anderson's campaign report dated August 7, 1863.
26. Fremantle, *Three Months*, 120; Boyles, *Reminiscences*, 40.
27. Varina D. Brown, *A Colonel at Gettysburg and Spotsylvania* (Columbia, SC: State, 1931), 77; Kennedy, *Civil War Battlefield Guide*, 118.

28. Jeffrey D. Wert, "Gettysburg," 27; Caldwell, *History of a Brigade,* 95–96; Kennedy, *Civil War Battlefield Guide,* 118.

29. Everson and Simpson, 250–251; Welch, 57–58.

30. Luther W. Minnigh, *Gettysburg: What They Did Here* (Gettysburg, PA: n.p., 1900).

31. *OR,* pt. 2, 607, 637. Based on Pettigrew's June 30 reconnaissance, Heth reported "a large force of cavalry near the town, supported by an infantry force." No Union infantry was present then, although the Confederates may have seen some Pennsylvania militiamen.

Chapter 1

1. David G. Martin, *Gettysburg July 1* (Cambridge, MA: Da Capo, 1996), 60.

2. *OR,* pt. 2, 607, 610, 661; Bradley M. Gottfried, *The Artillery of Gettysburg* (Nashville, TN: Cumberland, 2008), 26. The battery was also known as the Pee Dee Light Artillery. It was initially organized as the Pee Dee Rifles, Company D, First South Carolina Volunteers. The infantrymen later trained as artillerists.

3. *OR,* pt. 2, 677; *Charleston (S.C.) News and Courier,* December 15, 1934. Brunson called the Chambersburg Pike the "Baltimore pike," which is also basically correct.

4. Stephen Z. Starr, *The Union Cavalry in the Civil War,* 3 vols. (Baton Rouge: Louisiana State University Press, 1979), vol. 1, 424–425.

5. Martin, 82. McPherson's Ridge is actually two ridges; the Union line posted on the western-most height.

6. *OR,* pt. 2, 610, 678; Jeffrey D. Wert, "Gettysburg," 31; Carol Reardon and Tom Vossler, *A Field Guide to Gettysburg* (Chapel Hill: University of North Carolina Press, 2013), 19.

7. *OR,* pt. 2, 289, 660; Caldwell, *History of a Brigade,* 96; United Daughters of the Confederacy, South Carolina Division, John K. McIver Chapter, *Recollections and Reminiscences,* 6 vols. (Columbia, SC: State, 1911), vol. 5, 513; *The State* (Columbia, S.C.), July 3, 1938, containing Perrin's July 29, 1863 letter to Bonham.

8. *OR,* pt. 2, 656, 661.

9. Warner, *Generals in Gray,* 235. The South Carolina infantry brigade in Lt. Gen. A.P. Hill's Third Corps was officially known as the First Brigade or, more popularly, "McGowan's Brigade," in Pender's division at Gettysburg. Since the command's namesake, Brig. Gen. Samuel McGowan, was recuperating from a wound and not present, the brigade was led by Col. Abner Perrin at Gettysburg. To simplify the narrative, these troops are called "Perrin's brigade."

10. Bruce Allardice, *Confederate Colonels: A Biographical Register* (Columbia: University of Missouri Press, 2008), 76, 78, 274; *Charleston Mercury,* September 3, 1861, May 26, 1864; Brown, *Colonel at Gettysburg,* 89. McCreary went by Wick, his middle name, instead of Charles, his first name.

11. *Charleston Mercury,* August 19, 1861.

12. Michael A. Dreese, *Torn Families: Death and Kinship at the Battle of Gettysburg* (Jefferson, NC: McFarland, 2007), 148–150. Both Richard and James Carter were in the First South Carolina.

13. Clement A. Evans, ed., *Confederate Military History,* 12 vols. (Atlanta: Confederate, 1899), vol. 5, 433–434.

14. *Ibid.,* 463–464. Bowden married Mary Fleck in 1863; the exact date is not recorded.

15. *Ibid.,* 495–496.

16. *The State,* October 7, 1925.

17. Macon (Ga.) *Telegraph,* July 4, 1886.

18. United Daughters of the Confederacy, 5: 513. Crosson and other members of the Thirteenth South Carolina's Company G were from Prosperity, S.C., and the surrounding area.

19. Caldwell, 96; United Daughters of the Confederacy, 1: 342–343; *Lancaster News,* August 4, 1906; Evans, 5: 495–496.

20. *Augusta (Ga.) Chronicle,* September 4, 1910. Letter was written on August 2, 1863, near Orange Court House.

21. Evans, 5: 725; *OR,* pt. 2, 290; David G. McIntosh, *Review of the Gettysburg Campaign* (Pamphlet Collection, South Caroliniana Library, University of South Carolina), 21. Evans states that McIntosh was promoted to colonel "after Fredericksburg," which is erroneous. The *OR* list McIntosh as a major at Gettysburg. McIntosh also had helped organize the Pee Dee Artillery; thus, that battery is also sometimes referred to as "McIntosh's Battery."

22. *OR,* pt. 2, 606–607; Martin, 188; Caldwell, 97.

23. James Longstreet, *From Manassas to Appomattox* (Philadelphia: J.B. Lippincott, 1896), 353; Minnigh, 19, 21–22.

24. *OR,* pt. 2, 155–157; Carol Reardon and Tom Vossler, *The Gettysburg Campaign: June–July 1863* (Washington, D.C.: Center of Military History, United States Army, 2013), 22.

25. Caldwell, 97–98; *The State,* July 3, 1938; *OR,* pt. 2, 656; *Augusta Chronicle,* September 4, 1910, containing August 2, 1863, from Welch to his wife; Martin, 188, where Martin states this last halt by Pender was about 10:30 a.m.

26. *Augusta Chronicle,* September 4, 1910; Brown, *Colonel at Gettysburg,* 77–78; Thomas M. Littlejohn, "Recollections of a Confederate Soldier," copy in Twelfth South Carolina file, Gettysburg National Military Park; Boyles, *Reminiscences,* 40.

27. *OR,* pt. 2, 674–675; Martin, 188–189; Gottfried, *Artillery,* 34.

28. Minnigh, 23; Kennedy, *Civil War Battlefield Guide,* 117.

29. *OR,* pt. 2, 638; Reardon and Vossler, Gettysburg Campaign, 23. Heth's battle report does not state when this attack began, while Perrin's claim of about 1 p.m. appears to be too early. Other accounts mark the time as closer to 2 p.m., especially since Lee's arrival was apparently during this period.

30. Minnigh, 22–23; Martin, 368; Warner, *Generals in Gray,* 237–238. Though he was a North Carolinian, Pettigrew had strong ties to the Palmetto State as well. After graduating college in 1847 he

eventually settled in Charleston and opened a law practice. Elected to the South Carolina legislature in 1856, he also was active as an officer in the state militia and participated in the bombardment of Fort Sumter in 1861. He later joined the Hampton Legion and was soon elected colonel of the Twelfth South Carolina. Promoted brigadier general in early 1862, he was seriously wounded and captured at Seven Pines, then exchanged about two months later.

31. *OR*, pt. 2, 656.

32. Brown, *Colonel at Gettysburg,* 77; *OR*, pt. 2, 656–661; Caldwell, 97–98; *Confederate Veteran* 30: 53.

33. Reardon and Vossler, *Field Guide*, 137; R.K. Beecham, *Gettysburg: The Pivotal Battle of the Civil War* (Chicago: A.C. McClurg, 1911), 54; Minnigh, 27–28.

Chapter 2

1. *Confederate Veteran* 30: 53; Beecham, *Gettysburg*, 55; Gottfried, *Brigades of Gettysburg*, 643.

2. *Confederate Veteran* 30: 53; Caldwell, *History of a Brigade*, 97–98; Martin, 405; *OR*, pt. 2, 656–657. Scales's and Lane's brigades also moved "rapidly forward" and passed Heth's division, Maj. Engelhard of Pender's staff noted.

3. *The State*, July 3, 1938; Caldwell, *History of a Brigade*, 97–98; *Confederate Veteran* 30: 53; *OR*, pt. 2, 660–661; Brown, 79. Caldwell states that Pettigrew's command also contained Mississippians, which is erroneous.

4. *Charleston* (S.C.) *Courier*, July 16, 1863; *OR*, pt. 2, 657, 661.

5. Brown, 78–79; Martin, 396; James K.P. Scott, *The Story of the Battles of Gettysburg* (Harrisburg, PA: Telegraph, 1927), 234.

6. Gottfried, *Brigades of Gettysburg*, 643; Brown, 78–79; Martin, 396; Scott, *Story of the Battles*, 234. Wainwright was chief of artillery for the Union I Corps.

7. Abner Doubleday, *Chancellorsville and Gettysburg* (New York: Charles Scribner's Sons, 1912), 147; Mark M. Boatner, III, *The Civil War Dictionary* (David McKay, 1987), 427–428. Wadsworth's other brigade, led by Brig. Gen. Lysander Cutler, fought stubbornly to hold McPherson's Ridge before being moved into the Union line north of the Chambersburg Pike.

8. John P. Nicholson, Lewis Eugene Beitler, Paul L. Roy, and Pennsylvania Gettysburg Battle-field Commission, *Pennsylvania at Gettysburg: Ceremonies at the Dedication of the Monuments*, 2 vols. (Harrisburg, PA: E.K. Meyers, State Printer, 1893), vol. 2, 745–746.

9. John M. Vanderslice, *Where and How the Regiments Fought and the Troops They Encountered: An Account of the Battle Giving Movements, Positions and Losses of the Commands Engaged* (Philadelphia: G.W. Dillingham, 1897), 48–49, 57.

10. *OR*, pt. 2, 660–661; Caldwell, *History of a Brigade*, 98; *Yorkville* (S.C.) *Enquirer*, November 20, 1889.

11. Littlejohn, "Recollections"; Martin, 405; Boyles, *Reminiscences*, 40–41; *Charleston Courier*, July 16, 1863.

12. *OR*, pt. 2, 657, 661.

13. Nicholson et al., *Pennsylvania at Gettysburg*, 2: 879; Martin, 406; Cooper's battery and Capt. G.H. Reynolds' Battery E of the First New York Light Artillery relieved Hall's and Lt. John H. Calef's Battery A, Second U.S. Horse Artillery, the latter in Buford's command. Martin identifies Gardner as James "Garner," which is erroneous. Gardner did not note the fate of this Confederate flag bearer, who was apparently in Perrin's brigade.

14. Caldwell, *History of a Brigade*, 98–99; United Daughters of the Confederacy, 1: 342–343; *Lancaster News*, August 4, 1906; Boyles, *Reminiscences*, 40–41. Rufus Harling was listed as having sustained a severe facial wound at Gettysburg.

15. *The State*, July 3, 1938.

16. United Daughters of the Confederacy, 1: 323–324; *Edgefield Advertiser*, August 23, 1911; Brown, 84.

17. *OR*, pt. 2, 661; Scott, *Story of the Battles*, 234; Nicholson et al., *Pennsylvania at Gettysburg*, 2: 747–748; *OR*, pt. 1, 327–328.

18. *OR*, pt. 2, 661; Scott, *Story of the Battles*, 234; Brown, 80–84.

19. *OR*, pt. 2, 661; Daniel A. Tompkins, *Company K, Fourteenth South Carolina Volunteers* (Charlotte, NC: Observer, 1897), 19–20; United Daughters of the Confederacy, 5: 553. Allen's account is based on a postwar narrative written by Zena Payne for the United Daughters of the Confederacy chapter in Johnston, S.C. Thirty-four men in Company K of the Fourteenth S.C. were casualties at Gettysburg.

20. *The State*, July 3, 1938; Caldwell, *History of a Brigade*, 98.

21. *OR*, pt. 2, 662; *The State*, July 3, 1938.

22. *OR*, pt. 2, 662–663; Welch, *A Confederate Surgeon's Letters*, 63; *Augusta Chronicle*, September 4, 1910.

23. *Lancaster News*, August 4, 1906.

24. *OR*, pt. 2, 662–663; *Lancaster* (S.C.) *Ledger*, July 22, 1863; *Yorkville Enquirer*, August 28, 1879; Brown, 85. Brown was in the Fourteenth South Carolina but was describing color bearer losses in the Twelfth South Carolina.

25. *Yorkville Enquirer*, November 20, 1889; Caldwell, *History of a Brigade*, 98; Nicholson, *Pennsylvania at Gettysburg*, 2: 747–748, 879; *OR*, pt. 1, 327–328.

26. *OR*, pt. 2, 662–663.

27. *OR*, pt. 2, 662; Caldwell, *History of a Brigade*, 98; *The State*, October 7, 1925.

28. *OR*, pt. 2, 662; Caldwell, *History of a Brigade*, 98; *The State*, October 7, 1925.

29. *OR*, pt. 2, 662; *Yorkville Enquirer*, November 20, 1889; *Lancaster News*, August 4, 1906. Steele incorrectly identified Nisbet as "Alexander J. Nesbit" in this letter.

30. United Daughters of the Confederacy, 6: 170; *OR*, pt. 2, 662; *Yorkville Enquirer*, November 20, 1889.

31. *Augusta Chronicle*, September 4, 1910.

32. Evans, 5: 433–434; *Charleston Courier*, July 16, 1863; "Search for Soldiers," U.S. National Park Service. In a July 2 letter to the *Courier*, Armstrong wrote: "Sergeants Larken and Owens, our color bearers, were both dangerously wounded. They exhibited great gallantry during the fight." Armstrong made no mention of carrying the banner himself.

33. Nicholson, *Pennsylvania at Gettysburg*, 2: 880. Gardner identified the officer as Lt. Col. Alfred B. McCalmont of the 142nd Pennsylvania.

34. Nicholson, *Pennsylvania at Gettysburg*, 2: 747–748, 750; *OR*, pt. 1, 327–328. McFarland and Brown of the Fourteenth South Carolina met again at Gettysburg 19 years later, the Carolinian telling the Pennsylvanian that he had seen him fall seriously wounded near the Seminary. The soldier who bore McFarland to safety was Pvt. Lyman D. Wilson of the 151st's Company F.

35. *OR*, pt. 2, 662; *Confederate Veteran* 30: 53; United Daughters of the Confederacy, 3: 62–63; Ron V. Killian, *General Abner M. Perrin, C.S.A.: A Biography* (Jefferson, NC: McFarland, 2012), 106; Henry S. Huidekoper, *A Short Story of the First Day's Fight at Gettysburg* (Philadelphia: Bicking, 1906), 10; *Newberry* (S.C.) *Herald and News*, May 27, 1904; *The State*, August 16, 1913; Caldwell, *History of a Brigade*, 98.

36. Brown, 81, 84–85; *Edgefield Advertiser*, August 5, 1863; Beecham, Gettysburg, 92.

37. *OR*, pt. 1, 251; Brown, 82–83.

38. *OR*, pt. 1, 251; Brown, 82–83.

39. *OR*, pt. 2, 662; *Confederate Veteran* 30: 53; United Daughters of the Confederacy, 3: 62–63; Killian, *General Abner M. Perrin*, 106; Huidekoper, *Short Story*, 10; *Newberry Herald and News*, May 27, 1904; *The State*, August 16, 1913.

40. Beecham, Gettysburg, 95; Jeffrey D. Wert, "Gettysburg," 40; *Augusta Chronicle*, May 12, 1901; *OR*, pt. 2, 662. A mild debate flickered years later when some of Ewell's veterans claimed to be the first Confederates to enter Gettysburg on July 1. Their claims appear to be unfounded.

Chapter 3

1. Caldwell, *History of a Brigade*, 99–100.

2. *Augusta Chronicle*, September 4, 1910.

3. *OR*, pt. 2, 607, 662–663; *Lancaster News*, August 4, 1906; *Augusta Chronicle*, April 7, 1901; *Yorkville Enquirer*, November 20, 1889. Hill reported: "About 2:30…, the right wing of Ewell's corps made its appearance on my left, and thus formed a right angle with my line. Pender's division was then ordered forward, Thomas' brigade being retained in reserve, and the rout of the enemy was complete."

4. Caldwell, *History of a Brigade*, 99; *Columbia* (S.C.) *Guardian*, n.d., reprinted in *Charleston Courier*, September 12, 1863; *The State*, July 3, 1938; Brown, 82–83. Returning to Gettysburg in 1882, Brown noted: "The streets and fencing look now as they did then." He added that the only difference

was a hedge growing and spreading on the north side of Boundary Street where his Fourteenth South Carolina entered the town.

5. *Abbeville* (S.C.) *Press*, August 7, 1863.

6. *Abbeville Press*, August 7, 1863 (italics in the original); Brown, 83; *OR*, pt. 2, 658, 663.

7. Brown, 84. Brown noted that the "celebrated Iron Brigade was in our front" along with the 121st, 143rd, 149th, and 151 Pennsylvania, and some Maine troops.

8. Perrin's July 29, 1863, letter to Gov. Bonham, published in *The State*, July 3, 1938. Perrin did not identify the two other captured flags. The 104th New York, commanded by Col. Gilbert G. Prey, belonged to the I Corps' Second Division, First Brigade.

9. *OR*, pt. 2, 607; *OR*, pt. 1, 251; Robertson, *General A.P. Hill*, 214–215. In a November battle report, Hill claimed his men captured 2,300 prisoners and two fieldpieces. The I Corps casualties are from Abner Doubleday's report, stating that his troop strength of 8,200 was reduced to about 2,450.

10. *Augusta Chronicle*, November 18, 1907. The article states that McCreary was knocked "half-stunned from his horse." This appears to be inaccurate, since the Carolinians, other than Perrin, attacked on foot.

11. United Daughters of the Confederacy, 3: 62–63; Evans, 5: 526.

12. *The State*, July 3, 1938; *OR*, pt. 2, 663; United Daughters of the Confederacy, 3: 62–63; Evans, 5: 526.

13. Brown, 83; Tompkins, *Company K*, 19–20; *OR*, pt. 2, 660–664; *Edgefield Advertiser*, August 5, 1863; Reardon and Vossler, *Field Guide*, 149.

14. *The Laurens* (S.C.) *Advertiser*, January 18, 1911; Brown, 85; Evans, 5: 785, 788–789. It's unclear if Richmond Parson's death in 1863 was before or after Gettysburg. Company F was noted for its tall soldiers. Of 130 men in the ranks, sixty or so were at least six feet tall.

15. United Daughters of the Confederacy, 6: 335–336; Dreese, 150.

16. Evans, 5: 464, 546–547; *Augusta Chronicle*, January 14, 1909. Evans spells the captain's last name as "Dewbery," apparently inaccurate since his death notice and the National Park Service "Search for Soldiers" website identify him as Dewberry. The death notice is erroneous in listing him as leading Company I. He led Company E, Evans and the NPS website agree.

17. Boyles, *Reminiscences*, 41–42.

18. *Macon Telegraph*, July 4, 1886.

19. *OR*, pt. 2, 610, 639, 678; Jeffrey D. Wert, "Gettysburg," 31; Reardon and Vossler, Gettysburg Campaign, 19.

20. *OR*, pt. 2, 610, 674–675, 677–678; McIntosh, *Review*, 57; United Daughters of the Confederacy, 47; Gottfried, *Artillery*, 34.

21. Douglas Southall Freeman, *Lee's Lieutenants: A Study in Command*, abridged by Stephen W. Sears (New York: Simon & Schuster, 2001), 574; Clarence C. Buel and Robert V. Johnson, *Battles and Leaders of the Civil War: Being for the Most Part*

Contributions by Union and Confederate Authors, 3 vols. (New York: Century, 1887), vol. 3, 339–340.

22. *Augusta Chronicle*, April 7, 1901; *The State*, July 3, 1938.

23. *The State*, July 3, 1938; *OR*, pt. 2, 607, 613.

24. Warner, *Generals in Gray*, 8–9; William W. Hassler, "'Fighting Dick' Anderson," *Civil War Times Illustrated* 12, no. 10 (February 1974): 5; Freeman, *Lee's Lieutenants*, 37, 108; Jack D. Welsh, *Medical Histories of Confederate Generals* (Kent, Ohio and London: Kent State University Press, 1995), 8–9.

25. *OR*, pt. 2, 607, 613.

26. *Philadelphia Times*, March 17, 1882.

27. *Ibid.*

28. *Augusta Chronicle*, September 4, 1910; Brown, 85. Brown noted that Huot "returned with us on the final retreat."

29. *Lancaster Ledger*, July 22, 1863; *Camden* (S.C.) *Confederate*, July 17, 1863; *Laurens* (S.C.) *Advertiser*, April 8, 1903. The *Ledger* states erroneously that Warren belonged to the Thirteenth South Carolina. It is unclear whether Smith, whom Bagwell described as "Dr.," survived. Bagwell also writes that Pool was a lieutenant, which is inaccurate. His letter to the paper states the date of the battle was 1864, an obvious error which may have resulted from the passage of forty years since Gettysburg.

30. *Lancaster Ledger*, December 18, 1889.

31. Brown, 83–84.

32. Starr, *Union Cavalry*, 1: 428–429; *OR*, pt. 2, 695–696.

33. *OR*, pt. 2, 291, 696–697; Starr, *Union Cavalry*, 1: 428–430.

34. Fremantle, *Three Months*, 118.

35. *The State*, July 9, 1911.

36. *OR*, pt. 2, 366, 372; Dickert, *History of Kershaw's Brigade*, 149–150; *Confederate Veteran* 21: 433; Buel and Johnson, *Battles and Leaders*, 3: 331–332. Kershaw wrote that his brigade went "into camp at 12 p.m." on July 1, which appears to be erroneous. Kershaw himself may have ridden ahead of his troops, stating that "we" arrived about sunset and "reached the top of the range of hills overlooking Gettysburg, from which could be seen and heard the smoke and din of battle then raging in the distance." This may have been Ewell's troops in action on the Confederate left flank.

37. *Augusta Chronicle*, September 4, 1910. Welch identified this soldier as Milton Bossardt in at least two letters to his wife and as Milton Bossard in another. Neither Bossardt nor Bossard are listed in various brigade/regimental rosters.

38. *Confederate Veteran* 21: 433–434; *The State*, July 9, 1911; *Philadelphia Weekly Times*, May 6, 1882. William Shumate wrote the latter article for the Philadelphia paper headlined "With Kershaw at Gettysburg."

39. *OR*, pt. 2, 291, 696–697; Starr, *Union Cavalry*, 1: 428–429; Jeffrey D. Wert, *General James Longstreet: The Confederacy's Most Controversial Soldier: A Biography* (New York: Simon & Schuster, 1993), 281.

40. *OR*, pt. 2, 307–308.

41. *Ibid.*

Chapter 4

1. Buel and Johnson, *Battles and Leaders*, 3: 340–341.

2. Ezra J. Warner, *Generals in Blue: Lives of the Union Commanders* (Baton Rouge: Louisiana State University Press, 1964), 233–234, 315–316; Jeffrey D. Wert, "Gettysburg," 28.

3. *OR*, pt. 2, 317.

4. Buel and Johnson, *Battles and Leaders*, 3: 340–341.

5. *OR*, pt. 2, 290, 724–725; Edward G. Longacre, *The Cavalry at Gettysburg: A Tactical Study of Mounted Operations During the Civil War's Pivotal Campaign, 9 June–14 July 1863* (Lincoln: University of Nebraska Press, 1986), 17, 198–199.

6. *OR*, pt. 2, 290; U.R. Brooks, ed., *Stories of the Confederacy* (Columbia, SC: State, 1913), 171, 545; Evans, 5: 706–707; *Charleston* (S.C.) *News and Courier*, March 27, 1946.

7. Warner, *Generals in Gray*, 348; Longacre, *Cavalry at Gettysburg*, 17.

8. G.W. Beale, *A Lieutenant of Cavalry in Lee's Army* (Boston: Gorham, 1918), 192–194.

9. Henry Kyd Douglas, *I Rode with Stonewall—Being Chiefly the War Experiences of the Youngest Member of Jackson's Staff from the John Brown Raid to the Hanging of Mrs. Surratt* (Chapel Hill: University of North Carolina Press, 1940), 234; G. Moxley Sorrel, *Recollections of a Confederate Staff Officer* (New York and Washington: Neale, 1905), 261.

10. Welsh, *Medical Histories*, 91; Warner, *Generals in Gray*, 122–123; John Esten Cooke, *Wearing of the Gray: Being Personal Portraits, Scenes, and Adventures of the War* (New York: E.B. Treat, 1867), 245.

11. *OR*, pt. 2, 697, 724–725; Longacre, *Cavalry at Gettysburg*, 19, 198–199. The Union cavalry engaged were from the Cavalry Corps' Third Division, led by Brig. Gen. H.J. Kilpatrick.

12. *Yorkville Enquirer*, November 20, 1889; Brown, 85–86.

13. Littlejohn, "Recollections"; Brown, 86. When Brown returned to Gettysburg in 1882 he encountered the McMillans; "the old gentleman and his wife" were still living in the house. Nineteen years after the battle McMillan "still laments the loss of his earthly store," Brown wrote.

14. *Charleston Courier*, July 16, 1863.

15. *Macon Telegraph*, July 4, 1886.

16. *OR*, pt. 2, 678. The position is on what is now West Confederate Avenue.

17. *OR*, pt. 2, 366–367; Dickert, *History of Kershaw's Brigade*, 150.

18. *Philadelphia Weekly Times*, May 6, 1882. The tavern is also known as Bream's Tavern.

19. Dickert, *History of Kershaw's Brigade*, 151–152.

20. Buel and Johnson, *Battles and Leaders*, 3: 340.

21. *OR*, pt. 2, 366–367; Jay Jorgensen, *Gettysburg's Bloody Wheatfield* (Shippensburg, PA: White Mane, 2002), 32.

22. Dickert, *History of Kershaw's Brigade*, 152.

23. *Newberry Herald and News*, January 24, 1902;

Dickert, *History of Kershaw's Brigade*, 152. There are other variations of this event recalled by other soldiers.

24. Welsh, *Medical Histories*, 127; Evans, 5: 409–410; Freeman, *Lee's Lieutenants*, 659; *Newberry Herald and News*, July 4, 1894.

25. C. Vann Woodward, ed., *Mary Chesnut's Civil War* (New Haven, CT: Yale University Press, 1981), 69–70; Sorrel, *Recollections*, 238. It is unclear if Sorrel was a major or lieutenant colonel at Gettysburg.

26. John F. Marzalek, ed., *The Diary of Miss Emma Holmes—1861–1866* (Baton Rouge: Louisiana State University Press, 1994), 230–231; *Anderson (S.C.) Daily Intelligencer*, April 22, 1914.

27. *OR*, pt. 2, 283.

28. *Charleston Mercury*, July 20, 1863. The writer of this post-battle article was identified only as "Pee Dee."

29. Welsh, *Medical Histories*, 126; Warner, *Generals in Gray*, 170–171; Evans, 5: 408–409; *The State*, May 5, 1907; Dickert, *History of Kershaw's Brigade*, 228–229.

30. John A. Chapman, *History of Edgefield County from the Earliest Settlements to 1897* (Newberry, SC: Elbert H. Aull, 1897), 345–346; *Abbeville (S.C.) Press and Banner*, October 2, 1912; *Edgefield Advertiser*, September 1, 1915; Dickert, *History of Kershaw's Brigade*, 107–108, 112–113, 202–203, 272–273; *OR*, pt. 2, 283.

31. Chapman, *History of Edgefield County from the Earliest Settlements to 1897* (Newberry, SC: Elbert H. Aull, 1897), 345–346; *Abbeville (S.C.) Press and Banner*, October 2, 1912; *Edgefield Advertiser*, September 1, 1915; Dickert, *History of Kershaw's Brigade*, 107–108, 112–113, 202–203, 272–273; *OR*, pt. 2, 283.

32. Dickert, *History of Kershaw's Brigade*, 161–162; *The State*, March 16, 1930; *Columbia Guardian*, n.d., reprinted in *Charleston Courier*, September 18, 1863.

33. *Confederate Veteran* 16: 105; *The State*, February 24, 1907.

34. *OR*, pt. 2, 367; Jorgensen, *Gettysburg's Bloody Wheatfield*, 32.

35. Longstreet, 364–365; Buel and Johnson, *Battles and Leaders*, 3: 319–320; Gottfried, *Brigades*, 428.

36. Reardon and Vossler, *Field Guide*, 189; Warner, *Generals in Gray*, 174–175; Welsh, *Medical Histories*, 129.

37. *Charleston Mercury*, September 18, 1861; *Charleston Courier*, September 11, 1861; Evans, 5: 437; *OR*, pt. 2, 67. Bachman's father, the Rev. John Bachman, participated in the ceremonies for the Volunteers' departure.

38. *Charleston Mercury*, September 18, 1861; *Charleston Courier*, September 11, 1861; Evans, 5: 437; *OR*, pt. 2, 67.

39. Evans, 5: 672–674; *Charleston Courier*, September 11, 1861; Buel and Johnson, *Battles and Leaders*, 3: 320. *The Courier* identified the color bearer as "Jaeger." Henry's North Carolina batteries were Capt. A.C. Latham's Branch Artillery and

the Rowan Artillery, led by Capt. James Reilly. All four of Henry's batteries were posted "at advantageous points" in the Confederate line, each facing Round Top.

40. *Anderson Intelligencer*, July 16, 1902.

41. Evans, 5: 595–596; *Charleston Mercury*, June 3, 1862. Due to promotions and reorganization, Gilbert led the battery for about eight months, including Gettysburg.

42. *Charleston Mercury*, November 8, 1862; Gottfried, *Artillery*, 92.

43. Longstreet, 364–365; Buel and Johnson, *Battles and Leaders*, 3: 341; Hassler, "'Fighting Dick' Anderson," 10.

44. *OR*, pt. 2, 613–614; Robertson, *General A.P. Hill*, 219; C. Irvine Walker, *The Life of Lieutenant General Richard Heron Anderson of the Confederate Army* (Charleston, SC: Art, 1917), 267.

45. *Ibid*.

46. Buel and Johnson, *Battles and Leaders*, 3: 320–322.

47. *Ibid.*; *Anderson Intelligencer*, July 16, 1902.

48. Buel and Johnson, *Battles and Leaders*, 3: 320–322.

49. *OR*, pt. 2, 284; Buel and Johnson, *Battles and Leaders*, 3: 323–324, 341; Welsh, *Medical Histories*, 105, 129–130.

50. Jeffrey D. Wert, "Gettysburg," 48; Buel and Johnson, *Battles and Leaders*, 3: 324–325.

51. Buel and Johnson, *Battles and Leaders*, 3: 324–325; John B. Hood, *Advance and Retreat* (Secaucus, NJ: Blue and Grey, 1985), 59–60.

Chapter 5

1. Dickert, *History of Kershaw's Brigade*, 152.

2. *Confederate Veteran* 21: 434. Cabell was a Virginian.

3. *Ibid.*; Dickert, *History of Kershaw's Brigade*, 153; Reardon and Vossler, *Field Guide*, 170.

4. *Anderson Intelligencer*, June 29, 1882; United Daughters of the Confederacy, 2: 307.

5. Dickert, *History of Kershaw's Brigade*, 164.

6. *Charleston Mercury*, September 18, 1863, and October 17, 1863.

7. Buel and Johnson, *Battles and Leaders*, 3: 333–334.

8. Glenn Tucker, *High Tide at Gettysburg* (New York: Bobbs-Merrill, 1958), 241–242.

9. Evans, 5: 263; *OR*, pt. 2, 367.

10. Buel and Johnson, *Battles and Leaders*, 3: 334; *Philadelphia Weekly Times*, May 6, 1882.

11. *OR*, pt. 2, 372; Dickert, *History of Kershaw's Brigade*, 153; Clifford Dowdey, *Lee and His Men at Gettysburg: The Death of a Nation* (New York: Skyhorse, 1986), 220; Buel and Johnson, *Battles and Leaders*, 3: 334; *Anderson Intelligencer*, June 29, 1882; Tucker, *High Tide*, 271; Harry W. Pfanz, *Gettysburg: The Second Day* (Chapel Hill: University of North Carolina Press, 1987), 253.

12. Jeffrey D. Wert, "Gettysburg," 51; *Manning (S.C.) Times*, July 13, 1904; *OR*, pt. 2, 372. Maffett stated that the Rebel artillery opened fire about 3

p.m., prefacing Longstreet's assault at 4 p.m., both times erroneous.

13. Frye Gaillard, *Journey to the Wilderness: War, Memory, and a Southern Family's Civil War Letters* (Montgomery, AL: NewSouth, 2015), 93; David L. Shultz and Scott L. Mingus, *The Second Day at Gettysburg* (El Dorado Hills, CA: Savas Beatie, LLC, 2015), 310; D. Wyatt Aiken to "Dear Capt." (unidentified), July 11, 1863, University of South Carolina, South Caroliniana Digital Library. Aiken's letter was written "Near Hagerstown."

14. Dowdey, *Lee and His Men*, 220–221; Buel and Johnson, *Battles and Leaders*, 3: 334–335; Lafayette McLaws, "Gettysburg: Address of General McLaws Before the Georgia Historical Society," *Southern Historical Society Papers* 7 (1879): 73.

15. *Charleston Mercury*, September 18, 1863; *Confederate Veteran* 5: 521; "Search for Soldiers."

16. *The State*, February 24, 1907; *Edgefield Advertiser*, July 29, 1863; Aiken letter, July 11, 1863. Aiken wrote, "Barksdale & Kershaw moved on," seemingly implying that the brigades were in tandem, which is inaccurate. Clark survived Gettysburg but was killed at Chickamauga in September 1863. Roper's letter to Harling's father is first mentioned at the beginning of chapter 1.

17. *Anderson Intelligencer*, June 29, 1882; *Confederate Veteran* 21: 434.

18. Dowdey, *Lee and His Men*, 222; OR, pt. 1, 881–882; Pfanz, *Gettysburg: The Second Day*, 254–255. McGilvery's force consisted of two sections of Ames's and Thompson's batteries, and Hart's, Clark's, Phillips's, and Bigelow's batteries.

19. Gaillard, *Journey to the Wilderness*, 93; Dowdey, *Lee and His Men*, 222; OR, pt. 1, 881–882; Pfanz, *Gettysburg: The Second Day*, 254–255.

20. Buel and Johnson, *Battles and Leaders*, 3: 334–335.

21. Gaillard, *Journey to the Wilderness*, 93.

22. *Confederate Veteran* 21: 434; Greenville (S.C.) *Southern Enterprise*, July 29, 1863; Dickert, *History of Kershaw's Brigade*, 163, 355; Kershaw (S.C.) *Gazette*, February 26, 1880; OR, pt. 2, 369. Dickert identifies Leitner as W.Z. Leitner and W.S. Leitner, the latter erroneously.

23. *Philadelphia Weekly Times*, May 6, 1882; *Greenville Southern Enterprise*, July 29, 1863; *Confederate Veteran* 21: 434.

24. *Philadelphia Weekly Times*, May 6, 1882; *Greenville Southern Enterprise*, July 29, 1863; *Confederate Veteran* 21: 434.

25. *Anderson Intelligencer*, June 29, 1882; Edwin Kerrison to his sister (unidentified), July 7, 1863, Kerrison Family Papers, South Caroliniana Digital Library, University of South Carolina; *Manning Times*, July 13, 1904; Gottfried, *Brigades*, 406.

26. Dickert, *History of Kershaw's Brigade*, 162; *Charleston Mercury*, October 17, 1863. Henagan's whereabouts and actions during the battle are unclear.

27. *Charleston Mercury*, September 18, 1863; *Philadelphia Weekly Times*, May 6, 1882.

28. *Charleston Mercury*, September 18, 1863; *Philadelphia Weekly Times*, May 6, 1882; Dickert,

History of Kershaw's Brigade, 154; Dowdey, *Lee and His Men*, 222; Buel and Johnson, *Battles and Leaders*, 3: 335–336.

29. *Philadelphia Weekly Times*, May 6, 1882; *Anderson Intelligencer*, June 29, 1882. Regarding the color bearer, Kerrison may have been referring to the Third S.C. Battalion, the only such command in Kershaw's ranks.

30. Buel and Johnson, *Battles and Leaders*, 3: 335–336; Gaillard, *Journey to the Wilderness*, 94.

31. Jorgensen, *Gettysburg's Bloody Wheatfield*, 74; *Confederate Veteran* 21: 434; Pfanz, *Gettysburg: The Second Day*, 256.

32. Gottfried, *Artillery*, 124–126; Scott, Story of the Battles, 12–13.

33. Tucker, *High Tide*, 270–271; OR, pt. 2, 372.

34. Buel and Johnson, *Battles and Leaders*, 3: 335; Pfanz, *Gettysburg: The Second Day*, 254; J.L. Smith, *History of the 118th Pennsylvania Volunteers, Corn Exchange Regiment, from Their First Engagement at Antietam to Appomattox* (Philadelphia: J.L. Smith, 1905), 241.

35. Tucker, *High Tide*, 270–271; Warner, *Generals in Blue*, 537–538; Pfanz, *Gettysburg: The Second Day*, 256, 258; Smith, *History of the 118th Pennsylvania Volunteers*, 244.

36. *Charleston (S.C.) Evening Post*, May 30, 1899; Dickert, *History of Kershaw's Brigade*, 155.

37. *Charleston (S.C.) Evening Post*, May 30, 1899; Dickert, *History of Kershaw's Brigade*, 155.Barksdale was a member of the Laurens Briars militia unit before the war. He survived the conflict minus his right arm, lost at Chickamauga.

38. Reardon and Vossler, *Field Guide*, 227; Pfanz, *Gettysburg: The Second Day*, 259, 264; Jorgensen, *Gettysburg's Bloody Wheatfield*, 74, 81.

39. Evans, 5: 269–270; OR, pt. 2, 372; Aiken to "Dear Capt."; Jorgensen, *Gettysburg's Bloody Wheatfield*, 74, 81. Aiken wrote that the Fifteenth S.C. was "detached to join Sims," which is in error.

40. Gottfried, *Brigades*, 121, 124; Jeffrey D. Wert, "Gettysburg," 51; Tucker, *High Tide*, 273.

41. St. Clair Mulholland, *The Story of the 116th Regiment, Pennsylvania Infantry* (Philadelphia: F. McManus Jr., 1899), 409; Gottfried, *Brigades*, 121, 124; Robert L. Stewart, *History of the One Hundred and Fortieth Regiment, Pennsylvania Volunteers* ([Philadelphia]: Published by authority of the Regimental Association, 1912), 105–106.

42. Jorgensen, *Gettysburg's Bloody Wheatfield*, 98; Mulholland, *Story of the 116th Regiment*, 409.

43. Buel and Johnson, *Battles and Leaders*, 3: 336; Pfanz, *Gettysburg: The Second Day*, 278–279.

44. OR, pt. 2, 283, 368. No battle reports from Semmes's Brigade were found to be included in the *Official Records*. The OR note that Col. Goode Bryan of the Sixteenth Georgia in *Wofford's* (author's italics) Brigade was in command of Semmes's troops by July 7 and was probably Semmes' immediate successor when the latter was mortally wounded.

45. *The State*, March 16, 1930; Dickert, *History of Kershaw's Brigade*, 161–162; United Daughters of the Confederacy, 1: 294–295. O'Neale wrote that De Saussure "fell with a bullet through his heart,"

but this is questionable due to the claim of another Carolinian who said the colonel had a lethal head wound.

46. Buel and Johnson, *Battles and Leaders*, 3: 336; *OR*, pt. 2, 283, 368–369, 372.

47. [*OR*, pt. 2, 283, 368–369, 372.]

48. *Ibid.*; Aiken letter, July 11, 1863.

49. Mulholland, *Story of the 116th Regiment*, 125, 409.

50. *OR*, pt. 2, 369.

51. Mulholland, *Story of the 116th Regiment*, 125, 409.

52. Jeffrey D. Wert, "Gettysburg," 51; Thomas J. Craughwell, *The Greatest Brigade: How the Irish Brigade Cleared the Way to Victory in the American Civil War* (Beverly, MA: Fair Winds, 2011), 152–153.

53. Mulholland, *Story of the 116th Regiment*, 125–126, 409. Of July 2 at Gettysburg, Mulholland later stated, "This was some of the most severe fighting our division had ever done."

54. Buel and Johnson, *Battles and Leaders*, 3: 337.

55. Tucker, *High Tide*, 271; Pfanz, *Gettysburg: The Second Day*, 327, 329.

56. *Confederate Veteran* 21: 435; *Richmond* (Va.) *Enquirer*, August 5, 1863; Gaillard, *Journey to the Wilderness*, 94; *OR*, pt. 2, 369. The *Enquirer* letter was written on July 25, 1863, from Culpeper County, Virginia, by a soldier identified only as "L" Gaillard.

57. Buel and Johnson, *Battles and Leaders*, 3: 337; Gottfried, *Brigades*, 120, 148; Scott, Story of the Battles, 12–13.

58. *Charleston Mercury*, July 31, 1863.

59. United Daughters of the Confederacy, 1: 294–295; Dickert, *History of Kershaw's Brigade*, 161–162.

60. *Newberry Herald and News*, July 18, 1913; *OR*, pt. 2, 369; Aiken letter.

61. Jeffrey D. Wert, "Gettysburg," 52; Gottfried, *Brigades*, 271, 275, 296; Gaillard, *Journey to the Wilderness*, 94; United Daughters of the Confederacy, 2: 307.

62. Gaillard, *Journey to the Wilderness*, 94; United Daughters of the Confederacy, 2: 307.

63. Aiken letter; United Daughters of the Confederacy, 1: 294–295.

64. *Abbeville Press and Banner*, April 14, 1915; *Charleston Mercury*, September 18, 1863; Buel and Johnson, *Battles and Leaders*, 3: 337; Stewart, *History of the One Hundred and Fortieth Regiment*, 116. The unidentified old soldier who related the incident in the Abbeville paper spelled Reagan's name as "Reagen," which is inaccurate. Reagan died a few weeks earlier, prompting his friend to write about him.

Chapter 6

1. Albert Prince, diary, courtesy of Lt. Wade Hampton Camp No. 273, Sons of Confederate Veterans, Columbia, S.C. (www.wadehamptoncamp.org.); *OR*, pt. 2, 285, 429. At least twice Prince refers to Brig. Gen. Barksdale as a lieutenant, an obvious

error. The other three batteries led by Huger were Capt. G.V. Moody's Madison (Louisiana) Artillery and the Virginia batteries of Captains W.W. Parker and O.B. Taylor.

2. *OR*, pt. 2, 429–430; Prince diary.

3. *OR*, pt. 2, 610. Walker noted that Pegram, McIntosh, Lane and a portion of Garnett's battalion were put into position to the right of the Fairfield Road and about a mile in advance of their location on July 1.

4. *OR*, pt. 2, 674–675; McIntosh, *Review*, 57; *Treasured Reminiscenses*, United Daughters of the Confederacy, 47–48. In this latter work, compiled years after the war, McIntosh wrongly refers to Hurt's battery as "Hart's" battery. The Alabama officer who was killed was Lt. John W. Tullis. Some accounts stated that his left foot was smashed, resulting in his death.

5. Evans, 5: 595–596; *OR*, pt. 2, 429–430.

6. Prince diary; Evans, 5: 595–596; "Brooks Artillery" marker, West Confederate Avenue on the battlefield.

7. *OR*, pt. 2, 607–608, 613–614.

8. *Ibid.*; Hassler "'Fighting Dick' Anderson," 10, 40; Robertson, *General A.P. Hill*, 219.

9. *OR*, pt. 2, 607–608, 613–614; Hassler "'Fighting Dick' Anderson," 10, 40. Anderson described the Florida brigade as "Perry's," but it was led at Gettysburg by Lang.

10. *OR*, pt. 2, 621.

11. Hassler "'Fighting Dick' Anderson," 10, 40; Robertson, *General A.P. Hill*, 218–219; *OR*, pt. 2, 308, 608.

12. Walker, *Life of Lieutenant General*, 145.

13. *OR*, pt. 2, 658–659.

14. *OR*, pt. 2, 658, 663; Caldwell, 103–104; Evans, 5: 265; Brown, 85–86; Tompkins, *Company K*, 20–21; *Edgefield Advertiser*, August 5, 1863; Reardon and Vossler, *Field Guide*, 149.

15. *OR*, pt. 2, 658, 663; Caldwell, 103–104; Evans, 5: 265; Brown, 85–86; Tompkins, *Company K*, 20–21; *Edgefield Advertiser*, August 5, 1863; Reardon and Vossler, *Field Guide*, 149. At least one account states that James Ouzts was mortally wounded and died the next day, likely confusing his fall with the July 1 death of his brother.

16. J.B.O. Landrum, *History of Spartanburg County* (Atlanta: Franklin, 1900), 528–530. Douglass's volunteers were Isham Kirby of Company C and A. Willis, Company I, both of Spartanburg, David Suber of Company D, from Newberry, and Dick Taylor of Company K, who was from Lexington.

17. *Yorkville Enquirer*, November 20, 1889. Mullineax's rank is not known, nor is Sherrer's fate.

18. United Daughters of the Confederacy, 5: 553; Evans, 5: 546–547.

19. Boyles, *Reminiscences*, 42.

20. *New York Times*, June 4, 1921; Patricia Spain Ward, *Simon Baruch: Rebel in the Ranks of Medicine, 1840–1921* (Tuscaloosa: University of Alabama Press, 1994), 41–42; Dickert, *History of Kershaw's Brigade*, 163, 355; *Kershaw Gazette*, February 26, 1880.

21. (Sumter, S.C.) *Watchman and Southron*, October 25, 1922; United Daughters of the Confederacy, 6: 349–341; *Lancaster News*, May 9, 1916.

22. *Charleston Mercury*, September 18, 1863. Some accounts erroneously identify Easterling as "J.R." Easterling. It is unclear if he was a corporal at the time of his death; most sources identify him as a private.

23. *The Laurens Advertiser*, January 18, 1911, and April 25, 1898; United Daughters of the Confederacy, 5: 520–521; Dickert, *History of Kershaw's Brigade*, 361, 164; *Confederate Veteran* 23: 522. The Laurens paper identified Capt. Langston as "D.M.H.," which is incorrect. He also is identified as Capt. Mason Langston, which appears to be accurate.

24. *Lancaster Ledger*, July 29, 1863, August 12, 1863, and September 2, 1863; Dickert, *History of Kershaw's Brigade*, 356–357. Dickert's regimental rosters offer some differences in spelling and identities. In Company H, his spelling is Lt. G.C. "Brasington"; there are also two entries for Cpl. "J.M." Small.

25. *Charleston Mercury*, July 31, 1863.

26. United Daughters of the Confederacy, 1: 319 and 3: 64–65; *Augusta Chronicle*, July 3, 1938. Lt. William Daniel's letter was written on July 13, 1862, at "Camp McLaws" near Richmond. The May 22, 1879, issue of the *Edgefield Advertiser* stated that the Daniel brothers "fell standing side by side" with another soldier, Edward Mobley, which appears to be inaccurate since the brothers were in different companies. Reynolds apparently was not related to Union General John F. Reynolds.

27. *Newberry Herald and News*, July 17, 1914; Dickert, *History of Kershaw's Brigade*, 360.

28. *OR*, pt. 2, 372–373; *Edgefield Advertiser*, 29, 1863; *Charleston Mercury*, October 17, 1863.

29. United Daughters of the Confederacy, 5: 206–207; Evans, 5: 455.

30. Gaillard, *Journey to the Wilderness*, 93; *OR*, pt. 2, 372–373.

31. Aiken letter.

32. *Confederate Veteran* 21: 435; *Manning Times*, July 13, 1904.

33. *Confederate Veteran* 21: 435; *Manning Times*, July 13, 1904.

34. *Southern Enterprise*, July 23, 1863; Dickert, *History of Kershaw's Brigade*, 155, 353; *Confederate Veteran* 21: 435.

35. Evans, 5: 834; *Philadelphia Weekly Times*, May 6, 1882; United Daughters of the Confederacy, 67–68.

36. *Anderson Intelligencer*, June 29, 1882.

37. Dickert, *History of Kershaw's Brigade*, 155, 352; *OR*, pt. 2, 369; *Augusta Chronicle*, September 4, 1910. Kershaw and his brigade had already fought at Chickamauga and were posted near Chattanooga when the Gettysburg report was filed on October 1, 1863.

38. *Abbeville Press and Banner*, December 16, 1908; *Charleston Mercury*, August 28, 1863. Baruch's casualty list identified McDowell as a lieutenant.

39. McIntosh, *Review*, 64.

40. *OR*, pt. 2, 308.

41. Buel and Johnson, *Battles and Leaders*, 3: 341–342.

42. *Ibid.*

43. Gaillard, 94.

44. Frank A. Haskell, *The Battle of Gettysburg* (Boston: Mudge, 1908), 60–61.

Chapter 7

1. *Newberry Herald and News*, January 5, 1904; *Edgefield Advertiser*, April 21, 1915; Gerard A. Patterson, *Rebels from West Point* (New York: Doubleday, 1987), 161; Warner, *Generals in Gray*, 192–193; Welsh, *Medical Histories*, 143–144; Freeman, *Lee's Lieutenants*, 30–31, 134; Fremantle, *Three Months*, 120, 134; Jeffrey D. Wert, *General James Longstreet*, 48, 50, 53, 96–97; Dowdey, *Lee and His Men*, 164. Harriett was less than a year old when she died.

2. Buel and Johnson, *Battles and Leaders*, 3: 342–343.

3. Freeman, *Lee's Lieutenants*, 587; Kennedy, *Civil War Battlefield Guide*, 118.

4. *Anderson Intelligencer*, July 16, 1902; *The State*, August 6, 1911.

5. Dickert, *History of Kershaw's Brigade*, 154, 156, 162; *Philadelphia Weekly Times*, May 6, 1882.

6. Dickert, *History of Kershaw's Brigade*, 154. Capt. S.G. Malloy of the Eighth's Company C claimed the regiment went into combat with 215 in its ranks and "lost more than half of its number."

7. *The State*, August 6, 1911.

8. McLaws, "Gettysburg," 79; *Confederate Veteran* 21: 435.

9. United Daughters of the Confederacy, 67–68.

10. *OR*, pt. 2, 663; Brown, 85, 89; Gottfried, *Brigades*, 646. The Browns did not identify this soldier in the colonel's memoir.

11. United Daughters of the Confederacy, 1: 145–147; *Edgefield Advertiser*, August 5, 1863. Buzzard is listed as a sergeant in a casualty list submitted by Lt. J.H. Allen, who led Company K in the battle.

12. Welsh, *Medical Histories*, 128; *Anderson Intelligencer*, September 23, 1903. A letter to the paper relating this incident was signed "An Old Reb."

13. *OR*, pt. 2, 608, 614; Freeman, *Lee's Lieutenants*, 589; Gottfried, *Brigades*, 640.

14. Buel and Johnson, *Battles and Leaders*, 3: 342–343; Sorrel, *Recollections*, 173.

15. *OR*, pt. 2, 678. The battalion's casualties on July 2, as described by Brunson, do not include a breakdown of losses by the individual batteries. Zimmerman's casualties, if any, were obviously minimal, other than possibly some horses.

16. *Ibid.*; Gottfried, *Artillery*, 189.

17. Evans, 5: 595–596; Buel and Johnson, *Battles and Leaders*, 3: 326; *Anderson Intelligencer*, July 16, 1902; Gottfried, *Artillery*, 189.

18. *OR*, pt. 2, 430, 675. Woolfork's battery was not present in this position, being on detached duty.

19. *Anderson Intelligencer*, July 16, 1902; Buel and Johnson, *Battles and Leaders*, 3: 343, 371–372.

20. Buel and Johnson, *Battles and Leaders*, 3: 327; *Yorkville Enquirer*, November 20, 1889; *OR*, pt.

2, 614. Anderson stated the artillery battle began at 3:30 p.m., which is erroneous.

21. Aiken letter. Aiken was comparing the Gettysburg bombardment to the Crimean War siege of Sevastopol in 1854–1855. Either spelling is considered correct; Aiken's version is based on British accounts of the war. *OR*, pt. 2, 675, 678; McIntosh, *Review*, 75.

22. *Watchman and Southron*, June 7, 1913; *Anderson Intelligencer*, July 16, 1902. It is unclear whether the Reids were related.

23. Caldwell, 100–101. Caldwell wrote that the artillery bombardment opened about 4 p.m., which is inaccurate.

24. *OR*, pt. 2, 610; Dickert, *History of Kershaw's Brigade*, 157; *The State*, August 6, 1911. In the latter article, Hargrove also claimed that high above the artillery duel "a great American eagle was seen to pass and view the carnage as it swept the azure elements with its great wings." *The State*, August 6, 1911.

25. *Manning Times*, July 13, 1904.

26. Buel and Johnson, *Battles and Leaders*, 3: 372–373; *The State*, August 6, 1911. In *The State* article, Hargrove did not identify either of the brothers, stating only that the surviving one was "living in Marion" S.C., in 1911. *The State*, August 6, 1911.

27. Buel and Johnson, *Battles and Leaders*, 3: 344–345; *OR*, pt. 2, 608; Gottfried, *Brigades*, 646.

28. Gottfried, *Artillery*, 217; *OR*, pt. 2, 675; McIntosh, *Review*, 76.

29. *Watchman and Southron*, June 7, 1913; *Anderson Intelligencer*, July 16, 1902.

30. *Watchman and Southron*, June 7, 1913. Garden said that he never again saw the wounded Union officer.

31. *Ibid.* Garden stated that the order for the artillery to follow the infantry came from one of Longstreet's staff officers.

32. Fremantle, *Three Months*, 134; Buel and Johnson, *Battles and Leaders*, 3: 346–347. Longstreet wrote of this encounter with some variation. He quoted Fremantle as saying, "General, I would not have missed this for anything in the world." Buel and Johnson, *Battles and Leaders*, 3: 346–347. Longstreet also does not record his response, if any, to this remark. The exchange also is not detailed in Longstreet's war memoir.

33. Buel and Johnson, *Battles and Leaders*, 3: 346–347.; Longstreet, 395.

34. Buel and Johnson, *Battles and Leaders*, 3: 346–347.

35. *OR*, pt. 2, 608, 614–615. It is interesting to note that Longstreet of the First Corps ordered Anderson to halt his attack, rather than A.P. Hill, Anderson's commander in the Third Corps. Hill does not address this in his battle report.

36. *OR*, pt. 2, 608, 678; Brown, 87.

Chapter 8

1. Longacre, *The Cavalry at Gettysburg*, 17, 221–222; Jeffrey D. Wert, "Gettysburg," 65.

2. P.J. Malone, "Charge of Black's Cavalry at Gettysburg," *Southern Historical Society Papers* 16 (1888): 225; *Watchman and Southron*, February 2, 1910; Brooks, *Stories of the Confederacy*, 19. Brooks was sixteen in July 1863 and not present at Gettysburg. He served in the Sixth S.C. Cavalry.

3. *OR*, pt. 2, 290, 724; Evans, 5: 480–481; Warner, *Generals in Gray*, 184; Malone, "Charge of Black's Cavalry," 225. Chambliss, on Hampton's right, was leading Brig. Gen. W.H.F. "Rooney" Lee's brigade after Lee was wounded at Brandy Station and later captured. Lee was R.E. Lee's second son. Fitzhugh Lee's brigade was minus the First Maryland Battalion, which was serving with Ewell's corps.

4. Cooke, *Wearing of the Gray*, 257; J.H. Kidd, *A Cavalryman with Custer: Custer's Michigan Cavalry Brigade in the Civil War* (New York: Bantam, 1991), 87–88.

5. Nicholson, *Pennsylvania at Gettysburg*, 2: 800, 810–811; Buel and Johnson, *Battles and Leaders*, 3: 404; Longacre, *Cavalry at Gettysburg*, 221–222.

6. Malone, "Charge of Black's Cavalry," 226; Nicholson, *Pennsylvania at Gettysburg*, 2: 800, 810–811.

7. Malone, "Charge of Black's Cavalry," 226; Cooke, *Wearing of the Gray*, 257.

8. Malone, "Charge of Black's Cavalry," 226; Beale, *Lieutenant of Cavalry*, 193; Brooks, *Stories of the Confederacy*, 546.

9. Buel and Johnson, *Battles and Leaders*, 3: 405–406; Beale, *Lieutenant of Cavalry*, 193.

10. Nicholson, *Pennsylvania at Gettysburg*, 2: 800, 811.

11. Edward L. Wells, *Hampton and His Cavalry in '64* (Richmond, VA: B.F. Johnson, 1899), 75–76.

12. Perry letter, July 11, 1863.

13. Malone, "Charge of Black's Cavalry," 227.

14. *OR*, pt. 2, 714; *Southern Enterprise*, August 27, 1863; *Edgefield Advertiser*, July 29, 1863; Buel and Johnson, *Battles and Leaders*, 3: 406. Sgt. Butler was in the Second Cavalry's Company I. Confederate Brig. Gen. Albert Jenkins' Virginia brigade also fought in this battle, but his losses are not known.

15. *OR*, pt. 2, 698, 714; *Charleston Mercury*, September 8, 1863; Evans, 5: 456–457.

16. Eleanor D. McSwain, ed., *Crumbling Defenses, or Memoirs and Reminiscences of John Logan Black, Colonel C.S.A.* (Macon, GA: J.W. Burke, 1960), 12, 17, 32.

17. *Ibid.*; Longacre, *Cavalry at Gettysburg*, 232. Longacre states that Black had "gone home on leave after Brandy Station" and makes no mention of Black being wounded.

18. Warner, *Generals in Gray*, 183; *Charleston News and Courier*, n.d., reprinted in *Augusta Chronicle*, June 30, 1875. Stuart's Horse Artillery was led by Maj. Robert F. Beckham and also consisted of four Virginia batteries and a Maryland battery.

19. *Augusta Chronicle*, June 30, 1875; Robert J. Trout, *Galloping Thunder: The Stuart Horse Artillery Battalion* (Mechanicsburg, PA: Stackpole, 2005), 7; Evans, 5: 632–633; *Charleston Mercury*, June 3, 1862.

The battery was also known as the Hampton Horse Artillery but was best known as Hart's Battery until the war's end and during the postwar years.

20. Evans, 5: 832–833.

21. Evans, 5: 444–445. Wade Hampton noted that Hart's command "was, in all, 142 times under fire," but Bamberg was never wounded or captured, surrendering with Joe Johnston's army. After the war Bamberg returned to Barnwell County and went into the mercantile business in Bamberg. He also dabbled in livestock before becoming a banker.

22. McSwain, *Crumbling Defenses*, 41; Longacre, *Cavalry at Gettysburg*, 232; *OR*, pt. 2, 284–285; Brooks, *Stories of the Confederacy*, 282–283; Gottfried, *Artillery*, 238–239. Gottfried erroneously describes Bachman's command as the Palmetto Light Artillery.

23. Starr, *The Union Cavalry*, 1: 439–440; Longacre, *Cavalry at Gettysburg*, 240.

24. McSwain, *Crumbling Defenses*, 40; Longacre, *Cavalry at Gettysburg*, 240–241.

25. McSwain, *Crumbling Defenses*, 40; Longacre, *Cavalry at Gettysburg*, 240–241.

26. *OR*, pt. 2, 285.

27. Gottfried, *Artillery*, 241; Buel and Johnson, *Battles and Leaders*, 3: 347.

28. McLaws, "Gettysburg," 79.

29. *Confederate Veteran* 21: 435–436; Buel and Johnson, *Battles and Leaders*, 3: 338.

30. *OR*, pt. 2, 373; Allardice, 288; Dickert, *History of Kershaw's Brigade*, 227–228.

31. *OR*, pt. 2, 369; *Charleston Mercury*, August 18, 1863; Dickert, *History of Kershaw's Brigade*, 154, 161–162. Dickert on at least one occasion refers to De Saussure as commander of the Thirteenth S.C., which is erroneous. Some accounts identify John K. McIver as John F. McIver, also inaccurate.

32. Aiken letter; underlining is in the original. Aiken's claim of drunkenness is unsubstantiated.

33. United Daughters of the Confederacy, 68–69.

34. Derek Smith, *The Gallant Dead: Union and Confederate Generals Killed in the Civil War* (Mechanicsburg, PA: Stackpole, 2005), 162, 181.

35. Malone, "Charge of Black's Cavalry," 227.

36. *Confederate Veteran* 21: 436.

37. *Anderson* (S.C.) *Daily Mail*, n.d., reprinted in the *Abbeville Press and Banner*, February 10, 1915. Speer's narrative was published as part of his obituary after his death on January 31, 1915.

38. Fremantle, *Three Months*, 137; Buel and Johnson, *Battles and Leaders*, 3: 345.

Chapter 9

1. Caldwell, *History of a Brigade*, 102.

2. *Charleston* (S.C.) *Weekly News*, n.d., reprinted in the *Yorkville Enquirer*, June 15, 1882.

3. Dickert, *History of Kershaw's Brigade*, 160; *Manning Times*, July 13, 1904; *OR*, pt. 1, 882.

4. *Lancaster Ledger*, December 18, 1889; *Yorkville Enquirer*, November 20, 1889; Longstreet, 426.

5. Fremantle, *Three Months*, 137; Jeffrey D. Wert,

"Gettysburg," 66; *Augusta Chronicle*, September 4, 1910.

6. *OR*, pt. 2, 308–309; Jeffrey D. Wert, "Gettysburg," 66; Longstreet, 426–427.

7. *OR*, pt. 2, 308–430; *Camden* (S.C.) *Confederate*, October 23, 1863; *Charleston Courier*, September 16, 1863.

8. *OR*, pt. 2, 678. Brunson does not break down the losses for each of the battalion's batteries. His July 31 report indicates that Capt. T.A. Brander's battery, the Letcher Artillery from Virginia, was in the most action on July 1, "suffering considerably from the enemy's canister" while in infantry support (although the entire battalion sustained only two dead and eight wounded that day). No other battery is singled out in Brunson's battle report, including Zimmerman's battery.

9. *OR*, pt. 2, 676; McIntosh, *Review*, 80–81.

10. *Abbeville Press and Banner*, February 10, 1915; *OR*, pt. 2, 608, 663–664; United Daughters of the Confederacy, 1: 146–147; *The State*, July 3, 1938, May 11, 1892; Warner, *Generals in Gray*, 310–311; Welsh, *Medical Histories*, 216–218.

11. Dreese, 150; Brown, 85; Boyles, *Reminiscences*, 42.

12. Starr, *Union Cavalry*, 1: 442–443; Dickert, *History of Kershaw's Brigade*, 161; Buel and Johnson, *Battles and Leaders*, 3: 422–423.

13. Dickert, *History of Kershaw's Brigade*, 161; Buel and Johnson, *Battles and Leaders*, 3: 422–423.

14. *Yorkville Enquirer*, June 15, 1882; Hood, *Advance and Retreat*, 60; Edward G. Longacre, *Gentleman and Soldier: A Biography of Wade Hampton III* (Nashville: Rutledge Hill, 2003), 155; Buel and Johnson, *Battles and Leaders*, 3: 424.

15. United Daughters of the Confederacy, 3: 62–63 and 6: 335–336; Evans, 5: 524–525, 596. Some accounts state that Croft was left behind due to the seriousness of his injuries; this appears to be erroneous.

16. United Daughters of the Confederacy, 1: 294–295; Starr, *Union Cavalry*, 1: 442–443.

17. Kennedy, *Civil War Battlefield Guide*, 126, 134–135.

18. Starr, *Union Cavalry*, 1: 443, 447.

19. *OR*, pt. 2, 309, 311.

20. *OR*, pt. 2, 370, 373; Dickert, *History of Kershaw's Brigade*, 165; *Charleston Weekly News*, n.d., reprinted in the *Anderson Intelligencer*, May 11, 1882.

21. Winnsboro *News and Herald*, February 24, 1916; *Augusta Chronicle*, September 4, 1910.

22. *OR*, pt. 2, 676; McIntosh, *Review*, 80–81. McIntosh does not specify the batteries or guns which participated in these actions.

23. Jeffrey D. Wert, "Gettysburg," 66; Buel and Johnson, *Battles and Leaders*, 3: 379–380.

24. Gottfried, *Artillery*, 126. Carter belonged to the Twenty-second Massachusetts in William S. Tilton's brigade.

25. J. Howard Wert, *A Complete Handbook of the Monuments and Indications and Guide to the Positions on the Gettysburg Battlefield* (Harrisburg, PA: R.M. Sturgeon, 1886), 109, 162–163.

26. *Yorkville Enquirer*, June 15, 1882; Starr, *Union Cavalry*, 1: 447–448.

27. United Daughters of the Confederacy, 1: 294–295; *Charleston Mercury*, August 18, 1863.

28. Buel and Johnson, *Battles and Leaders*, 3: 425–426.

29. *Ibid.*; Evans, 5: 456–457, 494. It is unclear if Cagle was a lieutenant or a captain at the time.

30. *Yorkville Enquirer*, June 15, 1882; Buel and Johnson, *Battles and Leaders*, 3: 426–427.

31. Buel and Johnson, *Battles and Leaders*, 3: 426–427; Caldwell, *History of a Brigade*, 105–106.

32. Longacre, *Cavalry at Gettysburg*, 255; *Yorkville Enquirer*, June 15, 1882; Buel and Johnson, *Battles and Leaders*, 3: 426–427.

33. Longacre, *Cavalry at Gettysburg*, 255; *Yorkville Enquirer*, June 15, 1882; Buel and Johnson, *Battles and Leaders*, 3: 426–427.

34. Caldwell, *History of a Brigade*, 105–106; *Yorkville Enquirer*, June 15, 1882; Buel and Johnson, *Battles and Leaders*, 3: 426–427.

35. Fremantle, *Three Months*, 142; Longacre, *Gentleman and Soldier*, 156.

36. McSwain, *Crumbling Defenses*, 51–53. Black incorrectly identifies the blinded officer as "McKeever," but the circumstances and the nature of the officer's wounds leave little doubt that he was Capt. McIver.

37. United Daughters of the Confederacy, 69.

38. *Charleston Courier*, July 16, 1863; "Search for Soldiers"; *The State*, August 16, 1913. Hamilton is listed as a sergeant in the NPS "Search for Soldiers" data.

Chapter 10

1. Tucker, *High Tide*, 386–387; *Anderson Intelligencer*, November 10, 1915. Russell's statement appeared in an article about his November 9, 1915, death at age 74 in Anderson, S.C. President Lincoln, among others, was highly critical of Meade for his cautiousness in the pursuit.

2. *OR*, pt. 2, 676; McIntosh, *Review*, 81–82.

3. *OR*, pt. 2, 676; McIntosh, *Review*, 81–82.

4. *OR*, pt. 2, 609–610, 679. Gen. Hill and Col. R. Lindsay Walker, his chief of reserve artillery, both stated that the corps arrived on the 7th; Brunson recalled that it was on the 8th.

5. *OR*, pt. 2, 370, 374; Smith, *Gallant Dead*, 182–183. Nance identified the slain soldier as Beasely," which is incorrect.

6. Kerrison letter.

7. *Charleston Mercury*, July 31, 1863.

8. *Newberry Herald and News*, January 24, 1902; Dickert, *History of Kershaw's Brigade*, 166, 361.

9. O'Neall, John Belton, and John A. Chapman, *The Annals of Newberry* (Newberry, SC: Aull and Houseal, 1892), 589–590.

10. Aiken letter. If aware of Barksdale's death, Aiken doesn't mention it in this instance.

11. *Charleston Mercury*, July 18, 1863. All name spellings are from the article.

12. *OR*, pt. 2, 615, 676.

13. Perry letter.

14. *OR*, pt. 2, 609, 639; *Anderson Intelligencer*, May 11, 1882; *Lancaster Ledger*, December 18, 1889.

15. Willis Keith to Anna Bell Keith, July 9, 1863, and July 10, 1863. Based on the contents, Keith apparently started the first letter on July 8.

16. *OR*, pt. 2, 634; *Anderson Intelligencer*, May 11, 1882. The *Charleston Courier* on July 25, 1863 states Chambers was killed on July 13, which appears to be inaccurate.

17. *OR*, pt. 2, 310, 609, 634, 640; Caldwell, *History of a Brigade*, 107–108.

18. *OR*, pt. 2, 310, 609, 634, 640; Caldwell, *History of a Brigade*, 107–108.

19. *OR*, pt. 2, 310, 612, 676, 679; McIntosh, *Review*, 82; United Daughters of the Confederacy, 48. In the latter work (*Treasured Reminiscences*), a postwar account, McIntosh wrote that his casualties for the campaign totaled 24 killed and/or wounded, and 38 horses killed or "disabled." His official report, written shortly after his return from Pennsylvania, is likely the more accurate.

20. Dickert, *History of Kershaw's Brigade*, 166–167, 227; *OR*, pt. 2, 370, 374.

21. Evans, 5: 511–12. This history erroneously states Coker was in a hospital in Williamsburg, Md.

22. *OR*, pt. 2, 310, 609, 634, 640–641, 664.

23. *Ibid.* Thomas's brigade of Pender's division was not involved in this engagement, having moved over the Potomac before the Union attacks.

24. *Ibid.*; Caldwell, *History of a Brigade*, 107–108. Hill in his November 1863 Gettysburg report states that the cavalry assault was against the brigades of Archer and Pettigrew, but he makes no mention of Perrin's troops. Hill also claimed the action began about 10 a.m., conflicting with Heth's time frame.

25. *OR*, pt. 2, 310, 612, 676, 679; *The State*, July 3, 1938; Caldwell, *History of a Brigade*, 102.

Chapter 11

1. *OR*, pt. 2, 365. Barksdale's brigade left behind the most wounded in the division, numbering 224, with Kershaw's total second. The *Official Records* do not show that any wounded from Maffett's Third South Carolina remained in Gettysburg, although the regiment sustained losses in line with the rest of Kershaw's troops. It is unlikely that of the dozens of wounded Carolinians in the Third Regiment, none were serious enough to remain behind, such as the two "severely wounded" by artillery on July 3. This lapse may be due to lost or incomplete reports or due to the regiment's command change hours after the battle, Col. J.D. Nance returning to lead the Third and relieving Maj. Maffett.

2. Evans, 5: 650–651; *The State*, March 10, 1917.

3. *OR*, pt. 2, 338, 370; Kershaw's losses vary slightly in another *Official Records* tally on p. 329: 113 killed and 472 wounded for a total of 585, with no one missing. This is likely the more accurate

record. Rice's Third Battalion is sometimes identified as "James' battalion" in the *OR*.

4. *OR*, pt. 2, 364–365.

5. United Daughters of the Confederacy, 6: 339–341; Dickert, *History of Kershaw's Brigade*, 352; *Charleston Mercury*, September 18, 1863; Ward, *Simon Baruch*, 44–46. Wheeler identified the surgeon as "Knott," which is inaccurate. Dickert identified the surgeon as "J.H. Nott," also erroneous. At the time of the battle the two-story stone tavern, built in 1813, was connected to a large log house.

6. United Daughters of the Confederacy, 6: 339–341; Ward, *Simon Baruch*, 45–46.

7. *Union* (S.C.) *Times*, May 5, 1905.

8. *Confederate Veteran* 17: 168; Ward, *Simon Baruch*, 46–47.

9. *Confederate Veteran* 17: 168; Ward, *Simon Baruch*, 46–47; United Daughters of the Confederacy, 6: 339–341.

10. Malone, "Charge of Black's Cavalry," 227.

11. Boyles, *Reminiscences*, 43. J.C. Garlington, *Men of the Time, Sketches of Living Notables: A Biographical Encyclopedia of Contemporaneous South Carolina Leaders* (Spartanburg, SC: Garlington, 1902), 275–276.

12. [Boyles, *Reminiscences*, 43].

13. *Laurens Advertiser*, April 8, 1903.

14. Georgeanna Muirson Woolsey Bacon, *Three Weeks at Gettysburg* (New York: Anson D.F. Randolph, 1863), 16–18; *Edgefield Advertiser*, August 5, 1863; *The State*, December 14, 1930. Ms. Woolsey's married name was Bacon, but to avoid confusion I refer to her as Woolsey in the book.

15. Bacon, *Three Weeks at Gettysburg*, 16–18; *Edgefield Advertiser*, August 5, 1863; *The State*, December 14, 1930. It is unclear when and how Lt. Rauch was wounded or when he was brought to the Sanitary Commission facility. At least one account states Rauch died on July 16. His brother's identity is also unclear, although there were several other soldiers in the Fourteenth South Carolina named Rauch.

16. Dreese, 150; *Macon Telegraph*, July 4, 1886.

17. Baltimore *American*, n.d., reprinted in the *Charleston Courier*, July 29, 1863. More information about the identities of the Rev. Fuller and "Dr. Frazer" is not known.

18. *Manning Times*, July 13, 1904. The writer of this account was identified only as "Old Rock."

19. John B. Linn, "A Tourist at Gettysburg," *Civil War Times Illustrated* 29, no. 4 (September/October 1990): 26, 60–62; Dickert, *History of Kershaw's Brigade*, 374, 378. These graves were obviously identified in some crude fashion to allow Linn to make his remarks. The Eighth South Carolina soldier was apparently Cpl. J.B. Robbins of Company I; Linn identifies him as "J.B. Robins," which could have been a misspelling on the grave marker. It is unclear if any of the officers buried in the Rose family garden were Carolinians. Also, Linn's account about Trooper John Cullen lists him as belonging to the Sixth South Carolina Cavalry, which did not fight at Gettysburg. Cullen, if his name was correct,

belonged to the First or Second South Carolina Cavalry. Linn also states erroneously that Capt. Warren belonged to the Thirteenth South Carolina, which was in Perrin's brigade. At least one South Carolina newspaper also incorrectly identified Warren's regiment as the Thirteenth. How this mistake was made is a mystery, but Warren is on the roster of the Fifteen South Carolina's Company D.

20. Reardon and Vossler, *Field Guide*, 236.

21. J. Howard Wert, *Complete Handbook*, 109.

22. Dickert, *History of Kershaw's Brigade*, 166–167, 227; *OR*, pt. 2, 370, 374.

23. Everson and Simpson, *"Far, Far from Home,"* 256–258; Longstreet, 427; John B. Jones, *A Rebel War Clerk's Diary at the Confederate States Capital*, 2 vols. (Philadelphia: J.B. Lippincott, 1866), 1: 374. It is unclear exactly when Lee's army learned of Vicksburg's fall, but based on some of the South Carolinians' letters it was not before July 10 but within a few days of Simpson's note home on July 18. In his postwar memoir, Longstreet wrote simply: "On this retreat the army, already crippled of its pride, was met by the dispiriting news of another defeat at Vicksburg." Indeed, the Confederate War Department in Richmond did not receive "the sad tidings" of the disaster until July 8, with further confirmation the next day.

24. Hood, *Advance and Retreat*, 60; Longacre, *Gentleman and Soldier*, 157.

25. *OR*, pt. 2, 612, 679.

26. *OR*, pt. 2, 370; *Augusta Chronicle*, September 4, 1910.

27. Gaillard, *Journey to the Wilderness*, 93, 95.

28. Wade Hampton, letter to Mary F. Hampton, July 16, 1863, Hampton Family Papers, 1773–1974 (South Caroliniana Digital Library, University of South Carolina); *Richmond Examiner*, n.d., reprinted in the Augusta *Daily Constitutionalist*, July 25, 1863; Walter Brian Cisco, *Wade Hampton: Confederate Warrior, Conservative Statesman* (Washington, D.C.: Potomac, 2004), 121. Hampton to Wigfall, July 16, 1863 (Hampton Family Papers).

29. McSwain, *Crumbling Defenses*, 50–51.

30. *Ibid.*

31. *Charleston Courier*, August 5, 1863.

32. Willis Keith to Anna Bell Keith, July 19–20, 1863.

33. *Philadelphia Times*, March 17, 1882. In this article written from his home in Columbus, Ga., in 1882, Walker offered no identification of the dead soldier or the woman nor any timeline about his correspondence with the woman.

34. *OR*, pt. 2, 664; Evans, 5: 546–547.

35. *The State*, July 3, 1938.

36. *Ibid.*

37. *OR*, pt. 2, 344.

38. *Abbeville Press and Banner*, July 23, 1879. A lengthy firsthand account by Wells in this issue offers many details about his imprisonment.

39. *Anderson Intelligencer*, May 11, 1882.

40. Buel and Johnson, *Battles and Leaders*, 3: 439–440; "The Battle of Gettysburg", Stone Sentinels, http://stonesentinels.com.

Chapter 12

1. *York* (S.C.) *Observer*, October 30, 1988.

2. *Abbeville Press*, July 10, 1863; *Charleston Courier*, July 8, 1863.

3. Gaillard, *Journey to the Wilderness*, 93.

4. *Edgefield Advertiser*, July 22, 1863, and July 29, 1863; *Yorkville Enquirer*, July 22, 1863. The "D.R.D" letter was dated July 19, 1863, from Richmond.

5. *Edgefield Advertiser*, July 22, 1863, and July 29, 1863; *Yorkville Enquirer*, July 22, 1863; *Abbeville Press*, July 24, 1863.

6. *Lancaster Ledger*, July 22, 1863, and July 29, 1863.

7. *Abbeville Press*, July 24, 1863; Dickert, *History of Kershaw's Brigade*, 366; *Abbeville Press and Banner*, June 28, 1916. Dickert identified the lieutenant as "A.T. Thayler," which appears to be erroneous. Traylor is also identified as A.A. Traylor in some records. The *Edgefield Advertiser* on July 29, 1863, reported that Traylor was shot in the chest.

8. Taylor, Kohn, Poppinheim and Washington, *South Carolina Women*, 212–213; *Camden Confederate*, July 17, 1863.

9. Charles M. Furman to Frances E. Garden, July 22, 1863, Furman University Digital Library. Charles Furman was the son of James C. Furman, the first president of Furman University, and the grandson of the university's namesake. The soldiers mentioned are Sgt. LaBruce Mortimer and privates S.C. Miles, Edmund J. Mills, Thomas S. Gadsden, Charles J. Colcock and William F. Lawton, all of the Second South Carolina's Company I.

10. *Charleston Mercury*, August 15, 1863; italics in the original.

11. *Charleston Mercury*, January 6, 1864. It is unclear why Edwards's demise was so late in being published.

12. *Charleston Mercury*, July 22, 1863. The recipient of the letter appears to be Mr. H.T. Peake, although the last name is somewhat illegible.

13. *Charleston Mercury*, July 23, 1863. The article identified Mills's parents as Samuel S. and Mary E. Mills.

14. *Southern Enterprise*, July 23, 1863; *Charleston Mercury*, August 28, 1863.

15. Evans, 5: 505–506. The cause of Sara A. Casson's death was not reported.

16. Evans, 5: 581–582. The two other Fuller brothers, Anthony and Franklin, survived the war.

17. *Columbia* (S.C.) *Guardian*, n.d., reprinted in the *Charleston Courier*, July 15 and September 18, 1863; *Charleston Mercury*, July 18, 1863. The *Mercury* incorrectly stated that De Saussure's regiment was the Twelfth South Carolina. It was the Fifteenth South Carolina.

18. *Charleston Mercury*, July 25, 1863. The list was compiled on July 20 and submitted by C. Witsell, surgeon in charge of the First Division at the hospital complex.

19. *Edgefield Advertiser*, July 29, 1863; *Southern Enterprise*, August 27, 1863; Brooks, *Stories of the Confederacy*, 137.

20. *Charleston Mercury*, July 27, 1863.

21. *Yorkville Enquirer*, July 29, 1863; Longacre, *Gentleman and Soldier*, 158; Warner, *Generals in Gray*, 40–41. Butler was commissioned brigadier general to rank from September 1, 1863.

22. *Charleston Mercury*, July 31, 1863.

23. *Camden Confederate*, July 17, 1863, and August 7, 1863. The *Confederate* on July 17 incorrectly identified Cunningham's regiment as the Fifteenth South Carolina. Cunningham was born and lived in the Liberty Hill area near Camden.

24. *Charleston Mercury*, July 18, 1863. The name of the person who compiled the list was not included.

25. *Charleston Courier*, July 20, 1863. The list was sent from Kershaw's headquarters near Hagerstown on July 9.

26. *Charleston Mercury*, July 20, 1863. It is unclear when or where the article was written, but it was sent "For the Mercury."

27. *Charleston News and Courier*, December 3, 1933. Enoch Ayres served as a sergeant in the Eighth's Company I and later in Company L.

28. *Edgefield Advertiser*, August 5, 1863; *Abbeville Press*, August 7, 1863; *Charleston Mercury*, August 13, 1863.

29. *Baltimore American*, n.d., reprinted in the *Charleston Courier*, August 14, 1863; *The Charleston Mercury* on August 13 ran the complete list of Confederates from all states who had died at the hospital.

30. *Charleston Courier*, August 11, 1863, August 17, 1863, December 14, 1864.

31. *Charleston Mercury*, August 17, 1863. The writer was identified only as "E.McC," possibly a relative of Maj. C.W. McCreary, commander of the First South Carolina.

32. *Ibid.*; *Charleston Mercury*, September 9, 1863; Dickert, *History of Kershaw's Brigade*, 162.

33. *Yorkville Enquirer*, August 26, 1863; *Edgefield Advertiser*, October 7, 1863.

34. *Charleston Mercury*, August 13, 1863, and September 21, 1863. The September article states that Duffus was wounded on July 3, which is questionable since Perrin's troops were not actively engaged that day. Duffus was "the third son of Mr. James A. Duffus" of Charleston, the article also noted.

35. *Charleston Mercury*, July 18, 1863, and September 8, 1863. In the September article, the Brooks Artillery is referred to as "Rhett's Battery," its name when it was commanded by Capt. A.B. Rhett in 1862.

36. *Charleston Mercury*, September 18, 1863.

37. *Charleston Mercury*, October 5, 1863. The report was submitted to the paper by "T.A. Lafar" or "Lavar," who is not identified other than by his inky, barely intelligible name.

38. *Edgefield Advertiser*, October 14, 1863.

39. Dreese, 151.

40. *Charleston Courier*, January 9, 1864.

41. *New York Times*, June 4, 1921; Ward, 48–49.

42. *Charleston Mercury*, August 8, 1863; Ward, 48–51.

43. *Charleston Mercury*, August 28, 1863, and September 1, 1863.

44. Ward, 48–51; *Union Times*, May 5, 1905.

45. Boyles, 45–47, 55. Boyles spent some of his imprisonment on Bledsoe's Island in New York Harbor before being sent to Johnson's Island.

46. Derek Smith, *Gallant Dead*, 182; Caldwell, 102; Brown, 86; *The State*, July 3, 1938.

47. *Richmond Enquirer*, August 19, 1863.

48. *OR*, pt. 2, 686; Caldwell, 90, 113–114. McGowan was listed as the brigade commander as of August 31 but was not present for duty, still recuperating from his Chancellorsville wound. Hadden was killed in action at Deep Bottom, Virginia, in late July 1864.

49. *OR*, pt. 2, 656–657; Warner, *Generals in Gray*, 234–235.

50. *OR*, pt. 2, 681–682; Allardice, 191.

51. *OR*, pt. 2, 637.

52. *Columbia Guardian*, n.d., reprinted in the *Charleston Courier*, September 12, 1863.

53. *Charleston Mercury*, December 22, 1863; Longacre, *Gentleman and Soldier*, 158.

54. Welch, 66–67. An August 2 letter from near Orange Court House.

Chapter 13

1. *Charleston Courier*, December 14, 1864.

2. United Daughters of the Confederacy, 5: 206–207.

3. *Laurens Advertiser*, April 8, 1903.

4. *Union Times*, May 5, 1905.

5. United Daughters of the Confederacy, 1: 147 and 6: 339–341; *Watchman and Southron*, October 25, 1922.

6. *Macon Telegraph*, July 4, 1886.

7. Evans, 5: 788–789.

8. Derek Smith, "Potter's Raid—'Our Errand Through The State'" *North and South* 10, no. 2 (July 2007): 68.

9. Evans, 5: 456–457.

10. Winnsboro *News and Herald*, February 24, 1916.

11. *Anderson Intelligencer*, May 11, 1882.

12. *The State*, March 10, 1917; Evans, 5: 650–651.

13. United Daughters of the Confederacy, 1: 294–295.

14. *Confederate Veteran* 21: 435; Evans, 5: 653–654.

15. Malone, "Charge of Black's Cavalry," 224–228; *Watchman and Southron*, February 2, 1910. It is unclear where Malone was taken in New York, although in all likelihood it was Davids' Island.

16. Evans, 5: 455–456.

17. *Ibid.*, 5: 433–434, 495–496; Boatner, 822; *Charleston News and Courier*, August 16, 1930.

18. *Charleston Mercury*, October 17, 1863, August 28, 1863, September 1, 1863. It is unknown why the obituary was published so long after Powe's July 22 death was mentioned in Baruch's list. The best guess is that the family was still praying,

hoping and waiting to hear from Powe or wanted more proof that he was actually dead. The only relative identified in the obituary was his father, "Dr. Thomas E. Powe, of Chesterfield."

19. Evans, 5: 633–634.

20. *Ibid.*, 5: 832–833.

21. *Ibid.*, 5: 437.

22. *Ibid.*, 5: 672–674.

23. McSwain, *Crumbling Defenses*, 53; United Daughters of the Confederacy, 69.

24. Evans, 5: 463–464.

25. United Daughters of the Confederacy, 6: 335–336.

26. *Augusta Chronicle*, January 14, 1909; Evans, 5: 546–547, 596.

27. Evans, 5: 494–495. Cagle was a captain when the war ended, but when he was promoted from lieutenant is unclear.

28. Evans, 5: 511–512; Garlington, *Men of the Time*, 90. Garlington states that Cohen, as he identifies him, studied law after the war, but was more involved in "farming and merchandising." By 1902 Cohen was a vice president of the Bank of Darlington.

29. O'Neall and Chapman, *Annals of Newberry*, 589–590.

30. *The State*, May 11, 1892; United Daughters of the Confederacy, 3: 62–63; Evans, 5: 524–526.

31. *Columbia Guardian*, n.d., reprinted in the *Charleston Courier*, July 15, 1863; Dickert, *History of Kershaw's Brigade*, 308–309; *The State*, January 5, 1903. Wallace was promoted from captain to major after Chancellorsville.

32. J. Russell Wright, *Edgefield Advertiser*, September 1, 1915; Dickert, *History of Kershaw's Brigade*, 108.

33. United Daughters of the Confederacy, 5: 553; Garlington, *Men of the Time*, 177, 391.

34. *Edgefield Advertiser*, September 1, 1915; Dickert, *History of Kershaw's Brigade*, 182–183. The Blands were buried in Edgefield Village Cemetery, also called Willow Brook Cemetery.

35. *The State*, May 5, 1907; Dickert, *History of Kershaw's Brigade*, 228–229; *Charleston Mercury*, May 18, 1864.

36. Dickert, *History of Kershaw's Brigade*, 272.

37. Evans, 5: 771–772; Allardice, 288; Dickert, *History of Kershaw's Brigade*, 227–228. Maffett's servant, Harry, took the colonel's horse home, and both lived to "a ripe old age."

38. Dickert, *History of Kershaw's Brigade*, 202–203.

39. Dickert, *History of Kershaw's Brigade*, 197, 201–202.

40. Brooks, *Stories of the Confederacy*, 546; Charleston *News and Courier*, March 27, 1946; Garlington, *Men of the Time*, 176.

41. Evans, 5: 725; Dickert, *History of Kershaw's Brigade*, 162–163. Evans says McIntosh made colonel "after Fredericksburg," which is erroneous.

42. *New York Times*, June 4, 1921; Ward, *Simon Baruch*, 52, 55–56, 58–59.

43. *New York Times*, June 4, 1921; Ward, *Simon Baruch*, 52, 55–56, 58–59.

44. Garlington, *Men of the Time*, 275–276.

45. Warner, *Generals in Gray*, 122–123; *Richmond Examiner*, June 13, 1864; Longacre, *Gentleman and Soldier*, 158.

46. *Richmond Sentinel*, October 21, 1864; Columbia *South Carolinian*, October 15, 1864.

47. *Charleston News and Courier*, n.d., reprinted in the *Weekly Union* (S.C.) *Times*, February 14, 1879.

48. *Brooklyn Eagle-Ledger*, n.d., reprinted in the *Anderson Intelligencer*, May 27, 1880. The article identifies the U.S. representative as "Caulk," but I found no record of him.

49. *Augusta Chronicle*, March 28, 1961; Welsh, *Medical Histories*, 91–92; Warner, *Generals in Gray*, 122–123. The *Chronicle* article was published on the 143rd anniversary of Hampton's birth.

50. Fairfield *News and Herald*, April 18, 1894; *The State*, April 14, 1894; Dickert, *History of Kershaw's Brigade*, 58–60; Warner, *Generals in Gray*, 171; Welsh, *Medical Histories*, 127; Buel and Johnson, *Battles and Leaders*, 3: 338.

51. Fairfield *News and Herald*, April 18, 1894; *The State*, April 14, 1894; Dickert, *History of Kershaw's Brigade*, 58–60; Warner, *Generals in Gray*, 171; Welsh, *Medical Histories*, 127; Buel and Johnson, *Battles and Leaders*, 3: 338.

52. Warner, *Generals in Gray*, 8–9; Hassler, "'Fighting Dick' Anderson," 43.

53. *The State*, May 13, 1920, and November 1, 1920; *Tampa Daily Times*, n.d. ; Warner, *Generals in Gray*, 174–175; Welsh, *Medical Histories*, 129–130. The *State* article identified Law's wife only as the former "Miss Latta," her maiden name. The Laws' son, Will, and his family lived in Rock Hill, S.C., before moving to Florida shortly before the general's death. The *State* article also said Law was a major general, which appears to be inaccurate, as is the subhead spelling of his middle name, "McIver" instead of the correct McIvor.

54. Warner, *Generals in Gray*, 235; *OR*, pt. 1, 1,030; *Edgefield Advertiser*, May 25, 1864; *Camden* (S.C.) *Journal*, June 10, 1864.

55. *Charleston Mercury*, May 18, 1864; *Yorkville Enquirer*, April 26, 1865.

56. Evans, 5: 408–409; Welsh, *Medical Histories*, 126; Warner, *Generals in Gray*, 170–171.

57. McSwain, *Crumbling Defenses*, 12–14, 51.

58. *Fairfield* (S.C.) *Herald*, April 27, 1869; *Yorkville Enquirer*, November 2, 1882. It appears that Brewer was in the First South Carolina, based on National Park Service records. He is most likely Pvt. Marion Brewer of the First's Company H. Another soldier, identified as Pvt. Marion J. Brewer, was in the First's Company G. M.C. Brewer was a lieutenant in the Florence Rifles, active in a fire company and "an esteemed citizen," the *Enquirer* noted.

59. *Camden Journal*, January 1, 1878; *Macon* (Ga.) *Weekly Telegraph*, December 12, 1876; *Newberry Herald and News*, May 18, 1892. Fellers was a member of the Third South Carolina's Company C.

60. *The State*, May 11, 1892.

61. *Yorkville Enquirer*, March 29, 1877.

62. *Yorkville Enquirer*, April 18, 1888.

63. *The State*, December 11, 1895.

64. *Charleston* (S.C.) *Evening Post*, March 21, 1899; *Lancaster Ledger*, September 6, 1899. Parker's regiment in the army is unclear.

65. Fairfield *News and Herald*, July 19, 1893. Germany is also listed as J.W. Germany in a National Park Service roster of the Twelfth South Carolina.

66. *Lancaster Ledger*, February 8, 1902. Porter also was in the Twelfth's Company I.

67. *Edgefield Advertiser*, February 22, 1872; *Newberry Herald and News*, November 2, 1909. Mrs. Mays was 57.

68. Boyles, *Reminiscences*, 55–56; *Winnsboro News*, n.d., reprinted in the *Daily* (Columbia, S.C.) *Phoenix*, August 31, 1873; Fairfield *News and Herald*, October 18, 1882; *Edgefield Advertiser*, August 10, 1882; *Abbeville Press and Banner*, July 23, 1884.

69. Boyles, *Reminiscences*, 55–56; *Winnsboro News*, n.d., reprinted in the *Daily* (Columbia, S.C.) *Phoenix*, August 31, 1873; Fairfield *News and Herald*, October 18, 1882; *Edgefield Advertiser*, August 10, 1882; *Abbeville Press and Banner*, July 23, 1884.

70. *Bamberg* (S.C.) *Herald*, April 26, 1900; "Search for Soldiers," NPS. The *Herald* identified the officer as "Capt. M.R. Sharpe," which is erroneous.

71. *Union Times*, July 13, 1900.

72. *Newberry Herald and News*, January 8, 1909, March 21, 1911. The 1909 article states that Pope was a lieutenant; Dickert's roster shows him as a sergeant, which is correct. Young was Pope's first name.

73. *Newberry Herald and News*, January 5, 1904.

74. *Chicago Tribune*, n.d., reprinted in *Macon Weekly Telegraph*, February 14, 1871.

75. *New York Times*, December 15, 1888; *Anderson Intelligencer*, January 3, 1889; Warner, *Generals in Gray*, 192–193.

76. *Newberry Herald and News*, January 5, 1904; Warner, *Generals in Gray*, 192–193, 406; *Greenville News*, n.d., reprinted in the *Keowee Courier*, January 27, 1904.

Chapter 14

1. *Charleston* (S.C.) *Daily News*, August 26, 1869. Fitzhugh Lee was a brigadier general when he fought at Gettysburg.

2. *Confederate Veteran* 24: 326–327; *Charleston Daily News*, May 10, 1871; *The State*, July 1, 1913.

3. *Charleston Daily News*, May 15, 1871, and June 25, 1872; *The State*, July 1, 1913. Warren was among the Gettysburg slain returned on the steamer. He was reinterred in Camden's Quaker Cemetery but was erroneously listed among those buried at Magnolia Cemetery.

4. *Yorkville Enquirer*, August 12, 1891; *Laurens Advertiser*, August 27, 1902. Some 5,000 people attended the 1891 gathering, including relatives of the veterans.

5. *Watchman and Southron*, June 18, 1913; *Fort Mill* (S.C.) *Times*, June 19, 1913.

6. *Yorkville Enquirer*, April 3, 1901; *Fort Mill Times*, June 16, 1910.

7. *Newberry Herald and News*, July 18, 1913; Kingstree (S.C.) *County Record*, July 31, 1913;

Anderson (S.C.) *Mail*, n.d., reprinted in the *Keowee Courier*, July 16, 1913.

8. *Edgefield Advertiser*, July 2, 1913.

9. *Edgefield Advertiser*, April 21, 1915; Ezra J. Warner, *Generals in Blue*, 446–447. In the 1915 account, Wright also claimed that he was briefly captured at Chancellorsville and brought to Sickles for interrogation. He stated that he mentioned the Chancellorsville encounter to the old general, but Sickles did not recall it. Sickles died in May 1914.

10. Kingstree *County Record*, July 31, 1913.

11. *Anderson Mail*, n.d., reprinted in the *Keowee Courier*, July 16, 1913; *Newberry Herald and News*, July 18, 1913.

12. *Yorkville Enquirer*, July 8, 1913.

13. Kingstree *County Record*, July 31, 1913.

14. *Keowee Courier*, July 9, 1913.

15. Kingstree *County Record*, October 16, 1913.

16. *The State*, June 17, 1913, and October 16, 1915. It is unclear if Dunlap went to the 1913 Gettysburg reunion. In his quest to locate Weir, he also wrote to Gen. Irvine Walker, commander of the S.C. Confederate Veterans. According to Mrs. Glenn, five members of her family went off to war; four of them, including Weir, not surviving.

17. *Anderson Intelligencer*, May 29, 1914. The stricken veteran was identified as W.R. Mundy, a retired planter from Abbeville.

18. *Keowee Courier*, July 11, 1917.

19. *Pageland* (S.C.) *Journal*, April 4, 1917.

20. *Charleston News and Courier*, December 15, 1934.

21. *Columbus* (Ga.) *Daily Inquirer*, June 28, 1938.

Chapter 15

1. *Laurens Advertiser*, June 18, 1902, and August 12, 1908.

2. *Anderson Intelligencer*, April 4, 1906.

3. *Laurens Advertiser*, April 26, 1898; *Newberry Herald and News*, May 1, 1908. Langston died on April 20, 1898.

4. *Edgefield Advertiser*, August 23, 1911; *Augusta Chronicle*, March 3, 1907; United Daughters of the Confederacy, 1: 324–325. Brunson was in the Fourteenth South Carolina.

5. *Fort Mill Times*, November 30, 1911; *Augusta Chronicle*, December 9, 1911.

6. *Manning Times*, January 21, 1914; *Newberry Herald and News*, March 20, 1914.

7. *Keowee Courier*, September 23, 1914; *The State*, January 19, 1915.

8. *Anderson Intelligencer*, February 26, 1915; *Watchman and Southron*, February 20, 1915. The Intelligencer article states that Petty was in the Sixteenth South Carolina, which is erroneous. "Thirty" is the traditional number to signify the end of a newspaper story, or for Petty's life in this case. Boykin initially joined the Hampton Legion's cavalry, which was consolidated with the Fourth South Carolina Battalion in 1862 to form the Second South Carolina Cavalry.

9. *Lancaster News*, April 16, 1915. Black's rank

at Gettysburg is unclear; he entered the service as a corporal and was either a lieutenant or captain commanding his company at the Appomattox surrender.

10. *Keowee Courier*, June 2, 1915.

11. *Newberry Herald and News*, January 4, 1916; *Keowee Courier*, June 28, 1916.

12. *Union Times*, December 22, 1916; *Lancaster News*, May 9, 1916. Cudd was promoted corporal at some point in the war.

13. *Union Times*, November 24, 1916; *Watchman and Southron*, January 3, 1917. Smith's regiment and rank were not available.

14. *Abbeville Press and Banner*, February 28, 1917; *The State*, March 10, 1917; *Keowee Courier*, February 6, 1918.

15. *Abbeville Press and Banner*, November 8, 1918. This account describes William Hudgens as a captain, but other references note his rank as lieutenant. His father's first name, rank and regiment were not found. Information about Pvt. Hughes's father also is vague and unreliable.

16. *Union* (S.C.) *Daily Times*, May 17, 1922; *Yorkville Enquirer*, May 19, 1922; *Newberry Herald and News*, May 25, 1920. Information about the command in which Sease served at Gettysburg is sparse.

17. *Keowee Courier*, January 26, 1921; *Abbeville Press and Banner*, January 26, 1921; Brown, 87.

18. *Lexington* (S.C.) *Dispatch-News*, January 25, 1922.

19. *Charleston News and Courier*, August 26, 1925; Warner, *Generals in Gray*, 236–237. Perry was a Georgia brigadier later in the war, but was a colonel leading the Forty-fourth Alabama in Law's brigade at Gettysburg. It is unclear from the article whether Ervin's wife Margaret was still living when he died.

20. *The State*, October 7, 1925.

21. *Charleston Evening Post*, May 20, 1929; *Augusta Chronicle*, May 20, 1929. Due to the First South Carolina's heavy casualties on July 1, it is certainly believable that Williams was one of the color bearers.

22. *The State*, August 14, 1930, and September 8, 1930.

23. *The State*, March 16, 1930, and July 13, 1930.

24. *Charleston Courier*, July 10, 1931.

25. *The State*, August 13, 1932. It is unclear when Shealy was wounded or his rank—corporal or sergeant—at the time.

26. *Augusta Chronicle*, January 12, 1940.

27. *The State*, July 3, 1963.

28. *Charleston News and Courier*, June 23, 1963; *The State*, August 12, 1944. Seigler did not fight at Gettysburg, based on *The State*'s story about his death.

29. *The State*, March 16, 1930.

Appendix

1. *Yorkville Enquirer*, June 25, 1896.

2. *Laurens Advertiser*, April 1, 1903; *Keowee Courier*, April 8, 1903; NPS Soldier Search. The Laurens

paper states that Smith was captured on July 2, but
this appears unlikely based on the positions of the
armies and the battle situation that day. He was
most probably taken prisoner on July 5–6 after Lee's
retreat. The Smiths lived in the Mount Gallagher
section of Laurens County.

3. *Philadelphia Weekly Times*, May 6, 1882.

4. *Newberry Herald*, January 24, 1872; *Newberry
Herald and News*, October 3, 1905.

5. *Greenville News*, n.d., reprinted in the *Watchman and Southron*, December 2, 1884.

6. *Yorkville Enquirer*, November 20, 1906.

7. *St. Louis Globe-Democrat*, n.d., reprinted in
the *Watchman and Southron*, January 28, 1891.

8. *Camden Journal*, January 29, 1878.

9. Atlanta *Constitution*, June 1, 1894; Thomas J.
Mackey, "Hampton's Duel on the Battle-Field at Gettysburg with a Federal Soldier," *Southern Historical
Society Papers* 22 (January–December 1894): 125.
At least one author's bibliography incorrectly titles
Mackey's article "Duel of General Wade Hampton on the Battle-Field at Gettysburg with a Federal
Soldier."

10. *OR*, pt. 2, 698, 725.

11. Warner, *Generals in Gray*, 123; *Yorkville
Enquirer*, June 20, 1894.

12. *Yorkville Enquirer*, June 20, 1894.

13. Mackey, "Hampton's Duel," 125.

14. *Ibid.*; *The State*, June 16, 1894.

Bibliography

Accessible Archives. https://www.accessible.com/accessible.

Aiken, D. Wyatt. Letter to "Dear Capt." (unidentified). July 11, 1863. South Caroliniana Digital Library, University of South Carolina.

Allardice, Bruce S. *Confederate Colonels: A Biographical Register*. Columbia: University of Missouri Press, 2008.

Bacon, Georgeanna Muirson Woolsey. *Three Weeks at Gettysburg*. New York: Anson D.F. Randolph, 1863.

Bates, Samuel P. *History of the Pennsylvania Volunteers, 1861–65, Prepared in Compliance with Acts of the Legislature*. 5 vols. Harrisburg, PA: B. Singerly, State, 1869.

Beale, G.W. *A Lieutenant of Cavalry in Lee's Army*. Boston: Gorham, 1918.

Beecham, R.K. *Gettysburg: The Pivotal Battle of the Civil War*. Chicago: A.C. McClurg, 1911.

Boatner, Mark M., III. *The Civil War Dictionary*. Rev. ed. New York: David McKay, 1987.

Boyles, J.R. *Reminiscences of the Civil War*. Columbia, SC: n.p., 1890.

Brooks, U.R., ed. *Stories of the Confederacy*. Columbia, SC: State, 1912.

Brown, Varina D. *A Colonel at Gettysburg and Spotsylvania*. Columbia, SC: State, 1931.

Buel, Clarence C., and Robert V. Johnson. *Battles and Leaders of the Civil War: Being for the Most Part Contributions by Union and Confederate Authors*. 4 vols. New York: Century, 1887.

Caldwell, J.F.J. *The History of a Brigade of South Carolinians, Known First as "Gregg's" and Subsequently as "McGowan's Brigade."* Philadelphia: King and Baird, 1866

Catton, Bruce. *This Hallowed Ground: The Story of the Union Side of the Civil War*. Garden City, NY: Doubleday, 1956.

Chapman, John A. *History of Edgefield County from the Earliest Settlements to 1897*. Newberry, SC: Elbert H. Aull, 1897.

"Chronicling America: Historic American Newspapers." Library of Congress. https://chroniclingamerica.loc.gov/.

Cisco, Walter Brian. *Wade Hampton: Confederate Warrior, Conservative Statesman*. Washington, D.C.: Potomac, 2004.

Clark, Champ, and the Editors of Time-Life Books.

Gettysburg: The Confederate High Tide. Alexandria, VA: Time-Life, 1985.

Cooke, John Esten. *Wearing of the Gray: Being Personal Portraits, Scenes, and Adventures of the War*. New York: E.B. Treat, 1867.

Craughwell, Thomas J. *The Greatest Brigade: How the Irish Brigade Cleared the Way to Victory in the American Civil War*. Beverly, MA: Fair Winds, 2011.

Davis, William C. *Battle at Bull Run: A History of the First Major Campaign of the Civil War*. Baton Rouge: Louisiana State University Press, 1977.

Dickert, Augustus. *History of Kershaw's Brigade*. Newberry, SC: Elbert H. Hull, 1899.

"Documenting the American South." University of North Carolina at Chapel Hill. https://docsouth.unc.edu/.

Doubleday, Abner. *Chancellorsville and Gettysburg*. New York: Charles Scribner's Sons, 1912.

_____. *Reminiscences of Forts Sumter and Moultrie in 1860–'61*. New York: Harper, 1876.

Douglas, Henry Kyd. *I Rode with Stonewall: Being Chiefly the War Experiences of the Youngest Member of Jackson's Staff from the John Brown Raid to the Hanging of Mrs. Surratt*. Chapel Hill: University of North Carolina Press, 1940.

Dowdey, Clifford. *Lee and His Men at Gettysburg: The Death of a Nation*. New York: Skyhorse, 1986.

Draper, John William. *History of the American Civil War*. 3 vols. New York: Harper, 1870.

Dreese, Michael A. *Torn Families: Death and Kinship at the Battle of Gettysburg*. Jefferson, NC: McFarland, 2007

Evans, Clement A., ed. *Confederate Military History*. 12 vols. Atlanta: Confederate, 1899.

Everson, Guy R., and Edward W. Simpson, Jr., eds. *"Far, Far from Home": The Wartime Letters of Dick and Tally Simpson, Third South Carolina Volunteers*. New York and Oxford: Oxford University Press, 1994.

Freeman, Douglas Southall. *Lee's Lieutenants: A Study in Command*. Abridged by Stephen W. Sears. New York: Simon & Schuster, 2001.

Fremantle, Sir Arthur James Lyon. *Three Months in the Southern States: April–June, 1863*. Mobile, AL: S.H. Goetzel, 1864.

Furman, Charles M. Letter to Frances E. Garden. July 22, 1863. Furman University Digital Library.

Gaillard, Frye. *Journey to the Wilderness: War, Memory, and a Southern Family's Civil War Letters.* Montgomery, AL: NewSouth, 2015.

Garlington, J.C. *Men of the Time: Sketches of Living Notables: A Biographical Encyclopedia of Contemporaneous South Carolina Leaders.* Spartanburg, SC: Garlington, 1902.

Gottfried, Bradley M. *The Artillery of Gettysburg.* Nashville, TN: Cumberland, 2008

_____. *Brigades of Gettysburg: The Union and Confederate Brigades at the Battle of Gettysburg.* New York: Skyhorse, 2002.

Grimsley, Mark. "Robert E. Lee: The Life and Career of the Master General." *Civil War Times Illustrated* 24, no. 7 (November 1985).

Hagood, Johnson. *Memoirs of the War of Secession.* Edited by U.R. Brooks. Columbia, SC: State, 1910.

Hampton, Wade. Letter to Mary Fisher Hampton. July 16, 1863. Hampton Family Papers, 1773–1974, South Caroliniana Digital Library, University of South Carolina.

Haskell, Frank A. *The Battle of Gettysburg.* Boston: Mudge, 1908.

Hassler, William W. "'Fighting Dick' Anderson." *Civil War Times Illustrated* 12, no. 10 (February 1974).

Hassler, Warren W., Jr. *The First Day at Gettysburg: Crisis at the Crossroads.* Gaithersburg, MD: Butternut, 1986.

Hood, John B. *Advance and Retreat.* Secaucus, NJ: Blue and Grey, 1985.

Horn, Stanley F. *The Robert E. Lee Reader.* Indianapolis, IN: Bobbs-Merrill, 1949.

Huidekoper, Henry S. *A Short Story of the First Day's Fight at Gettysburg.* Philadelphia: Bicking, 1906.

Izlar, William V. *A Sketch of the War Record of the Edisto Rifles: 1861–1865.* Columbia, SC: State, 1914.

Johnston, Joseph E. *Narrative of Military Operations, Directed, During the Late War Between the States.* New York: D. Appleton, 1874.

Jones, John B. *A Rebel War Clerk's Diary at the Confederate States Capital.* 2 vols. Philadelphia: J.B. Lippincott, 1866.

Jorgensen, Jay. *Gettysburg's Bloody Wheatfield.* Shippensburg, PA: White Mane, 2002.

Keith, Willis W. Letter to Anna Bell Keith, July 8–9, 1863; Willis W. Keith to Anna Bell Keith, July 10, 1863; Willis W. Keith to Anna Bell Keith, July 19, 1863. Wilkinson-Keith Family Papers, College of Charleston (S.C.) Libraries and Lowcountry Digital Library.

Kennedy, Frances H., ed. *The Civil War Battlefield Guide.* Boston: Houghton Mifflin, 1990.

Kerrison, Edwin, to his sister (unidentified). July 7, 1863. Kerrison Family Papers, South Caroliniana Digital Library, University of South Carolina.

Kidd, J.H. *A Cavalryman with Custer: Custer's Michigan Cavalry Brigade in the Civil War.* New York: Bantam, 1991.

Killian, Ron V. *General Abner M. Perrin, C.S.A.: A Biography.* Jefferson, NC: McFarland, 2012.

Landrum, J.B.O. *History of Spartanburg County.* Atlanta: Franklin, 1900.

Linn, John B. "A Tourist at Gettysburg." *Civil War Times Illustrated* 29, no. 4 (September/October 1990).

Littlejohn, Thomas M. "Recollections of a Confederate Soldier." Twelfth South Carolina file, Gettysburg National Military Park.

Longacre, Edward G. *Gentleman and Soldier: A Biography of Wade Hampton III.* Nashville, TN: Rutledge Hill, 2003.

_____. *The Cavalry at Gettysburg: A Tactical Study of Mounted Operations During the Civil War's Pivotal Campaign, 9 June–14 July 1863.* Lincoln: University of Nebraska Press, 1986.

Longstreet, James. *From Manassas to Appomattox.* Philadelphia: J.B. Lippincott, 1896.

Mackey, Thomas J. "Hampton's Duel on the Battle-Field at Gettysburg." *Southern Historical Society Papers* 22 (January–December 1894).

"Making of America." Cornell University Library and University of Michigan. https://collections.library.cornell.edu/moa_new/.

Malone, P.J. "Charge of Black's Cavalry at Gettysburg." Richmond, VA: *Southern Historical Society Papers* 16 (January–December 1888).

Martin, David G. *Gettysburg July 1.* Cambridge, MA: Da Capo, 1996.

Martin, Isabella D., and Myrta Lockett Avery. *A Diary from Dixie, as written by Mary Boykin Chesnut, wife of James Chesnut, Jr., United States Senator from South Carolina, 1859–1861, and Afterward an Aide to Jefferson Davis and a Brigadier General in the Confederate Army.* New York: D. Appleton, 1905.

Marzalek, John F., ed. *The Diary of Miss Emma Holmes—1861–1866.* Baton Rouge: Louisiana State University Press, 1994.

McCrady, General Edward, Jr., and Hon. Samuel A. Ashe. *Cyclopedia of Eminent and Representative Men of the Carolinas of the Nineteenth Century with a Brief Historical Introduction on South Carolina by General Edward McCrady Jr., and on North Carolina by Hon. Samuel A. Ashe.* 2 vols. Madison, WI: Brant and Fuller, 1892.

McIntosh, David Gregg. *Review of the Gettysburg Campaign.* Pamphlet Collection, South Caroliniana Library, University of South Carolina.

McLaws, Lafayette. "Gettysburg—Address of General McLaws Before the Georgia Historical Society." Richmond, VA: *Southern Historical Society Papers* 7, 1879.

McSwain, Eleanor D., ed. *Crumbling Defenses, or Memoirs and Reminiscences of John Logan Black, Colonel C.S.A.* Macon, GA: J.W. Burke, 1960.

Miller, Francis Trevelyan, ed. *Photographic History of the Civil War.* 10 vols. Springfield, MA: Patriot, 1911.

Minnigh, Luther W. *Gettysburg: What They Did Here.* Gettysburg, PA: n.p., 1900.

Mulholland, St. Clair A. *The Story of the 116th Regiment, Pennsylvania Infantry.* Philadelphia: F. McManus Jr., 1899.

Murfin, James V. *The Gleam of Bayonets: The Battle of Antietam and the Maryland Campaign of 1862.* Baton Rouge: Louisiana State University Press, 1965.

Nicholson, John P., Lewis Eugene Beitler, Paul L. Roy, and Pennsylvania Gettysburg Battle-field Commission. *Pennsylvania at Gettysburg: Ceremonies at the Dedication of Monuments.* 2 vols. Harrisburg, PA: E.K. Meyers, State Printer, 1893.

O'Neall, John Belton, and John A. Chapman. *The Annals of Newberry.* Newberry, SC: Aull and Houseal, 1892.

Patterson, Gerard A. *Rebels from West Point.* New York: Doubleday, 1987.

Perry, William H. Letter to Benjamin F. Perry. July 11, 1863. South Caroliniana Digital Library, University of South Carolina.

Pfanz, Harry W. *Gettysburg: The Second Day.* Chapel Hill: University of North Carolina Press, 1987.

Pitzer, John E. *The Three Days Battle at Gettysburg.* Gettysburg, PA.: Pitzer House, 1900.

Prince, Albert. Diary of Pvt. Albert Prince of the Brooks Artillery. Courtesy of Lt. Gen. Wade Hampton Camp No. 273, Sons of Confederate Veterans, Columbia, S.C. www.wadehamptoncamp. org.

Reardon, Carol, and Tom Vossler. *A Field Guide to Gettysburg.* Chapel Hill: University of North Carolina Press, 2013.

_____. *The Gettysburg Campaign: June–July 1863.* Washington, D.C.: Center of Military History, United States Army, 2013.

Recollections and Reminiscences, 1861–1865, Through World War I. 6 vols. South Carolina Division, United Daughters of the Confederacy, 1992.

Reid, Whitelaw. *Ohio in the War: Her Statesmen, Her Generals, and Soldiers.* 2 vols. Cincinnati, OH: Robert Clarke, 1895.

Richardson, Elizabeth Buford. *A Geneological Record with Reminiscences of the Richardson and Buford Families.* Macon, GA: J.W. Burke, 1906.

Robertson, James I., Jr. *General A.P. Hill: The Story of a Confederate Warrior.* New York: Random House, 1987.

Ross, Fitzgerald. *A Visit to the Cities and Camps of the Confederate States.* London: William Blackwood, 1865.

Russell, William Howard. *My Diary: North and South.* Boston: T.O.H.P. Burnham, 1863.

Scott, James K.P. *The Story of the Battles of Gettysburg.* Harrisburg, PA: Telegraph, 1927.

"Search for Soldiers." U.S. National Park Service. https://www.nps.gov/civilwar/search-soldiers. htm.

Shultz, David L., and Scott L. Mingus, Sr. *The Second Day at Gettysburg: The Attack and Defense of the Union Center on Cemetery Ridge, July 2, 1863.* El Dorado Hills, CA: Savas Beatie, 2015.

Shumate, William. "With Kershaw at Gettysburg." *Philadelphia Times,* n.d.

Smith, Derek. *Civil War Savannah.* Savannah, GA: Frederic Beil, 1997.

_____. *The Gallant Dead: Union and Confederate Generals Killed in the Civil War.* Mechanicsburg, PA: Stackpole, 2005.

_____. "Potter's Raid—'Our Errand Through the State.'" *North and South* 10, no. 2 (July 2007).

Smith, J.L. *History of the 118th Pennsylvania Volunteers, Corn Exchange Regiment, from Their First Engagement at Antietam to Appomattox.* Philadelphia: J.L. Smith, 1905.

Sorrel, G. Moxley. *Recollections of a Confederate Staff Officer.* New York and Washington: Neale, 1905.

Starr, Stephen Z. *The Union Cavalry in the Civil War.* 3 vols. Baton Rouge: Louisiana State University Press, 1979.

Stewart, Robert L. *History of the One Hundred and Fortieth Regiment, Pennsylvania Volunteers.* [n.p.]: Published by authority of the Regimental Association, 1912.

Swinton, William. *The Twelve Decisive Battles of the War: A History of the Eastern and Western Campaigns, in Relation to the Actions that Decided Their Issue.* New York: Dick and Fitzgerald, 1871.

Taylor, Mrs. Thomas, Mrs. A.T. Smythe, Mrs. August Kohn, Miss M.B. Poppinheim, and Miss Martha B. Washington. *South Carolina Women in the Confederacy.* Columbia, SC: State, 1903.

Tompkins, Daniel A. *Company K, Fourteenth South Carolina Volunteers.* Charlotte, NC: Observer, 1897.

Trimpi, Helen P. *Crimson Confederates: Harvard Men Who Fought for the South.* Knoxville: University of Tennessee Press, 2010.

Trout, Robert J. *Galloping Thunder: The Stuart Horse Artillery Battalion.* Mechanicsburg, PA: Stackpole, 2005.

Tucker, Glenn. *High Tide at Gettysburg.* New York: Bobbs-Merrill, 1958.

United Daughters of the Confederacy, South Carolina Division, John K. McIver Chapter. *Treasured Reminiscences.* Columbia, SC: State, 1911.

U.S. War Department. *The War of the Rebellion: A Compilation of the Official Records of the Union and Confederate Armies.* 128 vols. Washington, D.C.: U. S. Government Printing Office, 1880–1901. Cited in notes as *OR.*

U.S. War Department. *Official Records of the Union and Confederate Navies in the War of the Rebellion.* 303 vols. Washington, D.C.: U.S. Government Printing Office, 1894–1922.

Vanderslice, John M. *Gettysburg: Where and How the Regiments Fought and the Troops They Encountered—An Account of the Battle Giving Movements, Positions and Losses of the Commands Engaged.* Philadelphia and New York: G.W. Dillingham, 1897.

Walker, C. Irvine. *The Life of Lieutenant General Richard Heron Anderson of the Confederate Army.* Charleston, SC: Art, 1917.

Walker, J.A. "Some Stirring Incidents." *Philadelphia Times,* March 17, 1882.

Ward, Patricia Spain. *Simon Baruch: Rebel in the Ranks of Medicine, 1840–1921.* Tuscaloosa: University of Alabama Press, 1994.

Warner, Ezra J. *Generals in Blue: Lives of the Union Commanders.* Baton Rouge: Louisiana State University Press, 1964.

_____. *Generals in Gray: Lives of the Confederate Commanders.* Baton Rouge: Louisiana State University Press, 1959.

Weber, John Langdon. *Fifty Lessons in the History of South Carolina*. Boston: Ginn, 1891.

Welch, Spencer Glasgow. *A Confederate Surgeon's Letters to his Wife*. New York: Neale, 1911.

Wells, Edward L. *Hampton and His Cavalry in '64*. Richmond, VA: B.F. Johnson, 1899.

Welsh, Jack D., M.D. *Medical Histories of Confederate Generals*. Kent, OH: Kent State University Press, 1995.

Wert, Jeffrey D. *General James Longstreet: The Confederacy's Most Controversial Soldier: A Biography*. New York: Simon & Schuster, 1993.

_____. "Gettysburg: The Special Issue." *Civil War Times Illustrated* 27, no. 4 (Summer 1988).

Wert, J. Howard. *A Complete Handbook of the Monuments and Indications and Guide to the Positions on the Gettysburg Battlefield*. Harrisburg, PA: R.M. Sturgeon, 1886.

Woodward, C. Vann, ed. *Mary Chesnut's Civil War*. New Haven, CT: Yale University Press, 1981.

Newspapers and Magazines

Abbeville (S.C.) *Press*
Abbeville (S.C.) *Press and Banner*
Advertiser (Mobile)
America's Civil War
American (Baltimore)
Anderson (S.C.) *Daily Intelligencer*
Anderson (S.C.) *Daily Mail*
Anderson (S.C.) *Intelligencer*
Anderson (S.C.) *Mail*
Atlanta Appeal
Atlantic Monthly
Augusta (Ga.) *Chronicle*
Augusta (Ga.) *Daily Constitutionalist*
Bamberg (S.C.) *Herald*
Brooklyn (N.Y.) *Daily Ledger*
Brooklyn (N.Y.) *Eagle Ledger*
Camden (S.C.) *Confederate*
Camden (S.C.) *Journal*
Century
Charleston (S.C.) *Courier*
Charleston (S.C.) *Daily Courier*
Charleston (S.C.) *Daily News*
Charleston (S.C.) *Evening Post*
Charleston (S.C.) *Mercury*
Charleston (S.C.) *Weekly News*
Charleston News and Courier
Charlottesville (Va.) *Chronicle*
Chicago Tribune
Civil War Times Illustrated
Columbia (S.C.) *Guardian*
Columbus (Ga.) *Daily Inquirer*
Confederate Veteran
Constitution (Atlanta)
County Record (Kingstree S.C.)
Daily (Columbia, S.C.) *Phoenix*
Daily Dispatch (Richmond)
Daily Richmond Enquirer
Edgefield (S.C.) *Advertiser*
Fairfield (S.C.) *Herald*
Fort Mill (S.C.) *Times*
Greenville (S.C.) *News*
Harper's New Monthly Magazine
Herald and News (Newberry, S.C.)
Keowee (Pickens, S.C.) *Courier*
Kershaw (S.C.) *Gazette*
Lancaster (S.C.) *Ledger*
Lancaster (S.C.) *News*
Laurens (S.C.) *Advertiser*
Lexington (S.C.) *Dispatch-News*
Macon (Ga.) *Telegraph*
Macon (Ga.) *Weekly Telegraph*
Manning (S.C.) *Times*
Military Heritage
Mobile Register
Mobile Tribune
New York Herald
New York Times
New York Tribune
Newberry (S.C.) *Herald and News*
News and Herald (Fairfield, S.C.)
News and Herald (Winnsboro, S.C.)
North and South
Pageland (S.C.) *Journal*
Philadelphia North American
Philadelphia Times
Philadelphia Weekly Times
Post and Courier (Charleston S.C.)
Richmond Enquirer
Richmond Examiner
Richmond Sentinel
South Carolinian (Columbia)
Southern Enterprise (Greenville, S.C.)
St. Louis Globe-Democrat
State (Columbia, S.C.)
Tampa Daily Times
Union (S.C.) *Daily Times*
Union (S.C.) *Times*
Watchman and Southron (Sumter, S.C.)
Weekly Union (S.C.) *Times*
Winnsboro (S.C.) *News*
World (New York)
York (S.C.) *Observer*
Yorkville (S.C.) *Enquirer*

Index